t t   re

Guide to
Literary London

Batsford London Library

Guide to Literary London

George G. Williams
assisted by Marian and Geoffrey Williams

B. T. Batsford Ltd
London

First published 1973
© George G. Williams 1973

Text printed in Great Britain
by Northumberland Press Ltd,
Gateshead, Co. Durham.
Books bound by Richard Clay
(The Chaucer Press) Ltd, Bungay, Suffolk,
for the publishers B. T. Batsford Ltd,
4 Fitzhardinge Street, London W1H OAH

ISBN 0 7134 0141 9

Contents

'By seeing London, I have
seen as much of life as the
world can show.'

Samuel Johnson
in Boswell's *Tour of the Hebrides*

Introduction

Why do museums everywhere preserve and exhibit Napoleon's snuff-box, Lincoln's shawl, Mary Stuart's slippers, and Carlyle's old black hat? And why do the natives of most respectable towns eagerly show you where Burns lodged, or Dylan Thomas is buried, or Washington slept, or King Arthur's horse trod? The reason is that mere objects and places seem, in some para-rational way, to reflect the aura of the great men with whom they were associated. Once upon a time, shrines and temples were built where heroes, saints, or gods were born, lived, or died. Pilgrims thronged to those places, and armies fought savagely to possess bits of real estate valueless except for their associations.

In earlier times, places associated with literary men, mere writers rather than saints or soldiers, went unnoticed in western Europe. But in the fourteenth century, with the 'Revival of Learning', Italians began to cherish their literary sites. By the sixteenth century, Englishmen too had awakened to the peculiar interest of literary sites in Italy, and then their own literary shrines. In the seventeenth century, one of London's chief tourist attractions was the house where Mr John Milton was born. In the eighteenth century, James Boswell, that astutely modern mind, observed that 'there is something pleasingly interesting, to many, in tracing so great a man through all his different habitations'—and then proceeded to list carefully all the London dwelling places of Dr Johnson. In the nineteenth century, Leigh Hunt confessed, 'I once had duties to perform that kept me out late at night, and severely taxed my health and spirits. My path lay through a neighbourhood in which Dryden had lived, and though nothing could be more commonplace, and I used to be tired to the heart and soul of me, I never hesitated to go a little out of my way that I might pass through Gerrard Street, and so give myself the shadow of a pleasant thought.' (How delightful and precise that last phrase—'the shadow of a pleasant thought'!) A little later on, the famous banker, poet, and man-about-town Samuel Rogers, with the poet Thomas Moore and the writer and wit Sydney Smith as companions, made a special trip to that same Gerrard Street to see that same house of Dryden. In the twentieth century, of course, the desire of people to see places associated with the lives of writers is almost universal—and has become the source of a vast tourist trade. Pilgrims flock to

1

the homes of Shakespeare, Scott, Dickens, and Dr Johnson as they once flocked to the shrines of saints.

Why do people visit literary places? Perhaps for no better reason than for climbing Mount Everest: Because it is there. On the other hand, a visit to the house where a great writer was born or died, to the church where he was baptized or married, to the streets along which he walked, to the places he frequented, to the home where he wrote, even to the grave where he is buried—this gives a peculiar sense of immediacy, of flesh-and-blood reality, of *humanness*, that mere reading of the printed page cannot possibly give. If there were no other reason for visiting literary sites, this would be enough.

But there *are* other reasons—by-products—that you, as a visitor to London, or even as a resident, will heartily appreciate after you have made any of the tours described in this book. First of all, the chances are good that, on each tour, you will learn something about literature, or literary men, that you did not know previously. Second, making the tours will give you continual variety in your London days—something else to do besides visiting another museum, or moping about your lodgings. Third, there is no better way of getting acquainted with London—the world's most fascinating city—than sallying out into its streets, walking along them with some plan or destination, visiting the lovely squares and ancient buildings, and penetrating into sections of the city that you would never see (and that, indeed, most Londoners never see) without making tours like those outlined here. Finally, and maybe most important of all, a thousand places in London, that city which has been so long a Mecca for a large part of the world, and which still attracts its annual millions from everywhere, acquire a peculiar, profound, and precious significance when you know that here, in this very spot, Chaucer lived, Shakespeare walked, Bunyan preached, Swift sat writing to his Stella, Dr Johnson held forth, Keats penned the 'Ode to a Nightingale', Blake composed *Songs of Innocence*—and on and on: the entire city, sometimes beautiful, often plain or merely commercial, usually jammed with traffic and filled with hurried, harried people, accumulates for you an indescribable and incalculable depth and richness of meanings.

Finding Your Way about London — The very first thing you should do when you step out on the streets of London is to buy a map of the city. The handiest map is the red-white-and-blue folding map that you will find for sale at every news-stand. This has the underground stations clearly marked, and the whole underground system charted in a simplified and unconfusing form.

For visiting most places in London, the underground is the quickest, easiest, and least expensive means of transportation. Buses may be useful—but the routes are so devious and stopping places so un-predictable to the uninitiated that they confuse even Londoners; and they are not nearly so fast (over long distances) as the underground trains. Taxis are next-best for London transportation; but they are not always to be had just when you want them, are subject to traffic tie-ups, and are relatively expensive. For these reasons, the tours described in this book are based on the underground system. Don't be afraid to tackle the underground. Study your map of London and the chart of the underground system, watch what other people do, observe the signs belowground—and you will have a fascinating experience.

If you lose your way, *ask somebody*. Everyone in London (even the native Londoner) is always asking directions. You will find that, if you are ordinarily polite in your manner, Londoners will be cheer-ful, courteous, even effusive, in helping you. But two other things you must never do: one is to try to make short-cuts, and the other is to circle around a block of buildings. London streets are so illogical and tricky that, if you do either of these things, you may expect to get lost.

In looking by name for a certain street, it is essential that you remember *what part* of London it is in. Londoners are great ones for using a good name over and over. For example, there are at least 27 different streets in 27 different parts of the city, named 'Victoria Road'; 23 different streets are called 'The Drive'; 38 have the designation 'Richmond'; and so on. Furthermore, you must be especially careful to note whether the street you are seeking is called, say, Windsor Avenue, Windsor Close, Windsor Court, Windsor Crescent, Windsor Drive, Windsor Gardens, Windsor Grove, Windsor Mews, Wind-sor Place, Windsor Road, Windsor Square, Windsor Street, Windsor Terrace, Windsor Walk, or Windsor Something-Else. Each of these places may be miles away from the others.

Americans are often confused to find that a street is called, for example, Southampton Buildings or Featherstone Buildings; or that many streets have the name 'Gardens', or 'Grove', or 'Terrace', or 'Villas' attached to them—yet have no gardens, groves, terraces, or villas within miles. Some streets have names without any suffix such as 'street', 'avenue', or 'road'; thus you will find merely Whitehall, Cornhill, Cheapside, The Poultry, Edge Hill, The Grove, and so on—all simple streets.

Another (really vexing) peculiarity of London streets is that they are likely to change names abruptly, every few hundred yards. Thus, you may walk straight along the same thoroughfare for five hundred yards, and find that you have been successively on John Street, Doughty Street, and Mecklenburgh Square; or in an unswerving half mile you may tread Southampton Place, Russell Square, Woburn Place, Tavistock Square, Upper Woburn Place, and Eversholt Street. Nor are these examples exceptional.

Finally, London's system of house-numbering—well, there is no system. Occasionally, you may find even and odd numbers on opposite sides of the street in regular order. More commonly, the numbers run consecutively up one side of a street (until it changes its name, whereupon it starts all over again), and down the other side, so that, say, No. 1 may be on your right, and No. 179 across the street immediately opposite No. 1. Sometimes the numbers on a street seem literally to have 'just growed' without rhyme or reason. Nor can you usually determine, from looking at your map, at which end of a street (if at either end) the numbering starts. About all you can do about these numbers is to thank heaven you are not a London postman.

Making the Tours Described Here — The tours described in this book have been arranged in three groups: Best Tours, Excellent Tours, and Good Tours. Within each of these categories, the separate tours have been arranged in a more-or-less descending order of interest. I hasten to add, however, that this arrangement depends entirely on my own individual tastes; anybody else arranging these tours would doubtless do it very differently. Moreover, your own special interests will determine the trips that will be most meaningful to you. In order to help you make decisions as to which tours you might like best, I have listed, at the beginning of each tour described, the names of persons who figure most prominently in the tour. By glancing over this list, you can make up your mind whether any particular tour is your special dish of tea. (Of course, if you don't care to take any of the tours, but *are* interested in certain writers, you can look up the latter in the index of this book, and make individual pilgrimages.)

The distances covered in the tours are not so long as to tire out any healthy tourist. The longest tour could be covered in less than an hour of steady walking—and you will not be walking steadily, but pausing to look, resting in parks and squares, sitting down in churches, and so on. The tours won't exhaust you; they will stimulate you— physically as well as intellectually and spiritually.

Side-trips (usually very short) off the main tours have occasionally been included. As a rule, these side-trips may not be worth the walking required, unless you are especially interested in the writer involved. These side-trips are indicated in the text by being enclosed in square brackets.

Italics (besides being used for book-titles) indicate sites (streets, squares, churches, house numbers, etc.) associated with persons mentioned (usually in capitals) in the immediately accompanying text. Italics are used also for the names of certain non-writers (artists, musicians, scientists, etc.) whose homes, studios, statues, and the like you may happen to pass on a literary tour. *Capitals* are used for the names of writers who have been physically associated with the sites mentioned in the accompanying text. Capitals are also used for the names of persons whose careers were intimately bound to literature —such as famous actors, publishers, play producers, etc.

The authors around whom each of the tours has been worked out are always of *major* literary importance. Nevertheless, it seemed a good idea to include *minor* authors who happened to lie handy along the route, and who will require no extra effort of the tourist who is passing that way anyhow.

The houses you will find at designated places may or may not be the original houses associated with the authors who stayed there. Often it was quite impossible for the author of this book to make up his mind whether a certain house is or is not the original. Sometimes a house may be old, yet its front or its interior may have been completely reconstructed; or large parts of it pulled down, and replaced by new parts, or not replaced at all. Sometimes a single old wall, or an old basement or foundation, or a set of windows, or a porch, has been retained, and all the rest of the original house demolished. Sometimes an old house has been completely swallowed up in a new, larger house; or a large house has been converted into a small house. Under such circumstances (and they are common), should we call the present house the original house? I don't know.... But there are certain rough rules-of-thumb that you may find helpful. If the date involved with the house is before 1666 (the year of the Great Fire), the house (unless it is a church or other public building) is almost certainly not the same one known to the author associated with it. If the date is from 1666 to 1750, there is a better, though still slight, chance that the house is the same. If the date is from 1750 to 1800, the chances are fair that it is the original house—unless it is within the City itself, that is, the ancient inner part of London. If the date is from 1800 to 1850, the chances are good; if from 1850 to 1900, the chances are excellent; if after 1900, the chances are better than excellent (except in the bombed-out areas) that the house is original.

The maps included in this book are not accurate as to scale, or complete as to detail. They are merely *charts*—as simplified and inaccurate as the diagrams of the underground railway system that you find in the underground stations. They are meant to help you, not to reflect accurate geography.

Some Apologies — Undoubtedly, mistakes have got into this book.

What book does not have them? Since this one involves thousands of localities and dates, as well as many hundreds of authors over the entire expanse of English literature, complete freedom from error would be a minor miracle. Some of the errors will be due to 'pure ignorance'; some to misprints and to slips in the process of compilation; and some to human lapses, as when I have caught myself inadvertently writing 'turn left', when I meant 'turn right', or '1970' when I meant '1870', or 'Street' when I meant 'Square', and so on. But I must also plead that some of the errors are not mine. Authorities often differ among themselves, so that I have repeatedly had to make decisions among several conflicting records. The best check has been the actual letters written by authors themselves—where letters exist and are available. Yet the editors of letters have been known to make mistakes; and authors themselves sometimes write down their own addresses, or the addresses of their correspondents, inaccurately. (At a time when Shelley was having serious matrimonial and financial troubles, and had just moved to Poland Street, he was gravely inconvenienced for some weeks because all letters addressed to him went to Portland Street. Possibly, in his agitation, he had headed his own letters 'Portland' instead of 'Poland'.) And then authors (like all the rest of us) habitually make errors in dating their letters and have bad memories as to the exact time they lived in certain places, and sometimes give addresses belonging to friends or relatives, and sometimes actually try to conceal their place of abode. Truth is an elusive quarry.

One thing I particularly regret is that many of the locations cited are too general—as when merely a street, and not a specific location on the street, is given. This weakness may be due to my inability to resolve conflicting opinions or reconcile differing records. Much more commonly, these too-generalized locations are due to vague records. House numbering was not generally used till the latter part of the eighteenth century. Instead, letters were addressed in some such terms as these: 'Mr So-and-so, Jermyn Street, at Mrs Brown's, over against the Cat and Castle', or 'Mr So-and-So, Briar Cottage, Liverpool Road', or 'Mr So-and-So, Bloomsbury Square'. When we remember that Mr So-and-So was probably only a temporary lodger with Mrs Brown, herself probably a tenant whose name does not appear in the tax records, and that the Cat and Castle may have existed only a few months, and has left not a trace behind—and that Briar Cottage was demolished long ago, and the part of Liverpool Road where it stood may now be called something else—and that Bloomsbury Square had dozens of houses—we can perceive the difficulty of being absolutely exact about certain locations.

Nevertheless, in spite of all the pitfalls, this book does contain a large store of sound information about literary London—more than has ever been previously collected in one place—and (I am convinced) a relative minimum of errors. If the user of this book does find serious inaccuracies, I hope he will tell me about them—if he is positive he is right. And if he finds that I have omitted important items (though he will probably think there is a plethora rather than a paucity here) I hope he will tell me about those items too.

G.W.

Part One

Best
Tours

Tour 1
Westminster

Jeremy Bentham

Richard Bentley

James Boswell

Isaac Hawkins Browne

Robert Browning

Edmund Burke

William Camden

Thomas Campbell

Thomas Carew

William Caxton

Mrs Susannah Centlivre

Geoffrey Chaucer

Charles Churchill

Winston Churchill

Colley Cibber

Jeremy Collier

Richard Cumberland

Charles Darwin

John Denham

Benjamin Disraeli

T. S. Eliot

Gilbert Frankau

Edward Gibbon

William Godwin

R. B. Cunninghame Graham

William Ernest Henley

Robert Herrick

Inigo Jones

Ben Jonson

John Keats

Mrs Charlotte Lennox

John Locke

Richard Lovelace

Sir Charles Lyell

James Macpherson

John Masefield

Harriet Martineau

Henry Milman

John Milton

Sir Thomas More

Sir Isaac Newton

Sir Gilbert Parker

Samuel Pepys

Matthew Prior

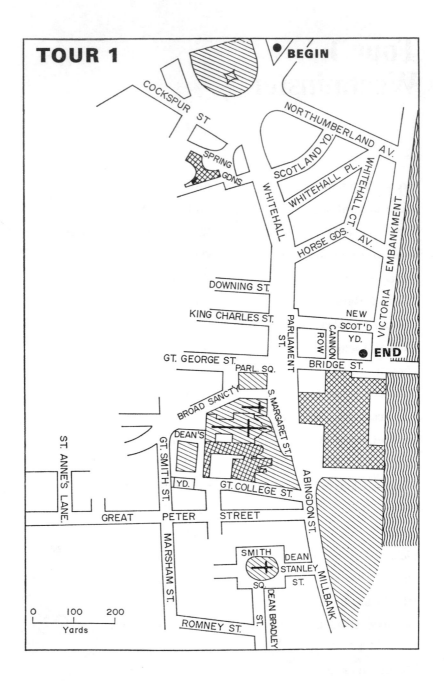

TOUR 1

BEGIN

COCKSPUR ST.

SPRING GDNS

NORTHUMBERLAND AV.

SCOTLAND YD.

WHITEHALL PL.

WHITEHALL CT.

WHITEHALL

HORSE GDS. AV.

VICTORIA EMBANKMENT

DOWNING ST.

KING CHARLES ST.

PARLIAMENT ST.

NEW SCOT'D YD.

GT. GEORGE ST.

CANNON ROW

END

PARL. SQ.

BRIDGE ST.

BROAD SANCT'Y

S. MARGARET ST.

DEAN'S

GT. SMITH ST.

ABINGDON ST.

ST. ANNE'S LANE.

YD.

GT. COLLEGE ST.

GREAT   PETER   STREET

MARSHAM ST.

SMITH SQ.

DEAN STANLEY ST.

DEAN BRADLEY ST.

MILLBANK

0   100   200
Yards

ROMNEY ST.

Henry Purcell	Alfred Tennyson
Sir Walter Raleigh	William Tyndale
Sir Owen Seaman	Nicholas Udall
George Bernard Shaw	Sir John Vanbrugh
Richard Brinsley Sheridan	George Villiers
John Skelton	Edmund Waller
Tobias Smollett	Horace Walpole
Thomas Southerne	H. G. Wells
Edmund Spenser	Sir Charles Hanbury Williams
Sir Richard Steele	

See also the lists printed below in Sections 9 and 12.

Leave the underground at the *Trafalgar Square Station.*

1. On 13 November 1887 (Bloody Sunday) several hundred thousand socialists and labour sympathizers had planned a vast protest meeting in *Trafalgar Square.* The police had forbidden the meeting. The poet William Morris, the dramatist George Bernard Shaw, the theosophist Mrs Annie Besant, and the poet and essayist Edward Carpenter were among the leaders marching on the square. These four, however, were halted by the police, and never reached their destination. But R. B. CUNNINGHAME GRAHAM (1852-1936), author, traveller, aristocrat, and liberal, did attain the square. From the north corner of the Strand (left rear of Lord Nelson on his column) Graham led a rush across the street against a police line protecting the square. A policeman bloodied Graham's head with a truncheon. and a police horse stepped on his great toe, taking the nail off. Graham was carted off to jail, where he spent a miserable night.

2. Immediately in front of Lord Nelson you will see an equestrian statue of King Charles I in the middle of the street. (The statue has stood here for over 300 years.) King Charles faces straight down the street called Whitehall. Cross over the street in front of Lord Nelson, and walk down the left side of *Whitehall.* On the other (right-hand) side of the street, directly to King Charles's right, and about where the street opens towards the huge, columned Admiralty Arch, the poet JOHN MILTON (1608-74) lived in 1649.

The area running just in front of the arch was, in the eighteenth century, a wide and fashionable residential area called *Spring Gardens*. COLLEY CIBBER (1671-1757), actor, theatre manager, autobiographer, dramatist, Poet Laureate, and victim of Alexander Pope (in the long satirical poem the *Dunciad*, lived in *Spring Gardens*, 1711-14.

On your side of Whitehall you will pass the small entrance of Craig's Court. Seven or eight doors down from this, the great nature poet JAMES THOMSON (1700-45) lived in his early London days, and here he worked on his poem 'Summer'. Almost directly across the street from this place stands the Admiralty—and beside it, to your right, you will see a small opening between buildings. This was once a residential place, called *Buckingham Court*, where MRS SUSANNAH CENTLIVRE (1667?-1723), the dramatist, lived and died. She wrote many lively, highly successful, and still enjoyable, comedies, and two tragedies.

[2A. A few steps farther along Whitehall, *Great Scotland Yard* opens to your left. It is now so changed from what once it was that visiting it may not be worth your while. In the seventeenth century it was not merely a street, but a wide 'yard' surrounded by buildings. The residences and offices of the Royal Architect were located here. INIGO JONES (1573-1652), architect, stage-designer, and writer of masques (dramatic productions related to the modern musical extravaganza), lived here—as did SIR JOHN DENHAM (1615-69), architect, poet, and dramatist, who died here; and also SIR JOHN VANBRUGH (1664-1726), flamboyant architect, and writer of coarse and witty prose comedies. JOHN MILTON resided here when he was Latin Secretary to the Council of State. Here he lost his only son (1650), as well as the sight of his left eye. The once-famous poet THOMAS CAMPBELL (1777-1844), author of the long didactic poem *The Pleasures of Hope* (and of the song 'Ye Mariners of England'), lived here for some years after his wife's death in 1829. *Susannah Maria Arne Cibber* (1714-66), singer and actress, daughter of the famous musical composer Dr Thomas Arne, and wife of the actor Theophilus Cibber (who was the son of the Poet Laureate Colley Cibber), lived on this street for a long time in the 1740's and 1750's.

[SIR JOHN DENHAM is remembered as the author of one of the first true nature poems in the language, 'Cooper's Hill', written in 1642. During the Civil Wars he intervened to save the life of the poet Edmund Waller, who had been accused of treason because of his somewhat wishy-washy behaviour in the wars. By way of explaining his intervention, Denham said, 'If Waller dies, *I* shall then be the worst poet in England!' While he was living in Scot-

land Yard, his young wife openly became the mistress of the Duke
of York (later, King James II), with Denham's full knowledge, and
possibly his consent and approbation—though his wife died early,
and scandal had it that Denham gave her poison in a cup of
chocolate.]

3. Continue down Whitehall, and turn left into Whitehall Place, the
next street beyond Great Scotland Yard. After passing the War Office
on your right, turn right at the first street, which is *Whitehall Court.*
Here *No. 2* is the address of the Authors' Club—which was also the
address of SIR OWEN SEAMAN (1861-1936), editor of *Punch* and author
of many humorous books and essays, from 1925 to 1930; and of SIR
GILBERT PARKER (1867-1932), novelist and politician, in the 1920's
and 1930's. After 1930, Sir Owen lived at *No. 9.* H. G. WELLS (1866-
1946), novelist, scientist and sociologist, lived at *No. 4* (Flat 120) for a
while. The dramatist GEORGE BERNARD SHAW (1856-1950) lived also
at *No. 4* (Flat 130), whenever he was in London from 1928 to 1945.
[3A. Continue down Whitehall Court. At its end, turn left, and walk
around the corner to the attractive gardens where stands a statue of
WILLIAM TYNDALE (d. 1536), humanist, Protestant reformer, translator of the Bible into English—who was executed in Antwerp for
his religious beliefs.... Now return to the foot of Whitehall Court,
from which you originally emerged.]

4. On the right, just beyond the Air Ministry, and almost opposite the
end of Whitehall Court, lies the entrance into *Whitehall Gardens.*
Turn into it. The place is now a paved car park—sadly unlike the
fashionable garden it once was. At what was *No. 8* (on your left, near
the entrance) lived CHARLES HANBURY WILLIAMS (1708-59), poet,
satirist, humorous writer, and diplomat. *No. 3*, farther down on your
left was the home of the parents of the poet *Charles Algernon Swinburne*; they moved out just before he was born. Still farther down,
at *No. 2*, lived the novelist and Prime Minister BENJAMIN DISRAELI
(1804-81), from 1875 to 1880.

5. Return to the place where you entered the 'Gardens' (on Horse-
guard Avenue), and turn left, towards Whitehall. Just at the corner,
on your left, stands the famous *Banqueting Hall.* Designed by INIGO
JONES (see above), it is regarded by architectural experts as 'one of
the noblest things in London'. In a previous hall on approximately
this site (built in 1581, but destroyed by fire in 1619) Shakespeare's
Othello is thought to have been first performed (1604). The original
building was renovated and virtually rebuilt from 1605 to 1607, and

was opened in January, 1608, with *The Mask of Beauty*, by BEN JONSON (1572-1637), poet, dramatist, and friend of Shakespeare. Innumerable other plays and masques by *Jonson, Thomas Campion, Francis Beaumont, James Shirley*, and many others were presented before the royal court here. From a window of the present building, King Charles I stepped out to the scaffold in Whitehall where he was beheaded (1649).

The Banqueting Hall is all that remains of Whitehall Palace—a huge rabbit-warren of houses, halls, wings, apartments, offices, and courtyards, that stretched from Great Scotland Yard more than halfway down to Big Ben. In the other (east-west) direction, it extended from the river almost to St James's Park. It began, in the thirteenth century, as the palace of the Archbishop of York, and had accumulated through the years into a vast pile when Henry VIII seized it from the reigning Archbishop of York, Cardinal Wolsey—at the same time that Wolsey himself was seized and charged with treason. Subsequent monarchs lived in it, along with their courtiers, mistresses, retainers, and *their* families, and enlarged upon it, until its final abandonment as a royal residence by William III (of Orange) about 1690. (Its damp location, near the river, aggravated his asthma.) Fires had destroyed various parts of it before this; but finally the whole thing (except the Banqueting House) burned to the ground in January 1698.

The poets *Sir Philip Sidney* and *Sir Walter Raleigh* took part in tournaments held within the palace Tilt Yard—which lay just opposite the Banqueting House, towards St James's Park; *Milton* worked within the palace; *Samuel Pepys* often had business here; and in other halls besides the Banqueting House playwrights presented comedies, tragedies, and masques before Queen Elizabeth I, King James I, Charles II, and all their courts.

A thoroughfare called *King Street* once ran beside (later on, right through) Whitehall Palace—from Charing Cross to Westminster Hall. It lay a little farther from the river than the present street called Whitehall. EDMUND SPENSER (1552?-99), author of *The Faerie Queene*, and the greatest poet, next to Shakespeare, of the Elizabethan Age, died in poverty on King Street; and THOMAS CAREW (1597-1639?), author of graceful 'cavalier lyrics', lived there.

Continue down Whitehall (noting the statue of *Sir Walter Raleigh* just down the street from the Banqueting Hall) till you reach *Downing Street*, on your right. *No. 10* is, of course, the official residence of the Prime Minister, who has, as a rule, lived here since the ministry of Sir Robert Walpole, 1721-42. Sir Robert's son, the letter-writer and novelist HORACE WALPOLE (1717-97), lived here with his father; and two Prime Ministers celebrated for their literary works as well as for their political accomplishments occupied this house: the novelist BENJAMIN DISRAELI (see above), and the historian WINSTON CHURCHILL (1874-1965). Before any of these, the poet and dramatist GEORGE VILLIERS, SECOND DUKE OF BUCKINGHAM (1628-87), lived at this spot.

The fascinating and slightly scandalous *London Journal* of the young JAMES BOSWELL (1740-95), later biographer of Dr Samuel Johnson, was mostly written in the young man's first permanent lodgings in London—just across the street from, and slightly beyond, the place occupied by No. 10. The novelist TOBIAS SMOLLETT (1721-77), who was a physician as well as a writer, established quarters for himself as a professional surgeon in a nearby house in 1744.

6. Return to Whitehall, and continue down it (it becomes Parliament Street) to *King Charles Street*, which is the next street entering from the right. At about this location, or a few yards farther down, *Axe Yard* formerly led off to the right. Here lived SAMUEL PEPYS (1633-1703), prominent as a government official in his own time, but remembered today as the author of the most honest, intimate, and charming diary ever written. He was living at this place when he made his first entry in the diary, January 1 1660.... Axe Yard was destroyed by the building of *Fludyer Street*, about 1767. On this street lived JAMES MACPHERSON (1736-96), author of the 'Ossianic poems', in 1792; and HARRIET MARTINEAU (1802-76), political writer and philosopher, and social reformer, lived here, at *No. 17*, from 1833 to 1839.... Fludyer Street was swept away in turn (1864-5), and replaced by government offices.

> JAMES MACPHERSON was a Scotsman who claimed to have discovered some manuscripts of ancient Gaelic poems, and to have translated them into modern English. Actually, they were his own work, but based on Gaelic myth. Dr Johnson declared at once that they were forgeries; but some other great literary men (including the poet Thomas Gray) believed them authentic. The controversy developed into a personal quarrel between Dr Johnson and Macpherson, with each man threatening bodily injury to the other. In any event, both were eventually buried in Westminster Abbey—and the Ossianic poems were translated into most languages of Western Europe, and became immensely popular.

7. Just opposite the entrance of King Charles Street, Derby Gate leads off from Whitehall. Turn into it. After a short block it becomes New Scotland Yard, where the Police Station (famed in many a spy and detective story) was located from the 1890's to the 1960's. But, just before you reach the police station, turn right into *Cannon Row*.

MATTHEW PRIOR (1664-1721), poet, wit, and diplomat, was brought up on this street in his uncle's Rhenish Wine House. SAMUEL PEPYS (see above) visited this wine house often to conduct business, drinking, and flirtations. Having dined one Mrs Lane here, he says that he 'did touse and feel her all over ... and indeed she has a very white thigh and leg'. JOHN LOCKE (1632-1704) was living in a little courtyard that led off the left-hand side of this street when his *Essay Concerning Human Understanding* (1690), one of the key books of philosophy, was published. JAMES MACPHERSON (see above) lived between this street and the river in 1779.... Follow Cannon Street down to Bridge Street, and here turn right, and reach Parliament Street. Cross the latter, and continue straight along Great George Street, with Parliament Square (trees and statues) on your left.

8. Opposite the far corner of Parliament Square, turn left (across Great George Street), and walk along in front of the Lincoln statue. Just to your left is a statue of *Benjamin Disraeli*, a successful novelist before he became Prime Minister. Veering slightly to your right, you will have no trouble reaching the main entrance of Westminster Abbey. Off to your right, beyond the open space before the Abbey, and just this side of a confluence of streets that you will note, once ran a thick wall, with a gatehouse almost directly in line with the Abbey entrance. This gatehouse served as a prison. SIR WALTER RALEIGH (1552?-1618) was brought here the day before his execution, and was taken from here to the scaffold at the other end of the Abbey. The night before his death he wrote here the little poem beginning, 'Even such is time'. Later on, the poet RICHARD LOVELACE (1618-57) was imprisoned here because of his royalist sympathies, and is said to have written the famous little poem 'To Althea, from Prison' (beginning 'Stone walls do not a prison make') while confined here. SAMUEL PEPYS was also imprisoned in the gatehouse (1690) on suspicion of having corresponded with the exiled King James II, as was the clergyman JEREMY COLLIER (1650-1726), on the same charge. Collier has a place in literary history because his *Short View of the Immorality and Profaneness of the English Stage* (1698) helped bring an end to the writing of comedies with broad speech and sexual implications that had characterized the Restoration period. COLLEY CIBBER (see above) was confined here for debt, in 1697.

9. Turn now to *Westminster Abbey* itself. Just to the right of the main door (before you enter) lies the Jerusalem Chamber. It was here that Henry IV (Chaucer's and Falstaff's king) was brought after he had had a fatal stroke in the Abbey; it had been predicted that he

would die in Jerusalem. The chamber was the regular meeting place of the scholars and literary men who had been commissioned to make that translation of the Bible now known as the King James Version— a monument of English literature. Remember that every person with a memorial in the Abbey is not buried here. This is true of SIR WINSTON CHURCHILL, whose memorial plaque you will see in the floor just as you enter the Abbey.

But look on the floor against the left wall for the grave of SIR CHARLES LYELL (1797-1875), the geologist who first established the age of the earth as being millions of years, instead of the few thousand allotted by orthodox biblical chronologists. Without him, Darwin could not have formulated the doctrine of evolution. Farther along on this same side, at the very end of the aisle, is the grave of CHARLES DARWIN (1809-82) himself. And a bit to the right of this is the tomb, with its monstrous memorial statuary, of the mathematician and physicist SIR ISAAC NEWTON (1642-1727).

Turn now into the right-hand (south) aisle, and go straight ahead until you reach a barrier where an attendant is stationed to demand your entrance fee. Do not pay it just yet, but turn sharply to the right, and find yourself in the world-famous 'Poets' Corner'. The wealth of literary associations here is overwhelming—what with the thronging memorials and crowded graves. Here you find the tomb of GEOFFREY CHAUCER, with the graves of ROBERT BROWNING, ALFRED TENNYSON, T. S. ELIOT, and JOHN MASEFIELD just in front of it; the grave of Shakespeare's friend the dramatist BEN JONSON, who was buried standing upright because (it is said) of some joke he had with Bishop Williams, dean of the Abbey, to the effect that Jonson could never hope to attain more than two square feet of Abbey space.

Most of the literary personalities buried in Poets' Corner, or in the adjoining St Faith's Chapel, or elsewhere in the Abbey, are included in the following list. The date given is the date of burial; the names asterisked have no monument in the Abbey.

JOSEPH ADDISON, poet, essayist, dramatist (1719)

FRANCIS BEAUMONT,* dramatist, collaborator with John Fletcher (1616)

APHRA BEHN, writer of coarse and witty comedies, and a novel 1689)

THOMAS BETTERTON, actor and adapter of Shakespeare's plays (1710)

ROBERT BROWNING, major Victorian poet (1889)

EDWARD BULWER-LYTTON, novelist (1873)

WILLIAM CAMDEN, historian, humanist, teacher (1623)

THOMAS CAMPBELL, poet (1844)

GEOFFREY CHAUCER, poet (1400)

MRS SUSANNAH CIBBER, singer and actress (1758)

WILLIAM CONGREVE, dramatist (1729)
ABRAHAM COWLEY, poet (1667)
WILLIAM D'AVENANT, poet and dramatist (1668)
JOHN DENHAM,* poet (1669)
CHARLES DICKENS, novelist (1870)
MICHAEL DRAYTON, poet and dramatist (1631)
JOHN DRYDEN, poet, dramatist, essayist, critic (1700)
T. S. ELIOT, American-born poet and dramatist (1965)
DAVID GARRICK, actor and dramatist (1779)
JOHN GAY, poet and dramatist (1732)
RICHARD HAKLUYT, geographer and historian (1616)
THOMAS HARDY, novelist and poet (1928)
AARON HILL, essayist, poet and dramatist (1750)
BEN JONSON, poet and dramatist (1637)
DR SAMUEL JOHNSON, essayist, poet, scholar, critic (1784)
THOMAS KILLIGREW,* dramatist and theatre manager (1683)
RUDYARD KIPLING, poet, writer of short stories, novelist (1936)
THOMAS BABINGTON MACAULAY, historian, poet, biographer (1859)
JAMES MACPHERSON, poet (1796)
JOHN MASEFIELD, poet and novelist, Poet Laureate (1967)
MATTHEW PRIOR, poet (1721)
HENRY PURCELL, musician (1695)
EARL OF ROSCOMMON,* poet (1685)
NICHOLAS ROWE, dramatist (1718)
RICHARD BRINSLEY SHERIDAN, dramatist (1816)
EDMUND SPENSER, poet (1599)
SIR WILLIAM TEMPLE, essayist, historian, statesman (1699)
ALFRED TENNYSON, poet (1892)
GEORGE VILLIERS, SECOND DUKE OF BUCKINGHAM, poet, dramatist, scholar (1687)

10. When you leave the Abbey, walk well out in front of the main door till you see an arched entrance on your left. Turn into it, and enter *Dean's Yard*—which was not originally a part of the Abbey, but had its name from being near the Abbey's deanery. Residences once occupied the region straight ahead of you (on the far side of the yard) as well as the area to your right. EDMUND BURKE (1729-97), states-man, essayist, and political philosopher lived here at one time. WIL-LIAM CAMDEN (1551-1623), scholar and historian, lived above a gate on the left-hand side of the Yard. MRS CHARLOTTE LENNOX (1720-1804), American-born novelist whom Dr Johnson admired, lived and died here. And EDWARD GIBBON (1737-94) made prolonged visits to his dearly beloved and motherly aunt, a Mrs Porten, who had a boarding

house for Westminster schooldays at the far (south) end of the Yard.

11. On your left, a gate through the wall leads to *Little Dean's Yard*. Though the public is not allowed to enter here, you may, perhaps, peek around the corner, and see *Ashburton House* stretching across the top of the Yard, to your left. Here the famous Cotton Library (now in the British Museum) was once kept. A fire in 1731 destroyed 114 of its 958 priceless medieval books. DR RICHARD BENTLEY (1662-1742), minor philosopher, famous critic, and 'generally conceded to have been one of the greatest of all English classical scholars', was visiting here on the night of the fire. He rushed about in his nightshirt and nightcap saving books. HENRY MILMAN (1791-1868), later Dean of St Paul's, lived in this house when he was a prebendary of the Abbey. Though Milman wrote several dramas on historical subjects, he is really memorable for his *History of the Jews* (1830)—the first English book to discuss the Jews objectively, as if they were any other historical nation instead of God's chosen people. The book evoked an ecclesiastical storm.

12. Surrounding Little Dean's Yard are the buildings of *Westminster School*, founded in the fourteenth century, and rejuvenated by Queen Elizabeth in 1560. NICHOLAS UDALL (1505-56), author of *Ralph Roister Doister*, first extant English comedy, was a master of the school; and WILLIAM CAMDEN (see above) was a later master. A list of boys who were students here, and later became celebrated figures, would include these:

WILLIAM CARTWRIGHT (1611-43), dramatist, poet, preacher.
CHARLES CHURCHILL (1731-64), satirical poet.
GEORGE COLMAN THE ELDER (1732-94), dramatist and theatre manager.
GEORGE COLMAN THE YOUNGER (1762-1836), dramatist and theatre manager.
ABRAHAM COWLEY (1618-67), poet and essayist.
WILLIAM COWPER (1731-1800), poet.
RICHARD CUMBERLAND (1732-1811), dramatist.
JOHN DRYDEN (1631-1700), poet, dramatist, essayist, critic.
JOHN DYER (1700?-58), poet.
EDWARD GIBBON (1737-94), historian.
RICHARD HAKLUYT (1552?-1616), geographer and historian.
GEORGE HERBERT (1593-1633), poet.
AARON HILL (1685-1750), poet and dramatist.
BEN JONSON (1572-1637), poet and dramatist.
NATHANIEL LEE (1653-92), dramatist.

MATTHEW ('MONK') LEWIS (1775-1818), novelist.
JOHN LOCKE (1623-1704), philosopher.
EDWARD MARSH (1872-1953), editor, biographer, critic.
A. A. MILNE (1882-1956), poet, dramatist, children's writer.
CHARLES MONTAGU, EARL OF HALIFAX (1661-1715), satirical poet.
MATTHEW PRIOR (1664-1721), poet.
NICHOLAS ROWE (1674-1718), dramatist.
ROBERT SOUTHEY (1774-1843), poet, historian, Poet Laureate.
CHARLES WESLEY (1707-88), hymn writer.

13. Leave Dean's Yard by the gate opposite the one you entered, and find yourself in *Great College Street*. To your right, as you leave the Yard, is the Church House, covering the spot once occupied by *No. 25*, where the poet JOHN KEATS (1795-1821) lived for a while in 1819. He left here to move nearer to his beloved Fanny Brawne, in Hampstead. At *No. 1*, near the river, lived WILLIAM ERNEST HENLEY (1849-1903), poet and editor, author (unfortunately) of 'Invictus'.

At this point, it would probably be better for you to walk on towards the river, and turn left on Abingdon Street. But if you have a special interest in some of the figures mentioned below, you may wish to continue with Sections 14 through 18.

14. From the place where you emerged from Dean's Yard, enter Tufton Street, and wind your way, via Little Smith Street, to *Great Smith Street*. SIR RICHARD STEELE (1672-1729), essayist, dramatist, journalist, theatre manager and politician, lived on this street in 1707. THOMAS SOUTHERNE (1660-1746), dramatist, died here. (The National Library for the Blind stands almost opposite the entrance of Little Smith Street into Great Smith Street.)

15. Turn left on Great Smith Street, and reach the crossing of Great Peter Street. If you think it worth your while (since nothing remains of the old buildings) turn right, into Great Peter Street, and, after two blocks, find *St Ann Street*, (formerly *Lane*) on your right. ROBERT HERRICK (1591-1674), 'greatest of the Cavalier poets', author of many well-remembered and exquisitely beautiful lyrics, spent his last years here. As a clergyman, he had been appointed to a living in the country; but he gave it up, and came to London, where he felt happier. HENRY PURCELL (1659-95), the musician (one of the two or three major musicians whom England has produced), also lived here.

16. Return along Great Peter Street the way you came, until you reach Great Smith Street once more. Here, turn right, on Marsham Street,

go two blocks, and turn left into *Romney Street*. CHARLES CHURCHILL (1731-64), satirical poet, was born on this street—his father being curate of the nearby church of St John the Evangelist. He wrote the highly successful *Rosciad*, a satire on leading actors and actresses of his time, was a friend of the unruly and dissolute politician John Wilkes, and a contributor to the latter's *North Briton*.

17. Continue to the end of Romney Street, and turn left, on Dean Bradley Street. Almost immediately, you will reach *Smith Square*, with the church of St John the Evangelist in the middle of it. CHARLES CHURCHILL (see above), became a lecturer and substitute curate for his father in the church—till his conduct (drunkenness, rowdiness, and wenching—a bit loose by even eighteenth-century standards) caused the parishioners to complain to higher authorities who made Churchill resign.

18. From the back of the church, move through Dean Stanley Street to Millbank, and turn left. (In the early nineteenth century the river ran nearer to Millbank than at present; and it was just here that David Copperfield, in *Dickens*'s novel, and Mr Peggotty saved the street girl Martha from suicide in the river.) If you care to visit the gardens between Millbank and the river, you will find Rodin's fine bronze statue of 'The Burghers of Calais'—and also a statue of Mrs Emmeline Pankhurst (1857-1928), early militant leader of the Women's Suffrage movement.

At the end of Millbank you will be back where you were at the end of Section 13—that is, at the beginning of Abingdon Street.

19. Walk up *Abingdon Street* towards the Abbey. On this street lived RICHARD BENTLEY (see above), scholar and critic; and also ISAAC HAWKINS BROWNE (1706-60), who wrote Latin poetry, as well as a delightful collection of imitations and parodies of contemporary poets (called *A Pipe of Tobacco*). Just to your right, where the gardens now lie, was once a collection of short streets and courts called Abingdon Buildings, where the dramatist RICHARD CUMBERLAND (1732-1811) was living in the late 1750's.

Abingdon Street runs into *Old Palace Yard* (now mostly a parking lot) with the ornate Victorian-Gothic Parliament Buildings (constructed 1840-52) to your right. The Yard was formerly an execution place, and here SIR WALTER RALEIGH (1552?-1618), historian, poet, philosopher, and adventurer, was executed. His last words were characteristic, and should be immortal. When the executioner suggested that he kneel before the block with his head to the east, Sir Walter answered: 'What matter how the head lie, so long as the heart be right?'

20. To the left juts out the *Henry* VII *Chapel* of Westminster Abbey. It is built on the site of a cottage in which GEOFFREY CHAUCER (1340?-1400), England's first great poet, lived his last few years, and died. The octagonal, spired building to the left of the chapel is the *Chapter House*. Next to this WILLIAM CAXTON (1422?-91), England's first printer, set up England's first printing press, and produced and sold England's first printed book.

21. Beyond the Old Palace Yard, and to the right, stands ancient *Westminster Hall*—dating from 1099, but virtually rebuilt by Richard II in 1394-9. It was the scene of many state trials, including that of the philosopher and humanist SIR THOMAS MORE (1478-1535), author of *Utopia*. Here Warren Hastings was tried—two of the more important members of the prosecution being EDMUND BURKE (see above) and the dramatist-politician RICHARD BRINSLEY SHERIDAN (1751-1816)—both of whom made famous orations against Hastings. (He was acquitted.) Lord Byron, a hot-headed ancestor of the poet, was tried for murder here. Since the Law Courts (Exchequer, Chancery, King's Bench, Queen's Bench, Common Pleas) were held, for centuries, in the open hall, or in stalls later built inside, along the walls—and since the floor and the walls were crowded with a multitude of other miscellaneous stalls of booksellers, stationers, seamstresses, and dealers in toys, novelties, and notions—it is likely that most London writers from Chaucer on to the mid-nineteenth century had business here at one time or another. Chaucer himself sat here as a member of Parliament in 1386.

22. *St Margaret's Church* stands on the left of the street, across from Westminster Hall. Built (or rebuilt) in 1504-23, and restored several times since, it has long been associated with the marriages and the burials of people important in government. Some *marriages* that have taken place here are those of JEREMY BENTHAM, Utilitarian philosopher; THOMAS CAMPBELL, poet; WINSTON CHURCHILL, statesman; GILBERT FRANKAU, poet and novelist; JOHN MILTON, poet (his second marriage); SAMUEL PEPYS, diarist; EDMUND WALLER, poet.

Burials in the church or churchyard include those of WILLIAM CAXTON, England's first printer; SIR WALTER RALEIGH (probably); JOHN SKELTON, Poet Laureate under Henry VIII; NICHOLAS UDALL; the wife of the poet JOHN DENHAM; and the second wife and the infant child of JOHN MILTON.

BEN JONSON (see above), poet and dramatist, spent his last years, and died, in a little cottage that stood between St Margaret's Church and Westminster Abbey.

Inside the church are two windows given by Americans—one in memory of SIR WALTER RALEIGH, with an inscription by the American poet *James Russell Lowell*; and the other in memory of JOHN MILTON, with an inscription by the American poet *John Greenleaf Whittier*. Verses on a memorial window to CAXTON are by *Alfred Tennyson*; those on a window to Queen Victoria are by *Robert Browning*.

23. Leave the church, and walk on up the street between Parliament Square and *New Palace Yard* (the fenced area on your right). During the last three years of his life, WILLIAM GODWIN (1756-1836), philosopher, novelist, and father of *Mary Godwin Shelley* (wife of the poet Shelley), held a sinecure as Yeoman Usher of the Exchequer; and with the position went a residence in one of the buildings (since removed) that fronted the Yard. Here Godwin died. This yard, too, was used as an execution place; and, later on, a pillory stood here. For everyone who cares about freedom of the press, it will be interesting to know that the last person to stand in the pillory here, and the last in England, was one John Williams, printer and bookseller, whose crime was that he had republished John Wilkes's *North Briton* —with its attacks on royal tyranny. But his punishment—like that of Defoe more than sixty years earlier—was a triumph for Williams and freedom. A great multitude came to cheer him, and when he was released, escorted him home. This was 14 February 1765.

The *Westminster Underground Station* is just across the street beyond the New Palace Yard. Here this tour ends—or you may go on from here to *Tour No. 16.*

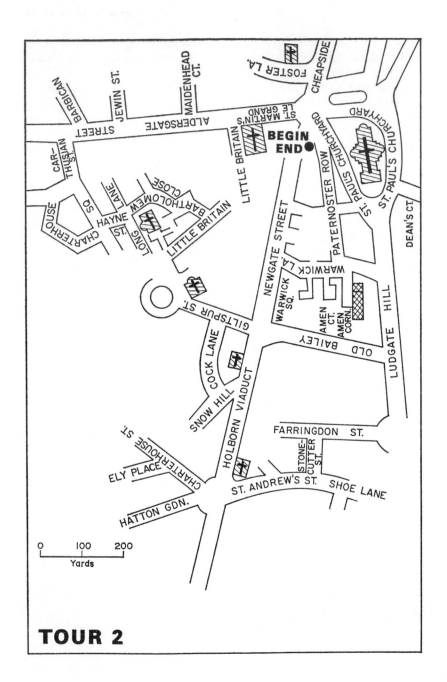

TOUR 2

26

Tour 2
Aldersgate and St Paul's

Joseph Addison

Roger Ascham

R. H. Barham

Max Beerbohm

Thomas Lovell Beddoes

Sir Richard Blackmore

Robert Bridges

Bronte Sisters

Thomas Browne

John Bunyan

William Camden

Thomas Campion

Thomas Chatterton

John Colet

William Cowper

Richard Crashaw

William Davenant

John Day

Daniel Defoe

Thomas Dekker

Walter de la Mare

Benjamin Disraeli

John Donne

George Dyer

John Foxe

Benjamin Franklin

Oliver Goldsmith

Ralph Griffiths

Henry Hallam

William Hazlitt

Robert Herrick

William Hogarth

Thomas Hood

William and Mary Howitt

John Hughes

Leigh Hunt

Washington Irving

Dr Samuel Johnson

Inigo Jones

Ben Jonson

Charles Lamb

Nathaniel Lee

Richard le Gallienne

Sir Roger l'Estrange

Thomas Linacre	Richard Savage
Robert Lloyd	Elkinah Settle
Richard Lovelace	Sir Philip Sidney
John Lyly	John Smith
Sir Thomas Malory	Sydney Smith
Christopher Marlowe	Tobias Smollett
George Meredith	Robert Southwell
Henry Hart Milman	Sir Richard Steele
John Milton	Henry Howard, Earl of Surrey
Thomas Nash	William Makepeace Thackery
George Peele	Anthony Trollope
Samuel Pepys	Edmund Waller
Thomas Percy	Thomas Watson
Samuel Purchas	John Wesley
Francis Quarles	Charles Williams
Ann Radcliffe	George Wither
James Ralph	Sir Thomas Wyatt
Sir Joshua Reynolds	William Wycherley
Samuel Richardson	John Wyclif
Henry Crabb Robinson	

Leave the underground at *St Paul's Station.*

1. Approximately on the site of the station itself stood the church of St Michael le Querne (burned down in the Great Fire of 1666), where SIR THOMAS BROWNE (1605-82), author of the baroque *Religio Medici* and *Hydrotaphia: or Urn-Burial*, was baptized.

2. Cross over the large street just in front of the station.
[2A. If you think it worth while, turn right, after crossing, and walk along Cheapside for one block, till you find *Foster Lane*, on your left. A few steps up it, on the right, stands *St Vedast's Church.* This

28

church, though it was badly bombed and has been much restored, was built by Sir Christopher Wren, 1670-3. In a previous church on the same spot the best of the Cavalier poets, ROBERT HERRICK (1591-1674), was baptized. A bit farther up Foster Lane, but on the left, stood *St Leonard's Church*, which was burned down in the Great Fire, but not rebuilt. In its churchyard was buried FRANCIS QUARLES (1592-1644), a vehement royalist and a pious poet whose volume of *Emblems* (poems to go with symbolic pictures) was 'the most popular book of verse in the seventeenth century'. Horace Walpole, more than a century later, remarked wittily: 'Milton had to wait till the world had done admiring Quarles.' The book went through more than 50 editions, and was popular for two and a half centuries after its first appearance (1635).... Now return to where you first crossed the large street after leaving the underground.]

You will find yourself at the entrance of *St Martin's le Grand*. You may notice a plaque here stating that SIR THOMAS BROWNE (see above) was born somewhere in this vicinity. The area immediately to your right was once occupied by *St Martin le Grand Collegiate Church*—where JOHN COLET (1467?-1519), early humanist, was a canon. Opposite this site, and on the left of the street, where part of the great General Post Office now stands, was *Northumberland House*, owned at one time by the Henry Percy (Hotspur) who figures in Shakespeare's *Henry* IV. BISHOP THOMAS PERCY (1729-1811), who, through his three-volume collection of medieval poems and ballads, *Reliques of Ancient English Poetry* (1765), contributed enormously to the revival of interest in the medieval world, lived here in the 1770's. On the right-hand side of the street, opposite the present General Post Office, stood the Old General Post Office, where the novelist ANTHONY TROLLOPE (1815-82) worked from 1834 to 1841.

3. Ahead of you, just this side of the church you can see on your left, the actual old *Aldersgate* lay across the street. From the thirteenth or fourteenth century there were residential apartments over the gate. Chaucer's friend *Ralph Strode*, to whom Chaucer dedicated his *Troilus and Criseyde*, lived in these gatehouse apartments in 1375—at a time when Chaucer himself was living in similar apartments over Aldgate. In the time of Elizabeth I the printer JOHN DAY (or DAYE) lived over Aldersgate; he printed *The Schoolmaster*, by Roger Ascham, a famous Renaissance discussion of education; William Tyndale's works; and *The Acts and Monuments of the Church* (called *The Book of Martyrs*) by the arch-Protestant and arch-Puritan JOHN FOXE (1516-87), who probably lived here with Day in 1567.

4. Just beyond this point, on your left, stands *St Botolph's Church.* The poet THOMAS HOOD (1799-1845), a humourist who, ironically, is remembered for his tragic 'The Song of the Shirt' and 'The Bridge of Sighs', was married here in 1825.

Along the far side of the church, the street called *Little Britain* leads off to the left. As early as the sixteenth century, and as late as the eighteenth, this street was famous for its printers and booksellers. England's first daily newspaper, the *Daily Courant* (1702), was first printed here, as were the *Spectator* papers—the latter apparently in the little court to your right, just after you enter the street. The boy who became DR SAMUEL JOHNSON (1709-84) lodged on this street with his mother when she brought him to London to be touched by the queen as a cure for the skin disease from which he suffered all his life. The American BENJAMIN FRANKLIN (1706-90) lodged here while working as a printer in 1725. At first he had for room-mate another American who had come over with him, the rascally poet JAMES RALPH (1705-62).

5. Now return to the main street which you left to enter Little Britain. It has become *Aldersgate Street.* Continue along it in the direction you were previously walking (northward).

The area alongside this street, on the right, farther up, was undergoing some drastic 'improvements' when this book was being prepared. Consequently, the next few streets mentioned may have disappeared by the time you are making this tour. But for the sake of the record, the following notes are included:

Just beyond the street now called London Wall, *Maidenhead Court* led away to the right. Here lived the poet JOHN MILTON (1608-74), in a house on the left, about halfway down the court, in 1643-5. His first wife left him while he was living here, and he immediately wrote his famous (and, for that time, shocking) pamphlet defending divorce.

Farther up Aldersgate Street, at *No. 35*, on the right, is the entrance to the new (1925) Ironmongers' Hall. Directly opposite this, on the left-hand side of Aldersgate Street, stood *Petre House* (or *Peterhouse*) where the poet RICHARD LOVELACE (1618-57) was imprisoned for political reasons in 1648.

A little farther up Aldersgate Street, *Jewin Street* entered from the right. JOHN MILTON, poet, and fighter for all liberal causes in politics and religion, lived near the far end of this street in the years immediately following the Restoration (1660). Here he wrote most of *Paradise Lost.*

6. Still farther up Aldersgate Street, the *Barbican* enters from the

right. JOHN MILTON (see above) lived here, 1645-7. His house was on the left, at about where the present *No. 17* stands. His father (and also, it is said, his father-in-law Richard Powell) died here in 1647.

7. Continue along Aldersgate Street, and on past the Aldersgate Station, on your left. Just beyond that station, Carthusian Street leads away to your left. Take this little street, and reach *Charterhouse Square*. On the far (north) side of the square, to your right, stand the buildings of the *Charterhouse*. This was a school, established early in the seventeenth century, for 'forty poor boys' of London, that remained here till 1872. Former students of the school include JOSEPH ADDISON (1672-1719), poet, dramatist and essayist; THOMAS LOVELL BEDDOES (1803-49), poet and dramatist; RICHARD CRASHAW (1612-49), one of the best of the 'metaphysical' poets; NATHANIEL LEE (1653?-92), dramatist; the lyric poet RICHARD LOVELACE (see above); SIR RICHARD STEELE (1672-1729), dramatist and essayist, who became friends with Addison while both were students here; WILLIAM MAKEPEACE THACKERAY (1811-63), the novelist; and JOHN WESLEY (1703-91), evangelist and founder of the Methodist Church. The Charterhouse was also a refuge for 80 destitute old men of London. And here ELKINAH SETTLE (1648-1724), once a famous and successful dramatist, a rival of Dryden during Charles II's reign, died penniless Thackeray's Colonel Newcome (of *The Newcomes*) attended school here, returned as a destitute old man, and died here. The dramatist and theatre manager WILLIAM DAVENANT (1606-68) had lodgings in the Charterhouse yard in 1655.

8. At the right-hand upper corner of Charterhouse Square, *Rutland Place* marks the site of the old Rutland House. Here WILLIAM DAVENANT (see above) was allowed by the Puritan government (which frowned on public theatrical spectacles) to produce his opera *The Siege of Rhodes* in 1656.

9. Return to the bottom of Charterhouse Square, right-hand (southwest) corner, cross a street, and take little Hayne Street, leading straight away from the square. Follow it on down, cross Long Lane, and enter Kinghorn Street (which opens directly opposite the end of Hayne Street). Follow this narrow, ancient passage till it runs into *Bartholomew Close*. On this winding street JOHN MILTON (see above), who had been a power in the Puritan government, hid, in the house of a friend, during the first few months of the Restoration; he feared that the returning king would seek vengeance on him—which might well have happened had it not been for his poetry, that 'one talent

31

which is death to hide'. The artist WILLIAM HOGARTH (1697-1764) (whose work has almost as much literary as artistic significance) was born on the lower part of this street—at about where *No. 58* now stands.

10. Bartholomew Close ends its winding in *Little Britain* once again. Formerly called Duck Lane, it was (in the seventeenth and early eighteenth centuries) noted for its bookshops. The diarist *Samuel Pepys* records that he came here often—to buy books and to kiss the pretty wife of a bookseller. Turn right, on this street. The great *St Bartholomew's Hospital* is on your left. Here ROBERT BRIDGES (1844-1930) poet (and Poet Laureate), was house surgeon (1870-82). In one year he saw 30,940 patients!

11. Follow Little Britain till it ends in an open area, with the great Smithfield Markets beyond. But turn sharp right, into the little way leading into *St Bartholomew the Great Church*—the remains (much restored) of a huge church built here in 1123. During the Peasants' Revolt (1381) Wat Tyler, leader of the revolt, was critically wounded by a sword blow from William Walworth, inflicted about where the hospital now stands. Tyler sought sanctuary in this church, while the king (Richard II) led the peasants off to a parley, about where the markets now stand. By promises he had no intention of keeping, the king persuaded the peasants to disperse. Meanwhile Walworth returned to the church, dragged Tyler from it, and beheaded him on a log in the open space before the church. In later centuries, hundreds (if not thousands) of 'heretics' were burned to death in this open space; and in 1306, the Scottish patriot William Wallace was hanged, drawn and quartered. A monument to him has been erected here. WILLIAM HOGARTH (see above) was baptized in the church; and the American printer, philosopher, and diplomat BENJAMIN FRANKLIN worked as a journeyman printer, in 1725, in a print shop that occupied the third floor of a building (connected with the Lady Chapel) at the back of the church.

12. Leaving the church, walk between the Wallace Memorial and the buildings on your left, and find (on your left) *St Bartholomew the Less Church*. INIGO JONES (1573-1652), architect, stage designer, and writer of dramatic masques, was baptized here. THOMAS WATSON (1557?-92), poet and friend of Christopher Marlowe, was buried here, as was JOHN LYLY (1554?-1606), poet, dramatist, and romancer.

13. Continue walking straight ahead, down Giltspur Street, for one

block, and then turn right, into *Cock Lane*. A house (now gone) about half way along this street, on your left, was the scene of the famous 'Cock Lane Ghost' episode—a typical *poltergeist* phenomenon that *Dr Johnson, Horace Walpole, Sir Joshua Reynolds,* and thousands of other people came here to investigate. *Hogarth* has a plate commemorating the event; *Goldsmith* wrote a pamphlet about it; and *Charles Churchill* wrote a poem ridiculing the great philosophers who were taken in. (During Chaucer's time, this was the only street on this side of the City where prostitutes were allowed to reside legally.)

14. Cock Lane runs into *Snow Hill*. Turn left on this street, and follow it down to Holborn Viaduct. JOHN BUNYAN (1628-88), preacher and author of *Pilgrim's Progress*, died at the house of a grocer friend of his which stood almost under your feet as you stand at the intersection.

15. When you have reached *Holborn Viaduct*, turn left on it. In a few steps you will reach, on your left, *St Sepulchre Church*. Here stood the Crusaders' church in the twelfth century; it was rebuilt in the fifteenth century; it suffered in the Great Fire of 1666, and was largely rebuilt, by Wren, in 1670-7; and it was partly rebuilt, repaired, or restored in 1738, 1837, 1875, 1880, and 1950. ROGER ASCHAM (1515-68), one of the early humanists, tutor of Queen Elizabeth I when she was a girl, author of *Toxophilus* (1554), a treatise on archery, and of *The Schoolmaster* (1570), one of the earliest English treatises on education, is buried here. CAPTAIN JOHN SMITH (1580-1631) adventurer, colonizer of Virginia, author of an autobiography and many books on America, is buried in the church.

16. On issuing from the church, turn back to your right, and walk across *Holborn Viaduct*. At its far end, where it runs into Holborn Circus, there stands, in the angle to your left, *St Andrew's Church*—built by Sir Christopher Wren, in 1686-7, where an older church had stood. It is the church by whose clock Dickens's David Copperfield timed his appointments with Agnes. Baptized in this church, or the older one, were the following: THOMAS CAMPION (1567-1720), a poet who wrote some of the most beautifully hushed and muted poems in English; RICHARD SAVAGE (1697?-1743), unfortunate poet who claimed to be the illegitimate son of titled parents, and who barely escaped the gallows for killing a man; ANN RADCLIFFE (1764-1823), Gothic novelist; and BENJAMIN DISRAELI (1804-81), novelist and Prime Minister, born of Jewish parents but baptized a Christian when he was twelve years old. Married here were WILLIAM HAZLITT (1778-

1830), essayist, and one of the finest and most perceptive of all literary critics—with CHARLES LAMB as best man and Mary Lamb as bridesmaid. (Lamb said later that he could hardly restrain his laughter during the ceremony because 'Anything awful makes me laugh'!); and RICHARD LE GALLIENNE (1866-1947), 'Aesthetic' poet. *Buried* here: the first wife of WILLIAM DAVENANT, dramatist and theatre manager (in 1654); JOHN HUGHES (1677-1720), poet, author of the epic *The Siege of Damascus*; and the father and the mother of Charles and Mary Lamb.

[16A. Cross over Holborn Viaduct, and find Charterhouse Street extending away to your right. Ascend this street a few steps, and then turn into *Ely Place*, entering Charterhouse from your left. On this short street WILLIAM COWPER (1731-1800), the poet, studied law with a solicitor in 1749—before a developing depressive state, that brought him close to madness, compelled him to retire to the country and, more or less, from life. At *No. 20* WILLIAM HOWITT (1792-1879) and his wife MARY (1799-1888), poets and novelists, writers of travel books and children's books, friends of most of the English writers of their time, lived in 1840. (Of all their works, the only one really remembered is the little poem, by Mary Howitt, beginning, 'Won't you walk into my parlour?'/Said the spider to the fly.') On the left-hand side of the street you will see *St Etheldreda's Church*, which is the thirteenth-century chapel of the great house of the Bishops of Ely that once stood here. John of Gaunt, Duke of Lancaster, who was the father of Henry IV and the brother-in-law of Geoffrey Chaucer, died here in 1399. Gaunt figures in Shakespeare's plays, and he seems to have been the original of several characters in Chaucer's poems. [16B. While on this side of Holborn, you may wish to return to Holborn Circus, and then turn right, up *Hatton Garden*. HENRY CRABB ROBINSON (1775-1867), lawyer and diarist, who knew almost everybody of literary importance in his generation, and wrote voluminously about all his acquaintances, lived at *No. 56* in 1810 and for several years thereafter.... Return now to St Andrew's Church.]

17. Walk down St Andrew Street, which leaves Holborn Circus directly in front of the church. This street quickly becomes Shoe Lane; and you will soon reach, on your left, the entrance to Stonecutter Street. Probably you should go a little distance beyond this last-named street, and (still walking along Shoe Lane) find narrow *Gunpowder Alley* on your right. In this little place, mean and poverty-stricken in the seventeenth century, the poet RICHARD LOVELACE (see above) died in extreme want.

18. Now return to *Stonecutter Street*, and enter it. On your left lay formerly the burial grounds of St Andrew's church; and here the 'marvellous boy' THOMAS CHATTERTON (1752-70), poet and lover of the Middle Ages, was buried after he had committed suicide (poison) before he had reached his eighteenth birthday. His bones were later removed from here.

19. Continue along Stonecutter Street till it ends in Farringdon Street. Turn right, on the latter. A block down this street, Fleet Lane enters from the left; and just beyond this stands the Congregational Memorial Hall, a large Gothic building. This hall occupies most of the site of old *Fleet Prison*. A prison existed here from Norman times; it burned down in the Great Fire of 1666, and was rebuilt (1671). It was burned down again by rioters in 1780, and again rebuilt; and it was finally abolished and torn down in 1846. Until the seventeenth century it was intended for important state prisoners; but eventually it was used for drunkards, disorderly persons, persons accused of misdemeanours and minor felonies, and (above all) persons imprisoned for debt. It was the scene, for centuries, of so much inhuman cruelty, vicious greed, and unspeakable suffering that the heart quails to think of it.

Among literary people who were confined in Fleet Prison were the following: HENRY HOWARD, EARL OF SURREY (1517-47), who introduced blank verse into English, imprisoned and later beheaded as a suspected traitor, mostly because of his kinship with Henry VIII's executed wife, Catherine Howard; SIR THOMAS WYATT (1503-43), suspected of some complicity in the misbehaviour of Anne Boleyn, Henry VIII's other executed wife; THOMAS DEKKER (1572?-1632), dramatist and satirist; THOMAS NASH (1567-1601), poet and satirist, for having helped Ben Jonson write the satirical comedy *The Isle of Dogs*; the poet JOHN DONNE (1572-1631), for having married without official consent; *William Herbert*, Earl of Pembroke (1580-1630), thought by many to be the 'Mr W.H.' to whom Shakespeare's sonnets were dedicated, and named outright in the dedication of Shakespeare's First Folio; WILLIAM WYCHERLEY (1640?-1716), one of the great writers of comedy in English, imprisoned seven years for debt; the poet RICHARD SAVAGE (see above); ROBERT LLOYD (1733-64), poet and essayist, imprisoned for debt. William Penn (1644-1718), Quaker leader and founder of the Pennsylvania colony, was also imprisoned here. Hogarth depicts the place in his *Rake's Progress*, and Dickens in the *Pickwick Papers*.

20. Continue down Farringdon Street to Ludgate Circus, and here

turn left into *Ludgate Hill*. Walk along the latter till you pass the entrance of Old Bailey, on your left, which formerly lay just outside the City Wall. The wall itself ran between Old Bailey and St Martin's Church a few steps farther along the street. As often happened in the Middle Ages, the apartments over Ludgate (which spanned the street here) were used as a prison. SIR THOMAS MALORY (d. 1471), author of *Morte d'Arthur*, a vigorously and dramatically written compilation of Arthurian legends from which later writers have mined innumerable stories, poems, and dramas, was kept for a time in this prison. He was imprisoned because he had become, in the north country that was his home, so lawless and violent a character that the difference between him and a highwayman was academic. Between Old Bailey and the church, at *No. 42*, stood the *London Coffee House* (1731-1868) where a club, of which *James Boswell* (Dr Johnson's biographer) was a member, met regularly. It is mentioned in Dickens's *Little Dorrit*. *St Martin's Church* was built by Wren to replace an older church destroyed in the Great Fire (1666). In the older church SAMUEL PURCHAS (1577-1626), who compiled the immense body of travel literature known as *Purchas His Pilgrims* (1625), was rector.

21. Turn back to *Old Bailey*, and ascend it. Much of this area has been rebuilt since the eighteenth century, and many old sites destroyed. About two-thirds the way up this street, Seacoal Lane intersects from the left. About a block down that lane, Green Arbour Court used to cut away to the right, to join what is left of Green Arbour Lane farther up the street. In a house on the right-hand corner of Seacoal and Green Arbour Lanes, OLIVER GOLDSMITH (1730-74), poet, essayist, novelist, dramatist, lived in 1758-9. A bit farther along Old Bailey, still on the left at *No. 68*, lived *Jonathan Wild* (1683-1725), a kind of eighteenth-century Al Capone who was finally hanged, and whose story has been told (part-fact, part-fiction) by both Daniel Defoe and Henry Fielding. A couple of doors still farther up the street the father of William Hogarth, the artist, had a school.

On the right-hand side of *Old Bailey*, at the corner where it joins Newgate Street, stands the massive and ornate pile of the Central Criminal Court building, erected 1902-7. It occupies part of the site of the ancient *Newgate Prison*, which stood on the corner, facing Newgate Street, where public executions took place from 1783 to 1868. SIR THOMAS MALORY (see above) was confirmed here for many years, and probably died here. Actually, his confinement seems to have been on a free-and-easy basis, since he was a man of distinction and good family, and had many warm friends. He used the library (a gift of Lord Mayor Dick Whittington, 1429) of the Gray Friars Monastery that stood just across Newgate Street from the prison; and he wrote his great work while in prison. Some other literary persons who have been imprisoned here are BEN JONSON (1572-1637), poet and dramatist, who had killed a man in a duel; the dramatist CHRISTOPHER MARLOWE (1564-93), for suspected complicity in a murder; EDMUND WALLER (1606-87), the poet, for being too lukewarm in support of both the commonwealth and the king; GEORGE WITHER (1588-1667), Cavalier poet; DANIEL DEFOE (1660-1731) first of England's great novelists, author of *Robinson Crusoe* and *Moll Flanders*, from 1702 to 1704, for political reasons; the strangely unlucky poet RICHARD SAVAGE (see above) for having killed a man in a tavern brawl. The Jesuit poet ROBERT SOUTHWELL (1561?-95) was taken from here to be hanged at Tyburn for having broken the law excluding Jesuits from England. In the yard of the prison were officially burned (1660) those books of *John Milton* that defended law and freedom against the Stuart theories of divine-right kingship.

22. Turn the corner around the Criminal Court building, and proceed to your right, along *Newgate Street*. To your left, on the far side of the street, occupying part of the site where the General Post Office now stands, was once the Gray Friars Monastery. Its library was used by SIR THOMAS MALORY (see above) and he was buried in its chapel. After the dissolution of the monasteries by Henry VIII, the site was occupied by *Christ's Hospital*—the famous charity school for poor boys of London, who were called 'bluecoat boys'. Among the boys who attended this school were the historian and humanist WILLIAM CAMDEN (1551-1623); the poet, critic, and philosopher SAMUEL TAYLOR COLERIDGE (1772-1834); the minor historian, and good friend of Charles Lamb, GEORGE DYER (1755-1841); the poet and friend of Keats LEIGH HUNT (1784-1859); the essayist CHARLES LAMB (1775-1834); the dramatist GEORGE PEELE (1558?-97), who lived in the place as a boy, his father being an employee there; and the novelist SAMUEL RICHARDSON (1689-1761). (The school was moved across the river into Sussex in 1902; and W. E. Henley wrote a very fine and affectionate sonnet on the occasion.)

23. Turn right, into Warwick Lane (the first major street you reach as you walk along Newgate from Old Bailey). The first small street on your right leads to *Warwick Square*, home of the Oxford University Press for many years. Here CHARLES WILLIAMS (1886-1945) poet, critic, and author of religious works, was a long-time editor.

24. Continue down Warwick Lane. Note, on your right, the entrance (under an arch) to *Amen Court*. In this court, at *No. 1*, lived and died RICHARD H. BARHAM (1788-1845), author of the *Ingoldsby Legends*, tales in verse and prose that were 'whimsical and grotesque, but stuffed with sound antiquarianism'.

25. Continue down Warwick Lane till you find *Amen Corner* on your right. There is a confusion of entry-ways here; but if you turn into any of them, and look about, you will discover *Stationers' Hall*, where every book published in Great Britain from 1557 to 1911 was supposed to be registered—a compilation invaluable to scholars. Somewhere in this small area SYDNEY SMITH (1771-1845), minister, reformer, and wit—who pops up all over London—was living in 1831.

26. Now cross back over Warwick Lane, and ascend a few steps into *Paternoster Square*. The entire area about here was bombed out during the Second World War, and has been rebuilt into a spacious shopping centre with modern buildings. Formerly, this was a book-publishing centre, and has many literary associations. Here GILBERT K. CHESTERTON (1874-1936), essayist, critic, novelist, and poet, did editorial work for a publisher in the 1890's. The Fisher Unwin publishing house was located at *No. 26* of the old square. It issued the first novels of Joseph Conrad: *Almayer's Folly* and *An Outcast of the Islands*. The same publisher also issued the first novel of John Galsworthy: *From the Four Winds* (written under the pseudonym 'John Sinjohn').

27. Some relics of the old *Paternoster Row* remain. Formerly it ran straight from Amen Corner to Cheapside. It was the centre of the London mercers' trade in the seventeenth century; and *Samuel Pepys* records going there several times (1660-6) to buy rich clothing. But in the eighteenth century it became a publishers' street, and remained so until well into the twentieth century. OLIVER GOLDSMITH (see above) lodged here (1757) with RALPH GRIFFITHS, who published the *Monthly Review* for which Goldsmith (along with the dramatists Arthur Murphy and George Colman the Elder) did a series of reviews. TOBIAS SMOLLETT (1721-71), best known as a novelist, edited the *Critical Review* here, 1756-8. The anonymous *Letters of Junius* (1769-72), the authorship of which still remains a mystery, were originally printed here—the manuscripts being sometimes tossed in at the open door of the printshop. The *Lyrical Ballads* (1798) of William Wordsworth and Samuel Taylor Coleridge—a volume that created a revolution in English poetry—was published at *No. 39*.

28. Some relics of *Ivy Lane* persist along the eastern side of Paternoster Square. SIR ROGER L'ESTRANGE (1616-1704), in the days of the Restoration, when he was riding high as licenser of the press and an enemy of free speech, had his office on Ivy Lane, and there published a journal. He is a significant literary figure because he was one of the earliest regular journalists in England, and because his translations of Spanish and Portuguese fiction helped further the development of fiction in England. One of the earliest clubs of which DR SAMUEL JOHNSON (1709-84) was a member met each Tuesday at the King's Head on this street.

Just opposite the entrance of Ivy Lane into Paternoster Row was the opening into *Paul's Alley*. At the corner of this stood the *Chapter Coffee House*, frequented by the boy poet THOMAS CHATTERTON (1752-70) in the months before he committed suicide. The novelists CHARLOTTE BRONTË (1816-55), author of *Jane Eyre*, and her sister ANNE (1820-49), author of *Agnes Gray*, stayed here on their first visit to London (1848). At about the same time, the novelist and poet GEORGE MEREDITH (1828-1909) was a clerk in a solicitor's office at *No. 44*.

29. Now make your way towards St Paul's Cathedral, and the street that encircles it. This encircling street is called *St Paul's Churchyard*. It was once the haunt of innumerable booksellers (that is, publishers). Several works of William Shakespeare (1564-1616) were first published here. Wheatley, in *London Past and Present* (1891), writes: 'At the sign of the White Greyhound in St Paul's Churchyard the first editions of Shakespeare's *Venus and Adonis* and *Rape of Lucrece* were published by John Harrison; at the Flower de Luce and the Crown appeared the first edition of the *Merry Wives of Windsor*; at the Green Dragon the first edition of *The Merchant of Venice*; at the Fox the first edition of *Richard* II; at the Angel the first edition of *Richard* III; at the Spread Eagle the first edition of *Troilus and Cressida*; at the Gun the first edition of *Titus Andronicus*; and at the Red Bull the first edition of *Lear*.' At a point almost opposite the outermost extension of the Cathedral's north transept (or a few yards west, towards the Cathedral's main entrance) was the shop where *Dr Johnson* (in one of the most celebrated of literary anecdotes) sold the manuscript of Goldsmith's novel *The Vicar of Wakefield*. A little farther west (at *No. 72*) was the shop of J. Johnson that published William Cowper's long poem *The Task* (1784), and also William Blake's *The French Revolution, a Prophecy* (1791) and also William Wordsworth's *An Evening Walk* (1793) and *Descriptive Sketches* (1793). In this shop *Blake* met the revolutionary social philosopher

William Godwin, the latter's wife *Mary Wollstonecraft*, and the American revolutionist *Tom Paine*. A group of booksellers meeting at *No. 60* decided to issue a multi-volume edition of the English poets, and to hire Dr Johnson to write the lives of these poets. This was the origin of Dr Johnson's great literary work, *Lives of the English Poets*.

30. Swing around to the front of St Paul's, with the statue of Queen Anne before it. To the Queen's left, the little street called Dean's Court leads off from St Paul's Churchyard. Here lived and died HENRY HART MILMAN (1791-1868), Dean of St Paul's. Poet, dramatist, historian, he was most famous for his *History of the Jews* (1829), which scandalized his generation because it presented the Jews historically, like any other nation, instead of religiously, as the chosen of God. It was the first significant English book in the development of what came to be called the 'Higher Criticism' of the Bible.

31. You will certainly wish to visit *St Paul's Cathedral*—even though it is cluttered with, probably, the world's ugliest collection of memorial monuments. (Undoubtedly, no uglier monument was ever imagined, and certainly not executed, than that to the Duke of Wellington in the centre of the north, or left aisle—with the Duke mounted on a horse 30 or 40 feet above the floor, and the horse mounted upon a succession of Victorian monstrosities. What a horse is doing in church, what it is doing mounted 30 feet in the air, and why the Duke should be deliberately concealed within the dark obscurity of the long arches, no rational person can explain.) In the north, or left, transept, almost at the choir, are statues of the great historian HENRY HALLAM (1777-1859), father of Arthur Henry Hallam, in whose memory Tennyson wrote his greatest poem, *In Memoriam*; and of DR SAMUEL JOHNSON (another horror!).

Continue along the north side of the church, and circle the choir. As you come down the ambulatory (alongside the choir) on the other, or south, side, note two monuments: that of JOHN DONNE (1572-1631), poet and Dean of the Cathedral, and that of HENRY MILMAN (see above). The DONNE monument is the only one saved from the burning of the old St Paul's that stood here until the Great Fire of 1666. It shows him as he originally posed for the artist—in his shroud.

As you leave the passage around the choir, turn left, and descend into the crypt of the cathedral. Here you will find the sarcophagi of Lord Nelson and the Duke of Wellington, as well as the graves of the following, among others:

Sir Christopher Wren (1632-1723), the architect who built so many churches in London after the Great Fire, and who was the architect of St Paul's (note the memorial tablet to him on the wall nearby, with the famous inscription, *Lector, si monumentum requiris, circumspice*, or 'Reader, if you seek a monument, look about you'); the American artist *Benjamin West* (1738-1820); the great landscape painter *J. M. W. Turner* (1775-1851); the painter and sculptor of animals, *Sir Edwin Landseer* (1802-73), who is responsible for the lions around the Nelson Monument in Trafalgar Square; *Sir John Millais* (1829-96), painter, one of the original Pre-Raphaelite Brotherhood that had an extraordinary influence on art and literature of the nineteenth century; *George Cruikshank* (1792-1878), caricaturist, who influenced Dickens and illustrated some of the latter's work; *Sir Arthur Sullivan* (1842-1900), the musician of the Gilbert-and-Sullivan partnership that created the immortal light operas. The last three persons mentioned are closely associated with English literature. Perhaps even more closely associated is SIR JOSHUA REYNOLDS (1723-92), painter, friend of Dr Johnson, member of Johnson's Literary Club, and author of some philosophical writings on art, whose grave is near Turner's. The grave of the poet WALTER DE LA MARE (1873-1956) is here; and just around the corner from it is the grave of MAX BEERBOHM (1872-1956), essayist and caricaturist—marked by a square stone with the letters 'M.B.'.

Besides graves, there are monuments in plenty to writers, among them the poet and artist *William Blake*, the historian of London *Sir Walter Besant*, the novelists *Edward Bulwer-Lytton* and *Charles Reade*, *T. E. Lawrence* ('of Arabia'), the poet and editor *W. E. Henley*, and *R. H. Barham* (see above). Perhaps it should be added that the inescapable SYDNEY SMITH (see above) was a canon of the Cathedral.

In the old St Paul's that burned in 1666 were buried *John of Gaunt* (1340-99), Chaucer's friend, patron, and brother-in-law, and subject of much of his poetry; the humanists THOMAS LINACRE (1460?-1524) and JOHN COLET (1467?-1519); the poet SIR PHILIP SIDNEY (1554-86); and the poet JOHN DONNE (see above). JOHN WYCLIF (1328-84), first translator of the Bible into English, was brought into the old cathedral to be tried for heresy; but upon Wyclif's friend and supporter, the powerful John of Gaunt (see above) threatening to drag the Bishop of London (who was trying the case) out of the Cathedral by the hair of his head, the trial broke up in disorder. In the early sixteenth century, the next translation of the Bible into English, by William Tyndale (d. 1536), was officially burned at about the spot where the statue of Queen Anne now stands before the Cathedral.

32. When you leave the Cathedral, turn left, and continue your cir-

cumambulation along St Paul's Churchyard. As you make the turn around the back of the Cathedral, you may see what the bombings have left of *St Augustine's Church*, where R. H. BARHAM (see above) was rector, 1842-5. Farther along St Paul's Churchyard, and to your right, stood *St Paul's School*, founded in 1512 by JOHN COLET (see above), Dean of the Cathedral, and not moved till 1884. The historian WILLIAM CAMDEN (1551-1623), the poet JOHN MILTON (see above), and the diarist SAMUEL PEPYS (1633-1703) were students here.

You are now only a few steps from *St Paul's Underground Station*, with which this tour commenced, and with which it ends. If you are of a mind to take another tour today, a three-minute ride on the underground will take you to *Holborn (Kingsway) Station*, where you may start on either *Tour 7* or *Tour 8*.

Tour 3
City Road to Blackfriars

Edward Alleyn	Thomas Hood
R. H. Barham	Dr Samuel Johnson
William Blake	Inigo Jones
Robert Bloomfield	Ben Jonson
James Boswell	John Keats
Samuel Boyse	Mrs Mary Manley
John Bunyan	Thomas Middleton
Richard Burbage	John Milton
Geoffrey Chaucer	Sir Thomas More
Henry Condell	Samuel Pepys
Daniel Defoe	William Shakespeare
John Donne	Mary Godwin Shelley
Desiderius Erasmus	Percy Bysshe Shelley
Henry Fielding	Henry Howard, Earl of Surrey
John Foxe	Frank Swinnerton
William Godwin	Francis Thompson
John Hawkesworth	Sir John Vanbrugh
John Heminge	Isaac Watts
Philip Henslowe	John Wesley
Robert Herrick	

Leave the underground at the *Old Street Station*.

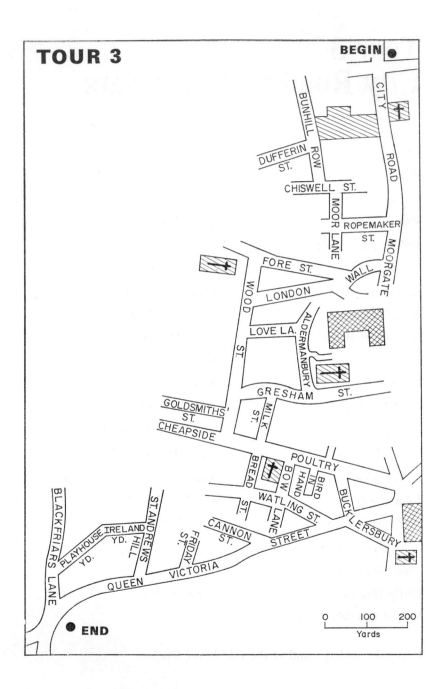

1. At the surface, turn *away* from a complex of branching intersections that you will see, and walk down *City Road.* (The house numbers will be decreasing if you are walking in the right direction.) A bit more than a block down the street, you will see, on your left, a few steps off the street, the bronze statue of JOHN WESLEY (1703-91), evangelist, father of Methodism, one of the most truly wonderful men who ever lived. His 'incomparable *Journal*' was called by the critic Augustine Birrell, 'the most amazing record of human exertion ever penned by man'. But what earns him a special place in a book like this is that in his work with the largely illiterate poorer classes he organized schools for teaching reading, and then supplied the learners with inexpensive books that he had caused to be printed. 'No man,' says the *Encyclopedia Britannica,* 'in the 18th century did so much to create a taste for good reading and to supply it with books at the lowest prices.' His long-time home, in which he died, stands just to the right of the statue; and directly behind it is the Wesley Chapel, opened by Wesley in 1788. Go through the Chapel to the little graveyard behind it, in which Wesley is buried—under a stone bearing a wordy and pompous inscription that Wesley himself, with his taste for direct writing, would certainly have deplored.

2. Return to City Road, cross over it, and enter *Bunhill Fields Cemetery,* just opposite the Wesley home. This was the Nonconformists' graveyard, 1685-1852. Step off about 40 paces from the gate of the cemetery, and look to your right. About 20 yards from you, the next-to-highest table-like tomb is the grave of ISAAC WATTS (1674-1748), poet and hymn-writer, author of 'O God, our help in ages past'. Several yards farther on, where a cross-walk cuts the main walk, is the tomb (to your left) of JOHN BUNYAN (1628-88), author of *Pilgrim's Progress;* and (to your right) stands an obelisk marking the grave of the pioneer novelist and early journalist DANIEL DEFOE (1660-1731), author of *Robinson Crusoe, Moll Flanders,* and other novels. Just beside this obelisk is a small blackened slab vaguely marking the grave of the mystic poet and artist WILLIAM BLAKE (1757-1827).

3. Walk on through the cemetery to *Bunhill Row* skirting its far side. Turn left on this street.
[3A. You may wish to turn right, off Bunhill Row, into Dufferin Street. Follow this to its end (two blocks) in Whitecross Street. Cross over the latter, and enter *Fortune Street.* Just to your right, along this street, stood the *Fortune Theatre,* built for PHILIP HENSLOWE and EDWARD ALLEYN (the actor), in 1600. Henslowe's full notes on specifications for this theatre are the chief source of our knowledge about

45

the architecture of the Elizabethan theatre. The Fortune burned down in 1621, was immediately rebuilt, and was destroyed by the Puritans in 1649.... Return to Bunhill Row.]

Continue along *Bunhill Row*. On your right, at about where a college stands in the 1970's, the poet JOHN MILTON (1608-74) lived from 1663 till his death here. In this house he finished *Paradise Lost*, and wrote *Paradise Regained* and *Samson Agonistes*.

4. Follow Bunhill Row to its end, and here make a short double turn, first to your left and then to your right, into Moor Lane. After one block along the latter, turn left, into *Ropemaker Street*. Though this street is wider, straighter, and more 'modern' than the original Ropemaker Alley that ran here, it was somewhere in this place that DANIEL DEFOE (see above) died while in hiding from some danger not now understood.

5. Ropemaker Street runs into *Moorgate*. Here turn right, and walk along the right-hand side of the street. At *No. 85* you will find, on the side of a modern building, a plaque announcing that the poet JOHN KEATS (1795-1821) was born on that site, above a livery-stable kept by his father.

6. At the next corner, turn right, into London Wall. This entire area suffered heavy bomb damage in the war, and was still under reconstruction when this book was being written. Follow London Wall a few steps, and bear right, past the front of the post office and telephone exchange into *Fore Street*. DANIEL DEFOE (see above) was born somewhere on this street.

7. A good long block beyond the post office and telephone exchange, a street formerly opened into Fore Street (where there is now a solid block of houses), and ran away to the right. Until the 1960's this was called Milton Street; and before that, it bore the name *Grub Street*. During the eighteenth century, this was the traditional home and gathering place of impoverished writers. Dr Johnson, in his *Dictionary*, defined *Grub Street* as 'the name of a street in London much inhabited by writers of small histories, dictionaries, and temporary poems; whence any mean production is called Grub Street'. One of the earlier inhabitants of the street was JOHN FOXE (1516-87) author of the *Book of Martyrs*, a history of Protestant martyrs; he died here.

8. Continue along Fore Street to *St Giles Cripplegate Church*. The present church dates from the late fourteenth century; but it was

badly damaged by fire in 1545, and extensively repaired. It was damaged again by bombing in 1940, and restored in the 1950's and 1960's. A child of the dramatist *James Shirley* (1596-1666) was baptized here; Oliver Cromwell and, probably, the poet and dramatist BEN JONSON (1572-1637) were married here; the philosopher, statesman and martyr SIR THOMAS MORE (1478-1535) and, probably, WILLIAM SHAKESPEARE (1564-1616) worshipped here. Among those buried here are JOHN FOXE (see above) and JOHN MILTON (see above), who was buried in the same grave with his father. The plaque marking Milton's grave is in the floor near the pulpit.

9. Leave the church, return to Fore Street, and turn right, at the first street behind the church, into *Wood Street*. (In passing, note the remnants of the old city wall that have been uncovered in the narrow little garden to your left as you descend Wood Street.) Walk on down Wood Street. Just beyond the next heavy traffic artery, Silver Street once led off to your right. WILLIAM SHAKESPEARE is known to have lived on this little street. Continue down Wood Street till you reach Love Lane, intersecting from the left. Turn here, and go one block, to *Aldermanbury*. Turn left on the latter, and walk on till you find, on your left, a tiny green plot with a pedestal and a bust of Shakespeare. This is a memorial to JOHN HEMINGE and HENRY CONDELL, friends and fellow-actors of Shakespeare, who collected and edited the famous First Folio edition (1623) of Shakespeare's plays. Without their work, the major part of Shakespeare's plays would have been lost to posterity. This little monument to them stands in what was formerly the churchyard of *St Mary Aldermanbury Church*, where the two were buried. The novelist and literary historian FRANK SWINNERTON (b. 1884) was a choir-boy here. The church was destroyed by the bombings of the Second World War.

10. Turn around and walk back along Aldermanbury till you find (on your left) a little passage leading off towards the great pile of the Guildhall that you can see beyond. This passage leads between the Guildhall (left) and St Lawrence Jewry Church (right). Perhaps you should visit the *Guildhall* first. This is the seat of government of the City of London. A hall was built here in 1411-25, and part of that hall (especially the crypt, which is open to the public) still survives. Since then, the hall has suffered the ravages of fire and age, and has been rebuilt, restored, repaired, and added to many times. The poet JOHN MILTON (see above) was married here to his second wife, in a civil ceremony. You may enter the Guildhall, and walk straight ahead to the Great Hall, where the poet HENRY HOWARD, EARL OF

SURREY (1517-47), who introduced blank verse into English, was tried for treason, and found guilty. It may be of interest that the inscription on the monument to William Pitt the Elder (which you will see here) was written by *Edmund Burke*, and that on the monument to Lord Nelson was written by the dramatist *Richard Brinsley Sheridan*. Note also a statue of Lord Mayor Beckford, father of the dissolute *William Beckford*, author of the celebrated Gothic novel *Vathek*. There is also a statue of *Winston Churchill.*

As you leave the hall by the wide entrance lobby, you will see stairs leading upward on your left, towards the Guildhall Library—one of the finest in London. The Catholic poet FRANCIS THOMPSON (1859-1907) used to come here to read in the days when he was a vagrant in London, but was finally forbidden entrance because his clothes were so ragged and dirty!

11. *St Lawrence Jewry Church*, just in front of the Guildhall, is a replacement (by Christopher Wren) of an ancient church burned down here in the Great Fire of 1666. In the previous church, SIR THOMAS MORE (see above) preached; and there is a stained-glass window in his memory in the church—as well as another window to WILLIAM GROCYN (1446?-1519), one of the early humanists, who worshipped here. THOMAS MIDDLETON (1570?-1627), dramatist and satirist, was baptized in the old church.

[11A. If you are interested in the rustic poet ROBERT BLOOMFIELD, whose quiet and simple nature poems are of a high quality, who influenced Wordsworth, and who came to London and went mad—you may, on leaving the church, double back alongside it on Gresham Street, walk on for two blocks to Coleman Street, and turn left into the latter. Up this you will find, on your right, Great Bell Alley, which leads on into *Telegraph Street*, where, at *No. 14*, a few houses from the corner, Bloomfield lived for a time.]

12. Walk back along Gresham Street towards Aldermanbury once again. Note *Milk Street* entering Gresham Street from your left. SIR THOMAS MORE (see above) was born on this little street in 1478.

13. Continue along Gresham to *Wood Street* again. Turn left on the latter. It was probably on this street (in the neighbourhood of Goldsmith Street, which enters Wood Street from your right, farther down), that ROBERT HERRICK (1591-1674), 'greatest of the Cavalier poets', was born; at any rate, when he was sixteen, he was apprenticed to a goldsmith uncle who had a shop on this street. Just beyond Goldsmith Street, on your right (some authorities put it on the left),

stood the old Cross Keys Inn, where *Dickens* first arrived in London as a boy, and where he had Pip (in *Great Expectations*) arrive. Just beyond this, where Wood Street enters Cheapside, still on your right, was a plot of ground with trees where rooks nested for many years. This was probably the place Wordsworth had in mind when he wrote, in 'The Reverie of Poor Susan', the lines in which the rooks were poetically transformed to a thrush:

> *At the corner of Wood Street, when daylight appears,*
> *Hangs a thrush that sings loud, it has sung for three years.*

14. Turn left, into Cheapside, and then right, into *Bread Street*. On this street, on your right, a house or two below the corner, stood the famous *Mermaid Tavern*—frequented by *Shakespeare, Ben Jonson, Christopher Marlowe, Sir Walter Raleigh, John Donne*, and *Beaumont* and *Fletcher*. Keats's poem has made it famous:

> *Souls of poets dead and gone,*
> *What Elysium have ye known,*
> *Happy field or mossy cavern,*
> *Choicer than the Mermaid Tavern?*

JOHN DONNE (1572-1631) was born on Bread Street; once neglected by criticism, he is now regarded as one of the very greatest of the English poets. The poet JOHN MILTON (see above) was born here in a house that became a tourists' Mecca even while Milton was alive. Though the precise location of the house is disputed, it seems to have stood at the entrance of a narrow court that opened on the left-hand (eastern) side of the street, beyond the third door after you left Cheapside.

15. Turn left on *Watling Street*—which is one branch of the ancient Roman road leading from Dover to the north. (But the main road seems to have been to the west, along what is now the long straight stretch of Edgware Road–Maida Vale–Kilburn High Road. The branch now called Watling Street connected with the main road.) After one block, turn left, on *Bow Lane*. At the end of this street, on your left, at the corner of Cheapside, stands the famous 'Bow Church' (St Mary le Bow). A Norman church dating from the eleventh century stood here till it burned down in the Great Fire, 1666. It was the sound of Bow Bells which, in the old legend, recalled *Richard Whittington* (afterward four times Lord Mayor) to London.

16. Turn right, on Cheapside, and walk about three blocks along it

till you reach, on your right, *Bird-in-Hand Court*. In a house that stretched over the passage leading from Cheapside into the court (at about *No. 76-8*) JOHN KEATS (1795-1821) was living in 1816-7. Here he wrote most of the poems that appeared in his first volume of *Poems* (1817), published while he was living here.

17. A few steps farther along Cheapside (which continues as Poultry) little *Bucklersbury* slants away to the right. The home of SIR THOMAS MORE (see above) was on this street when his daughter, who became Margaret Roper, was born. But the location of his house is unknown. The humanist DESIDERIUS ERASMUS (1466-1536) visited More here, and here wrote the witty *Moriae encomium*.

18. A little farther down the Poultry, but on your left, *Grocers' Hall Court* leads off. If the court is still there when you read this—the next-to-last house on the right was a tavern visited by Mr Pickwick and Sam Weller. In the court was a sponging-house (that is, a place where debtors were kept after their arrest, but before the legal courts had officially disposed of their cases) where the minor poet SAMUEL BOYSE (1708-49) was confined in 1742; his chief distinction (besides leading a singularly miserable life) was his use of the romantic and imaginative Spenserian stanza at a time when neo-classic criticism was regarding Edmund Spenser as a fool. He was also an early poet of nature; and he protested against the cruelties of hunting. JOHN HAWKESWORTH (1715?-73), editor of the periodical *The Adventurer*, contributor to many other periodicals, editor of Swift, and friend of Dr Johnson, lived in this court.

19. On the *Poultry* itself, at *No. 22*, lived the publishers and booksellers *Edward* and *Charles Dilly*, with whom JAMES BOSWELL (1740-95) often lodged when he came to London, and who published his *Life of Johnson* and *Tour of the Hebrides*. They were hosts here at the famous dinner where Dr Johnson met the spectacular but disreputable politician *John Wilkes*. At *No. 31* was born THOMAS HOOD (1799-1845), poet who, though a humorous writer, is chiefly remembered for his 'Song of the Shirt', a moving humanitarian poem. In this little street (at the sign of the 'Peacock') JOHN BUNYAN's *Pilgrim's Progress* was first published (1678).

20. At the end of the Poultry, where seven or eight streets intersect, you will see, to your right, the dark and ugly Mansion House, official home of the Lord Mayor of London. Turn sharp right, alongside it, and reach *St Stephen Walbrook Church* just beyond. This little

church (one of Wren's very finest) should be visited. Besides, SIR JOHN VANBRUGH (1664-1726), noted and flamboyant architect, as well as author of some of the wittiest comedies of his time, is buried in the church. A picture, 'The Martyrdom of St Stephen') on the left wall is by the famous American-born painter *Benjamin West* (1738-1820).

21. After visiting the church, turn back from it a few steps, and enter this end of Bucklersbury, on your left. As you walk along it, you will find, just around the corner, the remains of a Temple of Mithras (dating from Roman times). Then walk on down *Queen Victoria Street*. After a bit more than a block, you will reach a six-way inter-section—on the far side of which, in the angle between Watling and Queen Victoria Streets, you will find *St Mary Aldermary Church*, by Wren. In a previous church on this site, the diarist SAMUEL PEPYS (1633-1703) was married (1655); and the poet JOHN MILTON (see above) was married here to his third wife (1663). Chaucer's grand-father, *Richard Chaucer*, was buried here. Continue along Queen Victoria Street to the next cluster of intersecting streets. On the far side of the intersection, in the angle formed by Cannon and Queen Victoria Streets, formerly stood *St Mildred's Church*. This, the smallest of Wren's churches, was all but completely destroyed by the bombings of 1941, only the tower being left standing. In this church, in 1816, were married the poet PERCY BYSSHE SHELLEY (1792-1822) and his second wife MARY GODWIN (1797-1851), author of *Franken-stein*, and daughter of the philosopher WILLIAM GODWIN (1756-1836), who was a witness at the wedding.

22. Continue down Queen Victoria Street. The second street opening on your right is *Friday Street*. GEOFFREY CHAUCER (1340?-1400), giving testimony in the famous Scrope-Grosvenor lawsuit over which family had the right to bear a certain coat-of-arms, said (according to the court records of the time) 'that he was once in Friday Street, London, and walking up the street, he observed a new sign hanging out with these arms thereon, and inquired what inn had hung out these arms of Scrope.' ... Continue along Queen Victoria Street till you see, down a passageway on your left, *St Benet's Church*. The architect, stage designer, and dramatic writer INIGO JONES (1573-1652) was buried in a previous church on this site. The 'egregious novelist and journalist' MRS MARY MANLEY (1663-1724) was buried in the present church. And the novelist HENRY FIELDING (1707-54) married his second wife here.

23. Return to Queen Victoria Street, and continue along it till you find a street called St Andrew's Hill entering from your right. Turn into this street, walk a short block, and turn left, into *Ireland Yard.* WILLIAM SHAKESPEARE (1564-1616), the dramatist, bought a house on this street, on your left, approximately at the corner where you turned, or just below the corner, fronting St Andrew's Hill.

24. The entire area just ahead of you has been drastically rebuilt since the fifteenth century. Most of it was covered by the Blackfriars Monastery, with its many buildings and courtyards till Henry VIII dissolved the monasteries, in 1538. About ten years thereafter, the entire precincts, with all their buildings, were granted to Sir Thomas Cawarden, who happened to be Master of the Revels for the king. Properties within the precincts were rented out to shopkeepers and residents; and private theatricals, at first on a strictly amateur basis, began to appear in the area (probably in the halls of some of the noble tenants) as early as 1576. The boys in the schools at St Paul's, the Chapel Royal, and others were the actors in these plays. *James Burbage* (d. 1597) bought buildings for a theatre here the year before he died. The project was taken over by his son RICHARD BURBAGE (1567-1619), who was an actor in Shakespeare's company, and who played in many dramas by Shakespeare and by Ben Jonson. Their theatre became the *Blackfriars*, which was professional, and the first public theatre in London with a roof over it. Shakespeare bought an interest in it later on, and some of his plays were performed here. The Puritans always resented it because it was within the City itself, and tried repeatedly to suppress it—but without real success until all the theatres were closed in 1642. In 1629 a French company tried to produce here a play in which women took the parts of female characters; but the spectators, who were accustomed to boys or youths playing feminine parts, hooted and pelted the French players off the stage. If you continue walking along Ireland Yard, which leads into *Playhouse Yard*, you will walk through the former site of Blackfriars Theatre, which fronted towards what is now Blackfriars Lane.

BEN JONSON (see above), the dramatist, lived in Blackfriars precincts, 1607-16; and the painter *Sir Anthony Vandyke* (1599-1641) lived here from the time he came to England in 1632, and died here.

25. Follow Playhouse Yard to its juncture with *Blackfriars Lane*, and turn right on the latter. Almost immediately you will reach *Apothecaries' Hall*, dating from the seventeenth and eighteenth centuries, where the poet JOHN KEATS (see above) was a licentiate.

Now reverse your direction, and descend Blackfriars Lane towards the river. Cross over Queen Victoria Street, bear to your right, and find the *Blackfriars Underground Station*—where you will end this tour.

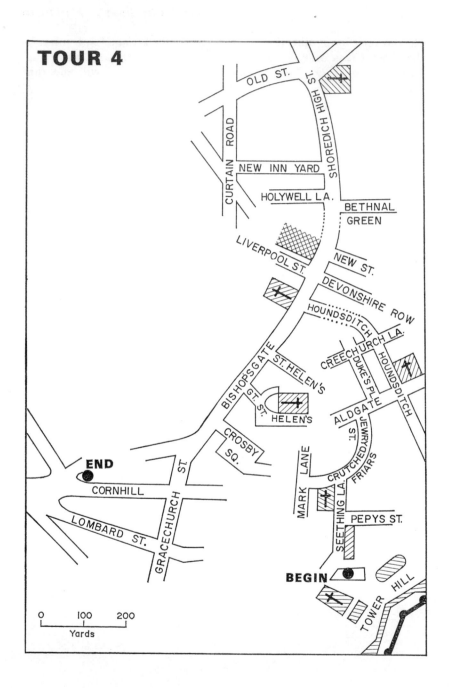

TOUR 4

OLD ST.

CURTAIN ROAD

SHOREDICH HIGH ST.

NEW INN YARD

HOLYWELL LA.

BETHNAL GREEN

LIVERPOOL ST.

NEW ST.

DEVONSHIRE ROW

HOUNDSDITCH

CREECHURCH LA.

BISHOPSGATE

ST. HELEN'S

GT. ST. HELEN'S

DUKE'S PLE.

HOUNDSDITCH

ALDGATE

CROSBY SQ.

END

CORNHILL

GRACECHURCH ST.

MARK LANE

JEWRY ST.

CRUTCHED FRIARS

LOMBARD ST.

SEETHING LA.

PEPYS ST.

BEGIN

TOWER HILL

0   100   200
Yards

54

Tour 4
Tower to Shoreditch

Joseph Addison

Edward Alleyn

Alexander Barclay

Aubrey Beardsley

Jeremy Bentham

James Burbage

Richard Burbage

Geoffrey Chaucer

George Crabbe

William Davenant

Daniel Defoe

Charles Dickens

T. S. Eliot

Robert Greene

Ben Jonson

John Keats

George Granville,
   Lord Lansdowne

George Lillo

Thomas Babington Macaulay

Sir Thomas Malory

Christopher Marlowe

Sir Thomas More

Thomas Otway

Sir Thomas Overbury

Samuel Pepys

Alexander Pope

Sir Walter Raleigh

John Wilmot, Earl of Rochester

William Shakespeare

Algernon Sidney

Henry Howard, Earl of Surrey

George Villiers,
   Duke of Buckingham

Isaac Watts

John Webster

George Wither

Sir Thomas Wyatt

Leave the underground at the *Tower Hill Station*. Depending on which exit you take from the station, you will see near you either the large, modern, easily recognizable Seaman's War Memorial, or the only church in the vicinity: Allhallows Barking.

1. *Allhallows Barking Church* was founded in the seventh century, added to or rebuilt every century thereafter, bombed badly in 1940, and rebuilt in the 1950's. From its tower (still standing) *Samuel Pepys* watched the spread of the Great Fire in 1666, as he reports in his diary. HENRY HOWARD, EARL OF SURREY (1517-47), the poet, was buried here, though his body was removed later. Americans will be interested in the facts that William Penn (1644-1718), founder of Pennsylvania, who was born nearby, was baptized here, and that John Quincy Adams, later President of the United States, was married here. Scholars may be interested to know that *William Thynne*, one of Chaucer's earliest editors, was buried in the old church, 1546.

2. The spot where the scaffold for executions stood lies on Tower Hill, just above and across the street from the Tower walls, and a few steps from the Seaman's War Memorial. The site is indicated by a pavement marker to Lords Kilmarnock and Balmerino, who were beheaded here in 1746. Lord Lovat of Fraser, last person to be officially beheaded in England, suffered here in 1747. The poet HENRY HOWARD, EARL OF SURREY (see above) was beheaded here in 1547. But besides Surrey, ALGERNON SIDNEY, republican and rebel (whose *Discourses Concerning Government* are of considerable historical and political importance, and who was beheaded here in 1683) seems to be the only person of literary importance who was executed on Tower Hill. THOMAS OTWAY (1652-85), the dramatist, died as a lodger in a tavern here; and William Penn was born at his parents' home on the Hill.

3. Of course, you will go on to visit the *Tower* itself. Many literary figures have been prisoner here—sometimes for a few days, sometimes for years, sometimes till they died here, and sometimes until they were taken away for execution. Among them have been WILLIAM DAVENANT (1606-68), the dramatist and theatre manager; LORD LANSDOWNE (GEORGE GRANVILLE) (1666-1735), poet, critic, friend of Pope; SIR THOMAS MALORY (d. 1471), author of that marvellous and stirring prose compilation of Arthurian legend known as *Morte d'Arthur*; SIR THOMAS MORE (1478-1535), statesman and philosopher, author of *Utopia*; SIR THOMAS OVERBURY (1581-1613), poet and essayist, who was treacherously poisoned here; SAMUEL PEPYS (1633-1703), the diarist, for a short while, because he was suspected of having corresponded with the Stuart Pretender to the throne; SIR WALTER RALEIGH (1552?-1618), who was taken from here and beheaded; the dissolute EARL OF ROCHESTER (JOHN WILMOT) (1647?-80), poet, who had forcibly abducted a lady; GEORGE VILLIERS, DUKE OF BUCKINGHAM (1628-87), dramatist and poet; GEORGE WITHER

(1588-1667), poet and dramatist, imprisoned for one of his satires; SIR THOMAS WYATT (1503?-42), poet, who wrote the first sonnets in English, imprisoned for some complicity in the misdoings of Anne Boleyn. ... *St Peter's ad Vincula*, the church within the Tower walls, is the burial place not only of Henry VIII's two executed queens, but also of SIR THOMAS MORE and SIR THOMAS OVERBURY.

4. When you leave the Tower, return towards Allhallows Barking Church, and, opposite the farther end of the church, turn right, into *Seething Lane*. One block up this street, Pepys Street enters from the right. About here, or a bit farther on, and on the right, SAMUEL PEPYS (see above), the diarist, had his home during the time that he was an official in the Navy Office, and was writing most of his diary. (The Navy Office itself was just beyond Pepys's house, but faced the next cross street: Crutched Friars.) On the left-hand side of Seething Lane, you will see *St Olave's Church*—which should be visited. The church dates from about 1450; but it was badly damaged by bombings in 1941, and has been restored. When you are inside the church, you will see, beyond the pulpit and altar, high up on your left, a marble bust of a woman looking intently out into the church itself. This represents Elizabeth, wife of SAMUEL PEPYS, and was placed there by her husband after her death so that he could look at her likeness during services (no doubt a pleasanter diversion than listening to the sermon). Both Pepys and his wife are buried in the crypt of this church.

[4A. At the end of Seething Lane, you may turn left, and go one block to *Mark Lane. Cyriac Skinner*, to whom Milton addressed a famous sonnet, and who was a friend and sometimes a volunteer secretary to the poet, was a merchant on this street, and lived here. ISAAC WATTS (1674-1748), the hymn-writer, was the minister at a Dissenting chapel that once stood on Mark Lane. ... Now return to the corner of Seething Lane and Crutched Friars.]

5. Turn right, on Crutched Friars, and follow it on till it becomes *Jewry*. On your right, before you reach India Street, a monastery once stood. After Henry VIII seized England's monasteries, he granted this property to the poet SIR THOMAS WYATT (see above), who built himself a fine town house here.

6. Continue on Jewry till it ends at *Aldgate*. Turn right. Twenty-five feet from the corner of Jewry, the foundations of the medieval gate in the City wall have been discovered, and corresponding foundations opposite them (between Duke's Place and Houndsditch) where a post

office has been located for many years. From 1374 to about 1385, the first of the great English poets, GEOFFREY CHAUCER (1340?-1400) occupied apartments above this gate. These apartments would have been over that portion of the street lying directly in front of the post office.

7. Just beyond the post office, *Houndsditch* (formerly the moat outside the City wall) runs into Aldgate High Street. At the corner stands *St Botolph's Church Aldgate*, where DANIEL DEFOE (1660-1731), the first of the great English novelists, was married on 1 January 1684.

8. Walk up Houndsditch to the first street, *Creechurch Lane*, entering from your left. Turn into this. At the end of the first block (last house on the left) JEREMY BENTHAM (1748-1832), the political philosopher, founder of the Utilitarian economic doctrine, was born.

9. Return to Houndsditch, and continue along it till you reach *Bishopsgate*, just across which you will see *St Botolph's Church without Bishopsgate*. In an older church here was baptized EDWARD ALLEYN (1566-1626), who became the foremost actor of his time, son-in-law of the theatre-owner Philip Henslowe, owner of the Rose and Fortune theatres and the Bear Gardens, founder of Dulwich College, and (by a second marriage) son-in-law of the poet John Donne. In the present church was baptized the poet JOHN KEATS (1795-1821). The infant son of the poet and dramatist BEN JONSON (1572-1637) was buried in the older church; and Jonson wrote a famous poem in memory of the child.

Walk on up *Bishopsgate* towards the Liverpool Street Station. From your right, one block up the street, enter little *Devonshire Row*—on or near which EDWARD ALLEYN (see above) was born. Still farther up Bishopsgate, the next street entering from the right is *New Street*, where DANIEL DEFOE (see above) lived for a time.

Just opposite is the Liverpool Street Station. It occupies part of the site of Old Bedlam (Bethleham Hospital), a hospital (so-called) for the insane, from the mid-thirteenth century to about 1675. Additional burial grounds for St Botolph's Church (called Bethlehem Churchyard) lay farther to the west, where the Broad Street Station now stands. Here ROBERT GREENE (1558?-92), poet, tale-teller, satirist, and dramatist, was buried. He was one of the first writers of his time to note (in a spitefully jealous passage) the rising star of Shakespeare; but Shakespeare, was not above stealing an occasional plot from Greene.

You now have a decision to make. (1) You may turn about, and walk back down Bishopsgate—a route which you will take eventually, anyhow. (2) Or you may walk on up Bishopsgate for nearly a mile, and then take a bus back to where you are now. (3) Or you may combine both walking and the bus to get you up Bishopsgate and back again. We suggest this last stratagem.

10. Catch a bus travelling up Bishopsgate. After about six blocks, Bishopsgate changes into *Norton Folgate*—a very short street, where CHRISTOPHER MARLOWE (1564-93) lived. But since no vestige remains of his habitation here, there is little point in stopping.

11. At the end of Norton Folgate (as it becomes Shoreditch High Street), *Worship Street* enters from the left. WILLIAM SHAKESPEARE (1564-1616) is said to have lived here, 'six doors from Norton Folgate'.

12. Some blocks farther along Shoreditch High Street, Bethnal Green Road enters from the right, and Holywell Lane from the left. *Leave the bus here.* In the area along the left-hand (western) side of Bishopsgate just beyond Holywell Lane there stood, in Shakespeare's time, lodging houses where lived RICHARD BURBAGE (1567?-1619), actor, theatre-owner, friend of Shakespeare, partner of Shakespeare in various theatrical ventures, and actor in many of Shakespeare's plays on their first appearance; and also JOHN WEBSTER (1580?-1625?), dramatist, author of the famous *The White Devil* and *The Duchess of Malfi*.

13. At the next corner beyond Holywell Lane, turn left on *New Inn Yard*, and follow it (about three blocks) to its juncture with Curtain Road, but do not cross the latter. To your right, as you stand at the intersection, stood England's first public theatre—called *The Theatre* —built in 1576 by JAMES BURBAGE (d. 1597), father of Richard Burbage (see above). Its approximate site is marked by a plaque at *Nos. 86-8 Curtain Road*, though actually it stood farther away from the road, in a large open space.

[13A. Two blocks to your left, down *Curtain Road*, just beyond the intersection with Hewett Street, and on the left-hand side of Curtain Road, stood England's second public theatre—the *Curtain*, built in 1577, and believed by some to have been the original 'wooden O' of Shakespeare's *Henry V*. (The name 'Curtain' does not refer to stage drapery, but to a 'curtain wall' at this location.)]

14. Continue to your right, up Curtain Road, to Old Street, and turn right. Go to the next juncture of main thoroughfares (about one block), with a church on the opposite side. This is *St Leonard's Church*, established about 900, rebuilt in 1740, bombed rather badly, and restored. JAMES BURBAGE (see above) and his son RICHARD BURBAGE (see above) were buried in this church—as were William Sly and Richard Cowley, original actors in some of Shakespeare's plays; Gabriel Spenser, the man whom Ben Jonson killed in a duel; and the Countess of Rutland, only child of Sir Philip Sidney. GEORGE LILLO (1693-1739), author of the play *The London Merchant* (1731), is also buried here. This play, though intrinsically worthless, is the first tragedy dealing with lower-class characters in a serious and naturalistic manner. It had tremendous influence on later drama in England, France, and Germany.

15. Now you should certainly take the bus, and ride back down Bishopsgate, about three blocks beyond St Botolph's Church. Just past a little church on your left (St Ethelburga's), get off at St Helen's Place, entering from the left. (Down this little street is the ancient Leathersellers' Hall, which may be worth visiting.) on *Bishopsgate*, just about opposite the entrance to St Helen's Place, stood (in the sixteenth and seventeenth centuries) the *Bull Tavern*. Plays were performed in its yard before the building of the *Theatre* on Curtain Road; and JAMES BURBAGE (see above) acted here. (The tavern was London headquarters of the carrier, and later employer of carriers, and livery stable keeper, Thomas Hobson—from whom comes the phrase 'Hobson's choice'.)

16. Walk on down Bishopsgate to *Great St Helen's* (on your left), which is the name of a street and also of the church to which the street leads. A certain WILLIAM SHAKESPEARE lived on this street in 1598, and may have been the poet; anyhow, the church, dating mostly from the thirteenth century, is one of the oldest and finest in the city, and should be visited.

17. Return to Bishopsgate, and descend it one block to *Crosby Square*, on your left. As you enter this, the area on your left, and ahead of you, was once occupied by the great house called *Crosby Place*, where noblemen lived and ambassadors were entertained. SIR THOMAS MORE (see above) bought and occupied the Place, 1518-23, when at the height of his power.

18. Return to *Bishopsgate*, and walk down it. At a house on your right, seven doors up from Cornhill (*No. 119* at that time), the poet

GEORGE CRABBE (1754-1832) lodged in 1780. A poet who, in the midst of the growing romantic movement, wrote with unflinching bitterness and realism about the brutish and miserable life of the English village, Crabbe had difficulty in getting a hearing. While lodged in this place, he wrote a desperate letter to Edmund Burke, asking for help; had Burke not answered favourably, Crabbe had resolved to drown himself.

19. Continue down Bishopsgate, and straight ahead down Gracechurch, till you find *Lombard Street* intersecting from your right. Turn into it. Just to your right, after you turn, is the entrance of Ball Alley, where Allhallows Church once stood. ALEXANDER BARCLAY (1475?-1552), the satirical poet who made a highly original and extremely free translation of the French poem *The Ship of Fools*, was rector here. A bit farther on, to your left, is the opening of *Plough Court*—at the bottom of which was the house (facing up the court) where the poet ALEXANDER POPE (1688-1744), the dominant critical and poetical influence of the eighteenth century, was born. Just beyond this court, but on the right-hand side of Lombard Street, stands *St Edmund's Church*, where JOSEPH ADDISON (1672-1719), poet, essayist, critic, and dramatist, was married (1716) to the widowed Countess of Warwick and Holland. Just beyond the church, *Birchin Lane* enters from the right; on this street THOMAS BABINGTON MACAULAY (1800-59), historian and essayist, passed two years of his infancy (1800-2). At *No 71 Lombard Street* stood (and probably still stands) the Lloyd's Bank in whose basement (Foreign and Colonial Department), the American-born and Nobel Prizewinning poet T. S. ELIOT (1888-1965) worked as a clerk for many years. You will find *Abchurch Lane* entering from your left. At about the nearer (eastern) corner of this and Lombard Street stood *Pontack's* (1688-1780), facing into Abchurch Lane. Long one of London's most fashionable eating places, it was frequented by *Sir Christopher Wren* and *Jonathan Swift*; *John Evelyn* visited it and mentions it in his diary; and it is mentioned in plays by Southerne, Sedley, Congreve, Steele, and Mrs Centlivre. At *No. 12 Lombard Street* AUBREY BEARDSLEY (1872-98), illustrator, artist, and occasional writer, worked briefly for a life assurance company (1891). Beardsley was one of the most creative spirits who ever lived, and his influence on art and literature dominated the last decade of the nineteenth century and the first decade of the twentieth. At *No. 2*, over a bank, lived the family of Maria Beadnall, who was the first serious love of the novelist CHARLES DICKENS (1812-70); her father, who was an official in the bank below, would not let Maria marry the impecunious young journalist—and her own

flirtatious on-again-off-again behaviour made Dickens miserable for years.

Go on to the end of Lombard Street, and find there, on your right, the *Bank Underground Station*—where this tour ends. If you have time and energy for other tours today, you may catch the train and, in less than ten minutes, be at the beginning of *Tours No. 2, No. 7,* or *No. 8.*

Tour 5
Southwark

Edward Alleyn	**Leigh Hunt**
Richard Baxter	**Dr Samuel Johnson**
Francis Beaumont	**Ben Jonson**
Eustace Budgell	**John Keats**
Geoffrey Chaucer	**Thomas Kyd**
William Combe	**Sir Thomas Malory**
W. H. Davies	**Philip Massinger**
Thomas Dekker	**F. D. Maurice**
John Donne	**George Peele**
Edward Dyer	**Henry Purcell**
John Fletcher	**William Shakespeare**
Oliver Goldsmith	**Christopher Smart**
John Gower	**Tobias Smollett**
Matthew Green	**Nahum Tate**
William Haughton	**Sir William Temple**
Benjamin Haydon	**Hester Lynch Thrale**
Philip Henslowe	**George Wither**

Leave the underground at the *Mansion House Station*. Turn right, along Queen Victoria Street; then half-right again, along Cannon Street; and then right again, along Queen Street—the approach to Southwark Bridge.

1. Cross *Southwark Bridge*. The view you get of the river and its commerce, the warehouses along the river, and St Paul's 'looming

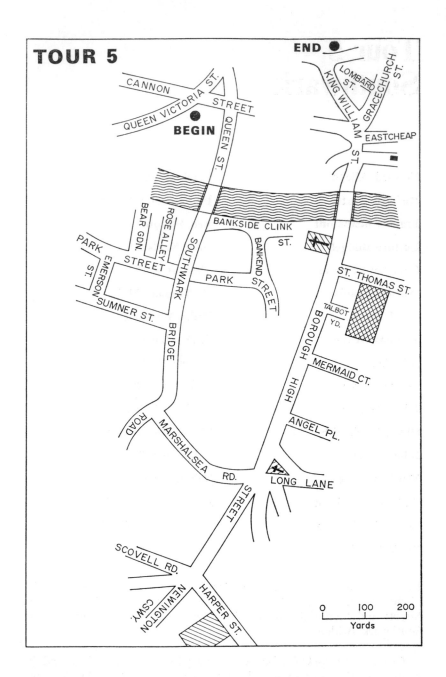

TOUR 5

CANNON

QUEEN VICTORIA ST.

STREET

BEGIN

QUEEN ST.

END

LOMBARD ST.

KING WILLIAM

GRACECHURCH ST.

ST.

EASTCHEAP

BANKSIDE CLINK

ST.

PARK

BEAR GDN.

ROSE ALLEY

SOUTHWARK

BANKEND STREET

STREET

EMERSON

ST.

PARK

ST. THOMAS ST.

SUMNER ST.

TALBOT YD.

BRIDGE

BOROUGH

MERMAID CT.

HIGH

ANGEL PL.

ROAD

MARSHALSEA

RD.

LONG LANE

STREET

SCOVELL RD.

NEWINGTON CSWY.

HARPER ST.

0   100   200
Yards

like a bubble o'er the town' is worth the walk—even if you should see nothing else interesting on this tour.

2. At the far end of the bridge, on the left, find stairs leading steeply down to the riverside. Descend them. You will now be on the famous (or infamous) *Bankside*. Here clustered, from the Middle Ages on into the seventeenth and eighteenth centuries, brothels, disreputable taverns, bear-baiting and bull-baiting gardens, and other places of shady fame. Walk along Bankside—with your back to the bridge, the river on your left, and great produce warehouses on your right. About 150 yards from the bridge (or two-thirds of the way to the next major turning, or corner, of the street), and about 50 feet to your right (in an area now covered over with warehouses) stood Shakespeare's *Globe Theatre*—the 'wooden O' referred to in *Henry V*.

Ahead of you, Bankside turns to the right. Just below the turning you will find *Clink Street* entering from the left. You need not explore this street. However, on Clink Street and Bankside lived the following persons significant in the Elizabethan or Jacobean theatre: EDWARD ALLEYN (1566-1626), greatest actor of his time, owner of the Rose and Fortune theatres, son-in-law (through his first wife) of the other famous theatre-owner Philip Henslowe, and son-in-law (through his second wife) of the poet John Donne; PHILIP HENSLOWE (d. 1616) himself, whose diary is an invaluable source-book on the Elizabethan theatre and stage; GEORGE PEELE (1558-97), brilliant dramatist and dissolute ne'er-do-well; the dramatists JOHN FLETCHER (1579-1625) and his collaborator FRANCIS BEAUMONT (1584-1616); PHILIP MASSINGER (1583-1640), who seems to have collaborated with Shakespeare in the play *Henry VIII*; and probably WILLIAM SHAKESPEARE himself.

In a later age, OLIVER GOLDSMITH (1730?-74), poet, dramatist, essayist, novelist, who had some training as a physician, practised medicine on Bankside in his early days.

On Clink Street stood the famous Clink Prison—meant mostly for debtors, indiscreet prostitutes, and rowdy persons. The dramatist PHILIP MASSINGER (see above) was imprisoned here, as was WILLIAM HAUGHTON (fl. 1598), who wrote the first full-length, altogether realistic comedy in English: *Englishmen for My Money* (1598). The prison stood just beyond where the railroad tracks plunge over the street towards the great railroad bridge that crosses the river alongside Southwark Bridge. (The name of the Clink Prison survives in a modern slang expression—as 'They put him in the clink'.)

3. Bankside leads on into *Bankend*. Continue down the latter—noting, on your right, the ancient *Anchor Inn* (*c.* 1775) which, though

picturesque, seems to have no intimate literary associations other than the fact that Dr Johnson visited it, and many people connected with the Elizabethan theatre undoubtedly visited its predecessor here. Continue straight ahead, cross the street, and find yourself walking along Park Street.

4. Somewhere along *Park Street*, on the right-hand side, very near your street crossing, stood the home of the wealthy brewer Henry Thrale and his wife HESTER LYNCH THRALE (1741-1821), diarist and letter-writer, long-time friend and hostess of DR SAMUEL JOHNSON (1709-84), who considered the Thrales' house his second home. While staying here, he is known to have written his *Life of Congreve*. His friends *Garrick*, *Reynolds*, and *Goldsmith* visited him and the Thrales here.

Now turn about, and walk back the way you came. At the first corner, turn left. You will still be on winding *Park Street*.

About half a block along the street, you will find (on your left) a largish plaque set into the wall of a brewery. It was once believed that the Globe Theatre (see above) had stood a few feet behind the plaque, on ground now occupied by the brewery—or perhaps twenty feet to your right as you face the plaque. But more recent research seems to have established that the Globe was nearer to Bankside—as indicated in a preceding paragraph. A bear-baiting garden was once almost directly behind you, as you stand looking at the plaque.

A brewery has stood on the site of the present brewery since the seventeenth or eighteenth century. Henry Thrale (see above) owned a brewery here—which is one reason for his establishing his home nearby, on Park Street, as mentioned above. (At that time, the street was called Dead Man's Place.) After Thrale's death, DR JOHNSON, who had been named an executor of Thrale's will, showed himself a competent businessman: he was able to sell the brewery for £135,000.

Continue along Park Street, going under the bridge, and note, on your right, *Rose Alley*, where stood the Rose Theatre of Edward Alleyn and Philip Henslowe (see above); and, a little farther on, the narrow street called *Bear Gardens*, whose name indicates its former association with this once-popular Sunday 'sport'.

5. At the next corner, turn left, on Emerson Street, and then left again, on Sumner Street. This leads back to the Bridge Road. Turn right, on this road, and walk along it three or four blocks, to *Marshalsea Road*, entering from your left. Turn into it. Just to your right as you enter this street once stood an old building that served as a home for down-and-outers. Here the 'hobo poet' W. H. DAVIES (1871-1940)

stayed while his first volume of poems was being published (at his own expense) in 1905.

6. Follow Marshalsea to the *Borough High Street*. Just across the street from where you have now arrived, you will see the *Church of St George the Martyr*. In its churchyard is buried NAHUM TATE (1652-1715), poet, author of operatic librettos, collaborator with Dryden in the satiric poem *Absalom and Achitophel*, 'improver' of Shakespeare (he has Cordelia, in *King Lear*, marry Edgar, and live happily ever afterward), and Poet Laureate. Dickens's Little Dorrit (with Mazy) passed a night in the vestry of the church; and was later married here. [6A. You may wish to turn right on Borough High Street, and follow it several blocks. The first main street on your right is *Lant Street*, where *Charles Dickens* had lodgings for a while, to be near his father, who was then in Marshalsea prison. Bob Sawyer (of the *Pickwick Papers*) had lodgings here (with Mrs Raddle), and was visited by Mr Pickwick. Two or three blocks farther along the Borough High Street, *Harper Street* intersects from the left. Turn into it, and after a few steps, find a recreation ground on your right. Here once stood the *Horsemonger Lane Jail* (Harper Street was once named Horsemonger Lane). Here LEIGH HUNT (1784-1859), poet, critic, essayist, and friend of Byron, Shelley, Tom Moore, and Keats, was confined for two years (1812-14) for libelling the Prince Regent (later George IV)—something of an impossibility, one would think, in light of the Prince Regent's character. *Byron* and *Thomas Moore* visited Hunt here, and dined with him (jail regulations were liberal in those days); and *Keats* and *Shelley* also visited him.
[6B. Return to the Borough High Street, and cross over it into *Scovell Road*. Ahead of you, and to your right, lay the old *King's Bench Prison*—from 1758 to 1870. The novelist TOBIAS SMOLLETT (1721-71) was confined here for three months (1759) for libelling an admiral; while here he wrote his novel *Sir Lancelot Greaves*. The poet CHRISTOPHER SMART (1722-71) died in this prison, where he had been confined for debt; WILLIAM COMBE (1741-1823) wrote all three of the *Tours of Dr Syntax* (verses to go with the satirical illustrations of Thomas Rowlandson) while being kept here for debt; BENJAMIN HAYDON (1788-1846), painter, autobiographer, and writer on art, who was a friend of Keats, and borrowed money from the poet when the latter could ill afford to lend, was confined here for debt.... Now return up the High Street to St George the Martyr Church.]

7. Just beyond the church, up the Borough High Street, stood the *White Lion Prison*; and just beyond that (near *Angel Place*) stood the

original *King's Bench Prison* (till 1758). THOMAS DEKKER (1572?-1632), dramatist and prose satirist, was kept in the latter six years for debt (1613-19). The non-conformist minister RICHARD BAXTER (1615-91), author of many religious works, scholar, saintly man, and victim of the infamous Judge Jeffreys, was also confined here. (Legend has it that Prince Hal was sent here by Judge Gascoigne for having insulted the latter on the bench.) As noted above, this prison was moved farther down the road in 1758. At about that time, the *Marshalsea Prison* was brought from farther up the road, and established on the site vacated by the King's Bench. This prison (granted new buildings in 1811) was the one in which Charles Dickens's father was confined for debt, and which played so large a part in the same novelist's *Little Dorrit*.

8. Continue up Borough High Street till you find *Mermaid Court* entering from your right. Just beyond this, and between this and the next street, stood the *Old Marshalsea* (see above) from the fourteenth century until about 1758. SIR THOMAS MALORY (d. 1477), author of that marvellous retelling of Arthurian legends, the *Morte d'Arthur*, was imprisoned here for a while—as well as in most other prisons of London at one time or another; BEN JONSON (1572-1637), poet and dramatist, was sent here for his part in writing *The Isle of Dogs* (1597); the poet GEORGE WITHER (1588-1677) 'wasted in despair' here (1613) for his satirical *Abuses Stript and Whipt*; and the poet JOHN DONNE (1572-1631) served time here for having married without official sanction.

9. Continuing up the Borough High Street, you will find, on your right, a little alley called *Talbot Yard*, with 'The Old Tabard Inn' at its entrance. This inn is, of course, not the same one from which the pilgrims of GEOFFREY CHAUCER's *Canterbury Tales* set out. But that inn was very near this spot, just down the alley from the present inn. It was pulled down in 1629.

Farther up Borough High Street, and again on the right, is the *George Inn*, dating from 1677, and mentioned by Dickens in *Little Dorrit*.

A little farther up High Street is *White Hart Yard*, where the White Hart Inn stood—an inn that stood there from about 1400 to 1889, and is mentioned in the *Paston Letters*, Shakespeare's *Henry VI* (Part II), and Dickens's *Pickwick Papers*.

10. The next large street leading off from the right is *St Thomas Street*, with *Guy's Hospital* a short distance down it, on the right.

Here the poet JOHN KEATS (1795-1821) studied medicine and the practice of surgery in 1815. And here the famous F. D. MAURICE (1805-72), theologian, novelist, founder of Christian Socialism (which powerfully influenced the fiction of Charles Kingsley and Mrs Gaskell), and a founder of the Working Men's College and Queen's College for Women, was chaplain to the hospital for ten years, 1836-46.

11. Continue up Borough High Street for a block or two, till you see an ancient church on your left. This is *St Saviour's*, or *Southwark Cathedral*. Descend the steps to it, and find the entrance on the far side. It is a fine old church, with parts of it dating back to the thirteenth century. The tower by which you enter is called the Beaufort Tower because it was built at the instigation of Cardinal Beaufort, who was the son of the poet Geoffrey Chaucer's sister-in-law, Katherine Swynford, by Chaucer's patron John of Gaunt. Chaucer's good friend, the poet JOHN GOWER (d. 1408) is buried here, and has a magnificent and well-preserved tomb on which lies his recumbent effigy, with the head resting on Gower's three greatest poetic works. In this church are buried the dramatists PHILIP MASSINGER (see above) and JOHN FLETCHER (see above). Also buried here are *Lawrence Fletcher*, co-owner, with Burbage and Shakespeare, of the Globe and Blackfriars Theatre; *Edmund Shakespeare*, actor, and brother of the poet; the poet SIR EDWARD DYER (1543-1607); the theatre-owner PHILIP HENSLOWE (see above).

12. When you leave the church, return the way you came, and continue across London Bridge. This is not the original bridge of song and story—which lay about 185 feet down river, to your right, and was demolished in 1832. It was succeeded by a bridge that was eventually sold to some American real-estate developers, and transported to Arizona, in the late 1960's. On the identical spot was built the present (wider) bridge. The massive stone piles supporting the old bridge downstream partially blocked the flow of the river—with the result that the current used to run swiftly and dangerously between the piles. A common sport was for daring boatmen to 'shoot the bridge' by rowing under it. The only son of SIR WILLIAM TEMPLE (1628-99) committed suicide by filling his pockets with stones, hiring a boatman to 'shoot the bridge', and then jumping overboard under the bridge. EUSTACE BUDGELL (1686-1737), periodical essayist, pamphleteer, kinsman and secretary of Joseph Addison, figure in Pope's *Dunciad*, committed suicide in the same way. Just to the left of the bridge some stone steps led down to the water. It was on those steps one dark night that Noah Claypole (in Dickens's *Oliver Twist*) over-

heard Nancy telling secrets that eventually caused Bill Sikes to murder her.

13. Walk on across the bridge, and to the farther bank of the river. As you continue walking straight ahead, you will see the Monument, off to your right. It was designed by Sir Christopher Wren to commemorate the Great Fire of 1666, and was finished in 1677. (Wren wanted to place a gigantic statue of Charles II atop the Monument but the King objected. 'After all,' he said, very sensibly, 'I didn't start the fire.') The bas-relief on the pedestal was carved by Caius Cibber—father of Colley Cibber (1671-1757), dramatist, actor, theatre-manager, Poet Laureate, and 'hero' of Pope's *Dunciad*. Near where you are standing (at the juncture of Arthur and King William Streets), there was once an apothecary's shop where OLIVER GOLDSMITH (see above) was a clerk for a while.

14. Continue straight along King William Street till it branches into a Y—with Gracechurch Street on the right and King William Street on the left.
[14A. By walking up Gracechurch Street one block, you will find, on your left, *Lombard Court*. In lodgings here the once-famous MATTHEW GREEN (1696-1737), author of a celebrated and still rather charming poem called *The Spleen*, lived and died.... Now return to King William Street.]
   In the open space at the lower end of Gracechurch Street, where five streets join, once stood the *Boar's Head Tavern*, where Falstaff, Prince Hal, and their cronies foregathered in Shakespeare's *Henry IV*. The spot was out in the present street, just in front of the entrance to the Monument Underground Station. (Actually, though the tavern had existed since the early sixteenth century, it was not in existence in the early fifteenth century, when Falstaff and Prince Hal lived.)

15. Walk up the left-hand branch of the Y—that is, *King William Street*. After a block, you will see, on your right. *St Clements Church*, where HENRY PURCELL (1659-95), greatest of English composers, was chief organist. At the far end of this street, on your right is *St Mary Woolnoth Church*. The building here is an eighteenth-century successor of an earlier church in which THOMAS KYD (1558-1594), a dramatist who had much influence on Shakespeare, was baptized. The present church figures in T. S. Eliot's poem *The Waste Land*: its bells 'kept the hours/With a dead sound on the final stroke of nine'. T. S. ELIOT (1888-1959) himself worked for some years at Lloyd's Bank, on nearby Lombard Street.

Just ahead of you, on the corner across the street, is the *Bank Underground Station*—where this tour ends. If you wish to make another tour today, you may reach, in five or six minutes by underground train, the starting points of *Tours No. 2, No. 7*, and *No. 8*.

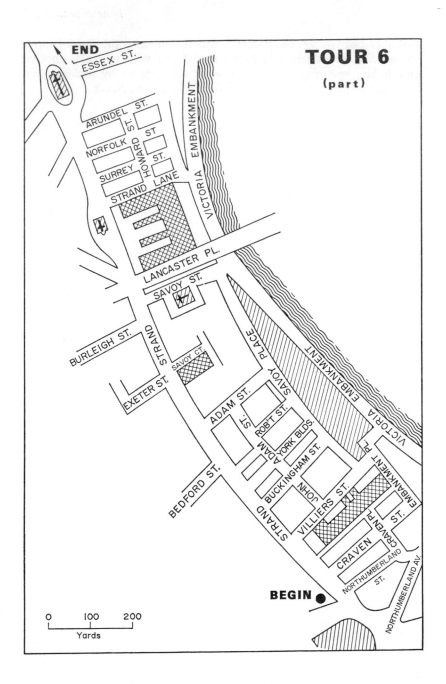

TOUR 6

(part)

END
ESSEX ST.
ARUNDEL ST.
NORFOLK
SURREY
HOWARD ST.
STRAND LANE
VICTORIA EMBANKMENT
LANCASTER PL.
SAVOY ST.
BURLEIGH ST.
EXETER ST.
STRAND
SAVOY CT.
ADAM ST.
ROBT ST.
SAVOY PLACE
VICTORIA EMBANKMENT
ADAM ST.
YORK BLDS.
BUCKINGHAM ST.
JOHN
VILLIERS ST.
BEDFORD ST.
STRAND
CRAVEN PL.
EMBANKMENT
CRAVEN ST.
NORTHUMBERLAND ST.
NORTHUMBERLAND AV.

BEGIN ●

0   100   200
Yards

Tour 6
The Strand and Fleet Street

Joseph Addison

Mark Akenside

Edwin Arnold

Francis Bacon

James Barrie

Topham Beauclerk

Thomas Lovell Beddoes

Arnold Bennett

Thomas Betterton

William Black

William Blake

James Boswell

Anne Bracegirdle

Eustace Budgell

Edmund Burke

Samuel Butler

Thomas Campion

D'Oyly Carte

Geoffrey Chaucer

John Cleland

Hartley Coleridge

Samuel Taylor Coleridge

William Congreve

Joseph Conrad

Abraham Cowley

William Cowper

George Crabbe

Edmund Curll

George Darley

William Davenant

W. H. Davies

Daniel Defoe

Sir John Denham

Charles Dickens

Isaac Disraeli

John Donne

Gawain Douglas

Michael Drayton

John Dryden

George Dyer

George Eliot

Ralph Waldo Emerson

John Evelyn

George Farquhar

Henry Fielding

Gilbert Frankau

Benjamin Franklin

Thomas Fuller

John Galsworthy

David Garrick

Edward Gibbon

William Godwin

Oliver Goldsmith

Harley Granville-Barker

Thomas Hardy

Frank Harris

William Hazlitt

Heinrich Heine

Aaron Hill

Thomas Hood

David Hume

Mrs Elizabeth Inchbald

Washington Irving

Lionel Johnson

Dr Samuel Johnson

Ben Jonson

Edmund Kean

John Keats

Hugh Kelly

Charles Kingsley

Henry Kingsley

Rudyard Kipling

Thomas Kyd

Charles Lamb

George Granville, Lord Lansdowne

Nathaniel Lee

Charlotte Lennox

George Henry Lewes

Bernard Lintot

John Locke

Richard Lovelace

E. V. Lucas

John Lyly

Herman Melville

Richard Middleton

Andrew Millar

A. A. Milne

John Milton

Mary Mitford

George Moore

Hannah More

Arthur Murphy

John Murray

John Middleton Murry

Sir Isaac Newton

Thomas Norton

Thomas Otway

Thomas Paine

Coventry Patmore

John Howard Payne

Samuel Pepys

Sir Walter Raleigh

Samuel Richardson

Dante Gabriel Rossetti

Jean-Jacques Rousseau

Thomas Rymer

Thomas Sackville

Sir Charles Sedley

Thomas Shadwell

Earl of Shaftesbury

George Bernard Shaw

Percy Bysshe Shelley

William Shenstone

Sarah Siddons

Sir Philip Sidney

James Smith

Tobias Smollett

Edmund Spenser

Sir Richard Steele

Sir John Suckling

Henry Howard, Earl of Surrey

Alfred Tennyson

William Makepeace Thackeray

Francis Thompson

James Thomson

Jacob Tonson

E. Temple Thurston

Richard Tottel

Mark Twain

William Tyndale

George Villiers

Voltaire

Izaak Walton

H. G. Wells

Wm. Hale White
  ('Mark Rutherford')

Oscar Wilde

George Wither

Peg Woffington

Mary Wollstonecraft

Virginia Woolf

Sir Thomas Wyatt

John Wyclif

Wynken de Worde

The Strand

Leave the underground at the *Trafalgar Square Station*. Spot the Nelson column, and the lion crouched at the admiral's left front. Follow the direction of the animal's gaze across the street to the entrance of Northumberland Street (*not* Northumberland Avenue).

1. On *Northumberland Street* (formerly Hartshorne Lane) BEN JONSON (1572-1637), poet, dramatist, and friend of Shakespeare, may have been born; anyhow, he spent his boyhood here with his mother and his stepfather, a bricklayer from whom young Ben learned the trade. A bit to the right of the place where you enter this street stood Northumberland House. Here OLIVER GOLDSMITH (1730?-1774), poet, dramatist, and novelist, calling on the Duke of Northumberland by appointment, mistook the elaborately uniformed footman for the Duke himself. Goldsmith was famous for such blunders.

2. Walk along the Strand to the next corner, and turn right, into *Craven Street. (Incidental intelligence:* On the left-hand corner, as you enter this street, stood a shop where Edward Gibbon, the historian, bought gold lace.) HERMAN MELVILLE (1819-91), the American novelist, lived briefly at *No. 25* when, as a sailor in his youth, he visited London. JAMES SMITH (1775-1839), one of the two brothers who wrote those immensely funny parodies of contemporary poets (*Rejected Addresses*), lived and died at *No. 27.* The poet HEINRICH HEINE (1797-1856), one of the very greatest figures in German literature, lived at *No. 32* while he was in London in 1827. MARK AKENSIDE (1721-70), poet, essayist, physician to the queen of George III, author of the long philosophical poem *The Pleasures of the Imagination* (1744), and one of the forerunners of the Romantic movement, lived at *No. 33* from 1759 to 1761. And BENJAMIN FRANKLIN (1706-90), the American statesman, diplomat, scientist, and author, had his residence at *No. 36* during the eighteen years (off and on) that he was in London as a representative of the Pennsylvania House of Assembly (1757-75).

3. At the lower end of Craven Street, turn left, into Embankment Place, and pass under Charing Cross Station and its railways. (This station covers the old Hungerford Stairs where CHARLES DICKENS worked as a boy in a shoe-blacking shop—an experience poignantly re-created in *David Copperfield*.)
[3A. You may wish to make an excursion into the green Embankment Gardens just ahead of you, where you will find memorials to *Robert Burns* and the musician *Sir Arthur Sullivan.* Nearby, on the Embankment itself, is a medallion to *W. S. Gilbert*.]

Beyond the station, turn left, into *Villiers Street. (Note:* Many streets hereabouts bear part of the name of GEORGE VILLIERS, DUKE OF BUCKINGHAM (1628-87), poet, dramatist, courtier, wit, who once owned the surrounding area. (Formerly, there was even an 'Of Alley'!) RUDYARD KIPLING (1865-1936), a young man who had made an enormous success in India with his stories and poems, came here, to

No. 43, on your right, to begin his conquest of England. Staying here (fifth floor, rooms 16, 17, 18), he wrote his novel *The Light that Failed*, saw the publication of a collection of his stories (*Life's Handicap*), and began publishing (in W. E. Henley's *National Observer*) the *Barrack-Room Ballads* that secured his fame. Almost across the street from the Kipling place, SIR RICHARD STEELE (1672-1729), charming essayist, dramatist, theatre manager, and member of Parliament, occupied a house in 1712. In this house the flamboyant Steele had a concert room that would seat 200 people. About ten years later, Steele occupied another house on the right-hand side of the street, farther up towards the Strand. The diarist JOHN EVELYN (1620-1706), who moved into London every winter, lived on this street in the winter of 1682-3.

4. Walk on to the *Strand*. At the corner (on your left) of Villiers Street and the Strand, the young JAMES BOSWELL (1740-95) reports having bought a sword from a dealer. He bought it on credit, and later, when he paid the man, lectured him for having been so trustful! Near here is *No. 33* occupied by the 'egregious FRANK HARRIS' (1856-1931) when he was editor of *Vanity Fair* in 1911. An enterprising and able editor, Harris wrote many (not too reliable) portraits and biographies of his contemporaries; and he capped the climax of scandal with his three-volume *My Life and Loves*, which (we may devoutly hope) is even less reliable than his literary portraits.

Farther to the right along the Strand is a site in which, just possibly, you may be interested. Since it is off the route of the rest of this tour, it should be mentioned here. On the southern (right-hand) side of the Strand, just opposite the entrance of Bedford Street (on your left) JOHN DRYDEN (1631-1700) lived, 1659-63. He was a dramatist, critic, poet, Poet Laureate, literary law-giver, and dominant literary figure of the Restoration.

5. You were left standing at the corner of Villiers Street and the Strand. To your right, in the angle (southeastern) formed by Villiers Street and the Strand, once stood *York House* and its outbuildings. It extended about two blocks to your right along the Strand, and down towards the river a bit farther than the Kipling House. York House was the lodging of the Archbishops of York from at least the early sixteenth century; but after many vicissitudes, the mansion and its outbuildings were finally demolished in the late seventeenth century, and replaced by a loosely integrated conglomeration of tenements, shops, offices, concert halls, and dwellings. The jurist, essayist, and philosopher, father of modern science, FRANCIS BACON (1561-

1626) was born here. GEORGE FARQUHAR (1678-1707), 'last of the Restoration dramatists', lived here, as did that other successful dramatist ARTHUR MURPHY (1727-1805), friend of Dr Johnson.

6. Turn right, along the Strand, go one block, and turn right again, into *Buckingham Street*. You are now entering the general region known as THE ADELPHI. All the area occupied by York House (see above) and Durham House (see below) had become disreputable slums by the mid-eighteenth century. They were bought up by the four Adam brothers (*adelphoi* is the Greek word for 'brothers'), Scottish architects and property developers. Between 1768 and 1774 the entire region was transformed into what became a wealthy and fashionable district. Following the example of the Duke of Buckingham in using his own names for the streets hereabouts, the Adam brothers named many of the new streets after themselves.

PEG WOFFINGTON (1714?-60), famous for her abilities both as actress and as lover, mistress of the great actor and dramatist David Garrick, lived at *No. 9* briefly, 1756-7. DAVID HUME (1711-76), the Scottish sceptical philosopher, was living at *No. 10* in 1766, when he was visited by JEAN-JACQUES ROUSSEAU (1712-78), French philosopher, whose ideas profoundly influenced the eighteenth-century movements towards Romanticism and democracy. The two had a great quarrel in the open street along here—because of their natural intellectual incompatibility, because of Hume's friendship with the son of one of Rousseau's critics in France, and because Hume persisted in talking in his sleep, a habit which Rousseau regarded as an insult to himself. In the twentieth century, *A. D. Peters*, literary agent for many of England's most celebrated modern writers, and himself a film producer, play producer, and drama critic, had his offices for many years at this same *No. 10*. SAMUEL PEPYS (1633-1703), the great diarist, lived at *No. 12* for ten years, 1679-88—in the same house that now stands here, though it has been much altered since Pepys occupied it. Pepys lived also at *No. 14* (not the same house today), the last on your right as you descend the street, 1688-1701. When Pepys moved out, the house was occupied by Robert Harley, Earl of Oxford, from 1701 to 1714. Harley was virtual Prime Minister of England, 1711-14, and was a friend of *Jonathan Swift*, who visited him here. Though Harley was no angel as a politician, literary scholars remember him favourably because he made a vast collection of medieval manuscripts and legal documents now residing, as the 'Harleian Library', in the British Museum. Across the street, at *No. 15* (rebuilt), the novelist CHARLES DICKENS (1812-70) lived briefly; and he had Miss Betsy Trotwood take rooms for David Copperfield here.

Later on, WILLIAM BLACK (1814-98), novelist of the Highlands and the Hebrides, lived at *No. 15*. The poet SAMUEL TAYLOR COLERIDGE (1772-1834) lodged for a while in 1799 at *No. 21*.

7. You should return now to *John Adam Street*, where it crosses Buckingham Street. Turn right (eastward) on John Adam Street. On your left you will note a plaque marking the former dwelling-place of *Thomas Rowlandson* (1756-1827), well-known caricaturist and humorous or satirical depicter of English social life around 1800. Nearby, at *No. 17*, lived the modern caricaturist *Bruce Bairnsfeather* (1888-1959), who did for the British infantryman of World War I what Bill Mauldin did for the American infantryman of World War II. Bairnsfeather's most famous character was 'Old Bill'. *Sir Cedric Hardwicke*, motion picture actor, also lived at *No. 17*, as did HARLEY GRANVILLE-BARKER (1877-1946), actor, play producer, and dramatist. Right opposite the end of Robert Street, on your left was the home of ISAAC DISRAELI (1766-1848), author of numerous books of biography and anecdote about literary persons, and father of the novelist Benjamin Disraeli. At the extreme end of John Adam Street, where it intersects Adam Street, on the right-hand corner, at *Nos. 1-4*, stood the Adelphi (or Osborn's) Hotel, where the historian EDWARD GIBBON (1737-94) stayed on his return from Europe with the completed manuscript of the last three volumes of his history of *The Decline and Fall of the Roman Empire*. The poet GEORGE CRABBE (1754-1832) also lodged here on a protracted visit to London.

8. Turn right, off John Adam Street, into the street known as *York Buildings*. JOHN MIDDLETON MURRY (1889-1957), critic, editor, literary biographer, husband of Katherine Mansfield, was living at *No. 18* in 1925. The mother of CHARLES DICKENS was living at *No. 31* in 1831 —and Charles was living with her part of the time.

9. Return to John Adam Street, continue along it for one block, and turn right, into *Robert Street*. The continuous building bearing *Nos. 1-3*, on your right, was the home, in the 1820's, of THOMAS HOOD (1799-1845), who wrote mostly humorous verses and essays, but is remembered for his great poem of social protest, 'The Song of the Shirt', and his tragic poem 'The Bridge of Sighs'. The American artist *Joseph Pennell* (1860-1926), friend and biographer of Whistler, lived here from 1909 to 1917. Other writers who have lived in this building are the popular novelist E. TEMPLE THURSTON, in 1909-10; Nobel Prize-winning novelist and dramatist JOHN GALSWORTHY (1867-1933), in 1917-18; and novelist and dramatist JAMES BARRIE

(1860-1937), for many years. Barrie lived on the top floor, with windows to the river.

10. At the bottom of Robert Street, *Adelphi Terrace* runs away to the left. Turn left into it. TOPHAM BEAUCLERK (1739-80), amateur scholar, charming personality, member of Dr Johnson's Literary Club, and 'loved by Dr Johnson with signal devotion', lived (1772-6) at *No. 3*. D'OYLY CARTE (1844-1901), impresario of the Gilbert and Sullivan light operas, and builder of the Savoy Theatre, lived at *No. 4* during the last thirteen years of his life. DAVID GARRICK (1717-79), his century's greatest actor, a theatre manager and dramatist, friend of Dr Johnson and member of the Club, lived from 1772 at *No. 5*, and died there—a house that was near the centre of the Terrace. Garrick and his wife often had as a house guest the novelist and dramatist HANNAH MORE (1745-1833), whose home was Bristol. Eventually, a vast, formidable and expensive apartment complex rose here; and JAMES BARRIE (see above) lived at *No. 3*, 1909 till his death. JOHN GALSWORTHY (see above) lived in the same building, 1913-16; and the dramatist GEORGE BERNARD SHAW ('The Sage of Adelphi Terrace') (1856-1950) lived here from about 1900 to 1919. THOMAS HARDY (1840-1928), poet and novelist, worked with an architectural firm in this building, at *No. 8*, in the 1870's. JOHN MIDDLETON MURRY (see above) had the editorial offices of his *Athenaeum* magazine at *No. 10*; and at the far end of the Terrace, on the nearer corner of Adam Street, was the editorial office of the magazine edited by the poet THOMAS HOOD (see above).

The entire area about here—from Adelphi Terrace up to the Strand, and from Robert Street over to Adam Street (to the east)— was once occupied by *Durham House* (official residence of the Bishops of Durham), its outbuildings, and its grounds. SIR PHILIP SIDNEY (1554-86) lived in this house with his father when he was a child; and the place was later granted, by Queen Elizabeth, to SIR WALTER RALEIGH (1552?-1618), poet, historian, geographer, adventurer, explorer, soldier, and courtier, who lived here.

A huge shopping centre under one roof (called the 'New Exchange') was established in this area, up alongside the Strand, in 1609, and lasted till 1737. *Samuel Pepys* records shopping here often; scenes in plays by Etherege, Dryden, and Wycherley are laid here; Shakespeare's *Othello* was first printed in a shop here; and the place is often mentioned in the *Tatler* and the *Spectator*.

At the end of Adelphi Terrace, turn left, on Adam Street, and reach the Strand once more. Turn right. As you walk along what is now a solid block of buildings, you are passing the entrances of two streets no longer existing. The first, *Salisbury Street*, opening on your right about five doors along the Strand, was the home, at *No. 13*, of the young poet, dramatist, novelist, and teller of fairy tales OSCAR WILDE (1854-1900) in 1879-80. Here the young 'professor of aesthetics' entertained Lillie Langtry, Ellen Terry, Sir Henry Irving, and Sarah Bernhardt.

The other lost street—about seven doors beyond Salisbury—was *Cecil Street*, where JOSEPH ADDISON (1672-1719), poet, dramatist, essayist, critic, and statesman, had lodgings for a while. Here also was living EDMUND KEAN (1787?-1813), the actor, when he first made a sensational success in the part of Shylock. And GEORGE MOORE (1852-1933), Irish novelist and poet, who wrote the first truly naturalistic novel in English, lived at *No. 17* in 1881-3.

11. Just beyond this block of ghost-streets is little *Savoy Court* and its adjoining *Savoy Theatre*. This was built by D'OYLY CARTE (see above) especially for the presentation of the Gilbert and Sullivan operas—hence the generic name of the latter: 'Savoy Operas'. The theatre opened with *Patience* in 1881.

12. At about this place (opposite the entrance of Exeter Street) the very handsome *Beaufort Buildings* were constructed, late in the seventeenth century. They surrounded a courtyard lying to the right (south) of the Strand, and communicated with the latter by a narrow passage. In a house torn down to make room for them was born AARON HILL (1685-1750), who wrote dramas, conducted periodicals, managed theatres, composed odes, and was a friend of John Gay and Alexander Pope. HENRY FIELDING (1707-54), the novelist, lived for a while with his sister in the Beaufort Buildings, as did his contemporary, TOBIAS SMOLLETT (1721-71), in 1750. In 1751 *Dr Thomas Arne*, the musician, lived in the house that Smollett had vacated—at the bottom of the courtyard.

13. Just across the *Strand*, between Exeter and Burleigh Streets, once stood *Exeter House*, where was born ANTHONY ASHLEY COOPER, EARL OF SHAFTESBURY (1671-1713), whose book of essays, *Characteristics of Men, Manners, Opinions, Times* (1711), had enormous influence on the moral ideas of the century, as well as on matters of taste and concepts of human nature. JOHN LOCKE (1632-1704), philosopher of empiricism and proponent of political theories on which are based the American Declaration of Independence and American Constitution, lived in Exeter House (1667-76) as 'family physician, tutor, and private friend' of the first Earl of Shaftesbury. Here he wrote much of

his most famous work, the *Essay Concerning Human Understanding.* At *No. 372,* about where this Exeter House stood, a concert hall (Exeter Hall) was built in the nineteenth century. Here the famous *Jenny Lind* (1820-87), who was worshipped hardly short of idolatry in her time, sang the soprano part (written especially for her) of Mendelssohn's *Elijah* (1848). Farther along the same side of the street the poet SAMUEL TAYLOR COLERIDGE (1772-1834) had lodgings in 1806.

14. Back on the right-hand (south) side of the Strand, between *Nos. 103* and *104,* there was formerly a little outlet called *Fountain Court.* Here the great poet and great artist WILLIAM BLAKE (1757-1827) lived from 1821, and here died. *Fountain Tavern* stood at the head of this court, at the corner of the Strand. *Jonathan Swift* patronized this tavern, and it was social headquarters for many Tories opposed to the Whig ministry of Sir Robert Walpole.

15. From somewhere along here, and for several blocks ahead of you, to your right, once stood the great palace of the *Savoy.* In the fourteenth century it was owned by John of Gaunt, father of Henry IV, and husband of the Blanche of Lancaster, about whose death GEOFFREY CHAUCER (1340?-1400) wrote the *Book of the Duchess* (1369). A few years after Blanche's death, Gaunt took for his mistress the young widow Katherine Swynford, who was Chaucer's sister-in-law. He lived with Katherine for 20 years, and eventually married her. Much of Chaucer's poetry reflects his interest in the rich and powerful Gaunt; and in the great poetic romance *Troilus and Creseyde* Chaucer, it is believed, gave a fictionalized account of the romance between Gaunt and Katherine. JOHN WYCLIF (1328-84), religious reformer and first translator of the Bible into English, preached in the Savoy. The palace was burned down by the peasants in the revolt of 1381, and not rebuilt until the time of Henry VII. The Cavalier poet GEORGE WITHER (1588-1667) lived within the precincts of the Savoy, and died there. JOHN LYLY (1554?-1606), poet, dramatist, and prose romancer, had lodgings in the place in the 1570's and 1580's, and here wrote his *Euphues*—a book that had an extraordinary effect on the English style (a style satirized in Shakespeare's *Love's Labour's Lost*). JOHN CLELAND (1709-89), author of the lively pornographic novel *Fanny Hill* lived here for many years in an old house fronting the river.

16. *Savoy Street* is the next one entering the Strand from your right. A few steps down this street stands the *Queen's Chapel of the Savoy* —originally built (1505) where the old palace chapel had stood, and

rebuilt in 1864 after a fire. THOMAS FULLER (1608-61), historian and antiquarian, author of the celebrated *Worthies of England,* preached here. GEORGE WITHER (see above) and the poet GAWAIN DOUGLAS (1472?-1522), a major figure in the Chaucerian tradition of poets, are buried here. A window inside the chapel commemorates the theatre impresario D'OYLY CARTE (see above).

17. Return to the Strand, and walk a few steps along it. About here JACOB TONSON (1656-1736), publisher and bookseller, had his shop from 1710 to 1742. He published the poems of Edmund Spenser (six volumes) in 1715, and the *Spectator* papers (eight volumes) in 1712-15. This was the third shop of the Tonson company—the first having been in Chancery Lane in the late seventeenth century, and the second at Gray's Inn Gate.

A few doors farther along the *Strand* (about where *Lancaster Place* now lies, or perhaps a little farther on) stood the shop of another famous publisher and bookseller, ANDREW MILLAR (d. 1768), who had established a shop still farther along the Strand (opposite St Clement Danes Church) in 1728, and who moved to this new location in 1742. Millar was a friend and publisher of James Thomson, Henry Fielding, and David Hume. Still later, Millar's apprentice, Thomas Cadell, took over the business, and published, at this spot, Gibbon's *Decline and Fall,* William Collins's *Odes,* Dr Johnson's *Dictionary,* Fielding's *Tom Jones,* and Hume's *History of England.* The disreputable book publisher EDMUND CURLL (1675-1747) lived and had a shop about here in the 1720's.

18. Along this same brief stretch of the Strand, *Lancaster Court* once led off to your right—occupying pretty much the site of the present *Lancaster Place* leading to Waterloo Bridge. In Lancaster Court was located the Lancaster Coffee House, which was frequented by JAMES THOMSON (1700-48), author of the *Seasons,* the first (and still the best) major nature poem in the language; he had his mail delivered here. *Alexander Cruden* (1701-70), who made a concordance of the Bible that has been a model for all subsequent biblical concordances, lived in Lancaster Court.

19. Continuing along the Strand, you will find (on your right) the vast and overpowering *Somerset House*—a building of 1776-86 which has been called 'perhaps the finest example of classical architecture in London', and which is certainly massive, coldly menacing, and inhuman enough to be Roman. Where it stands there was once another Somerset House, used in the seventeenth century as a palace for

the queens of England. In that older house were frequently performed plays and masques by Francis Beaumont, Thomas Campion, George Chapman, Samuel Daniel, Thomas Dekker, Michael Drayton, Ben Jonson, and others—with stage sets and decorations by Inigo Jones. CHARLOTTE LENNOX (1720-1804), American-born novelist who moved to London, became a friend of Dr Johnson and Samuel Richardson, and achieved enormous popularity, had apartments in the old Somerset House Complex before it was pulled down.

Today's Somerset House is occupied, for the most part, by government offices, including the Probate and Divorce Registry. Here may be seen the original wills of William Shakespeare, Sir Isaac Newton, Dr Samuel Johnson, and Charles Dickens.

The farthest (easternmost) wing of the building (as you walk along the Strand) is *King's College*, founded in 1829, and now a part of the University of London. Among literary men who were students at King's College were CHARLES KINGSLEY (1819-75), poet and novelist; his brother HENRY KINGSLEY (1830-76), novelist; EDWIN ARNOLD (1834-1904), once celebrated for his long poem *The Light of Asia,* about the Buddha; DANTE GABRIEL ROSSETTI) (1828-82), poet and painter, one of the original Pre-Raphaelite Brotherhood; and THOMAS HARDY (see above), who came here as a mature man, learned Greek, and read the fatalistic Greek dramas that influenced his own philosophy.

(In the middle of the street about here stands *St Mary-le-Strand Church*, built 1714-17, and consecrated in January, 1724. It has no special literary associations—except that the father and mother of Charles Dickens were married here, 1809.)

During the rest of your walk along the *Strand*, you will be dodging in and out of little streets entering it from your right (south). It may be less confusing for you, therefore, if we now list certain other literary sites on the Strand itself.

No. 142 was the home of *John Chapman*, the publisher, in the mid-nineteenth century, and here he sometimes lodged literary personages —among them the American poet and essayist RALPH WALDO EMERSON (1803-82), on his visit to England in 1848; the novelist GEORGE ELIOT (MARY ANN EVANS) (1819-80) in 1851-3; and MARK RUTHERFORD (WILLIAM HALE WHITE) (1831-1913) in 1853. Here George Eliot first met GEORGE HENRY LEWES (1817-78), novelist, dramatist, biographer, and critic, with whom she lived from about that time until his death; here she met also the philosopher *Herbert Spencer*. At *No. 149* the great actress MRS SARAH SIDDONS (1755-1831) lived for a time. At *No. 162* stood the *Somerset Coffee House*, which Boswell sometimes visited, and where the manuscripts of the still anonymous 'Letters of Junius' were occasionally left for the printer. MRS ELIZABETH INCHBALD (1753-1821), actress, dramatist, novelist, and charming person, was living at *No. 163* in 1809. WILLIAM GODWIN (1756-1836), philosopher who influenced many of the Romantic poets, and father-in-law of the poet Shelley, had bookshops at *No. 165* (1783-4) and *No. 195* (1823). *No. 186* (between Norfolk and Arundel Streets) was the publishing house of Chapman and Hall. In their shop CHARLES DICKENS (1812-70), the novelist, bought and read the copy of the *Old Monthly Magazine* in which his first published fiction (contributed anonymously) had appeared. Chapman and Hall later published the *Pickwick Papers, Nicholas Nickleby, Master Humphrey's Clock, The Old Curiosity Shop, Barnaby Rudge, A Christmas Carol, Martin Chuzzlewit, The Chimes, The Cricket on the Hearth,* and *Dombey and Son* from this place. At *No. 213* was George's Coffee House, frequented by ARTHUR MURPHY (see above), the dramatist, and by the poet WILLIAM SHENSTONE (1714-63), who is significant in literary history as one of the first poets to write about nature, the simplicity of rural life, and his own emotions—an important precursor of Romanticism.

20. Beyond St Mary-le-Strand, *Surrey Street* opens on your right. Here the diarist JOHN EVELYN (see above) lived in 1696, on his annual winter move into town. The dramatist WILLIAM CONGREVE (1670-1729) lived on this street with his friends Mr and Mrs Edward Porter in 1706, and off-and-on thereafter till his death here. The French sage and satirist VOLTAIRE (1694-1778) visited Congreve here—and was intensely irritated because Congreve wanted to be regarded as an English gentleman instead of as a great writer.

21. About halfway down Surrey Street, *Howard Street* intersects from the left. Here lived ANNE BRACEGIRDLE (1663?-1748), lovely actress, and member of Congreve's theatrical company. He was in love with her, but they did not marry—nor did either of them ever marry. She was a sister of Mrs Edward Porter (see above).

22. Return to the Strand, and continue along it to *Norfolk Street*, entering from your right. At *No. 13*, and then at *No. 32*, the poet PERCY BYSSHE SHELLEY (1792-1822) lodged in 1816, much troubled by debt and marital problems. WASHINGTON IRVING (1783-1859), the American writer, lodged at *No. 35* on his first visit to London, 1805; and MARY MITFORD (1787-1855), poet, novelist, dramatist, and bluestocking, lived at this same *No. 35* in the 1830's, and gave literary receptions here. The poet and critic SAMUEL TAYLOR COLERIDGE (1772-1834) lived at *No. 42* in 1816. From here he went to the home

of Mr Gillman, at Highgate, who had a reputation for being able to help drug addicts break the habit. Mr Gillman knew that Coleridge (who had the opium habit) was coming, and was determined not to take him; but Coleridge's powers of persuasion were so great that Mr Gillman not only took him in, but kept him as a permanent guest for the remainder of his life! ALFRED TENNYSON (1809-92), the most celebrated of the Victorian poets, lodged, in 1842, 'at the last house, at the bottom of the street, on the left'. Down next to the river Peter the Great of Russia, was lodged when he first came to London, 1698; and William Penn, founder of Pennsylvania, lived at the last house, next to the river, on the right as you descend the street. Addison's Sir Roger de Coverley sometimes stayed on this street when he was in London.

23. Return to the Strand, and find the next street along it entering from the right: *Arundel Street*. Some lesser literary figures who lived on this street were the following: THOMAS RYMER (1641-1713), who collected what he called *Foedera*—20 volumes of important state papers from the Middle Ages through the Renaissance—and was an influential literary critic who supported neo-classic 'rules' and common sense so strongly that he ignored human nature; EUSTACE BUDGELL (1686-1737), Addison's cousin and secretary, who conducted a literary periodical and contributed to the *Spectator*; GEORGE DARLEY (1795-1846), the Irish writer of 'ecstatic' poetry, prose tales, dramatic criticism, fanciful comedy, and heavy tragedy, who lived at *No. 35* in 1822-3; and (on a considerably higher level of literature) COVENTRY PATMORE (1823-96), Roman Catholic poet associated with the Pre-Raphaelites, at *No. 12* in the 1840's. *No. 37*, at the corner, was, in the eighteenth century, the location of the Crown and Anchor Tavern, where *Dr Johnson* and *Boswell* often came, and where Johnson quarrelled with Percy. The American actor and playwright JOHN HOWARD PAYNE (1791-1852), who wrote *Home, Sweet Home*, lived at *No. 29* for two years (1825-7).

24. When you return to the Strand, you will see *St Clement Danes Church* in the middle of the street just ahead of you. It is said to have acquired its name because a colony of Danes was settled nearby before the Norman Conquest. The church, built here in 1681 by Sir Christopher Wren, was badly damaged by bombs in 1941; but it has been rebuilt in its original style. The old steeple remained, though the bells that sang 'Oranges and Lemons' were thrown to the ground and broken. They have been recast from the original metal; and oranges and lemons are still distributed to children at a special ser-

vice held in March. DR SAMUEL JOHNSON (1709-84), the great lexico-grapher, scholar, essayist, critic, and talker, attended services regularly here, and (until the bombing) his pew (No. 18) was still pointed out. A peculiarly ugly statue of him stands on the outside at the far end of the church, near the Law Courts.

Baptized here were Florence, daughter of the poet EDMUND SPENSER (1552?-99); SIR CHARLES SEDLEY (1639?-1701), courtier, whose wit, life, and poetry were brilliant and licentious; and ANTHONY ASHLEY COOPER, EARL OF SHAFTESBURY (see above). The wife of the poet JOHN DONNE (1572-1631) is buried here (1617); and so is GEORGE GRANVILLE, LORD LANSDOWNE (1666-1735), critic, poet, statesman, friend of Alexander Pope, the poet. NATHANIEL LEE (1653?-1692), the dramatist (who went mad, recovered, and 'died in a drunken fit') is buried here, as is also that other unfortunate dramatist THOMAS OTWAY (1651-85).

25. To the left (north) of the church, the little street called *Clement's Inn* opens into the Strand. H. G. WELLS (1866-1946) had a sleeping place at *No. 6* in 1902-3. The spot was formerly occupied by an Inn of Chancery, where Falstaff first met Justice Shallow, and which was the 'Shepherd's Inn' of Thackeray's *Pendennis*.

26. The next street on the right is *Essex Street*—on the site of the former Essex House, which belonged to the Earl of Essex, favourite of Queen Elizabeth I, patron of the poet Edmund Spenser, and husband of the widow of the poet-romancer Sir Philip Sidney. Methuen and Company, publishers, occupied *No. 36* for many years. One of their editors was E. V. LUCAS (1868-1938) critic, biographer, and auto-biographer. Here were published two major novels by ARNOLD BENNETT (1867-1931): *Hilda Lessways* and *Clayhanger*; and three novels by JOSEPH CONRAD (1857-1924): *The Secret Agent, Under Western Eyes*, and *Chance. No. 43* was the office of *Merry England*, the Roman Catholic journal edited by *Wilfred Meynell* (husband of the poet Alice Meynell). Here Meynell and the forlorn and ragged poet FRANCIS THOMPSON (1859-1907), author of 'The Hound of Heaven', first met—and Thompson was saved (quite literally) from the gutter. The novelist HENRY FIELDING (1707-54) lived briefly on this street; and at *No. 40*, the Essex Head Tavern, *Dr Johnson*, late in life, tried to establish a new club.

27. Beyond Essex Street, the next street entering the Strand from the right (south) is *Devereux Court*. Here the *Grecian Coffee House* once stood—on your right, as you descend the street, and just above the

corner where a passage leads off to the right, at *No. 19*. This coffee house is mentioned in Steele's *Tatler, No. 1*, where the author promises that 'all ... accounts of learning' shall be written from here. Joseph Addison mentions it in *Spectator, No. 1*. Others known to have come here often were *Sir Isaac Newton*, the poet *Mark Akenside*, and *Oliver Goldsmith*. A club of booksellers (publishers) met here regularly in the 1760's and 1770's; among its members were *Tom Davies* (who introduced Boswell to Johnson) and *James Dodsley*, brother and successor of the more famous Robert Dodsley. THOMAS LOVELL BEDDOES (1803-49), writer of visionary romances, verse tragedies, and strange, sinister lyrics, lived at *No. 2* (1824) and then at *No. 6* (1825).

28. On this side of the *Strand*, somewhere between Essex Street and Temple Bar (see below) lived the poet and dramatist BEN JONSON (1572-1637), and, a century later, the poet WILLIAM SHENSTONE (see above).

At this point of the tour you may wish to do one of the following:

(1) You may wish to enter the visitors' galleries of the great Law Courts buildings on the left-hand side of the Strand, opposite Essex Street, and hear some of the trials going on there. (All cases heard are *civil*.)

(2) You may find that you have no more time for the present tour today—and may wish to retrace your steps along the Strand, almost to Somerset House, and there, at the *Aldwych Underground Station*, end this tour.

(3) You may wish to go forward to the next street on the right (Middle Temple Lane), enter it, and explore the Temple. If you make this choice, turn to the latter part of Tour No. 7 for directions.

(4) Or you may wish to continue the present tour to its conclusion. If you make this choice —

29. Walk on along the Strand. Just at the end of the Law Courts buildings you will see, in the middle of the street, what Mr F. R. Banks calls, in an excess of charity, the 'ineffectual' Temple Bar Memorial. Surmounted by its griffin, and flanked by Queen Victoria and the Prince of Wales, it is a simple horror. Here was the site of Temple Bar—which was, for centuries, some kind of bar, chain, or gateway marking the limits of the authority of the City of London, beyond it. Here the reigning sovereign, coming from Westminster, must still pause and formally ask permission of the Lord Mayor to pass on into the City. At about this spot DANIEL DEFOE (1660-1731), England's first great novelist, author of *Robinson Crusoe* and *Moll Flanders*,

stood in the pillory for having written *The Shortest Way with Dissenters*—in which he ironically advocated the exile or execution of all Dissenters, himself being a Dissenter! The authorities put him in the pillory because they were foolish enough to have been taken in by the joke. But the experience was a triumph for Defoe: the people thronged about, and wreathed him and the pillory with flowers.

Fleet Street

30. Continue walking along the right-hand side of what has now become *Fleet Street*. You had just as well be on this side because all the literary sites you may wish to note on the other side have disappeared, and 'left not a rack behind'. Right opposite the gate of Middle Temple Lane (opening on your right, beneath an arch) stood the *Cock Tavern*, from the mid-seventeenth century to the late nineteenth. Here the diarist *Samuel Pepys* made merry (in the company of women friends, and without his wife) in the 1660's; and here the poet *Alfred Tennyson*, two centuries later, enjoyed himself (without women friends) and wrote a poem about the place. *Charles Dickens*, the novelist, often came here; after his time, however, the tavern was transferred to the opposite side of the street, farther down.

Still on the left-hand (or north) side of the street, two doors from the traffic artery of Chancery Lane leading off from Fleet Street, IZAAK WALTON (1593-1683), who wrote *The Compleat Angler*, had an ironmonger's shop. Farther on, at the far (southeastern) corner of Chancery Lane (though some authorities say the place was nearer the Law Courts buildings) stood the *King's Head Tavern*, on the second floor; underneath it was the shop of the printer-bookseller Richard Marriot, who issued the works of Izaak Walton in 1665. Later on, the famous bookseller JACOB TONSON (see above) opened his first shop at this place (*c*. 1680), and here published many of the works of JOHN DRYDEN.

31. Back on the right-hand (south) side of *Fleet Street*, at *No. 1*, was the famous *Devil Tavern*, dating from near the middle of the sixteenth century. Here BEN JONSON (see above), poet, playwright, and friend of Shakespeare, helped establish the Apollo Club—one of the earliest of London's literary clubs. Later on, *Samuel Pepys* frequented the Tavern; still later, *Addison, Steele*, and *Swift* came here; and still later, *Dr Johnson* and his friends came regularly. In 1751 Dr Johnson gave an all-night party here, with MRS CHARLOTTE LENNOX (see

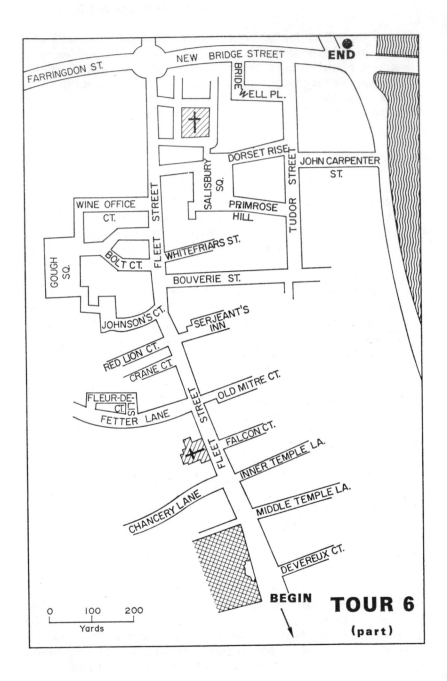

FARRINGDON ST.

NEW BRIDGE STREET

END

BRIDE WELL PL.

DORSET RISE

JOHN CARPENTER ST.

SALISBURY SQ.

WINE OFFICE CT.

FLEET STREET

PRIMROSE HILL

TUDOR STREET

GOUGH SQ.

BOLT CT.

WHITEFRIARS ST.

BOUVERIE ST.

JOHNSON'S CT.

SERJEANT'S INN

RED LION CT.

CRANE CT.

OLD MITRE CT.

FLEUR-DE-LIS CT.

FETTER LANE

FLEET STREET

FALCON CT.

INNER TEMPLE LA.

CHANCERY LANE

MIDDLE TEMPLE LA.

DEVEREUX CT.

BEGIN

0   100   200
Yards

TOUR 6

(part)

90

above) as the honoured guest, by way of celebrating the lady's first published novel.

32. Continue along *Fleet Street*, past the gate to Middle Temple Lane. Two doors beyond the gate, at *No. 7* (now absorbed by *No. 10*), was the printing house of RICHARD TOTTEL (1530?-1594?), who published the translations from the Latin *Aeneid* by HENRY HOWARD, EARL OF SURREY (1517-47)—the first blank verse (1554) ever seen; and he published also the famous *Book of Songs and Sonnets* (1557) known as *Tottel's Miscellany*, which preserves all other known poems by Surrey, as well as the poems of SIR THOMAS WYATT (1503-42), who introduced the sonnet into English. This book of Tottel's is the first flower of what became the richest of all periods in English poetry. The same location was occupied, in the eighteenth century, by the publisher BERNARD LINTOT (1675-1736), who published the works of Sir John Vanbrugh, Sir Richard Steele, John Gay, and Alexander Pope. The latter's *Rape of the Lock* and translations of the *Iliad* and the *Odyssey* were issued here. (Later on, Pope quarrelled with Lintot, and satirized him in the *Dunciad*.) On the upper floor was *Dick's Coffee House*, patronized by Steele and Joseph Addison, and mentioned in the *Tatler*. At this coffee house the young poet WILLIAM COWPER (1731-1800) read in a newspaper an item that, in his sick mind, he interpreted as an invitation for him to commit suicide—and he rushed out and attempted it.

33. Above the gateway of *Inner Temple Lane*, the next opening on your right, EDMUND BURKE (1729-97), philosopher and statesman, took lodgings when he first arrived in London in 1750.

34. *Falcon Court*, the next opening on your right, takes its name from a printing shop called 'The Falcon'. This shop was established here by WYNKEN DE WORDE (d. 1535), successor of William Caxton, England's first printer. Here was printed the first tragedy in English: *Gorboduc* (1565), by THOMAS SACKVILLE (1536-1608) and THOMAS NORTON (1532-84). Over Falcon Court was *No. 32 Fleet Street*, where the publisher JOHN MURRAY (1776-1843), founder of a great publishing house, started his business in London. Here were published (1809) early numbers of the *Quarterly Review*. Just beyond, at about *No. 39*, at 'The Mitre' bookstore, John Milton's *Paradise Regained* (1671) and *Samson Agonistes* (1671) were first offered for sale. Two years later, at 'The Blue Anchor', a bit farther along the street, near the corner of Old Mitre Court, Milton's minor poems were first sold.

35. Next to the near (western) corner of *Old Mitre Court* and Fleet Street stood the famous *Mitre Tavern*, where DR SAMUEL JOHNSON (1709-84) and his circle used to meet. Many of the finest Johnsonian anecdotes originated here. A few steps down Old Mitre Court, at what was then Brown's Coffee House, the poet SAMUEL TAYLOR COLE-RIDGE (see above) was living in 1810. (In the middle of Fleet Street, right opposite Old Mitre Court, one Sarah Malcolm was hanged, in 1733, for the murder of three other women. The scene was painted by Hogarth.)

36. The second small court opening into Fleet Street beyond Old Mitre Court is *Serjeant's Inn*. Here ABRAHAM COWLEY (1618-67), poet and essayist, was born. Cowley was once very famous.

37. Now cross to the other (north) side of Fleet Street, drop back a few steps to Fetter Lane, cross it, and reach *St Dunstan's in the West Church*, hemmed in by buildings on three sides. The poet MICHAEL DRAYTON (1563-1631) lived beside the end of the church nearest you, at about *No. 186*. The church itself, though built on a site occupied by a church since the thirteenth century, dates only from 1833, and is not very exciting. Many booksellers clustered in sheds and shacks about the walls of the older church. One of the three shops where Milton's *Paradise Lost* (1667) was first sold was here—as was also the shop of the 'unspeakable' EDMUND CURLL (1675-1747), who pirated great men's writing at will, and was satirized by Pope. The first quarto of *Hamlet* (1604) was first sold here, and so was a quarto (1600) of *A Midsummer Night's Dream*. WILLIAM TYNDALE (d. 1536), humanist, translator of the New Testament into English, was pastor of this church, 1528-36. He fled from here to Holland to escape persecution for heresy, but was there arrested and executed. The poet JOHN DONNE (1572-1612) was vicar till his death; and Donne's friend IZAAK WALTON (see above) was a vestryman. Walton's *Compleat Angler* was first sold by Richard Marriot, a bookseller in the churchyard. The poets THOMAS CAMPION (1567-1620) and THOMAS CAREW (1595?-1639?) were buried here. The bells of this church are the ones that figure in Dickens's story *The Chimes*.

40. Till the early twentieth century, the buildings crowded about the church constituted *Clifford's Inn*—a complex of shops, gardens, pass-ageways, and residences—an inn of court since the fourteenth century. HARTLEY COLERIDGE (1796-1849), eldest son of the poet Samuel Taylor Coleridge, and himself a brilliant mind, but with too much of his father's tragic weakness, lodged here in 1822. The minor

historian GEORGE DYER (also distinguished as being the fourth husband of his laundress) lived here from 1792 till his death in 1841. He was a correspondent and friend of Scott, Coleridge, Southey, and Lamb. The last letter that Lamb wrote was to Mrs Dyer, concerning a book he thought he had left at her house. 'If it is lost,' he wrote, 'I shall never eat tripe again.' SAMUEL BUTLER (1835-1902), novelist, author of *The Way of All Flesh* and *Erewhon*, lived here from 1879 till his last illness. LIONEL JOHNSON (1867-1902), whose quiet poetry and intense Catholicism seem incongruous with his habitual alcoholism, lived here, 1901-2. He left his rooms one bitter winter evening to go to a nearby tavern, where he died. VIRGINIA WOOLF (1882-1941), novelist, lived here in 1912. And that unabashed novelist-poet-dramatist-adventurer GILBERT FRANKAU (1884-1952) had rooms here in the 1930's.

[40A. Now turn about and return to *Fetter Lane*. Up this street a very short distance, at *No. 10-11*, were the offices of *Woman*, the magazine that ARNOLD BENNETT (1867-1931) edited in 1897. A bit farther up, little *Fleur-de-Lis Court* enters from the right. The poet JOHN DRYDEN (see above) is reputed to have lived at the corner of this court and Fetter Lane—at about where *No. 16* now is; but the authority for this is not too sound. In the court itself, at *No. 17½*, at the Chapel of the Scottish Corporation, SAMUEL TAYLOR COLERIDGE (see above) delivered, in 1818, a series of lectures on the highly inclusive topic of 'Language, Literature, and Social and Moral Questions'. Farther on up *Fetter Lane*, at *No. 77*, lived TOM PAINE (1737-1809), American-born writer who was also a born revolutionist. His *Rights of Man* and *Common Sense* were highly influential in justifying the American Revolution; but he was kicked out of England for supporting the French Revolution. Swift's Lemuel Gulliver lived on this street.... Now return to Fleet Street.]

41. Turn about, re-cross the bottom of Fetter Lane, and walk on along Fleet Street once more—with buildings on your left and traffic on your right. At the corner was a bookshop, called the 'Flower de Luce', that printed many of the plays of Dekker, Day, Webster, and Heywood. Soon you will reach a tiny hole-in-the-wall opening on your left; this is *Crane Court*. At the far end of the court was a house owned by Dr Edward Browne, son of Sir Thomas Browne (1605-82), author of the baroque prose masterpieces *Religio Medici* and *Hydrotaphia: or Urn-Burial*. The Royal Society bought this house, and met here (with SIR ISAAC NEWTON as president) from 1710 to 1780. Later, the house was bought by the Philosophical Society for its meetings—

and here SAMUEL TAYLOR COLERIDGE (see above), one of England's great poets, and probably her greatest literary critic, delivered his lectures on Shakespeare. From *No. 9* the first numbers of *Punch* were issued, and from *No. 10* the first numbers of the *Illustrated London News*. (*Incidental Intelligence:* In this little court lived Dr Nicholas Barebone, highly successful property developer and insurance man, son of Praise-God Barebone. It is said that Nicholas was christened 'If-Jesus-Christ-Had-Not-Died-For-Thee-Thou-Hadst-Been-Damned Barebone'—a name shortened by his enemies to 'Damned Barebone'!)

42. Return to Fleet Street, continue along it a few steps, and turn left into *Red Lion Court*. The *Gentleman's Magazine* (most famous periodical in England in the eighteenth century) was issued from the 'Cicero's Head' here, 1779-81, and again 1792-1820.

43. Return to Fleet Street, walk along it a few steps, and turn left into *Johnson's Court*. Though this was not named after DR SAMUEL JOHNSON, the Doctor lived here, at *No. 7*, from 1765 to 1776, and here wrote his *Tour of the Hebrides*, and prepared his edition of Shakespeare. The house has long since vanished. In this court was published, in the nineteenth century, the *Old Monthly Magazine* to which CHARLES DICKENS (1812-70), the novelist, contributed some of his early humorous sketches—a project that developed into the *Sketches by Boz*. In the early twentieth century the little volume of simple Blake-like poems, called *The Soul's Destroyer*, by W. H. Davies (1871-1940), who had been a beggar, tramp, and itinerant peddler, was first published here—at the author's expense. The book attracted the attention of George Bernard Shaw, who recommended Davies to the right people, and helped him become a financially solvent writer.

44. Johnson's Court leads on into *Gough Square*. Here is 'Dr Johnson's House', where the Doctor lived from 1748 to 1758, and where his *Dictionary* was prepared. While living here he wrote the essays for his periodical, the *Rambler*; and his wife died here. The house, with its many mementos of Dr Johnson, is open to the public for a small fee, and should certainly be visited. The dramatist HUGH KELLY 1739-77), whose technically 'sentimental' comedies rivalled Goldsmith's and Sheridan's in popularity in the 1760's and 1770's, lived and died in Gough Square.

45. You can leave Gough Square by *Bolt Court*—which opens on the side of the square nearest Fleet Street. In this court DR JOHNSON lived

from 1770, and here he died in 1784, with the novelist Fanny Burney in attendance below. Here he was visited by some of the most distinguished people in England, and here he prepared what is probably his greatest piece of writing, *The Lives of the Poets*.

46. When you have reached Fleet Street again, turn left, and walk on a short distance, past several slits-in-the-wall, to another slit-in-the-wall named *Wine Office Court*. Enter it, and find the famed *Cheshire Cheese Tavern* on your right. This ancient tavern has a great deal of authentic 'atmosphere' as well as a considerable amount of synthetic 'campiness'. Though Boswell nowhere mentions it, the place advertises that it was frequented by *Dr Johnson, Goldsmith, Boswell*, and the rest of the Johnsonian circle—which may well be true. At any rate, in a room on the second floor, the Rhymers' Club used to meet regularly in the 1890's. Some of the more prominent members or associates of the Club (which issued two volumes of its own poetry) were *Arthur Symons, Ernest Dowson, Lionel Johnson, W. B. Yeats, John Davidson, John Gray*, and *Richard Le Gallienne. Oscar Wilde* was a visitor here, as was the French poet *Paul Verlaine*. Farther along the court, at *No. 6* (rebuilt), OLIVER GOLDSMITH (1730?-74), poet, essayist, dramatist, novelist, had lodgings in 1760. Here he wrote some, or all, of his novel *The Vicar of Wakefield*, which Dr Johnson sold for him to pay his rent. Wine Office Court extends on past the Goldsmith house, and turns to the right. This right-hand extension (leading into Shoe Lane) was formerly called *Gunpowder Alley*. Here died RICHARD LOVELACE (1618-57), in abject poverty. One of the finest of the Cavalier poets, he is remembered for two poems containing the lines, 'Stone walls do not a prison make,/Nor iron bars a cage', and 'I could not love thee, dear, so much,/Loved I not honour more'.

47. Return to Fleet Street; and at Shoe Lane cross over to the other (south) side of Fleet. Turn right, and walk *back* along Fleet. You will pass *No. 85*, the old offices of *Punch*, where Thackeray's *Vanity Fair* was first published. You will pass also the entrance of *Whitefriars Street* (formerly called Water Lane); at the Black Lion Inn on this street, a few doors off Fleet, the young JAMES BOSWELL (1740-95), Dr Johnson's biographer, spent his first night in London. This same inn was the scene of Boswell's night with the fair Louisa—a scene dramatically (not to say lusciously) recounted in Boswell's *London Journal*.

48. A little farther along Fleet Street, enter *Bouverie Street*, on your left. At *No 3* WILLIAM HAZLITT (1778-1830), essayist and critic, lived

in 1829, just before he moved over to Soho to die. Farther down, at
No. 10, were the later offices of *Punch*, where MARK TWAIN (1835-
1910), the American humourist, was entertained on July 9, 1907. At
No. 11 were the offices of Bradbury and Evans, publishers. Here were
published the following novels by CHARLES DICKENS (see above):
David Copperfield, Bleak House, Hard Times, and *Little Dorrit*. Here
also were published the following novels by WILLIAM MAKEPEACE
THACKERAY (1811-63): *Pendennis, Vanity Fair*, and *The Virginians*.
At the bottom of this street, in 'Temple Chambers', on your right,
A. A. MILNE (1882-1956), dramatist and story writer, creator of
Christopher Robin and Winnie-the-Pooh, had lodgings in 1903.

The area you are walking through, as well as that to your left, was
once covered by the buildings and grounds of the Whitefriars Monastery. After the dissolution of the monasteries in the sixteenth
century, the main hall of Whitefriars was converted into a theatre—
possibly before the building of any regular professional theatre in
London. The theatre was approximately in the angle formed by
Bouverie Street and Magpie Alley, which enters from your left as you
descend Bouverie Street. Apparently, this theatre was abandoned or
dismantled about 1608, and another theatre built on the same site, or
nearby, about 1610. Plays by Ben Jonson, George Chapman, Beaumont and Fletcher, Nathaniel Field, and others were performed here.

49. Turn left, off Bouverie Street, into Tudor Street, and walk two
blocks, to what is called *Dorset Rise*, on your left. Turn into it. This
is a relatively new street running to the right of an older street, now
vanished, called *Salisbury Court*. On Salisbury Court (on your left,
as you ascend Dorset Rise) lived SIR JOHN SUCKLING (1609-42?),
Cavalier poet and (farther up) THOMAS SHADWELL (1642?-92), poet
and dramatist, Poet Laureate. Still farther up lived JOHN DRYDEN
(1631-1700), poet, dramatist, critic, and also Poet Laureate. Shadwell
and Dryden were friends when they were neighbours here; but they
later disagreed on politics, and satirized each other in some fairly
vicious poems.

50. Dorset Rise ends in *Salisbury Square*. Here, in the far left-hand
(north-west) corner of the square, lived SAMUEL RICHARDSON (1689-
1761), one of the first and one of the greatest English novelists. He
brought into the novel a concern for character, psychology, emotion,
and details of domestic life. He had also his quite extensive printing
house in this square. Here he wrote *Pamela* and *Clarissa Harlow*; and
here OLIVER GOLDSMITH (see above) worked on the proofs of *Clarissa*.

51. In *Salisbury Court*, leading out of the far right-hand (north-east) corner of the square, the diarist SAMUEL PEPYS (1633-1703) was born.

52. Turn to your right, leave the square, and reach *St Bride's Church*. A church stood here from very early times; but it was rebuilt (1670-84) by Sir Christopher Wren. This Wren church was gutted in the blitz of 1940—though the steeple and most of the exterior walls were left standing. It was rebuilt according to Wren's original design in 1956-7. SAMUEL PEPYS (see above) was baptized here in a font that still survives. JOHN DENHAM (1615-69), poet who wrote 'Cooper's Hill', perhaps the first out-and-out nature poem in English since the Middle Ages, was married here. The early printer WYNKEN DE WORDE (see above) was buried in the church; so was RICHARD LOVELACE (see above); so was THOMAS SACKVILLE (1536-1608), poet, co-author of *Gorboduc*; and so was SAMUEL RICHARDSON (see above). The first three were buried in the old church, and the precise locations of their graves were lost when Wren rebuilt the church. The Richardson family grave was in the centre aisle, near the middle of the church, and Samuel Richardson was buried there. The Richardson gravestone survived the bombing; but, on last inspection, was leaning against the outside back wall of the church. (There is a macabre, but well-authenticated, story to the effect that an American scholar, specializing in Richardson, rushed over to London immediately after the Second World War, and visited St Bride's. He found the coffins and corpses that had been exposed by the bombings now stacked to one side, waiting for reinterment, and rebuilding of the church. The scholar found the body of Richardson, and touched him on the nose!) The poet, pamphleteer, and patriot JOHN MILTON (1608-74) lived for a while in a house fronting the churchyard. This house seems to have been on the left-hand corner (near the church) of the little passage through which you leave the churchyard and attain Fleet Street.

53. Walk on out to *Fleet Street*, and turn right. You will pass *No. 96*, where were located the offices of Taylor and Hessey, publishers, and the residence of John Hessey. This firm published the *Elia* essays of CHARLES LAMB (1775-1834), and also the poems of JOHN KEATS (1795-1821)—including *Endymion, Lamia, Isabella*, and *The Eve of St Agnes. Keats* himself spent much time at this place. The poet THOMAS HOOD (see above) was also published by the firm (which issued the *London Magazine*, for which Hood wrote regularly), and he too was often here, as was the poet JOHN CLARE (1793-1864) in the 1820's.

54. Continue along Fleet Street till you reach thronging Ludgate

Circus. Keep to the right, and turn along *New Bridge Street*. On your right, a block or two down this street, you will find the entrance of a little street called Bridewell Place. There is no point in exploring it; but it may be interesting to know that the area extending from Bridewell Place ahead of you at least one block, and to your right at least one block, was formerly (1555-1863) occupied by *Bridewell Prison*. This institution originally existed for two purposes: the brief imprisonment (and sometimes flogging) of vagrants and disorderly persons (usually common prostitutes), and a refuge and training place for homeless apprentices. THOMAS KYD (1558-94), dramatist, author of *The Spanish Tragedy*, which influenced Shakespeare's *Hamlet*, was imprisoned (on the charge of atheism) and tortured here. Under torture, he implicated the poet and dramatist Christopher Marlowe as an author of atheistic writing. (Marlowe was murdered shortly thereafter, while Kyd was still in prison, under mysterious circumstances suggesting that something more than atheism was involved in the misdoings of the two dramatists.)

55. At the next corner, turn right, on Tudor Street. After three short blocks, turn left, on *John Carpenter Street*. This was formerly called Salisbury Court, and was an extension almost straight down from the Salisbury Court and Salisbury Square that you have already seen. On the left-hand side of the street lived THOMAS BETTERTON (1635?-1710), greatest actor of his time, theatre owner and manager, adapter of Shakespearean plays for the Restoration stage.

At the end of the street, still on the left, stood what is generally known as the *Dorset Garden Theatre*—so called because it was built on what had been the gardens, or spacious backyard, of Dorset House which stood higher up towards Fleet Street. A theatre was originally built here in 1629—the seventeenth theatre ever built in England. In 1642 the Puritans suppressed all the public playhouses; and this theatre was not opened again till 1660—after rebuilding and renovation. WILLIAM DAVENANT (1606-68), poet, dramatist, and theatre manager, was licensed, in 1660, by the restored King Charles II, to present plays in London. He rented this theatre in January, 1661, and occupied it till June of the same year, when he moved to the theatre in Lincoln's Inn Fields that he had been preparing. After his death, his widow and Thomas Betterton (see above), with several others, acquired the site of the old theatre (which had burned down in the Great Fire of 1666), and here built a magnificent new theatre: the Duke's Theatre, with a fine front towards the river. It opened in 1671 with John Dryden's *Sir Martin Mar-all*. All the plays of THOMAS OTWAY (1652-85), except *The Atheist*, were first produced here. For a time this was perhaps the chief theatre of London, but towards the end of the seventeenth century it became less fashionable, and was given over to wrestlers, tumblers, and spectaculars. It was finally demolished in the 1720's.

56. Walk on down the street to Victoria Embankment, and turn left. Almost immediately you will find yourself at the wide area where the Embankment, New Bridge Street, and Blackfriars Bridge converge. In the portion of this vacant area nearest to you lay once a little square called *Chatham Place*. Here, at *No. 14*, in the upper left-hand (north-west) corner, not far from the Victoria statue, DANTE GABRIEL ROSSETTI (1828-82), poet, painter, Pre-Raphaelite, lived for ten years (1852-62), and here he brought his bride, that extraordinary Elizabeth Siddal, who died (or committed suicide) here. (Rossetti had written a series of sonnets for her, and in his grief had the manuscript of the poems laid on her breast, and buried with her. Ten years later, his friends persuaded him to have the poems disinterred, and they were published as *The House of Life*.)

You are now at the end of this tour, and you may cross over the wide area just mentioned (if you can dodge the traffic successfully), and catch a train at the *Blackfriars Underground Station.*

[56A. If, by chance, you should be interested in that strange and tragic figure RICHARD MIDDLETON (1882-1911), who committed suicide in Brussels, and was a 'beat' long before the heyday of the beats, you can cross Blackfriars Bridge, and find, just below it, *No. 7 Blackfriars Road* where Middleton lived in 1906. Also just below the bridge, on the right-hand side, was the old Surrey Institution 'Rotunda' where SAMUEL TAYLOR COLERIDGE (see above) gave a series of lectures on Shakespeare, and WILLIAM HAZLITT (see above) gave a series on the comic writers of England. Much farther down, on Dolben Street (once called George Street), opening on the left, lived MARY WOLLSTONE-CRAFT (1769-97), ardent feminist writer, who married the philosopher-novelist William Godwin, and became the mother of Mary Godwin Shelley, second wife of the poet Percy Shelley. Still farther down Blackfriars Road, at *No. 26 Nelson Square*, PERCY BYSSHE SHELLEY (1792-1822) himself lived unhappily with Mary Godwin in 1814—before his first wife died.... Now go back across the bridge, and end the tour.]

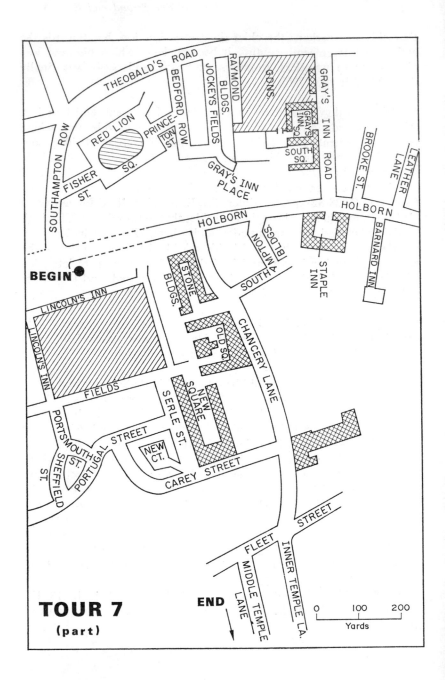

TOUR 7
(part)

BEGIN

END

0   100   200
Yards

Tour 7
Inns of Court and Vicinity

(There are now four Inns of Court in London: Gray's Inn, Lincoln's Inn, Middle Temple, and Inner Temple. Physically, they are collections of buildings that house dining halls, lecture rooms, libraries, private offices of lawyers, and residential flats occupied by students or lawyers or almost anybody else—and their families. Their official function is to sponsor legal lectures, give examinations, and admit applicants to the practice of law in England.)

Sir Norman Angell

Francis Bacon

James Barrie

Elizabeth Barry

Maurice Baring

Arnold Bennett

Jeremy Bentham

E. C. Bentley

Thomas Betterton

James Boswell

James Boswell, Jr.

Anne Bracegirdle

Alexander Brome

James Bryce

John Buchan

Edward Bulwer-Lytton

Edward Burne-Jones

Frances ('Fanny') Burney

Samuel Butler

John Byrom

William Camden

Thomas Campbell

Thomas Carew

George Chapman

Thomas Chatterton

Richard Church

Samuel Taylor Coleridge

Jeremy Collier

Churton Collins

George Colman The Elder

George Colman The Younger

William Congreve

William Cowper

William Davenant

A. J. Dawson

John Denham

Charles Dickens

Benjamin Disraeli

Richard Watson Dixon

John Donne

John Dryden

Havelock Ellis

Sebastian Evans

John Evelyn

Henry Fielding

John Forster

Benjamin Franklin

James G. Frazer

John Galsworthy

David Garrick

George Gascoigne

William Gascoigne

John Gay

Mary Godwin

Oliver Goldsmith

Philip Guedalla

H. Rider Haggard

Frederick Harrison

William Hazlitt

Thomas Holcroft

Anthony Hope (Hawkins)

Bishop Richard Hurd

Lionel Johnson

Dr Samuel Johnson

Inigo Jones

Ben Jonson

Thomas Killigrew

Charles Lamb

Walter Savage Landor

Nathaniel Lee

Richard Le Gallienne

John Locke

Thomas Lodge

Thomas Babington Macaulay

Arthur Machen

Katherine Mansfield

Edward Marsh

John Marston

Frederick D. Maurice

Mayhew Brothers

E. H. W. Meyerstein

Thomas Middleton

Joe Miller

John Milton

Harold Monro

Sir Thomas More

William Morris

Arthur Murphy

John Middleton Murry

Sir Henry Newbolt

John Henry Newman

Sir Harold Nicolson

Thomas Norton

Thomas Otway

Thomas Love Peacock

F. C. Philips

Eden Phillpotts

Mackworth Praed

J. B. Priestley

Bryan Waller Procter
('Barry Cornwall')

James Quin

Mrs Ann Radcliffe

Charles Reade

Joseph Ritson

Henry Crabb Robinson

Samuel Rogers

Dante Gabriel Rossetti

Thomas Rymer

Charles Sackville, Earl of Dorset

Thomas Sackville

Victoria Sackville-West

William Shakespeare

Percy Bysshe Shelley

Richard Brinsley Sheridan

James Shirley

Sir Philip Sidney

Robert Southey

Richard Steele

John Suckling

Jonathan Swift

Arthur Symons

Alfred Tennyson

William Makepeace Thackeray

Jacob Tonson

Martin Tupper

Edmund Waller

Izaak Walton

Bishop William Warburton

John Warren, Lord De Tabley

Sidney Webb

John Wilmot, Earl of Rochester

George Wither

William Wordsworth

William Butler Yeats

Israel Zangwill

See also the addendum at the end of this tour.

Leave the underground at the *Holborn* (*Kingsway*) *Station*. Find Southampton Row, and walk up it. From the station you can walk in only one direction, and still be on Southampton Row.)

1. After two very short blocks, turn right, into Fisher Street, and reach

Red Lion Square. In 1826 *Charles Lamb,* the essayist, sat for a portrait at *No. 3,* Henry Mayer being the painter. At *No. 17* the poet-painter DANTE GABRIEL ROSSETTI (1828-82) lived in 1851, in the early days of the Pre-Raphaelite Movement; and that other painter-poet WILLIAM MORRIS (1834-96) lived with the Pre-Raphaelite painter EDWARD BURNE-JONES (1833-98) and the Pre-Raphaelite poet RICHARD WATSON DIXON (1833-1900), from 1856 to 1859, at this same *No. 17.* Morris, Burne-Jones, and others had a decorator's shop at *No. 8* from 1860 to 1865, and here designed (and sometimes fabricated) carpets, wallpaper, furniture, metal work, stained glass, and so on. At *No. 31* F. D. MAURICE (1805-72) (professor, theologian, journalist, novelist, founder of Christian Socialism established the Working Men's College in 1854). Some lecturers in the college were *Dante Gabriel Rossetti, John Ruskin, Thomas Woolner, Frederic Harrison,* and *H. G. Wells.*

2. Leave Red Lion Square by Princeton Street, across the square from the place where you entered. Reach *Bedford Row,* and turn right. The last house on your left in this street was occupied by WILLIAM WARBURTON (1698-1779), who became a bishop, but has been well described as 'a brash and inferior personage'. A friend of Alexander Pope, he was the one who made the poor suggestion that Colley Cibber would make a good hero for the second edition of Pope's *Dunciad.*

3. At the far end of Bedford Row, turn left, go a block, descend some steps, and then bear right, into little *Gray's Inn Place.* EDWARD MARSH (1872-1953)—editor of the *Georgian Poetry* series of anthologies (1913-21), author of a memoir of Rupert Brooke, and friend of almost everybody who mattered (from Winston Churchill, whose secretary he was, on down)—lived at *No. 3* from 1899 to 1903; and his friend MAURICE BARING (1874-1945), playwright, novelist, poet, critic, and diplomat, lived at the same *No. 3* from 1899 to 1930. Another playwright, novelist, poet, critic, and scholar, E. H. W. MEYERSTEIN (1899-1952) lived at the same *No. 3* during his last fourteen years.

4. Return the way you came, to the beginning of Gray's Inn Place, and turn half-right into a little street with houses on only your right-hand side. This is called *Raymond Buildings.* EDWARD MARSH (see above) lived at *No. 5* from 1903 to 1940. To visit him came, at various times, along this little street, the poets *Rupert Brooke, Lascelles Abercrombie, W. W. Gibson, W. H. Davies, Edmund Blunden, Walter de la Mare, Ralph Hodgson, Robert Nichols, John Freeman, John*

Drinkwater, J. C. Squire, Leslie Shanks, Harold Monro, W. J. Turner, Siegfried Sassoon, and many more.

5. Continue on to *Theobald's Road*, turn right, and continue along it. You will pass, on your left, *No. 22*, where BENJAMIN DISRAELI (1804-81), novelist and Prime Minister, was born.

6. Continue along Theobald's Road two blocks to *Gray's Inn Road*. Turn right. A short distance down this street you will find, on your right, a little gateway into a small and narrow courtyard with houses (or flats) along the opposite side. These are the *Verulam Buildings* (named after Francis Bacon, Baron Verulam), where, at *No. 4*, ARTHUR MACHEN (1863-1947), novelist, essayist, and translator of Casanova, lived in the 1890's, and wrote his *Hill of Dreams.*

7. Go back outside, and continue down Gray's Inn Road to another small gate on your right—leading through some buildings to a paved square beyond. In a building composing the gatehouse JACOB TONSON (1656-1736), bookseller who published most of the famous works of Addison, Steele, Pope, and Dryden, had his business from about 1698 to 1712. Forty years later, the shop was owned by 'Osborne, the bookseller, whom Johnson immortalized by knocking down'.

8. Now walk on into the paved square itself: *Gray's Inn Square* (formerly, Coney Court). SIR FRANCIS BACON (1561-1626), essayist, philosopher, jurist, father of modern scientific thought, kept chambers here, at *No. 1*, for nearly 50 years. The poet LIONEL JOHNSON (1867-1902), one of the *Yellow Book* group of aesthetes of the 1890's, lived at *No. 7* from 1895 to 1899.... You are now within the precincts of GRAY'S INN, one of London's famous Inns of Court.

9. From the gate where you entered Gray's Inn Square, you will see, off in the far left-hand corner, a narrow opening between buildings. Make for it, and pass through it. You will then find *Gray's Inn Gardens* on your right. Still lovely today, these peaceful gardens were praised by Bacon (his essay 'Of Gardens' is inspired by them), by *Pepys, Addison* and *Lamb*. All these people are known to have walked the paths here; and *Sir Walter Raleigh* records a long conversation he had with Bacon in the gardens. As late as the 1960's two old catalpa trees (much propped up) were still alive on either side of the main path; these are said to have been planted at the direction of Bacon from slips that Sir Walter Raleigh brought from America. The place was a fashionable promenade for fine ladies (as well as those not so fine) in

the time of Charles II, and on into the eighteenth century. In October and November, 1814, when the poet PERCY BYSSHE SHELLEY (1792-1822) was in danger of arrest for debt (mostly incurred by his first wife, Harriet) he and MARY GODWIN (1797-1851), author of *Frankenstein*, and afterwards Shelley's second wife, used to meet secretly in these gardens on Sundays. They met on Sundays because people could not be arrested for debt on the sabbath, and they met secretly because William Godwin, the liberal-minded philosopher who was Mary's father, and who had written in support of what many would have called 'free love', became a very proper father indeed when he found his daughter in love with, and being courted by, a man who already had one legal wife!

10. Leave the gardens, and return to Gray's Inn Square by the same narrow passage that you previously traversed. Once you are in the square, note the first building on your immediate right—which is *Gray's Inn Hall*. It was built in 1556-60, bombed in 1941, and restored according to the original designs. Here WILLIAM SHAKESPEARE'S *Comedy of Errors* was first performed (1594). Before that, GEORGE GASCOIGNE (1539?-1623), poet, had produced here (1566) his *Jocasta* —a translation-adaptation of an Italian play—and his *The Supposes* (also 1566), translated from the Italian as one of the very earliest prose comedies produced in England.

Turn to your right through a narrow passage, and enter *South Square*. When you emerge into this square, you will see another passage straight ahead of you, on the far side of the square. In the building immediately to the left of this second passage, CHARLES DICKENS (1812-70) worked in a law office as a youth. At *No. 8* (bombed out and rebuilt) lived JOSEPH RITSON (1752-1803), antiquarian and one of the first scholars who had a meticulous respect for his sources, and there he died. Later on, THOMAS BABINGTON MACAULAY (1800-59), historian, popular poet, and government official, lived at the same *No. 8*.

Many other literary figures, besides those mentioned, have been associated with Gray's Inn as members, students, or residents. Among these are the following:

E. C. BENTLEY (1875-1956), novelist, was a student.

SAMUEL BUTLER (1612-80), satirical poet, is believed to have been a student.

JOHN BYROM (1692-1763), shorthand expert and eccentric poet, was a resident here, 1723-5.

WILLIAM CAMDEN (1551-1623), historian, was a student.

GEORGE CHAPMAN (1559-1634), dramatist and poet, whose translation of Homer was immortalized by Keats, was a student.

JEREMY COLLIER (1650-1726), clergyman, whose essay, *A Short View of the Immorality and Profaneness of the English Stage* (1698), had considerable influence in 'cleaning up' the licentious Restoration stage, was a lecturer here.

BARRY CORNWALL (BRYAN WALLER PROCTER) (1787-1874), poet, was a student.

GEORGE GASCOIGNE (see above), poet, was a student.

WILLIAM GASCOIGNE (1350?-1419), chief justice, who figures in Shakespeare as an enemy of Falstaff, was a student.

OLIVER GOLDSMITH (1730?-74), poet, dramatist, and novelist, was a resident briefly in 1764.

DR SAMUEL JOHNSON (1709-84) was a resident briefly in 1759.

THOMAS MIDDLETON (1570?-1627), dramatist, was a student.

JAMES SHIRLEY (1596-1666), dramatist, lived here.

SIR PHILIP SIDNEY (1554-86), poet, romancer, soldier, critic, lived here.

ROBERT SOUTHEY (1774-1843), poet, historian, and biographer, (he became Poet Laureate) lived here in 1797.

SIR JOHN SUCKLING (1609-42), cavalier poet, lodged here.

SIDNEY WEBB (1859-1947), civil servant and extremely influential writer on behalf of socialism, was a student.

11. Go on through the second passage mentioned above (leading past the offices where Dickens worked), and reach Holborn. Here turn left, cross Gray's Inn Road, and go a block to *Brooke Street*. Turn left on this street, and find (on your left) *No. 39*, where THOMAS CHATTERTON (1752-70), the young poet, committed suicide.

THOMAS CHATTERTON, the 'marvellous boy' of Wordsworth, made giddy by the vision of a romantic medieval world that was just appearing after a century of neo-classic common sense, learned to read from the medieval manuscripts stored in the Bristol church where his father was sexton, began to write 'medieval' poems before he was twelve, wrote a sheaf that he pretended were by the medieval monk Rowley, and tried to get them printed and accepted as true medieval works. After he had brought his poems to London, he failed to convince the experts that they were actually medieval, failed to receive favourable notice, failed to make any money; and, standing on the brink of starvation, he took arsenic, and ended his life before he had reached his eighteenth birthday.

12. Return to Holborn, and walk on to the next street beyond Brooke. This will be Leather Lane. In the area between these two streets (later occupied by a vast insurance company) was *Furnival's Inn*, one of the Inns of Chancery. SIR THOMAS MORE (see above) was a student here.

But by the eighteenth century it had degenerated into a collection of lodging houses. CHARLES DICKENS (1812-70), the novelist, lived in Furnival's Inn (*No. 13* and then *No. 15*) while he was writing the *Pickwick Papers*, 1834-7. JAMES BARRIE (1860-1937), novelist and dramatist, lived here in 1888.

13. Cross over Holborn, and reverse your direction along it. Just opposite the site of Furnival's Inn, between *Nos. 22* and *23 Holborn*, the little passage of *Barnard's Inn* leads off into a kind of courtyard. The poet SAMUEL TAYLOR COLERIDGE (1772-1834) lived at *No. 7* (now gone) for a few weeks in 1804; and Pip, in Dickens's *Great Expectations*, lodged here.

14. Walk on along *Holborn*. At the place marked by *No. 19* MRS ANN RADCLIFFE (1764-1823), the 'Gothic' novelist, was born. In the next block you will see some half-timbered ('black-and-white') buildings looking incongruously antique in modern London. This is *Staple Inn*, formerly an Inn of Chancery. The original buildings were erected during the latter half of the sixteenth century, were rebuilt in the eighteenth century, were struck by a V-bomb in 1944 and rebuilt (or restored) again in 1955. Enter the first gateway you reach, and you will find yourself in a small and attractive courtyard surrounded by doors opening into stairways and apartments. DR SAMUEL JOHNSON (1709-84) lived at *No. 2*, up under the roof, in the years 1759-60, and is supposed to have written his novel *Rasselas* here; he completed it in two weeks in order to get money to defray his mother's funeral expenses. The poet WILLIAM WORDSWORTH (1770-1850) lived for seven months with his brother in Staple Inn on returning from France. RICHARD LE GALLIENNE (1866-1947), who typifies so many of the weaker aspects of the Aesthetic movement, lived at *No. 19* in 1891. Staple Inn figures in Dickens's *Bleak House, The Uncommercial Traveller*, and *Edwin Drood*.

15. Return to Holborn, and turn left along it. Within a short distance you will reach a street known as *Southampton Buildings*, entering from your left. Turn into it. Though it is now a street of huge and miserably ugly commercial buildings, it has many literary associations. THOMAS LOVE PEACOCK (1785-1866), novelist and poet, was living here in 1814, and the poet PERCY BYSSHE SHELLEY (see above) stayed with him, dodging creditors, trying to arrange a separation from his wife Harriet, and courting Mary Godwin (who became his second wife). THOMAS HOLCROFT (1745-1809), actor, playwright, and novelist (and friend of Coleridge, Lamb, Godwin, and Tom Paine)

lived here about 1780. WILLIAM HAZLITT (1778-1830), essayist and critic, lived at *No. 34* in 1829, and at *No. 9* in 1820. In the latter place (nine doors from Holborn, right-hand side of street) he fell in love with his landlord's daughter (though he was already married), and wrote one of his best books, *Liber Amoris*, about this bitterly unhappy affair. *No. 21* (at the far end of the street) was the Southampton Coffee House, where Hazlitt presided each evening over a kind of literary *levée*. CHARLES LAMB (1775-1834), the essayist, lived at *No. 34* from 1810 to 1817, and in 1830. SAMUEL TAYLOR COLERIDGE (see above), poet and critic, stayed with Lamb a few weeks in 1811, while Coleridge was lecturing in London.

16. Southampton Buildings winds on into *Chancery Lane.* You should now explore the adjoining few blocks of this street. RICHARD LE GALLIENNE (see above) lived at *No. 69* in 1896 and 1898. The little journal *Rhythm* (which failed almost immediately) had its office, which was also the flat of its editors, at *No. 57.* The editors were JOHN MIDDLETON MURRY (1889-1957), critic and literary biographer, and his mistress (later, wife) KATHERINE MANSFIELD (1888-1923), considered by many to be the finest short-story writer in English literature. The virile and original poet HAROLD MONRO (1879-1932) established at *No. 93* the office of *Poetry Review* (1911), a magazine that had a strong impact on the development of the 'new' poetry of the time.
[16A. You may wander down Chancery Lane as far as *Cursitor Street,* entering from your left. Turn into it, and then left again, into *Took's Court.* Here, in the early nineteenth century, was a famous sponging-house. (A sponging-house was a kind of halfway house where debtors were confined until they either paid their debts or were sent to prison for non-payment.) RICHARD BRINSLEY SHERIDAN (1751-1816), dramatist and politician, spent most of the last year of his life in this sponging house. Rawdon Crawley of Thackeray's *Vanity Fair,* was taken here; and Mr Snogsby, of Dickens's *Bleak House,* lived in Took's Court.]

17. Turn around, and walk back up Chancery Lane the way you came, keeping on the left-hand side of the street, paralleling a wall at your elbow. The Elizabethan dramatist and poet *Ben Jonson* is said to have worked as a mason on this wall, and especially on the gate which opens through the wall just beyond (and opposite) the place where you emerged from Southampton Buildings. Enter this gate; you will then be between the precincts of LINCOLN'S INN. On your right you will see a massive group of classical buildings called the *Stone Buildings*—with their 'grandiose pedimented elevation'. The Nobel

Prize-winning novelist and dramatist JOHN GALSWORTHY (1867-1933), author of *The Forsyte Saga* had chambers at *No. 5* in 1890-4.

18. Walk on past the Stone Buildings, and turn left. Almost at once you will reach an open courtyard. This is *Old Square*. The building immediately ahead of you as you enter the square is the Chapel. The poet JOHN DONNE (1572-1631) laid the cornerstone of this building, and was its first chaplain. Others who preached regularly in this chapel were WILLIAM WARBURTON (see above), who became Bishop of Gloucester, a foolish and arrogant man, and who wrote a huge anti-deistic book, a book vindicating the alliance between church and state, and a vicious attack on Methodism, as well as becoming a friend of Alexander Pope, and putting the latter up to some of his most ill-advised satires; RICHARD HURD (1720-1801), who became Bishop of Worcester, was a friend of Warburton, but was also admired by Thomas Gray, and was an influential figure in the rise of Romanticism because of his two books condemning imitation in poetry and (more significantly) his *Letters on Chivalry and Romance* (1762) (in which he praised Edmund Spenser at a time when Spenser's fanciful and imaginative genius was not generally recognized), and pioneered in that 'medievalism' which so captivated writers like Scott and Coleridge in the next generation; and FREDERICK D. MAURICE (1805-72), who wrote one novel and many religious works, but is best remembered as the founder of the Christian Socialist movement, which inspired novelists like Charles Kingsley (in *Alton Locke*) and Mrs Gaskell (in *Mary Barton*), and was a forerunner of a socialism that attracted many great writers later in the century.

The first large building on your right beyond the Chapel (and perpendicular to the latter) is Old Hall, dating from 1492; and the other buildings surrounding Old Square are mostly from the sixteenth and seventeenth centuries. MARTIN TUPPER (1810-99), the ridiculously moralistic poet-philosopher who attained enormous popularity and repute among the Victorians, lived here as a student, at *No. 10*; and the poet and critic RICHARD CHURCH (1893-1972), whose profound and intellectual poetry should be better known, lived on the top floor of *No. 13* in 1935-40. The first London home of SIR HENRY NEWBOLT (1862-1938), imperialistic poet, novelist, historian, and public servant, was at this same *No. 13*. Sergeant Snubbin of Dickens's *Pickwick Papers* had offices in this square; and Lincoln's Inn figures in *Bleak House.* . . . Note the gardens lying off in front of the Chapel. They were frequented and praised by the diarist *Samuel Pepys* and by *Sir Richard Steel*, (who wrote about them in the *Tatler—Nos. 13* and *100*—and in *The Theatre—No. 3.*

19. Turn about and leave Old Square. Outside, turn left, and continue straight ahead into *New Square*. ARTHUR MURPHY (1727-1805), actor, friend of Dr Johnson, author of a dozen successful comedies and half that number of successful tragedies, lived for 23 years at *No. 1.* JOHN GALSWORTHY (see above) read law at *No. 2* before 1890; CHARLES DICKENS (see above) was a law clerk *No. 8* (1827); LIONEL JOHNSON (see above) lodged at *No. 8* in 1899; and the great Romantic poet WILLIAM WORDSWORTH (see above) stayed, on at least two occasions (1795, 1796) with his friend Basil Montagu at *No. 7* (far right-hand corner of the square). FREDERICK HARRISON (1831-1923), who was a lawyer, and who wrote poetry, a novel, biographies, and books on law, sociology, and politics, lived at the same *No. 7* in the 1860's.

Some other students or residents of Lincoln's Inn have been

JEREMY BENTHAM (1748-1832), Utilitarian philosopher.

JAMES BRYCE (1838-1922), diplomat, jurist, historian.

EDWARD BULWER-LYTTON (1803-73), novelist and dramatist.

THOMAS CAMPBELL (1777-1844), poet and critic.

GEORGE COLMAN THE ELDER (1732-94) and his son GEORGE COLMAN
    THE YOUNGER (1762-1836), both of them actors, theatre managers,
    and dramatists.

JOHN DENHAM (1615-69), poet and dramatist, author of 'Cooper's
    Hill'.

BENJAMIN DISRAELI (1804-81), novelist and Prime Minister.

SEBASTIAN EVANS (1830-1909), lushly romantic poet.

DAVID GARRICK (1717-79), actor, theatre manager, dramatist.

THOMAS LODGE (1587?-1625), poet and romancer.

THOMAS BABINGTON MACAULAY (see above).

SIR THOMAS MORE (1478-1535), philosopher, statesman, saint.

JOHN HENRY NEWMAN (1801-90), theologian, poet, cardinal.

CHARLES READE (1814-84), novelist—whose studying here seems to
    have consisted mostly of dining the required number of times in the
    Hall.

HORACE WALPOLE (1717-97), novelist and letter-writer.

JOHN WARREN, LORD DE TABLEY (1835-95), poet who 'of all the lesser
    poets of the period missed greatness by the narrowest margin'
    (Chew).

GEORGE WITHER (1588-1667), Cavalier poet.

20. Leave New Square, and turn to the left, through an arch. You will be guided by the sight of a street with heavy traffic, and some trees beyond. The trees are in *Lincoln's Inn Fields*—a fine broad square laid out by Inigo Jones in 1618, and supposed to be the same

size as the base of the Great Pyramid. (It is smaller.) You will emerge at a corner of the square. Look diagonally across the square to the (north-western) corner opposite you. Down to the right of that corner, and facing the square, is the Soane Museum, a fascinating hodge-podge of antiquities in a building (designed by Soane) that is itself a museum piece. On the place where the museum stands JOHN DRYDEN (1631-1700), dramatist, poet, and critic, lived in a previous house in 1663. On the nearer side of this same place the poet JOHN MILTON (1608-74) had a house whose garden backed up to the square, but which faced the other way. Milton lived here (1647-9) at the same time when his *Tenure of Kings and Magistrates* was published. This bold and liberal work furnished ideas and diction for John Locke's *Two Treatises on Government*—which, in turn, furnished ideas and diction for the American Declaration of Independence.

On the (western) side of the square to the *left* of the corner diagonally opposite you, stands a series of old houses dating back to the seventeenth and eighteenth centuries. JOHN FORSTER (1812-76), literary and dramatic critic, literary biographer, friend of Dickens, and author of a three-volume biography of the latter, lived at *No. 58*. This was the house of Mr Tulkinghorn in Dickens's *Bleak House*, and here *Dickens* first read aloud *The Chimes* (to Forster and other friends). The poet CHARLES SACKVILLE, EARL OF DORSET (1638-1706), who wrote the song beginning, 'To all you ladies now at land', lived at *No. 59*, in 1700-1; and DANTE GABRIEL ROSSETTI (see above), painter and poet, lived at the same place in 1862. ALFRED TENNYSON (1809-92), most famous of the Victorian poets, stayed at *No. 60* in 1854; and the poet THOMAS CAMPBELL (1777-1844) lived at *No. 61* from 1837 to 1841.

21. Walk along the bottom (south side) of the square. On your left the Royal College of Surgeons (Ionic columns) occupies the spot where Lady Dorothy Sidney lived in 1660-5; she was the 'Sacharissa' to whom EDMUND WALLER (1606-87) addressed many of his early poems. At the next corner of the square you will reach the beginning of little *Sardinia Street*—much shortened and altered since the eighteenth century. Once there stood on this street (to your left as you walk from Lincoln's Inn Fields) a small Roman Catholic chapel where the novelist FRANCES ('FANNY') BURNEY was married in 1793, and where the famous sculptor Joseph Nollekens (1737-1823) was baptized. Just across the street from the chapel, the American printer BENJAMIN FRANKLIN (1706-90) had lodgings when he was a journey-man printer in London in the 1720's.

22. From the (south-west) corner of Lincoln's Inn Fields, where Sar-

dinia Street begins, turn left into little Portsmouth Street, leading away from the square. What purports to be, and is *not*, Dickens's original 'Old Curiosity Shop' stands a few steps down this street. In front of this shop, Sheffield Street branches off to the right from Portsmouth. Follow Sheffield till it reaches Portugal Street.

[22A. At about this spot, a *Vere Street* once ran athwart Sheffield Street. On this Vere Street stood a sponging-house where SIR RICHARD STEELE (1672-1729), essayist and dramatist, was confined for debt on more than one occasion—but never for more than a day or two at a time. An Irishman, he made money easily, spent it freely, and had acquired any number of loyal friends to help him out in a pinch. THOMAS KILLIGREW (1612-83), dramatist and theatre manager, had a temporary theatre on this street; and at this theatre (immediately after the Restoration of Charles II had made theatres legal once more) Killigrew rushed into production Shakespeare's *Henry* IV, *Part One*. In this theatre on 8 December 1660, an English woman played the part of a woman for the first time in any public English theatre. The part was that of Desdemona in *Othello*.]

Turn left, into *Portugal Street*. After you have passed two small streets opening on your right as you walk along Portugal Street, you will reach a long unbroken block extending along the right-hand side of the street. Farther to your right, at this place, there once extended the *burial-grounds* of St Clement Danes Church, in the Strand. Among literary people buried here were THOMAS OTWAY (1652-85), dramatist, known for his ability to depict intense tragic emotion; NATHANIEL LEE (1653?-92), dramatist, author of tragedies with classical settings; THOMAS RYMER (1641-1713), historian and influential neo-classic critic; and JOE MILLER (1684-1738), comic actor, whose name was attached by a publisher to the famous *Joe Miller's Jests*.

Farther along *Portugal Street*, on the left-hand side, almost directly opposite the entrance of Carey Street, three different theatres have been built successively on approximately the same land. Whatever their official names, each of these theatres was known as the 'Lincoln's Inn Fields Theatre'.

In 1660 a covered tennis court here was converted into the *Duke's Theatre* by SIR WILLIAM DAVENANT (1606-68), who was a dramatist as well as a manager. This theatre had movable painted scenes, the first ever shown on anything like so full a scale in any public English theatre. *Samuel Pepys* was a frequent member of the audience at this theatre. About three years after Davenant died, his company moved (November, 1671) to a luxurious theatre newly built in Dorset Gardens; and three months later (February, 1672) the King's Company, under THOMAS KILLIGREW (see above) moved into the old theatre after the company had been burned out of its regular location in Drury Lane.

Killigrew's company moved back to Drury Lane when it was rebuilt (March, 1674); and the Duke's Theatre became a tennis court again.

The second theatre here was built by WILLIAM CONGREVE (1670-1729), one of the greatest and the wittiest of the English dramatists, together with THOMAS BETTERTON (1635?-1710), probably the most celebrated actor of his time. The leading women of their company were ANNE BRACEGIRDLE (1663?-1748), with whom Congreve was in love, and ELIZABETH BARRY (1658-1713), 'the greatest tragic actress of her day'. The theatre opened in April, 1695, with the premier production of Congreve's *Love for Love*—and with King William III present.

Christopher Rich and his son John Rich tore down this theatre, and built another on the same spot. It was opened in December, 1714. JAMES QUIN (1693-1766) was the chief actor here. He was famous for many comic portrayals, particularly that of Falstaff. The *Beggar's Opera* of JOHN GAY (1685-1732) was first produced here (January, 1726), and was such an enormous and long-lasting success that it gave rise to a joke: 'The play made Gay rich, and Rich gay.' This was abandoned in December, 1732—and was the last theatre here. Among literary people who have lived on this street were WILLIAM DAVENANT (see above), who had lodgings behind his theatre here, and died here; JOHN WILMOT, EARL OF ROCHESTER (1647-80), poet and courtier, who lived 'in the house next to the Duke's playhouse'; and EDEN PHILLPOTTS (1862-1960), novelist, dramatist, and poet, who lived at *No. 4* around 1900.

23. At the end of Portugal Street, turn right, into Serle Street. At the corner where you turn stood, in the eighteenth century, Serle's Coffee House, known to have been frequented by *Joseph Addison* and the poet *Mark Akenside*. Continue to the intersection with *Carey Street*. On the left-hand corner here JOHN LOCKE (1642-1704), the philosopher, lived for a while. At the right-hand corner was the entrance to *New Court*—a hollow square of buildings where ARNOLD BENNETT (1867-1931), the novelist, worked in a law office on first coming to London. The place and some of the people Bennett knew here figure in his very first novel, *A Man from the North*. Just across the street, where the law court buildings now stand, there was once another courtyard called Boswell Court (after a sixteenth-century Boswell). By coincidence, DR SAMUEL JOHNSON (1709-84) lived here (1738-41). The poet WALTER SAVAGE LANDOR (1775-1864) lodged in the court in

1801. The MAYHEW brothers—HENRY (1812-87), HORACE (1816-72), and AUGUSTUS (1826-75)—were born at *No. 26*. All of them were writers of farces and fiction, Horace was an artist, and Henry was a sociological writer as well.

24. Turn left on Carey Street, and reach *Chancery Lane*. Turn right. THOMAS CAREW (1595?-1639?), diplomat, court official, friend of Ben Jonson, one of the finest of the Cavalier poets, lived with his parents, when he was young, along this part of the street. IZAAK WALTON (1593-1683), who has earned a permanent place in English literature with one book, *The Compleat Angler* (1653), lived at the next-to-the-last house on your right before you reach the Strand. Across the street from where Carey Street intersects Chancery Lane stands the *Public Record Office*, where national archives and legal records are deposited. A museum within the building displays many documents of literary interest. Among these are letters from Sir Philip Sidney, Edmund Spenser, Francis Bacon, Ben Jonson, John Milton, James Boswell, Sir Walter Scott, and others; a manuscript poem by Shelley; signatures on documents by Shakespeare and John Bunyan; the earliest specimen of English printing done in England: the 'Abingdon Indulgence' (1476) ... and so on.

The Temple

25. When you reach Fleet Street (at the end of Chancery Lane), cross over it, turn right, and go a short block—till you reach a narrow passage (under an arch) leading away to your left. This is *Middle Temple Lane*—and you are now within THE TEMPLE. The latter is officially divided into the 'Middle Temple' and the 'Inner Temple', though there is no easily recognizable geographic line between the two. Just to your left, as you enter Middle Temple Lane from Fleet Street is the building where JONATHAN SWIFT'S *A Tale of a Tub* was published.

26. Farther down, on your right, you will find a largish car park, which is *Brick Court*. There has been a good deal of rebuilding here in recent years, especially since the bombings of 1940-1. At *No. 2* lived (1768-74) and died OLIVER GOLDSMITH (1730-74), that extraordinary Irishman who is famous in English literature as a poet, novelist, dramatist and essayist; and Sir William Blackstone (1723-80), the great jurist, lived on the floor below Goldsmith, and complained of the noise made by his 'revelling neighbour'. WILLIAM

115

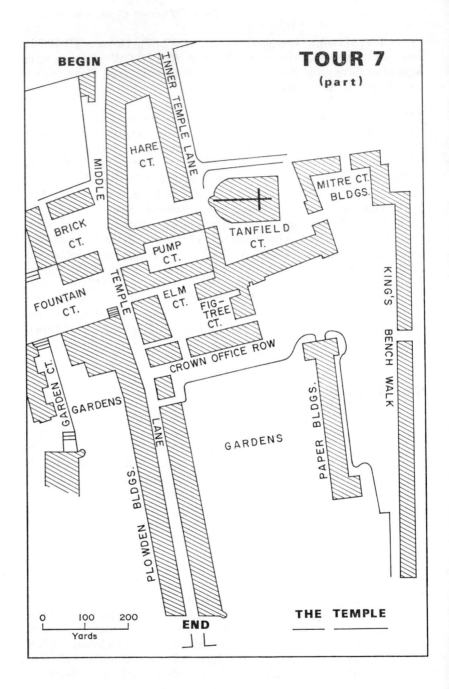

BEGIN

TOUR 7
(part)

INNER TEMPLE LANE

HARE
CT.

MITRE CT.
BLDGS.

MIDDLE

BRICK
CT.

PUMP
CT.

TANFIELD
CT.

TEMPLE

FOUNTAIN
CT.

ELM
CT.

FIG-
TREE
CT.

KING'S BENCH WALK

GARDEN CT.

GARDENS

CROWN OFFICE ROW

GARDENS

PAPER BLDGS.

PLOWDEN BLDGS.

LANE

0   100   200
Yards

END

THE TEMPLE

MAKEPEACE THACKERAY (1811-63), the novelist, lived at *No. 3* in 1865; and MACKWORTH PRAED (1802-39), poet, essayist, member of Parliament, political satirist, lived and died at the same place. ANTHONY HOPE (HAWKINS) (1863-1933), author of *The Prisoner of Zenda* occupied *No. 1* in the 1880's; and the great anthropologist and folklorist SIR JAMES GEORGE FRAZER (1854-1941) lived (part of the time) at the same place in the 1920's. JOHN BUCHAN (1875-1940), novelist and statesman, lodged briefly at *No. 4* in 1900.

27. Continue down Middle Temple Lane till you find another open space on your right—this one with trees instead of cars. It is *Fountain Court*. Just ahead of you, at the corner, you will see an impressive building with a broad flight of steps leading up to an arched door. This is *Middle Temple Hall*, where Shakespeare's *Twelfth Night* was first acted (1602), before Queen Elizabeth I. ARTHUR SYMONS (1865-1945), poet and critic, who introduced the French Symbolist poets to England, edited the *Savoy* (started, with Aubrey Beardsley, because the *Yellow Book* was deemed too tame), and was in general, as someone said, 'the ringmaster of the *fin-de-siècle* circus', lived in an apartment off this court from 1890 to 1901. HAVELOCK ELLIS (1859-1939), who was a physician, poet, essayist, critic, and socio- logical writer, but who is better known for his multi-volume work on the *Psychology of Sex*, lived with Symons (see above) in 1893-4; and WILLIAM BUTLER YEATS (1865-1939), the Nobel Prize-winning Irish poet and dramatist, lived here, 1895-6. Charles Dickens described this court fondly, in *Martin Chuzzlewit*, as the meeting place of Ruth Pinch, her brother, and her lover.

28. Walk on to the back of Fountain Court, and turn left, down some steps, into *Garden Court*. Thomas Jefferson Hogg (1792-1862), friend and biographer of Shelley, expelled from Oxford along with Shelley, lived in *No. 1* in 1816; JAMES BOSWELL, JR. (1778-1822), son of the great Boswell, friend of Sir Walter Scott, and editor of a variorum edition of Shakespeare, lived and died at *No. 3*; and OLIVER GOLD- SMITH (see above) lived at *No. 2*, opening on the library staircase. The garden you see to your left here was probably the one in which (tra- ditionally, and perhaps apocryphally) the Lancastrians and Yorkists identified themselves by plucking red or white roses. Their differences led to the Wars of the Roses—which Shakespeare has used in his *Henry* VI plays, and in *Richard* III.

29. Return, the way you came, to Middle Temple Lane, cross over to its other side, turn left, and re-ascend the Lane a few steps—till

you find a passageway leading off under some buildings to a court beyond. Walk through the passageway into the court—which is *Pump Court*. HENRY FIELDING (1707-54), novelist and dramatist, author of *Tom Jones*, rented chambers at *No. 4* for life. The poet WILLIAM COWPER (1731-1800) is said to have had rooms here. MARION ST JOHN WEBB (d. 1930), writer of children's books, lived at *No. 1*.

30. Walk on through Pump Court, pass under the cloisters at the far end, and emerge into large *Tanfield Court. No. 2* here was the address of GEORGE GREENE (1853-1921), novelist, poet, and critic, during his last years. He is best remembered, no doubt, as the editor of the two anthologies of poetry issued by the Rhymers' Club in the 1890's.

To your right stood the old *Inner Temple Hall*, destroyed by the bombings in 1941, and entirely rebuilt (1952-5). In the old hall was produced the earliest English tragedy, *Gorboduc* (1561), by THOMAS NORTON (1523-84) and THOMAS SACKVILLE (1536-1608). Officially, it was first performed before Queen Elizabeth I at Whitehall in January, 1562; but it had its first showing here. Many other famous plays were performed here during the sixteenth and seventeenth centuries— including plays by Beaumont and Fletcher, James Shirley, William Davenant, Thomas Otway, William Wycherley, and John Dryden.

31. Across Tanfield Court from the hall, and to your left as you enter the court, you will see *Temple Church*. Its entrance is on the side facing the court. You should go inside the church and look around; for though it was bombed during the Second World War, much still remains of its twelfth-century architecture, and many ancient effigies repose on its floor. JOHN MARSTON (1575-1634), dramatist and satirist, was buried here; and the essayist CHARLES LAMB (1775-1834) was baptized here. The famous jurist *John Selden* (d. 1654) is buried here, and *Bishop Ussher* (1581-1656) preached the funeral sermon. (Ussher, it will be recalled, calculating the age of the earth from the chronologies in the Bible, determined that the earth was created in 4004 B.C., and finished on Friday, 23 October, at six in the evening.)

32. When you leave the church, double back to the nearer (rounded) end, mount some steps, and turn right, walking parallel with the church at your right. Here you will find a raised stone slab with the words 'HERE LIES OLIVER GOLDSMITH'. Actually, however, the location is only approximate. Goldsmith was buried within a few feet of this stone, but the precise spot is unknown. The buildings just above the grave (a little to the left) are called *Goldsmith Buildings*, though they are of much more recent construction than Goldsmith's time.

118

33. Return to the rounded end of the church, and find opposite it a passage leading into *Hare Court*. In a building immediately to your right JAMES BOSWELL (1740-95), Dr Johnson's biographer, lived in the early 1760's, so as to be near the Doctor, who was at that time lodged a bit farther up the lane. At *No. 1* WILLIAM MAKEPEACE THACKERAY (see above) studied law. At *No. 3* of this court lived ISRAEL ZANGWILL (1864-1926), from about 1910 almost to the time of his death, and here he wrote his novels and stories of Jewish life in London. (In a house where *No. 2* now stands lived the infamous Judge Jeffreys, of the Bloody Assizes.)

34. Leave Hare Court by the way you entered, and turn left, up *Inner Temple Lane*. The houses here are comparatively new, but the lane itself is redolent of the eighteenth century. The poet WILLIAM COW-PER (see above) occupied lodgings for a while on this lane in 1752. CHARLES LAMB (see above) and his sister *Mary* stayed, from 1808 to 1817, at *No. 4*. DR SAMUEL JOHNSON lived at *No. 1*, from 1760 to 1765. EDGAR MIDDLETON (1894-1939), dramatist and novelist, lived at *No. 3*.

35. Unfortunately, you will now have to retrace your steps to the Temple Church, and around it. But this time, instead of entering the church, walk on past it, and find the passage ahead of you leading on into broad King's Bench Walk. Over to your left, blocking the end of the Walk, are the *Mitre Court Buildings* (rebuilt after the bombings), where CHARLES LAMB (see above) and his sister *Mary* lived (1800-8) at *No. 16* before moving into Inner Temple Lane. The poet ALFRED TENNYSON (1809-92), also lived in these buildings for a short while, and the novelist A. J. DAWSON was living in *No. 8* around 1905-6.

36. Cross over to the far side of *King's Bench Walk* and find the following places. OLIVER GOLDSMITH (see above) lodged at *No. 3* before he moved into Brick Court; and HENRY CRABB ROBINSON (1775-1867), who was a friend of most of the important literary people of his day, and wrote about them in his diaries, later occupied (1822-9) the same *No. 3*. SIR NORMAN ANGELL (1872-1967), Nobel Peace Prizewinner, and author of many books on behalf of peace and democracy, lived at *No 4*; and SIR HAROLD NICOLSON (1886-1968), historian, literary biographer, diarist, and diplomat, and his wife VICTORIA SACKVILLE-WEST (1892-1962), poet and novelist, kept this same *No. 4* as their town lodgings from 1930 to 1945. GEORGE MOORE (1852-1933), poet, outrageous autobiographer, and first truly naturalistic English novelist,

lived at *No. 8* from 1888 to 1896. The once-popular novelist-drama-tist F. C. PHILIPS (1849-1921) was living at *No. 12* in 1910-11; and the novelist H. RIDER HAGGARD (1856-1925), author of *King Solomon's Mines* and *She*, wrote his novel *Mr Meeson's Will* (about a will tattooed on the back of its feminine beneficiary) while he was living at *No. 13*. GEORGE COLMAN THE YOUNGER (see above) had rooms somewhere on the Walk.

37. When you have reached the lower end of King's Bench Walk, turn about and ascend on the other (right-hand) side. The buildings to your left are known as the *Paper Buildings*. SAMUEL ROGERS (1763-1855), wealthy poet (he refused the Poet Laureateship), conversation-alist, bonvivant, and friend of most of the important writers of his time, lived in these buildings, 1800-3. And the novelist-playwright JOHN GALSWORTHY (see above) had offices at *No. 3* in the 1890's. (Sir John Chester, of Dickens's *Barnaby Rudge*, lived here, probably at *No. 3;* and Stryver, in *A Tale of Two Cities*, had offices here.)

38. When you have reached the end of this row of buildings, turn left, into *Crown Office Row* (which faces the gardens on your left). About midway along this row of buildings, you will see a plaque that marks the site of the house where CHARLES LAMB (see above) was born. WILLIAM MAKEPEACE THACKERAY (see above) lived at *No. 10* (his building is gone) in 1848-50; and J. B. PRIESTLEY (1894-   ), novelist and dramatist, lived briefly at *No. 5* in 1939-40, before being chased out by the bombings.

39. Near the far end of Crown Office Row, just before you would pass under an archway, turn right, through a narrow passage. You will find yourself in *Elm Court*, which has been thrown together with *Fig Tree Court*, since the bombings. The poet WILLIAM COWPER (see above) lived in Fig Tree Court at one time during his stay in the Temple—and here he tried to hang himself with a garter. But, as he wrote later, 'By the eternal Providence of God, the garter which had held me till the bitterness of temporal death was past, broke before eternal death had taken place upon me'. His laundress heard him fall, rushed into the room, and resuscitated him. The novelist F. C. PHILIPS (see above) lived at *No. 1 Elm Court* for a while; and CHURTON COLLINS (1846-1908), essayist, critic, scholar, literary bio-grapher, had rooms at *No. 3 Elm Court* in the 1870's.

40. From this court, take the passage at the upper left-hand corner back again to *Middle Temple Lane*. Turn left here, and keep walking

on down the Lane, past places where you have already been. Just beyond Middle Temple Hall and beyond Crown Office Row, you will see some buildings that are called the *Plowden Buildings*. HENRY CRABB ROBINSON (see above), the diarist, lived at *No. 2* from 1832 to 1836; and *No. 3* was occupied successively by the novelist and diplomat JOHN BUCHAN (see above), and PHILIP GUEDALLA (1889-1944), journalist, historian, and biographer.

Keep walking on down this lane, through a passage, and out on Victoria Embankment. Turn right, on the latter, and find, a short distance away, the *Temple Underground Station*. By this time your feet will certainly be so tired that they will demand to be taken home for the day.

Addendum

Among literary persons, not previously mentioned, who lived in *Middle Temple*, either as members or as residents, are the following; all of them must have walked often along Middle Temple Lane, and frequented its courts:

WILLIAM ARCHER (1856-1924), critic and dramatist, who introduced Ibsen to England.

ALFRED AUSTIN (1835-1913), Poet Laureate succeeding Tennyson.

R. D. BLACKMORE (1825-1900), novelist, author of *Lorna Doone.*

EDMUND BURKE (1729-97), essayist and statesman.

WILLIAM CONGREVE (see above), dramatist.

WILLIAM DAVENANT (see above), dramatist and theatre manager.

JOHN DAVIES (1569-1626), poet.

THOMAS DE QUINCEY (1785-1859), essayist and critic, author of the autobiographical *Confessions of an English Opium Eater.*

JOHN EVELYN (1620-1706), the diarist.

HENRY FIELDING (1707-54), novelist.

JOHN FORD (b. 1586), dramatist.

W. S. GILBERT (1836-1911), poet, and librettist of the immortal Gilbert-and-Sullivan operas.

THOMAS MOORE (1779-1852), Irish poet, friend of Byron.

SIR THOMAS OVERBURY (1581-1613), author of prose sketches describing typical 'characters', in the Theophrastan manner.

SIR WALTER RALEIGH (1552-1618), adventurer, colonizer, statesman, historian, poet.

NICHOLAS ROWE (1674-1718), dramatist, 'last of the Elizabethans'.

THOMAS SHADWELL (1642?-92), poet, playwright, Poet Laureate, first friend and then enemy of Dryden.

RICHARD BRINSLEY SHERIDAN (1751-1816), dramatist.

JOHN WEBSTER (1580?-1625?), dramatist, author of *The White Devil* and *The Duchess of Malfi*.

WILLIAM WYCHERLEY (1640?-1716), dramatist.

Among the *Inner Temple* literary people not previously mentioned are

FRANCIS BEAUMONT (1584?-1616), dramatist, who collaborated with John Fletcher.

EDMUND BOLTON (1575?-1633?), poet and historian.

SIR FRANCIS DOYLE (1810-88), poet of the Kipling school—well before Kipling.

ARTHUR HENRY HALLAM (1811-33), poet, in memory of whom Tennyson wrote *In Memoriam*.

LESLIE STEPHEN (1832-1904), man of letters, editor, literary biographer, editor of the *Dictionary of National Biography*, and father of the novelist Virginia Woolf.

Tour 8
Bloomsbury

Dr Mark Akenside

Herbert Asquith

Margot Asquith

Mrs Anna Laetitia Barbauld

Topham Beauclerk

Clive Bell

George Borrow

Mrs Golding Bright
('George Egerton')

Thomas Burke

Sir Edward Burne-Jones

Francis ('Fanny') Burney

Samuel H. Butcher

Thomas Campbell

Colley Cibber

Arthur Hugh Clough

Churton Collins

William Cowper

Mrs Pearl Craigie
('John Oliver Hobbes')

Richard Cumberland

Charles Darwin

W. H. Davies

William de Morgan

Charles Dickens

Isaac Disraeli

Ernest Christopher Dowson

George du Maurier

John Passmore Edwards

T. S. Eliot

Ralph Waldo Emerson

Chester B. Fernald

Edward Fitzgerald

Johnston Forbes-Robertson

E. M. Forster

Harold Frederic

Roger Fry

David Garnett

David Garrick

William Godwin

Charles Gounod

Thomas Gray

Graham Greene

Gordon Hake

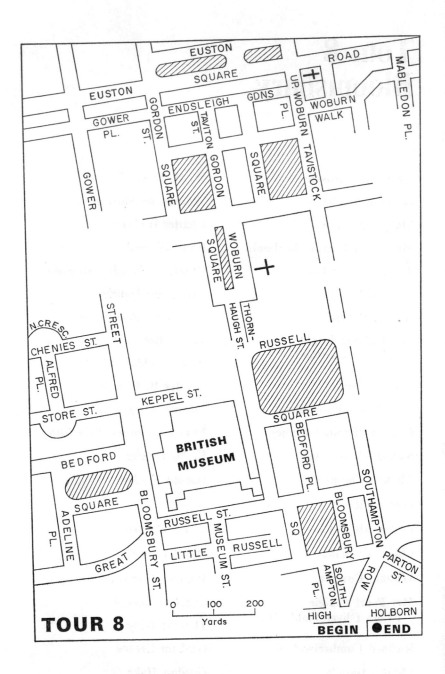

TOUR 8

Yards
0   100   200

BEGIN ●END

Joseph Hatton

Nathaniel Hawthorne

William Hazlitt

Theodore Hook

Thornton Leigh Hunt

Anthony Hope (Hawkins)

Dr Richard Hurd

John Keats

John Philip Kemble

W. P. Ker

John Maynard Keynes

D. H. Lawrence

Richard le Gallienne

Amy Levy

Eliza (Lynn) Linton

Arthur Machen

Desmond MacCarthy

Katherine Mansfield

Henry W. Massingham

Frederick D. Maurice

Francis Meynell

Charlotte Mew

James Mill

J. E. Millais

Mary Russell Mitford

Harold Monro

Ottoline Morrell

William Morris

John Middleton Murry

Cardinal John Henry Newman

Sir Harold Nicolson

Edgar Allan Poe

Adelaide Proctor

Bryan W. Proctor
    ('Barry Cornwall')

Dorothy Richardson

Henrietta Robertson
    ('Henry Handel Richardson')

Henry Crabb Robinson

Christina Rossetti

William Michael Rossetti

Victoria Sackville-West

Sir Charles Sedley

Mary Godwin Shelley

Percy Bysshe Shelley

Sir Richard Steele

Gertrude Stein

James Strachey

Lytton Strachey

Algernon C. Swinburne

A. J. A. Symons

Lewis Theobald

Henry D. Traill

Sir Herbert Beerbohm Tree

Anthony Trollope

Arthur Waley

Mrs Humphry Ward	**Leonard Woolf**
H. G. Wells	**Virginia Woolf**
Thomas Wolfe	**William Wordsworth**
Mary Wollstonecraft	**William Butler Yeats**

Leave the underground at the *Holborn (Kingsway) Station.* Orient yourself with Southampton Row on your right, and Kingsway on your left—then walk straight forward, along High Holborn.

1. After one block along High Holborn, turn right, into *Southampton Place.* At the far end of this street, on the left (next to Bloomsbury Square), was born COLLEY CIBBER (1671-1757), 'actor and theatre manager, Poet Laureate and prose polemist, autobiographer and dramatist'—and King of Dunces in Pope's vicious satire the *Dunciad.* CARDINAL JOHN HENRY NEWMAN (1801-89) spent much of his early life at *No. 17.* Newman, as one of the leaders of the Oxford Movement, attempted to recall the Anglican Church to its traditional heritage—and carried the attempt so far that he himself ended by becoming a Roman Catholic.

2. Walk on into *Bloomsbury Square.* Here lived and died the profligate poet SIR CHARLES SEDLEY (1639-1701), brilliant wit and satirist. DR MARK AKENSIDE (1721-70), author of the long and historically important *The Pleasures of the Imagination,* man of letters in general, and physician to the queen of George III, also lived somewhere on this square at one time. *No. 45,* at the right-hand corner of Southampton Place and the square, is the townhouse of the Earls of Chesterfield. Dr Johnson's *Lord Chesterfield* undoubtedly stayed in the place—but this was not his regular home in London. SIR RICHARD STEELE (1672-1729), dramatist and originator and editor of the *Tatler,* lived (1712-15) in what was then the fifth house on your right (east side) up from Southampton Place. At *No. 12* lived the modern historian *Demetrius Boulger* (1853-1928); and the philosopher *Herbert Spencer* (1820-1903) lived briefly (1853) at *No. 29.* The first house on the left-hand (west) side of the square was the long-time home of ISAAC DISRAELI (1761-1848), father of the Prime Minister Benjamin Disraeli, and author of several volumes of sidelights on English authors and English literature. (He wrote the original *Curiosities of Literature* here.) *No. 12* was the home of Eliza Polidori, aunt of the literary Rossettis; and here the poet CHRISTINA ROSSETTI (1830-94) often stayed for long periods. GERTRUDE STEIN (1874-1946), the American 'modern' writer lodged, with her brother Leo, at *No. 20* in 1902, just after having

failed to get her medical degree at Johns Hopkins University. At the far left-hand (north-west) corner of the square (facing down the length of the square) lived BISHOP RICHARD HURD (1720-1801), whose essays against literary imitativeness, and whose interest in the Middle Ages and in Spenser, influenced the growth of the Romantic movement.

3. *Bedford Place* leads away from the far end of Bloomsbury Square. RICHARD LE GALLIENNE (1866-1947), poet, essayist, critic (and father of the actress Eva Le Gallienne) lived, in 1900, at *No. 34.* RICHARD CUMBERLAND (1732-1811), once-famous dramatist, died at *No. 30*, the home of his friend Henry Fry.

4. At the end of Bedford Place is *Russell Square*. Off to your right you will see a row of hotels facing the square. At the site of the *Imperial Hotel* the poet THOMAS GRAY (1716-71), author of what has long been the best-known English poem, 'An Elegy in a Country Churchyard', lodged (1759-60) so as to be near the British Museum, where he was studying. The American novelist THOMAS WOLFE (1900-38) stayed at the earlier Imperial Hotel, on this site, in 1924.

[4A. *Southampton Row* extends to your right from the corner of the square nearest the Imperial Hotel. The family of EDGAR ALLAN POE (1809-49) lived at *No. 83* from about 1815 to 1817, while the young poet-to-be was in boarding school in London; the child was often here with his foster parents.]

In what follows, the numbers on *Russell Square*, are arranged in descending order.

The Osbornes (in Thackeray's *Vanity Fair*) lived at *No. 96*, and the Sedleys at *No. 62*. The American poet and essayist RALPH WALDO EMERSON (1803-82) stayed at *No. 63* on his visit to London in 1833. The poet WILLIAM COWPER (1731-1800) lived at *No. 62* while he was a law student in London; and MRS HUMPHRY WARD (1851-1920), novelist and editor, and niece of Matthew Arnold, lived, with her husband, at *No. 61* in the 1880's. MARY RUSSELL MITFORD (1785-1855), fiction-writer, dramatist, and poet, lived at *No. 56*. While living here in 1836, she wrote: 'Mr Wordsworth, Mr Landor, and Mr White dined here. I like Mr Wordsworth.... Mr Landor is a very striking-looking person, and exceedingly clever. Also we had a Mr Browning, a young poet, and Mr Proctor, and Mr Morley, and quantities more of poets.' HENRY CRABB ROBINSON (1775-1867), the diarist, who knew and wrote about everybody of the slightest literary importance in his time, lived at *No. 30* from 1842 till his death. *No. 24* was, for many years, the editorial office of Faber and Faber, and also the London address of T. S. ELIOT (1888-1965), American-born Nobel Prize-winning poet, and Faber editor. At *No. 13* lived Sir George Williams (1821-1905), founder of the Y.M.C.A.—in whom the author of this book has an understandable interest. And *No. 5* was the home of FREDERICK DENISON MAURICE (1805-72), theological writer, novelist, one of the founders of the Christian Socialist movement and the Working Men's College.

5. Leave Russell Square at the corner near the Eliot address (that is, at Thornaugh Street, on which lived Basil Montagu, friend of WILLIAM WORDSWORTH, whom the poet visited for some weeks in 1806 and 1807), and walk on to *Woburn Square*. On the right-hand side of the square stands Christ Church (1833), which contains an altarpiece with paintings by SIR EDWARD BURNE-JONES (1833-98), one of the most important of the Pre-Raphaelite painters, in memory of CHRISTINA ROSSETTI (1830-94), lyric poet of great depth and sensitivity, who lived near here. SIR FRANCIS MEYNELL (b. 1891), poet and specialist in typography, son of Wilfred and Alice Meynell (the poet), lived at *No. 39* in the 1930's.

6. Until the 1930's, *Torrington Square* ran along parallel to the entire length of Woburn Square, one block to your left (west). But the area of the former square, as well as the intervening block, is mostly occupied by the expansion of the University of London. On this square, at *No. 30*, CHRISTINA ROSSETTI (see above) lived from 1876 till her death there in 1894; and her brother WILLIAM MICHAEL ROSSETTI (1829-1919), also a writer of some consequence, lived with her during most of that time. *No. 61* was the home of CHURTON COLLINS (1848-1908), essayist, critic, literary biographer, from 1883 to 1896.

7. Cross over the street at the far end of Woburn Square, and reach *Gordon Square*. This was the headquarters (especially before 1920) of the famous 'Bloomsbury Group' of brilliant but highly eccentric (in both the intellectual and the sexual sense) of writers, artists, and personalities. The goings and comings of this group, its intricate and ever-shifting combinations of heterosexual and homosexual relationships, its *ménages à trois* and *à quatre* (masculine-feminine, masculine, or feminine), and the doings of many other brilliant people on the fringes of the group have been studied in Michael Holroyd's two-volume life of *Lytton Strachey* (1967, 1968). The children of Sir Leslie Stephen (1832-1904), the great editor, historian, and biographer, were at the centre of the group; but almost as important was the Strachey family. Other important members were CLIVE BELL (1881-

1964), art and literary critic, husband of Vanessa Stephen; LEONARD WOOLF (1880-1969), editor, historian, and sociologist, husband of Virginia Stephen; DAVID GARNETT (b. 1892), novelist, critic, and voluminous autobiographer (he tells a great deal about the Bloomsbury Group); E. M. FORSTER (1879-1968), the novelist; DESMOND MACCARTHY (1878-1952), editor and critic; JOHN MAYNARD KEYNES (1883-1946), economist, whose theories revolutionized national and international economics; ARTHUR WALEY (1889-1966), translator of Oriental poetry (to whom is due any knowledge of Chinese poets and poetry that most Americans and Englishmen may possess); the poet T. S. ELIOT (see above); ROGER FRY (1866-1934), artist and art critic, who seems to have been at least half in love with Vanessa Bell; and Duncan Grant (b. 1885), an artist. This list is far from complete, of course; nor, in what follows, is there any attempt to date the occupancy of certain houses by members of the group. It should be understood, furthermore, that several members may have lived at the same address at the same time—either in the same or in different flats. If the reader wishes more precise information in all these matters, he should consult Holroyd's book, mentioned above.

Duncan Grant and Vanessa Stephen Bell lived at *No. 37* and *No. 39 Gordon Square*; *David Garnett* at *No. 37*; *Ralph Partridge* (editor and editorial assistant) with Frances Marshall (who became his wife) and with Dora Carrington (who became Lytton Strachey's more-or-less mistress, and Partridge's mistress) at *No. 41*; the Freudian psychologist *James Strachey* (brother of Lytton) and his wife Alix also lived at *No. 41*, as did Lydia Lopokova, who became the wife of John Maynard Keynes. The Stephen family took *No. 46* in 1904, after the death of their father, Sir Leslie; during World War I, *Clive* and *Vanessa Bell* and Duncan Grant had rooms at *No 46*; and *John Maynard Keynes* and his wife Lydia lived there from 1922. The Strachey family lived at *No. 51* after the death of their father; and here LYTTON STRACHEY (1880-1932), author of the *Life of Queen Victoria*, and father of modern biography, lived off-and-on until it became his regular address after his mother's death. Oliver Strachey and his daughter Julie lived at *No. 42*; and Adrian Stephen and his wife Karin at *No. 50*. *Clive Bell* and his wife Vanessa also lived at *No. 50*, as did *Arthur Waley* in 1930 and 1955-60.

No. 5 Gordon Square was the editorial office (1930-1) of the Fascist magazine *Action*, edited by Sir Oswald Mosley, with the help of SIR HAROLD NICOLSON (1886-1968), editor, diarist, historian, husband of the poet and novelist VICTORIA SACKVILLE-WEST (1892-1962). Nicolson should have known better; and, learning better, he withdrew from the Fascist movement. Among other writers who have lived on

Gordon Square, the following may be mentioned: GORDON HAKE (1809-95), poet and physician, at *No. 42* in 1840-1; and HENRY D. TRAILL (1842-1900), poet and dramatist, literary biographer and editor of the multi-volume *Social History of England*, at *No. 47*.

Across the street from Gordon Square is *University Hall*, where ARTHUR HUGH CLOUGH (1819-61), the sceptical and melancholy poet who was a friend of Matthew Arnold, and subject of the latter's great elegiac poem *Thyrsis*, lived while teaching at University College, London. In passing, it may be noted that the poet THOMAS CAMPBELL (1777-1844) and the philosopher JAMES MILL (1773-1836) were largely responsible for the founding of University College.

[7A. *Taviton Street* opens at the far right-hand corner of Gordon Square (as you entered the latter from Woburn Square). Up this street, at *No. 19*, DAVID GARNETT (see above) and Francis Birrell (son of the man of letters, critic, and politician Augustine Birrell) had a book-shop; and the basement of the place later became the site of the Nonesuch Press, managed by SIR FRANCIS MEYNELL (see above).]

8. Move over to your right (eastwards) from Gordon Square to *Tavistock Square*. At *No. 6* SAMUEL H. BUTCHER (1850-1910), the Greek scholar, translator of Aristotle and of Homer, author of several books on Greek civilization, lived early in this century. THOMAS BURKE (1886-1945), the novelist whose subject was the East End and the waterfront of London (see his *Limehouse Nights*) was living at *No. 33* in the 1930's. VIRGINIA WOOLF (1882-1941), the novelist (and one of the daughters of Sir Leslie Stephen, mentioned above) and her husband LEONARD WOOLF (see above) lived at *No. 52* till the Second World War. The place was bombed out, and Virginia Woolf committed suicide soon afterward.... Now go on to the far right-hand (north-east) corner of Tavistock Square, where it joins with Woburn Place. Just across the latter, and facing the Square (that is, facing west, or south-west) stood *Tavistock House*. Here CHARLES DICKENS (1812-70) lived for ten years, 1850-60, and here he wrote *Bleak House*, *Hard Times*, *Little Dorrit*, *A Tale of Two Cities*, and the beginning of *Great Expectations*. He built a small theatre in the garden, and gave amateur performances in which he played the leading parts. Later on, CHARLES GOUNOD (1818-93), the French composer of operas (e.g., *Faust* and *Romeo and Juliet*) lived in the same house.

9. Leave Tavistock Square by *Upper Woburn Place*—which leads away from the far (north-east) corner of the square. (You will see a church a short distance up this street, on your right.) MRS PEARL

CRAIGIE ('JOHN OLIVER HOBBES') (1867-1906), dramatist and novelist, lived at *No. 24* as a child.

10. A short block up from Tavistock Square, *Woburn Walk* leads off to the right of Upper Woburn Place. At *No. 5* of this narrow 'street' the great Irish poet and dramatist WILLIAM BUTLER YEATS (1865-1939) lived from 1896 to 1917. He lived on the second floor with a mistress (the novelist *Olivia Shakespear*) whom he called 'Diana Vernon'; but later he occupied most of the house. After he married and moved away, Maud Gonne (who was his love and ideal during most of his life, and to or about whom much of his poetry was written) occupied the house. DOROTHY RICHARDSON (1882-1957), the first novelist to bring 'stream of consciousness' technique into English fiction, lived in an attic room across the street from Yeats.

[10A. Go to the end of Woburn Walk, then slant away leftward on Flaxman Terrace, till you reach *Mabledon Place*. The poet PERCY BYSSHE SHELLEY (1792-1822) and his wife MARY GODWIN SHELLEY (1797-1851) lodged at *No. 19* in 1817.... Return to Upper Woburn Place.]

11. Turn right, and continue along Upper Woburn Place (past St Pancras Church) to *Euston Road.*

[11A. Before reaching Euston Road, you may wish to make a little side trip along *Endsleigh Gardens*, opening on your left. Here, at *No. 5*, WILLIAM MICHAEL ROSSETTI (see above), brother of the more famous Dante Gabriel Rossetti and Christina Rossetti, lived, 1880-7. At *No. 7* the minor but poignant poet AMY LEVY (1861-89), who wrote a volume of poems called *A Minor Poet*, as well as two other small volumes of poetry and a novel—committed suicide at the age of twenty-eight, by breathing charcoal fumes.]

On *Euston Road* just opposite St. Pancras Church, ERNEST CHRISTOPHER DOWSON (1867-1900), the finest lyric poet writing in English in the 1890's, had lodgings at one time during his unhappy life. H. G. WELLS (1866-1946), novelist and social philosopher, lodged with his aunt at *No. 181* when he first came to London, and was a science student at the South Kensington College, 1884-7. He walked from here all the way to the college for his daily classes. Here he met his cousin Isabel, whom he later married—and soon divorced.

12. *Euston Square* (now an exceptionally ugly commercial area with few or none of its old literary sites untouched) lies just to the left of the corner where you entered Euston Road. Cross the road, and reach the square. *No. 11* was the home, in the early nineteenth century, of one Charles Aders, who was the friend of many literary men. On one

occasion he had here as his dinner guests the poet *William Words-worth* (who fell asleep), the essayist *Charles Lamb*, the poet *Samuel Taylor Coleridge*, the poet and man-about-town *Samuel Rogers*, and the sculptor *John Flaxman*. The poet *William Blake* and the diarist *Henry Crabb Robinson* (who also knew almost everybody of literary importance in his time) were frequent guests here. THORNTON LEIGH HUNT (1810-73) lived at *No. 4* from 1863 to 1865, and at *No. 26* from 1866 to 1872. A journalist and son of Leigh Hunt (poet and friend of Keats and Byron), this Thornton Leigh Hunt was the man with whom the wife of George Henry Lewes, critic and journalist, fell in love. Lewes, who had previously advocated the freedom of woman in matters of love, put up no strong objection to his wife's liaison with Hunt; and he himself shortly afterwards began his famous and lasting liaison with George Eliot (Mary Anne Evans). The ROSSETTI family, consisting then of Frances, CHRISTINA, and WILLIAM, lived at *No. 56* from 1869 to 1879.

13. At the far (east) end of Euston Square, cross back over Euston Road, and descend *Gordon Street*. At *No. 1* WILLIAM MORRIS (1834-96), the 'English Leonardo', who was poet, painter, printer, worker in tapestries and stained glass, social reformer, and philosopher, lived (1856) with EDWARD BURNE-JONES (1833-98), one of the best-known and most successful of the Pre-Raphaelite painters. CHARLOTTE MEW (1869-1928), a slight but profound poet, spent most of her life at *No. 9* (bombed out in 1940).

14. Almost immediately turn aside, to your right, into *Gower Place*. WILLIAM GODWIN (1756-1836), the revolutionary political philosopher and novelist, whose ideas influenced most of the early Romantic poets, lived at *No. 44* from 1827 to 1833.

15. After one block, turn left, into *Gower Street*. Many of the literary sites on this street have disappeared; nevertheless, mentioning them seems worth while. The imaginative person may be able to people the street, at any rate, with dream-figures of literary personages who once walked and lived there.

At *No. 147 Gower Street* Mrs John Dickens, mother of CHARLES DICKENS (see above) set up, in 1823, a dame school by which she vainly hoped to make some kind of living while her husband was in debtors' prison, and her son was working in the shoe-blacking factory described in *David Copperfield*. Louis Kossuth, the Hungarian patriot, lived for a while (1858-9) at *No. 129*. CHARLES DARWIN (1809-82), the great biologist whose 'theory of evolution' upset the entire intellectual world, lived (1839-42) at *No. 110. Simeon Solomon,* a painter who was a tragic figure, but a significant influence on the Aesthetic movement of the 1880's and 1890's, lived at *No. 106.* W. P. KER (1855-1923), the literary critic and historian, lived at *No. 95* from the 1890's until his death. *No. 92* was the home of CHESTER B. FERNALD (1869-1938), dramatist and fiction writer. The poet and novelist D. H. LAWRENCE (1885-1930) 'touched down for a few days' at *No. 73* the last time he was in England (1925). At *No. 69* WILLIAM DE MORGAN (1839-1917) was born. A member of the Pre-Raphaelite and socialist circles of the later nineteenth century, and a celebrated artist in ceramics, he became (after the age of 65) a highly successful novelist. A little farther along the street stands the Royal Academy of Dramatic Art, founded in 1904 by SIR HERBERT BEERBOHM TREE (1853-1917), long the manager of Her Majesty's Theatre.

(*Now make the side-trip described in Sections 16-20 below*)

MRS ELIZA LYNN LINTON (1822-98), one of the very early female journalists, and a novelist, lived (1869-71) at *No. 28 Gower Street.* (Though she herself lived a highly independent and non-conformist life, she became a violent anti-feminist; and though she was essentially kind, she was so wittily sharp-tongued that she 'collected probably the largest and most distinguished set of enemies of anyone of her period'.) ANTHONY HOPE (SIR ANTHONY HOPE HAWKINS) (1863-1933), novelist and dramatist, whose best-known novel is *The Prisoner of Zenda,* lived (1921-5) at *No. 14.* LADY OTTOLINE MORRELL, friend (and lover) of many of the Bloomsbury group, especially Lytton Strachey and Bertrand Russell, held court, in the 1920's and 1930's, at *No. 10.* J. E. MILLAIS (1829-96) was living with his parents at *No. 7* when, with *D. G. Rossetti* and *Holman Hunt,* he helped establish the Pre-Raphaelite Brotherhood—which had far-reaching effects on both art and literature. *Dorothy Brett,* friend of many literary figures in the first third of the twentieth century (and especially of D. H. Lawrence) was living (1917) at *No. 3.* The impecunious KATHERINE MANSFIELD (1888-1923), short-story writer, and her lover (later, husband) JOHN MIDDLETON MURRY (1889-1957), critic, literary biographer, and editor, lived at the same address at the same time (above Brett); and JOHN MAYNARD KEYNES (see above), the economist, lived on the floor below. Dorothy Brett wrote a life of Lawrence; and it was she who motivated him to become a painter as well as writer.

Side-Trip

16. Just beyond the Academy of Dramatic Art, turn right, into

Chenies Street. FRANCES ('FANNY') BURNEY (1752-1840), novelist, friend of Dr Johnson, author of *Evelina*, lived with her sister Charlotte at *No. 23* around 1812-13.

[16A. A few steps along Chenies Street, you may turn right into *Ridgmount Gardens*. For many years the poet and playwright GEORGE EGERTON (MRS GOLDING BRIGHT) lived at *No. 59*; and at *No. 87* lived JOSEPH HATTON (1841-1907), novelist and dramatist.]

17. Farther along Chenies Street, *North Crescent* opens on your right. The poet ALGERNON CHARLES SWINBURNE (1837-1909), whose lush paganistic poetry scandalized the Victorian world, lived at *No. 12*.

18. *Alfred Place* opens just opposite North Crescent. Turn left into it. THOMAS CAMPBELL (see above), the poet, lodged on this street in 1837.

19. At the end of Alfred Place, turn left, on *Store Street*. MARY WOLLSTONECRAFT (1759-97), one of the first feminists in England, lived here while writing her *Vindication of the Rights of Women* (1792). She became the wife of the philosopher William Godwin, and the mother of Mary Godwin, who became the second wife of the poet Shelley.

20. Store Street leads straight on, across Gower Street, into *Keppel Street*. ANTHONY TROLLOPE (1815-82), one of the major Victorian novelists, was born at *No. 6*; and Charles Dickens's poor father, an unworldly Mr Micawber always harassed by debts, died in a house on this street.

21. Now return to Gower Street, and continue your previous course along it. Soon you will reach *Bedford Square*, on your right. Some more-or-less significant literary figures have lived here; they are listed in the numerical order of their house numbers: A. J. A. SYMONS (1900-41), literary historian and critic, at *No. 17*; HENRY W. MASSINGHAM (1860-1924), editor of the *Nation*, at *No. 21* in his last years; Sir Johnston Forbes-Robertson (1853-1937), the actor, at *No. 22*; BARRY CORNWALL (real name, BRYAN WALLER PROCTOR) (1787-1874), poet, dramatist, literary biographer, friend of Charles Lamb and his group, at *No. 25*—where his daughter, the celebrated moralizing poet ADELAIDE PROCTER (1825-64) was born; HAROLD FREDERIC (1856-98), American-born realistic novelist, at *No. 39* (1887-92); ANTHONY HOPE (HAWKINS) (see above) at *No. 41* (1903-17); Herbert Asquith, the Prime Minister, author of several historical-autobiographical books,

and his wife MARGOT ASQUITH (1864-95), novelist, wit, and auto-biographer, at *No. 44* in the 1920's; Philip Morrell, M.P., and his wife OTTOLINE MORRELL (see above), who played a notable part in the lives of several literary figures, including the novelist D. H. Lawrence and the philosopher Bertrand Russell, at *No. 44* in the second decade of the twentieth century; and JOHN PASSMORE EDWARDS (1823-1911) at *No. 51* around 1900.

> JOHN PASSMORE EDWARDS was one of the most extraordinary of men. Born poor, he made a fortune in the publishing business, and gave most of the fortune away. An early Chartist (seeking liberali-zation of England's labour laws), he lectured on behalf of temper-ance, promoted the shorter working week for labour, organized international conferences for peace, worked for the abolition of capital punishment and of flogging in the army and navy, opposed the Crimean and South African wars, and fought the opium trade (while his country was fighting a war to perpetuate it). With his own money he erected 24 free libraries, and even more free hospitals, founded several art galleries and contributed to the support of many more, erected drinking fountains at many places in London and elsewhere, and placed memorial busts of Hogarth, Lamb, Keats, Ruskin, Dickens, Emerson, and other writers in many public places.

22. Leave Bedford Square at the corner (south-west) diagonally opposite the one where you entered the square. You will be on *Adeline Place* (formerly Caroline Street), where MRS ANNA LAETITIA BARBAULD (1742-1825), poet, editor, and literary biographer, lived in the 1780's. JOHN PHILIP KEMBLE (1757-1823), the famous Shakes-pearean actor, and manager of Drury Lane and Covent Garden Theatres, lived at *No. 12* in the late 1790's.

23. Adeline Place leads into *Great Russell Street*. Turn left on this street. [Shortly after you turn, you will see *Bloomsbury Street* leading off to your left. The novelist and dramatist THEODORE HOOK (1788-1841) was born on this street, at *No. 3*. To the right of Great Russell Street, *Wyan's Court* once led away, but has long since disappeared. LEWIS THEOBALD (1688-1744), poet, critic, scholar, editor of Shakes-peare, lived here. He pointed out so many errors in Alexander Pope's edition of Shakespeare that Pope grew furious, and made him the hero of the satirical poem the *Dunciad*.] The arrangement of house numbers on *Great Russell Street* is somewhat erratic. Some of the numbers mentioned below no longer exist—but they are included for the record. The arrangement that follows is in regular numerical order.

No. 14, W. H. DAVIES (1871-1940), poet who spent his youth as a hobo in Britain and America, became a friend of Bernard Shaw, and has been compared to William Blake, from 1916 to 1922; *No. 17*, GEORGE BORROW (1803-81), novelist and essayist who was also, like Davies, a wanderer, a peddler in his youth, in 1829; *No. 24*, the American novelist and short-story writer NATHANIEL HAWTHORNE (1804-64), on a visit to London in 1857-8; *No. 36*, ARTHUR MACHEN (1863-1947), novelist and literary critic, translator of the *Memoirs* of Casanova, in 1893, though he moved to *No. 98* immediately after his marriage, and there commenced the translation of the *Memoirs*; *No. 38*, HAROLD MONRO (1879-1932), a poet who deserves considerable respect in his own right, but is better known as the founder of the *Poetry Review* (1911), the *Chapbook* (1919), and the Poetry Bookshop (here, 1926-36), all of which had an extraordinary influence on English poetry, from 1911 to 1930; *No. 48*, GEORGE DU MAURIER (1834-96), artist and novelist, grandfather of the novelist Daphne du Maurier, in the early 1860's, though he moved from here in 1863, and stayed till 1866 at *No. 91*; *No. 62*, the Pre-Raphaelite painter EDWARD BURNE-JONES (1833-98) and his wife (who was a sister of the mothers of Rudyard Kipling and Stanley Baldwin), 1861-5.

Houses with the following numbers may not occupy the exact sites of present houses with the same numbers: *No. 100-101*, TOPHAM BEAUCLERK, dear friend of Dr Johnson, and member of the latter's Literary Club, who had an immense library here; *No. 109*, WILLIAM HAZLITT (1778-1830), essayist and critic, and friend of most of the important figures of the Romantic movement, who stayed here with his brother, 1804-7; *No. 119*, the poet PERCY BYSSHE SHELLEY (1792-1822), in 1818.

[23A. You will soon reach the British Museum, on your left. On your right, directly in front of the Museum, is the entrance to *Museum Street*. A few steps down it, at *No. 7*, GEORGE BORROW (see above) lived in 1830. This street crosses *Little Russell Street*, which runs parallel to Great Russell. On this small street, at *No. 18*, W. H. DAVIES (see above) lived in 1914.]

24. The *British Museum* must be visited, of course. Some items in the Museum that should be of particular interest to those who have bought this book ought to be mentioned. Once inside the main door that faces Great Russell Street, turn to the left, and then to the right, past the great Assyrian winged bulls, and walk on into the Egyptian Sculpture Gallery straight ahead of you. In the centre of the aisle you will find the *Rosetta Stone*, with its inscription in three forms of writing that gave the key to the translation of Egyptian hieroglyphics. Halfway down this gallery, turn to the left, and keep going till you

reach the Duveen Gallery, where the *Elgin Marbles* are kept. JOHN KEATS wrote a sonnet about these marbles, and the sight of them inspired him to write what is certainly one of the two or three greatest short poems in English: 'Ode on a Grecian Urn.'

Return (if you can bear to ignore all the treasures about you) to the Entrance Hall where you started out. Go a few steps farther into it, and note the main staircase on your left. Just opposite it is the entrance to the Grenville Library. Pass through this, and on beyond it to the Manuscript Salon and the Bible Room, and (to the left of them) the King's Library. Explore all these galleries. (They occupy the site of the former home of the great actor JOHN PHILIP KEMBLE.) You will find there on public exhibition more items of literary significance than you can possibly imagine.

Among the holograph manuscripts of books exhibited may be mentioned Jane Austen's *Persuasion*, Bishop George Berkeley's *Treatise Concerning the Principles of Human Knowledge*, Elizabeth Barrett Browning's *Sonnets from the Portuguese*, Robert Browning's *The Ring and the Book*, the seventeenth-century Samuel Butler's *Hudibras*, the nineteenth-century Samuel Butler's *Erewhon*, Lewis Carroll's *Alice in Wonderland*, Thomas Chatterton's *Rowley Poems*, Joseph Conrad's *Lord Jim*, George Eliot's *Mill on the Floss*, John Galsworthy's *Forsyte Saga*, Thomas Hardy's *Tess of the D'Urbervilles*, James Joyce's *Finnegan's Wake*, Samuel Pepys's *Diary*, Alexander Pope's translations of Homer, Sir Walter Scott's *Kenilworth*, Bernard Shaw's *St. Joan* (in shorthand, with the names of the actors written in), Lawrence Sterne's *A Sentimental Journey*, Jonathan Swift's *Journal to Stella*, a play by William Makepeace Thackeray, Oscar Wilde's *The Importance of Being Earnest*, and many more.

There are holograph poems by the following: Matthew Arnold, Emily Brontë, Rupert Brooke ('If I should die, think only this of me'), Robert Burns, Lord Byron, Samuel Taylor Coleridge, William Cowper ('John Gilpin's Ride'), Thomas Gray ('Elegy in a Country Churchyard'), A. E. Housman, John Keats ('Hyperion'), Rudyard Kipling ('Recessional'), William Morris, Christina Rossetti, Dante Gabriel Rossetti, Percy Bysshe Shelley ('When the Lamp is Shattered'), Algernon Charles Swinburne ('Atlanta in Calydon'), Alfred Tennyson, William Wordsworth, and many others.

Holograph letters include the following—from Francis Bacon, James Boswell, Thomas Browne, Lord Byron (from Greece, swearing he will never sell Newstead Abbey), the historian William Camden, Thomas Carlyle, Lord Chesterfield (to his son), Samuel Taylor Coleridge (to his patrons the Wedgwoods, of pottery fame), William Congreve, William Cowper (criticizing Dr Johnson's prejudiced criticisms of Milton), Charles Darwin (answering a criticism of his *The Origin of Species*), Daniel Defoe, John Donne (from prison), John Dryden, John Evelyn, Henry Fielding, David Garrick (to Edward Gibbon), Thomas Hobbes, David Hume (about securing a pension for J.-J. Rousseau), Henry James (to Edmund Gosse), Dr Samuel Johnson (to Warren Hastings), John Keats, Charles Lamb (telling about the famous occasion when he dined with William Wordsworth, Samuel Taylor Coleridge, Thomas Moore, and Samuel Rogers), Isaac Newton, Alexander Pope, Sir Walter Raleigh, Samuel Richardson, Robert Louis Stevenson (to Edmund Gosse), Jonathan Swift, Alfred Tennyson, George Vanbrugh, Horace Walpole (to Thomas Chatterton), John Wesley, James McNeill Whistler (to Swinburne), William Wordsworth (on the death of Coleridge), Sir Thomas Wyatt.

And, of course, there are ancient manuscripts by the score—many of them unique copies. Among these are *Beowulf* (unique), *Sir Gawain and the Green Knight* (unique), Layamon's *Brut* (1205), *Ancrene Riwle* (thirteenth century), Thomas Hoccleve's *De Regimine Principium* (with an excellent portrait of Chaucer), John Gower's *Confessio Amantis*, *Piers Plowman*, an early Wyclifite translation of the Bible (owned by John of Gaunt's brother Thomas, Duke of Gloucester, who was murdered by Richard II, who was in turn murdered by Gloucester's nephew Henry IV), the *Anglo-Saxon Chronicle* (unique), the Venerable Bede's *Ecclesiastical History of the British People* (a manuscript contemporary with Bede himself), a grant by the Saxon King Eadred to a nun for '£2 of purest gold' (A.D. 948), the Earl of Essex's death warrant signed by Queen Elizabeth I, several different versions of *Magna Carta*, and so on.

In addition, one can see displayed here many other ancient manuscripts from the civilizations of Greece, Rome, Italy, France, and so on.

25. When you leave the Museum, turn left, on Great Russell Street, and follow it to where it intersects *Southampton Row*. At *No. 7* EDWARD FITZGERALD (1809-83), 'translator' of Omar Khayyam, lived in the early 1830's.

Just ahead you will find the *Holborn (Kingsway) Underground Station*, where you began this tour, and may end it.

Tour 9
Covent Garden

Joseph Addison

Dr John Armstrong

Dr Thomas Arne

Jane Austen

Arnold Bennett

Bishop George Berkeley

Thomas Betterton

William Blake

Barton Booth

James Boswell

Isaac Hawkins Browne

Edmund Burke

Frances ('Fanny') Burney

Samuel Butler

Lord Byron

D'Oyly Carte

Giovanni Casanova

Mrs Susannah Centlivre

George Chapman

Colley Cibber

Mrs Susannah (Arne) Cibber

Theophilus Cibber

Samuel Taylor Coleridge

George Colman The Elder

George Crabbe

Edmund Curll

William Davenant

Thomas Davies

Mrs Mary Delaney

Thomas De Quincey

Charles Dickens

John Dryden

John Evelyn

Henry Fielding

Edward Fitzgerald

Benjamin Franklin

John Galsworthy

Edward Garnett

David Garrick

W. S. Gilbert

William Godwin

Radclyffe Hall

Thomas Hardy

William Hazlitt

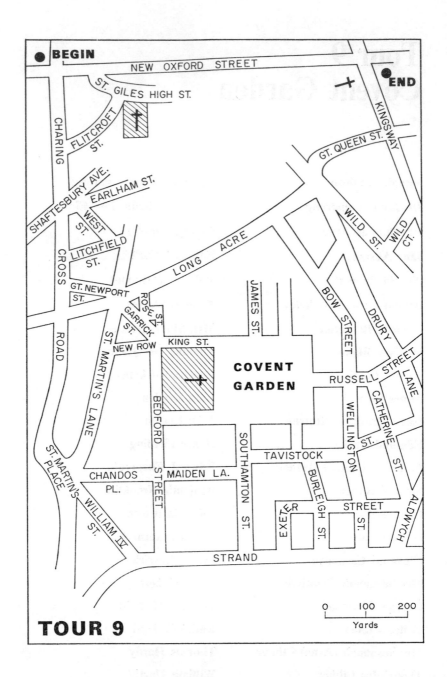

BEGIN

NEW OXFORD STREET

ST. GILES HIGH ST.

CHARING

FLITCROFT ST.

SHAFTESBURY AVE.

EARLHAM ST.

WEST ST.

LITCHFIELD ST.

CROSS

GT. NEWPORT ST.

ROAD

ST. MARTIN'S LANE

ST. MARTIN'S PLACE

WILLIAM IV ST.

ROSE ST.

GARRICK ST.

NEW ROW

KING ST.

BEDFORD STREET

CHANDOS PL.

MAIDEN LA.

LONG ACRE

JAMES ST.

COVENT GARDEN

SOUTHAMTON ST.

STRAND

BOW STREET

RUSSELL

WELLINGTON ST.

TAVISTOCK

BURLEIGH ST.

EXETER

STREET

DRURY

CATHERINE STREET

WELLINGTON ST.

GT. QUEEN ST.

KINGSWAY

WILD ST.

WILD CT.

LANE

ALDWYCH

END

0   100   200

Yards

TOUR 9

W. E. Henley

Edward Herbert

Aaron Hill

A. E. Housman

Mrs Elizabeth Inchbald

Sir Henry Irving

Washington Irving

Douglas Jerrold

Dr Samuel Johnson

Inigo Jones

Thomas Killigrew

Charles Lamb

Sir Roger L'Estrange

Richard Lovelace

Andrew Marvell

Mary Russell Mitford

Lady Mary Wortley Montagu

Hannah More

John Payne

Thomas Love Peacock

Ambrose Philips

Alexander Pope

Beatrix Potter

Matthew Prior

Sir Joshua Reynolds

Nicholas Rowe

Charles Sackville

Sir Charles Sedley

Percy Bysshe Shelley

Richard Brinsley Sheridan

Thomas Sheridan

James Shirley

Sir Richard Steele

Sir John Suckling

Sir Arthur Sullivan

Frank Swinnerton

Alfred Tennyson

Ellen Terry

Francis Thompson

Hester Lynch Thrale

Bishop James Ussher

Voltaire

Edmund Waller

John Wesley

John Wolcot ('Peter Pindar')

William Wycherley

Leave the underground at the *Tottenham Court Road Station.* You may have quite a problem finding your way across, or around, St Giles Circus, and on into St Giles High Street; but, with the help of the map, you will eventually make it. (In the early fifteenth century the public gallows stood in the Circus. In 1417 a special new gallows was raised for the hanging and burning of the Lollard martyr Sir John Oldcastle. He has a certain literary significance because Shakespeare, who never had much regard for the mere facts of history, originally gave the name of Sir John Oldcastle to the character now known as Sir John Falstaff. Shakespeare changed the name to Falstaff only because the Oldcastle descendants threatened a libel suit for ridicule of their ancestor. Evidence of the original name remains, however, in *Henry* IV *Part 1*, where Prince Hal once addresses Falstaff as 'My old lad of the castle.')

1. Leaving St Giles Circus behind, proceed down *St Giles High Street* till you reach, on your right, *St Giles-in-the-Fields Church*. A church has stood here since about 1100; but the present edifice dates from only about 1733. *Baptized* in the preceding or the present church were COLLEY CIBBER (1671-1757), poet, dramatist, actor, theatre manager, Poet Laureate, victim of Pope in the *Dunciad*; Allegra Byron (illegitimate daughter of the poet Byron and Claire Clairmont) in 1818; and the two children of the poet Percy Bysshe Shelley and his wife Harriet Westbrook Shelley, also in 1818. *Buried* here were GEORGE CHAPMAN (1559?-1634), dramatist and translator, whose translation of Homer inspired one of John Keats's finest sonnets; JAMES SHIRLEY (1596-1666), dramatist, who, with his wife, died of shock and exposure caused by the Great Fire (the pair are buried in the same grave); ANDREW MARVELL (1621-78), poet, best remembered for 'To his Coy Mistress'; EDWARD HERBERT, LORD CHERBURY (1583-1684), poet (brother of the much greater poet George Herbert), philosopher, and author of a swashbuckling autobiography that Errol Flynn could have made into a wildly successful film; and SIR ROGER L'ESTRANGE (1616-1704), royalist, journalist, politician, enemy of free speech, prolific pamphleteer (he tried to answer some of Milton's pamphlets), and translator of some early Spanish and Portuguese romances that figure in the history of the English novel. A literary association once removed may be of interest. When *George Villiers, Duke of Buckingham* (1628-87), poet, dramatist, and profligate, was in process of killing the Earl of Shrewsbury in a duel, the Duke's mistress (who happened to be the Earl's wife) stood by, dressed as a page, obligingly holding the Duke's horse: this remarkable lady is buried here. An old wooden pulpit in the left (north) aisle was taken from a church on West Street (see below) where *John Wesley*, founder of the Methodist Church, used the pulpit regularly.

2. When you emerge from the church, turn left on either Denmark or Flitcroft Street, and reach Charing Cross Road. Turn left, and find (at the corner of Phoenix Street a short distance down) the *Phoenix Theatre*, which opened (1930) with the first performance of Noel

Coward's *Private Lives*. Continue down Charing Cross Road till you reach *Cambridge Circus*. Off on the far side of the Circus (to your right) you will see the large *Palace Theatre*. This was built (1890), as the 'Royal English Opera House', by D'OYLY CARTE (1844-1901), the impresario of the Gilbert-and-Sullivan light operas. The theatre was opened with the performance of *Ivanhoe*, an operatic version of Scott's novel, composed by SIR ARTHUR SULLIVAN (1842-1900).

3. Opposite the Palace Theatre, on the lower left-hand side of the Circus, lies the entrance of *West Street*. Walk down it, and find, on your left, the arched doorway (at about *No. 10-11*), which is what remains of a chapel where JOHN WESLEY (1703-91) often preached from 1742 until his death. His brother *Charles Wesley* (famous hymn-writer) and George Whitefield (1714-70) also preached here. At the corner of the next street, on your left, is the *Ambassadors Theatre* (opened 1913). John Galsworthy's *Escape* was first produced here (1926); *Paul Robeson* (in O'Neill's *Emperor Jones*) made his first English appearance here (1925); and the first London appearance of Lennox Robinson's famous and popular *The Whiteheaded Boy* was here (1920). Just across the street from the Ambassadors is the *St Martin's Theatre* (opened 1916). The following plays were first produced here: John Masefield's *Pompey the Great* (1920); John Galsworthy's *The Skin Game* (1920), *Loyalties* (1922), *The Forest* (1924); J. C. Squire's *Berkeley Square* (1926); Noel Coward's *The Queen Was in the Parlour* (1926); and the first London performances of Karel Capek's *R.U.R.* (1922).

4. Little *Litchfield Street* enters West Street from your right at about this point. Somewhere on Litchfield Street THOMAS DE QUINCEY (1785-1859), essayist, critic, and autobiographer, lodged during his early starvation days in London. Mozart, the musician, also lodged on this street.

5. Walk on along West Street (it turns slightly to your left) till you reach the traffic artery of Upper St Martin's Lane. Turn right, and walk a block to *Great Newport Street*. Here, just around the corner to your right, SIR JOSHUA REYNOLDS (1723-92), painter, art theorist, and friend of Dr Johnson, lived at *No. 5* for seven years (1753-60). At *No. 7* lived JOHN WOLCOT ('PETER PINDAR') (1738-1819), the satirist, who got himself imprisoned for his cleverness. (At the lower corner of the juncture of this street with St Martin's Lane, the Wedgwoods, of pottery fame, established a warehouse and showrooms, 1768.)

6. Cross over St Martin's Lane (to your left) into *Long Acre*. Here the first 'street' opening on your right is a dirty little alley called Rose Street. Opposite the entrance of the latter, on the left-hand side of Long Acre, at *No. 137*, JOHN DRYDEN (1631-1700), poet, dramatist, critic, Poet Laureate, lived for many years (1669-87). His house was not pulled down till two centuries later. WILLIAM HAZLITT (1778-1830), the critic, lived at *No. 139* for a while. MATTHEW PRIOR (1664-1721), wit, diplomat, and gracefully sparkling poet, had at least one mistress (wife of a common soldier) living on this street; he spent much time with her, and addressed her as 'Chloe' in many poems. Another mistress of his, Betsy Cox, to whom he addressed his 'Emma' poems, seems also to have lived on this street. The unfortunate Cavalier poet RICHARD LOVELACE (1618-57) is said to have spent part of his unhappy life on this street, living in a cellar.

7. Turn off Long Acre into *Rose Street*. JOHN DRYDEN (see above) was assaulted and severely beaten on this street, the night of 18 December 1679, when he was on his way from Will's Coffee House (see below) to his Long Acre home. His assailants were ruffians hired by the corrupt character and witty poet John Wilmot, Earl of Rochester (1647?-80), who had satirized Dryden in a poem, and had been effectively answered by Dryden in another poem. SAMUEL BUTLER (1663-78), author of the once-famous poem *Hudibras* (a satire on the Puritans) died in poverty in lodgings here. And MRS MARY DELANEY (1700-88), bluestocking, and author of six volumes of letters and auto-biographical gossip, lived on this street after her first marriage. EDMUND CURLL (1675-1747), 'the unspeakable Curll', who was pilloried for publishing obscene books, was living here when he published an unauthorized (perhaps stolen) edition of Alexander Pope's letters.

8. Follow Rose Street across Floral Street, and reach *Garrick Street*. Depending on whether you followed *all* the windings of Rose Street, you will find the famous *Garrick Club* (for dramatists, actors, and other theatre people) either just before you, or a bit to your left, at *No. 15*. Founded in 1831, it moved here from King Street (see below) in 1859. Its membership has included virtually all significant (and many insignificant) theatre people in England since its founding.

9. Turn right, on Garrick Street, and reach *St Martin's Lane* again. AMBROSE PHILIPS (1675?-1749), essayist, critic, poet, judge, friend of Steele, and enemy of Pope, lived (1720-5) just across St Martin's Lane,

lower corner, as you emerge from Garrick Street. (A few steps to your left, at *Nos. 60-2*, the Chippendales, makers of fine furniture, had their establishment.) At *Nos. 74-5* stood (1692-1760) Old Slaughter's Coffee House, frequented by *Boswell*, the artist *Hogarth*, and the painter (and friend of Keats) *Benjamin Haydon*.

[9A. The first intersecting street to your left, as you descend St Martin's Lane, is *New Row*. Here DR JOHNSON, when he first came to London (1737) dined regularly at the 'Pine Apple'. He told Boswell: 'I dined very well for eightpence, with very good company ... several of them had travelled; they expected to meet every day, but did not know one another's names. It used to cost the rest a shilling, for they drank wine; but I had a cut of meat for sixpence, and bread for a penny, at that I was quite well served, nay, better than the rest, for they gave the waiter nothing.']

Just opposite the entrance of New Row, on St Martin's Lane, stands the *New Theatre*, which opened in March 1903. Dion Boucicault was a manager, and John Gielgud produced plays here; it was the home of the Old Vic Theatre Company (with Laurence Olivier) from 1944 to 1950. This theatre saw the first public London productions of Somerset Maugham's *Caroline* (1916), James Barrie's *The Old Lady Shows Her Medals* (1917), A. A. Milne's *Mr Pim Passes By* (1920), Noel Coward's first play *I'll Leave It to You* (1920), Bernard Shaw's *Saint Joan* (1924), Aldous Huxley's *The Gioconda Smile* (1948), and T. S. Eliot's *The Cocktail Party* (1950). (One block beyond this theatre, *Cecil Court* intersects from the right. At *No. 7* on this little street was published the 'aesthetic' magazine *The Dome*, in the late 1890's.) In the second block beyond the New Theatre, and also on your right, stands the *Duke of York's Theatre* (opened 1892). Many of the plays of J. M. Barrie were first produced here: *Peter Pan* (1904), *Pantaloon* and *Alice-Sit-by-the-Fire* (both in 1905), *What Every Woman Knows* (1908), *Old Friends* and *The Twelve-Pound Look* (both in 1910), and *Rosalind* (1912). Other plays first produced here were John Galsworthy's *Justice* (1910) and Bernard Shaw's *Misalliance* (1910).

SIR JOHN SUCKLING (1609-42), Cavalier poet, lived somewhere on St Martin's Lane in the last years of his life. Before the First World War, there used to assemble regularly in *St George's Restaurant*, on this street, the following poets: *Edward Thomas* (killed in the war), *Ralph Hodgson, W. H. Davies, Walter de la Mare, John Freeman, Gordon Bottomley, Rupert Brooke*, and the American *Robert Frost*. At Talbot House, also on this street, lived the novelist RADCLYFFE HALL, author of the delicate and beautiful but (in its day) sexually sensational novel, *The Well of Loneliness*.

10. St Martin's Lane debouches into *St Martin's Place*, with its statue of Edith Cavell (nurse shot as a spy by the Germans in the First World War). Turn right, at this place, and see the National Portrait Gallery that more-or-less faces Nurse Cavell. You *must not* miss this gallery; it has many fine portraits of British writers—often done by men closely associated with the writers in various groups or movements. Beyond the gallery stands a statue of SIR HENRY IRVING (1838-1905), the great Shakespearean actor associated so long with Ellen Terry at the Lyceum Theatre. The statue occupies approximately the site of Dickens's 'Old Curiosity Shop'. At *No. 8* THOMAS HARDY (1840-1928), poet and novelist, worked with an architectural firm when he first came to London. On your right, well beyond the National Gallery, you will see the *Garrick Theatre* (opened 1889, with Arthur Wing Pinero's *The Profligate*). W. S. Gilbert (of Gilbert-and-Sullivan fame) financed the building of this theatre; and his own *The Fairies' Dilemma* was produced here (1904). Pinero's *Lady Bountiful* (1891) and *Iris* (1901) were first produced here—as were Henry Arthur Jones's *Whitewashing Julia* (1903) and *The Chevalier* (1904); and also J. M. Barrie's *The Wedding Guest* (1900). Just beyond the theatre was Kegan Paul's publishing house—which first issued A. E. HOUSMAN'S *A Shropshire Lad* (1896), at the author's own expense.

11. Return to the foot of St Martin's Lane, and turn left into William IV Street—which branches into a Y. (As this is being written, vast commercial 'improvements' are being considered for this area, and may have been perpetrated by the time you read this.) Take the left-hand arm of the Y, into Chandos Place, and on into *Maiden Lane*. ANDREW MARVELL (see above) lived here, at *No. 9*, in the last year of his life; and VOLTAIRE (1694-1778) lodged at the White Perruke, somewhere to your right on this street, in 1727, and was here visited by *Congreve, Pope*, and the poet *Edward Young*. The great artist *J. M. W. Turner* (1775-1851) was born at *No. 21* (on your right, eight doors beyond Bedford Street), where his father was a barber. In the basement of *No. 21* was the Cider Cellar Tavern, which was frequented by the novelist-Prime Minister *Benjamin Disraeli* and the novelist *William Makepeace Thackeray*, who, in *Pendennis*, calls it the 'Back Kitchen'. It might be mentioned also that, in a house somewhere on this street, young *James Boswell* records that he 'first experienced the melting and transporting rites of love'—with a lady of the town.

12. You will soon reach *Southampton Street*. Turn right. At *No. 11* (fourth door on the left-hand side) lived *Thomas Linley*, the musical composer for Drury Lane Theatre. One of his beautiful daughters,

Elizabeth, a singer, became the wife of the dramatist Richard Brinsley Sheridan—who fought several duels over her, and eventually eloped with her. These adventures formed a basis for some of the plot of Sheridan's great comedy *The Rivals*.

13. When you reach the Strand, turn left, and (after three blocks) left again, into *Wellington Street*. Here you will immediately notice (if it is still standing when you read this) the *Lyceum Theatre*. Here SIR HENRY IRVING (see above) was actor-manager from 1878 till his death in 1905. During all this time his leading lady was ELLEN TERRY (1848-1929), the great actress who was a friend and correspondent of George Bernard Shaw. On the same side of the street, at *No. 11*, CHARLES DICKENS, owner and editor, published his magazine *All the Year Round* (1859-70). The magazine published serially the editor's *A Tale of Two Cities* and *The Uncommercial Traveller*. Before he started this magazine, Dickens had published another, *Household Words* (1850-9), at *No. 16* on this street. This magazine published Dickens's *Hard Times* serially. The first street-crossing you reach is Exeter Street. Wellington Street covers the site here of the house of 'Mrs Norris, a stay-maker', with whom DR SAMUEL JOHNSON (1709-84) lodged when he first came to London, in 1737. Here he finished his poem *London*, and wrote part of his drama *Irene*.

14. Continue along Wellington Street for one more block, and then turn left, into Tavistock Street. You will soon reach *Southampton Street* again. On this street, looking right down Tavistock Street, is *No. 27*, which was the home of the greatest actor of the eighteenth century, DAVID GARRICK (1717-79) from the year of his marriage (1749) to 1772. Garrick, who was also a dramatist, was a friend of Dr Johnson and a member of the latter's Literary Club. Turn right, on *Southampton Street*. At *No. 17* (the third door on your right) was born W. S. GILBERT (1836-1911), poet and playwright, librettist of the Savoy light operas.

15. Continue along Southampton Street till you reach Covent Garden. We shall explore it in more detail presently; but just now you should turn to the left until you reach the church that you will see in that direction, and then turn and walk along in front of the columned portico of the church. (The film versions of both *Pygmalion*, by George Bernard Shaw, and *My Fair Lady*, the musical derived from the play, used this church portico for the first scene, in which Professor Higgins first encounters Eliza Doolittle.)

Immediately beyond the church, turn left on *King Street*. NICHOLAS

147

ROWE (1674-1718), dramatist and Poet Laureate, 'last of the Shakespeareans', died in lodgings on this street. THOMAS ARNE (1710-78), who composed music for Milton's *Comus*, set many of Shakespeare's songs to music, composed operas, and was official musician for the Drury Lane Theatre, and his sister Susannah, who became MRS THEOPHILUS CIBBER (1714-66), famous actress and singer, were born on this street, at *No. 31*, well along on your right. SAMUEL TAYLOR COLERIDGE (1772-1834) lived at *No. 10*, on your left, during 1801-2. The Garrick Club was established (1831) at *No. 35*, almost opposite the Coleridge place; and DAVID GARRICK (see above) himself lodged briefly at *No. 27* in 1748. Almost opposite the Garrick place, and in the last house on your left (corner of King and Bedford Streets) the Communist Party of Great Britain had its headquarters from 1920 to the present writing.

16. Turn left on Bedford Street, and then left again into the foregarden of *St Paul's Church, Covent Garden*. Designed by INIGO JONES (1573-1652), architect who figures also in the history of drama, this church was consecrated in 1638. It burned down in 1795, and the present church was built on the same spot according to Jones's original designs. It has long been attended by the theatrical people of the neighbourhood; and many are buried here. LADY MARY WORTLEY MONTAGU (1689-1762), letter-writer, wit, and bluestocking, was baptized here, as was W. S. GILBERT (see above). Among those buried here are SAMUEL BUTLER (see above), author of *Hudibras* (in the churchyard, 'in the north part next to the church at the east end. His feet touch the wall. His grave is 2 yards distant from the pilaster of the dore'.); WILLIAM WYCHERLEY (1640?-1716), the great realistic dramatist of the Restoration period (in the crypt); JOHN WOLCOT ('PETER PINDAR') (see above), next to Butler; MRS SUSANNAH CENTLIVRE (1667?-1723), actress and author of many highly successful plays; THOMAS DAVIES (1712?-85), bookseller, publisher, and actor, who first introduced Boswell to Dr Johnson; DR THOMAS ARNE (see above), musical composer; *Thomas Linley* (see above), musician and father-in-law of Sheridan; *Grinling Gibbons* (1648-1721), the woodcarver; the parents of the painter *J. M. W. Turner*, with an inscription by their son. The ashes of ELLEN TERRY (see above), actress, repose in a silver urn in a dark cylindrical case high up against the wall near the altar, on your right as you enter the church. BISHOP JAMES USSHER (1581-1656), the biblical scholar whose concepts of world chronology dominated thought even into the late nineteenth century, preached here. Esther, sister of FRANCES ('FANNY') BURNEY (1752-

1840), the novelist, married her cousin here in 1770, and Fanny was in attendance.

17. Return to *Bedford Street* and continue down it. At the near corner, where Bedford Court now enters from the right, THOMAS SHERIDAN (1719-88), elocutionist, friend of Dr Johnson and later estranged from him, and father of the dramatist Richard Brinsley Sheridan, had a house that looked straight down Henrietta Street, to your left. A visitor to Sheridan described what he saw from the front window one day when Dr Johnson was expected for dinner: 'I perceived him at a good distance, walking along Henrietta Street with a peculiar solemnity of deportment, and an awkward sort of measured step. At that time the broad flagging at each side of the street was not universally adopted, and stone posts were in fashion, to prevent the annoyance of carriages. Upon every post, as he passed along, I could observe, he deliberately laid his hand; but missing one of them, when he had got at some distance he seemed suddenly to recollect himself, and immediately returning back, carefully performed the accustomed ceremony, and resumed his former course, not omitting one till he gained the crossing.' On the upper corner (to your left) of Bedford and Henrietta Streets once stood a tavern called 'The Castle'. Here RICHARD BRINSLEY SHERIDAN (1751-1816), dramatist, theatre owner, and politician, had his third duel with one Captain Matthews over some remark the latter had made about Miss Elizabeth Linley (see above). (The duel had commenced in Hyde Park, but, because of the crowd that gathered, adjourned to a tavern at Hyde Park Corner—and then, for the same reason, to the Castle. Sheridan disarmed Matthews.)

Bedford Street has long been a street of publishers. At *No. 21* (in front of the church) W. E. HENLEY (1849-1903), poet, critic, and editor, had offices, as editor of the *National Review*, in the 1890's. Here also Heinemann published many novels by JOHN GALSWORTHY (1867-1933). At *No. 16*, just beyond Bedford Court, Macmillan published *Alice in Wonderland* (1865); and at *No. 15* Warne published the Peter Rabbit stories of BEATRIX POTTER (1866-1943). The novelist FRANK SWINNERTON (b. 1884) was long an editor of Dent and Company, at *No. 29*.

18. Turn left, into *Henrietta Street*. At *No. 22* (second door on your left) the American WASHINGTON IRVING (1783-1859) paid an extensive visit to a friend in 1824. Farther along this side of the street, on the corner with Covent Garden, stood Tom King's Coffee House—one of the most celebrated disorderly houses of eighteenth-century London.

It figures in novels by Fielding and Smollett, and was pictured by Hogarth. On the right-hand side of the street, at *No. 11*, Chapman and Hall issued many of the novels of CHARLES DICKENS. At *No. 10* the novelist JANE AUSTEN (1775-1817) visited her brother, then living here, for some months in 1813. At *No. 9 Grant Richards* established a publishing house that issued many of the 'new' writers just before and after 1900. At *No. 8* lived the actress Frances Maria Kelly, whom CHARLES LAMB (1775-1834), the essayist, loved, and to whom he proposed by letter in 1819—only to be refused by letter the same day. *No. 3* was the address of the publishers Duckworth and Company, whose most famous reader was EDWARD GARNETT (1867-1937), discoverer and encourager of many writers, including John Galsworthy, whose second and third novels were published here, and also D. H. Lawrence. On Henrietta Street were the home and shop of John Partridge (1644-1715), the astrologer and almanac maker, whose fearless predictions Swift ridiculed in the *Bickerstaff Papers*. HANNAH MORE (1745-1833), novelist, playwright, bluestocking, philanthropist, lived on this street in 1777.

19. Beyond Southampton Street, and facing into Covent Garden, once stood a row of houses called *Tavistock Row*. Here lived the satirist JOHN WOLCOT ('PETER PINDAR') (see above), three doors beyond Southampton Street; and WILLIAM GODWIN (1756-1836), novelist and philosopher, father-in-law of the poet Shelley, in the late 1780's and early 1790's.

20. The other two sides of Covent Garden (besides the one next to the church and the one next to Henrietta Street and the old Tavistock Row) were once fronted by a columned cloister called the Piazza, built by the architect and dramatist INIGO JONES (see above) in 1633-4. Jones's work has disappeared, but has been replaced (at the present writing) by a heavy imitation thereof. The cloister ran in front of residences that were once highly fashionable. On the north side of Covent Garden (the side at right angles to the columned portico of the church), James Street enters from the left. In the third house beyond James Street THOMAS KILLIGREW (1612-83), dramatist and theatre manager, lived from 1636 to 1640, and in 1661-2. In the next (fourth) house beyond James Street lived LADY MARY WORTLEY MONTAGU (see above). CHARLES MACKLIN (1697?-1797), the actor and dramatist, lived (1753-5) in the next (fifth) house; and *William Hogarth* (1697-1764), the artist, lived for many years in the next (sixth, and last) house. In the nineteenth century the Tavistock Hotel replaced most of the residences just mentioned; and Mart Street (1932) swept some

of them away. (A supper club in the hotel was frequented by Colonel and Clive Newcome, of Thackeray's novel.)

At the extreme end of this north side of the Garden a passageway led, for many years, to the Covent Garden Theatre. Just this side of the passageway stood, in the eighteenth century, the *Great Piazza Hotel*. Here, on the evening of 6 April 1763, young JAMES BOSWELL (1740-95) and two friends 'had some negus and solaced our existence', and here Boswell repaired again on 5 June after a love-bout made unsuccessful by his temporary impotence. The dramatist RICHARD BRINSLEY SHERIDAN (see above) came here for a glass of wine after watching his Drury Lane Theatre burn to the ground. 'A man may surely be allowed,' he said, 'to take a glass of wine at his own fireside.' Later on, the place became the *Piazza Hotel*, where CHARLES DICKENS stayed in 1844 and 1846, and had Steerforth (in *David Copperfield*) visit. EDWARD FITZGERALD (1809-83), translator of Omar Khayyam, stayed here in 1844.

Turn the corner, and walk along the east side of Covent Garden— that is, the side facing towards the church. In the corner here stood the *Shakespeare's Head Tavern*, where JAMES BOSWELL once took two girls of the street, and 'solaced my existence with them, one after the other, according to their seniority'. The house had been previously the residence of Bubb Dodington (1691-1762), wit, eccentric, and friend of writers. John Rich (1682-1761), actor, manager of the Lincoln's Inn Fields Theatre, and builder of the first Covent Garden Theatre (1732), lived in a house to the rear of the Shakespeare's Head for seventeen years (1743-60); and GEORGE COLMAN THE ELDER (1732-94), dramatist, essayist, poet, and manager of theatres, lived briefly in the same house, 1772-4.

Next door to the Shakespeare's Head stood the famous *Bedford Coffee House*. Here many who had been to the plays at the Covent Garden and Drury Lane Theatres nearby, or had taken part in the plays, loved to congregate after performances. Some of these patrons of the Bedford were the actor-dramatists *David Garrick* and *Samuel Foote*, the novelist-dramatists *Henry Fielding* and *Oliver Goldsmith*, the dramatists *Richard Brinsley Sheridan* and *Arthur Murphy*, the actors *Macklin* and *James Quin*, the satirist of actors *Charles Churchill*, the poets *Pope* and *William Collins*, the novelist and gossip *Horace Walpole*.

GEORGE BERKELEY (1695-1753), the philosopher, lived a door or two from the Bedford in 1726.

Farther down this (eastern) side of the Garden, Russell Street enters from your left—directly opposite the portico of the church. Cross over Russell Street, and continue along this side of the Garden. At your left, on the corner of Russell Street, stood the old *Hummums Hotel*, facing the Garden. *Dr Johnson* and *Boswell* patronized it; JOHN WOLCOT ('PETER PINDAR') (see above) frequented it; GEORGE CRABBE (1754-1823), the realistic poet, lived here when he came to town in his more prosperous days; ALFRED TENNYSON (1809-92) stayed here on a London visit, 1844.

EDMUND BURKE (1729-97), the statesman-philosopher, records (in a letter to the famous agriculturist Arthur Young) that, in 1771, he sold, in the Covent Garden produce market, carrots that he had grown in his own garden, and that brought him £14. This entire neighbourhood must be haunted by the ghost of the Roman Catholic poet FRANCIS THOMPSON (1859-1907), author of 'The Hound of Heaven', who slept many nights in alleys and doorways about Covent Garden, in the church portal, in the theatre porch, in boxes and crates in the Garden, during the time when he was a virtual beggar and an opium addict, and before he was discovered and rescued by Wilfrid Meynell. Sometimes he sold matches to theatre-goers, or held their horses.

Covent Garden and its Piazza figured in much literature of the seventeenth and eighteenth centuries—in Dryden, Shadwell, Wycherley, Otway, Fielding, Walpole, and others. Pickpockets and thugs thronged about it; riots and other disturbances seem to have been commonplace; and many of its taverns, respectable enough in daylight, turned into little more than bawdy houses after dark.

21. Turn back, and enter Russell Street. Two doors from the corner house, on your right, stood *Button's Coffee House*, established in 1712, where JOSEPH ADDISON (1672-1719), poet, essayist, and dramatist, presided over literary gatherings, and 'gave his little senate laws' (as the envious Alexander Pope sneered). Among this 'little senate' were SIR RICHARD STEELE (1672-1729), essayist and dramatist; AMBROSE ('NAMBY PAMBY') PHILIPS (1675?-1749), poet and essayist; and COLLEY CIBBER (1671-1757), actor and dramatist. *Alexander Pope*, with his friends *Jonathan Swift*, *John Gay*, and *Dr John Arbuthnot*, likewise frequented the place at times—until Pope quarrelled with both Addison and Philips. (Philips hung up a rod with which he promised to chastise Pope if that venomous little satirist ever again showed up at Button's.) Later on, the building that housed Button's became a private residence, where MRS ELIZABETH INCHBALD (1753-1821), actress, novelist, dramatist, and lovable woman, lived for many years, after moving there in 1787.

Directly across the street from Button's was *Tom's Coffee House* (*No. 17*), established in 1700. It was mentioned in the *Tatler*, and was frequented by *David Garrick, Colley Cibber, Dr Johnson, Oliver Goldsmith,* the dramatists *Arthur Murphy* and *George Colman the Elder,* and the novelists *Henry Fielding* and *Tobias Smollett.* The Coffee House was above the ground floor, which was inhabited by the bookseller T. Lewis, who, from here, issued Pope's epoch-making *Essay on Criticism* (1711).

No. 8 (the house was still standing in the late 1960's) was the bookshop of THOMAS DAVIES (see above), where *James Boswell* and *Dr Samuel Johnson* first met, in a celebrated encounter.

Farther along the street, on the left-hand corner with Bow Street, stood the most famous coffee house of them all, at *No. 21* (sometimes called *No. 1 Bow Street*). This was *Will's Coffee House,* established in the latter part of the seventeenth century. JOHN DRYDEN (see above) presided here, even as *Addison* later presided at Button's, but, apparently, over a more varied audience—not merely literary men, but also politicians, noblemen, clergymen, and scholars. WILLIAM WYCHERLEY (see above), the dramatist, came here, and introduced the young ALEXANDER POPE (1688-1744). *Steele,* in the first number of the *Tatler,* announced that he would write articles about poetry from Will's Coffee House (and he mentions the place in over 60 numbers thereafter); and *Addison,* in the first number of the *Spectator,* wrote: 'Sometimes I am seen thrusting my head into a round of politicians at Will's.' CHARLES LAMB (see above), lived with his sister *Mary* at this same No. 20-21 from 1817 to 1823, and here wrote the earlier *Essays of Elia.* The Lambs had 'literary evenings' on Wednesdays— and since they knew everybody of literary importance in London at that time, almost everybody of literary importance in London at that time must have walked this street. At *No. 19* was the bookshop at which *Lamb* purchased his copy of Beaumont and Fletcher that he gossips about in 'Old China'.

JOHN EVELYN (1620-1706), the diarist, lodged on this street, at *No. 17,* in 1659; THOMAS BETTERTON (1635-1710), greatest Shakespearean actor of his time, manager of various Restoration theatres, opener of the original Haymarket Theatre, and dramatist, lived on this street, and died here. Joseph Taylor (1586-1652), actor, one of the original performers of several of Shakespeare's plays (he is said to have been the original Iago), and of plays by Beaumont and Fletcher, as well as being an associate of Heminge and Condell (actors and editors of Shakespeare's First Folio) lived on this short street, 1634-41. The poet DR JOHN ARMSTRONG (1709?-79) died here. He was a friend of James Thomson, David Hume, and Tobias Smollett, and author of a long and much-praised blank verse didactic poem called *The Art of*

Preserving Health (1744)—as well as what was then considered a scandalous poem: *The Oeconomy of Love* (1736).

22. Turn right, off Russell Street, into *Wellington Street* again. COLLEY CIBBER (see above) lived (1721-40) on the right-hand side, as you walk down from Russell Street, and three doors up from Tavistock Street; here he wrote his autobiography, *Apology for His Own Life*. BARTON BOOTH (1681-1733), Shakespearean actor and theatre manager, associate of Thomas Betterton (see above) lived and died at the same place.

23. Turn left at *Tavistock Street*. The first short block you traverse was formerly known as York Street, and has been rebuilt. Here, in a room at the back of the place since occupied by *No. 36*, THOMAS DE QUINCEY (1785-1859) wrote his *Confessions of an English Opium-Eater*. At *No. 38* THOMAS LOVE PEACOCK (1785-1856), novelist and poet, lived in 1819. HENRY MAYHEW (1812-87), dramatist, journalist, one of the founders of *Punch*, humanitarian sociological writer, lived and died at *No. 8*.

[23A. The continuation of Tavistock Street across Catherine Street was, until the end of the nineteenth century, a narrow pedestrian way called *Russell Court*—since widened into the present street. The Star Tavern stood in Russell Court in the eighteenth century; and here the adventurer and memoirist GIOVANNI CASANOVA (1723-98) was introduced, by the tavern keeper, to various girls as prospective bedmates —but the Continental connoisseur found them all unsatisfactory in appearance or manner, and refused them all.]

24. Turn left, into *Catherine Street*. After a few steps you will be passing in front of the famous *Drury Lane Theatre*, officially the 'Theatre Royal'. After the Restoration, Charles II issued a kind of dual monopoly to his friends WILLIAM DAVENANT (1606-68) and THOMAS KILLIGREW (1612-83)—both of them dramatists and directors—for all professional theatrical productions in London. Killigrew began constructing the Theatre Royal in 1661, and opened it in 1663 —with Beaumont and Fletcher's *The Humourous Lieutenant*. Nell Gwynn is supposed to have sold oranges in this theatre before she became the mistress of Charles II. At that time, the main entrance of the theatre was on the opposite side, at the end of a passage opening into Drury Lane (hence its name). This theatre burned down in 1672; and a new theatre, designed by Sir Christopher Wren, replaced it in 1674, with JOHN DRYDEN (see above) as chief playwright supporting

it. AARON HILL (1685-1750), poet and dramatist, was manager briefly in 1709. COLLEY CIBBER (see above), who became Poet Laureate and was satirized (most unjustly) by Pope in the *Dunciad* (Cibber was made King of Dunces), was manager from 1710 to 1740. SIR RICHARD STEELE (see above), dramatist and essayist, was at one time one of the lessors; and DAVID GARRICK (see above), great actor, dramatist, and friend of Dr Johnson, was manager from 1747 to 1775. RICHARD BRINSLEY SHERIDAN (see above), dramatist and politician, was manager from 1776 to 1788, and part owner till 1809.

Later on, under the management of J. B. Kemble (of the great acting family), the theatre was virtually rebuilt in 1794; but it burned down in 1809. It was rebuilt; and the fourth (and present) theatre was opened, with Shakespeare's *Hamlet* and a prologue by Lord Byron, in 1812. Among the famous actors and actresses, besides Garrick himself, who have appeared at the Drury Lane are *Charles Kemble, Edmund Kean, Charles Macready, Anne Bracegirdle, Mrs Oldfield,* and *Mrs Siddons.*

Adjoining the theatre, at the corner of Catherine and Russell Streets, the Rose Tavern once stood. It figures in the diary of Samuel Pepys, in plays by Thomas Shadwell and George Farquhar, in songs by Tom D'Urfey, in John Gay's poem 'Molly Magg of the Rose', in the *Tatler* and the *Spectator*, in Boswell's *Journal*, and in a print by William Hogarth. *Edward Gibbon,* the historian, records having dined here with his father and the playwright and poet *David Mallet* in 1763. The place was pulled down in 1776.

25. Turn left on Russell Street, and then right, on *Bow Street*. On the left-hand (west) side, in the next house to the corner, lived for a while EDMUND CURLL (see above).

What was the fourth house from Russell Street (still on the left-hand, or western, side of Bow Street) was the residence of HENRY FIELDING (1707-54), one of England's greatest novelists. He was a police magistrate, and held court in the lower front room of this house, 1749-54. What was the sixth house from Russell Street (still on the left-hand side of Bow Street) was the one where the actor-manager-dramatist CHARLES MACKLIN (see above) and DAVID GARRICK (see above) took turns living with the beautiful actress Peg Woffington, with whom both were in love, and who, apparently, cared for both men—a sensible, if not strictly moral, arrangement, much to be preferred to duelling and murder. Beyond this house, and where the present columned theatre stands, was the house of WILLIAM WYCHERLEY (see above), who set the style in witty, outspoken prose comedy in the Restoration period. He died in this house—two weeks after he (a man of seventy-five) had married a young girl to prevent a hated nephew from inheriting his fortune.

On the same side of the street you will see the lofty Greek portico of the *Covent Garden Theatre*. This is the fourth theatre building that has occupied approximately this site. The first building (which was much farther back from the street) was opened in 1732 by John Rich, with Congreve's *The Way of the World*. This building was later so enlarged and modified that it became a new theatre, which opened in 1792. This building burned down in 1808, and was replaced in 1809. This third building burned in 1856, and was replaced by the present building in 1858. Actors and actresses associated with this theatre have been *James Quin* (1693-1766), *John Kemble* (1757-1823), *Peg Woffington* (1714?-60), *Mrs Susannah Cibber* (1714-66), and *Mrs Sarah Siddons* (1755-1831), who made her farewell to the stage here.

Right across the street from the Wycherley house stood the *Cock Tavern*. Wycherley's wife was so jealous that she allowed him to visit no tavern but this, and then insisted that he keep open the windows fronting her house opposite—so that she could maintain a constant check on his behaviour. In this tavern, one night in 1663, SIR CHARLES SEDLEY (1639-1701), dramatist and author of many witty and salacious poems and songs, was drinking with Sir Thomas Ogle and CHARLES SACKVILLE (later, EARL OF DORSET) (1638-1706), another witty, satirical, and salacious poet and courtier. The three became superbly drunk, went out on the balcony of the tavern, removed their clothes, and proceeded to harangue the assembled citizens below, accompanying their lecture with many indecent gestures and actions, and a wealth of blasphemy. The crowd mobbed them, and they were barely rescued by the police. They were fined heavily—but Charles II, amused by the episode, and himself no model of propriety, paid their fines. The musician DR THOMAS ARNE (see above) lived on this side of the street, at *No. 33*, in 1778; and the sculptor *Grinling Gibbons* (1648-1721) lived at *No. 15* during the last 33 years of his life.

(Just beyond the theatre, *Broad Court* opens on your right. At or near the corner with Bow Street, and on the upper (north) side, stood the *Wrekin Tavern*, a favourite resort of eighteenth-century devotees of the theatre. Here DOUGLAS JERROLD (1803-57), dramatist, novelist, humorous writer, and WILLIAM GODWIN (see above) met regularly as members of the same club. As a boy, Jerrold lived with his father along this same street.)

26. Continue along Bow Street till you reach *Long Acre* once again. On this street, exactly opposite the end of Bow Street, once stood *St Martin's Hall*, which later became the *Queen's Theatre*, which later

was converted into a publishing house. In 1858 Dickens gave his first series of paid readings in St Martin's Hall; and in 1867 SIR HENRY IRVING (see above) and ELLEN TERRY (see above) acted together for the first time, in the Queen's Theatre.

27. Turn right, on Long Acre, and follow it on across, and past, Drury Lane. Here, turn sharp right, down Wild Street. After one block, turn left, into *Wild Court*. Here, at *No. 12*, lived the actor THEOPHILUS CIBBER (1703-58), son of COLLEY CIBBER (see above), with his wife, the singer and actress SUSANNAH ARNE CIBBER (see above), during the short time that the two lived together. In a printing office, about midway along the right-hand side of the street, BENJAMIN FRANKLIN (1706-90), the American philosopher and diplomat, worked as a journeyman printer, 1723-6.

28. Retrace your steps to the top of Wild Street, and turn right, into *Great Queen Street*. Just to your right, where the huge Freemasons' Hall was erected, lived (1777-82) RICHARD BRINSLEY SHERIDAN (see above) while working on *The School for Scandal*. JAMES BOSWELL wrote much of his *Life of Johnson* in a house that also stood on the site of the Freemasons' Hall. Just opposite this place, at *No. 31*, WILLIAM BLAKE (1757-1827), artist and poet, worked for three years as an engraver's apprentice. SIR JOSHUA REYNOLDS (1732-92), the great painter, and friend of Dr Johnson, also served an apprenticeship on this street. DR THOMAS ARNE (see above), the musician and composer, lived at *No. 66* in 1748; MARY RUSSELL MITFORD (1787-1855), novelist and dramatist, lived briefly at *No. 50* during the 1820's; and at *No. 25* was born JOHN PAYNE (1842-1916), poet, scholar, Pre-Raphaelite, and translator of Villon, Omar, Hafiz, Heine, etc. Near the far end of the street, on the right, at a spot later occupied by a Methodist mission, lived (1753-8) the poet and writer of light verse ISAAC HAWKINS BROWNE (1706-60). SIR CHARLES SEDLEY (see above) had a house on this street; and Dr Johnson's friend HESTER LYNCH SALUSBURY (1741-1821), who became MRS THRALE, lived somewhere on this street when she was a child (1748).

On the left-hand side of the street, just where Newton Street enters, stood a theatre (1882-1959) that enjoyed a multitude of names during its career. It gave the English public première of Ibsen's *A Doll's House* (1889); of Synge's *Playboy of the Western World* (1907), with the visiting Abbey Players; and of various plays by Arnold Bennett and Eden Phillpotts. It even attempted a production of Thomas Hardy's unproduceable *The Dynasts* (1913).

29. At the end of Great Queen Street, turn left, on *Kingsway*. Follow this until you see, on your left (second block), a church (built 1910). It stands on the site of the house where Mary Lamb, sister of CHARLES LAMB (see above), stabbed their mother to death in a fit of insanity (1796).

Just beyond the church, you will find the *Holborn (Kingsway) Underground Station*, where this tour ends.... Or you may wish to undertake, from here, *Tour No. 7* or *Tour No. 8*.

Tour 10
St James's

Joseph Addison

Mark Akenside

John Arbuthnot

Herbert Asquith

Margot Tennant Asquith

Gertrude Atherton

Francis Bacon

Aubrey Beardsley

James Beattie

Mrs Annie Besant

Arnold Bennett

Richard Bentley

Bishop George Berkeley

William Blake

George Borrow

James Boswell

John Buchan

Eustace Budgell

Edmund Burke

Lord Byron

Thomas Campbell

Edward Carpenter

Mrs Susannah Centlivre

Lord Chesterfield

George Colman The Elder

George Colman The Younger

William Congreve

James Fenimore Cooper

Charles Cotton

George Crabbe

Olive Custance

Sir John Davies

Mrs Mary Delaney

Charles Dickens

Benjamin Disraeli

James Dodsley

Robert Dodsley

Lord Alfred Douglas

Thomas D'Urfey

George Eliot

George Farquhar

Henry Fielding

Samuel Foote

Sir Philip Francis

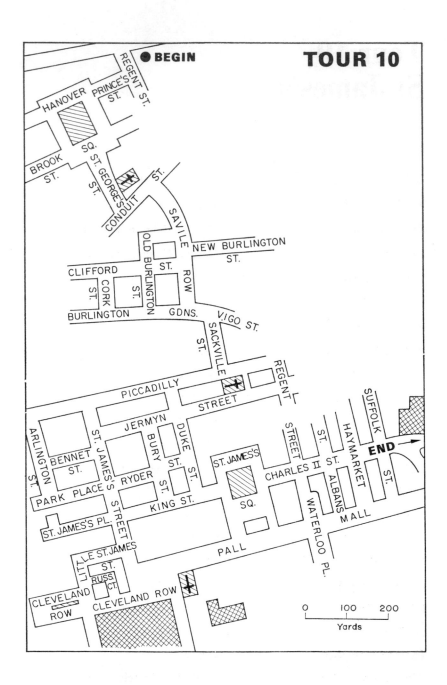

BEGIN

TOUR 10

REGENT ST.

PRINCE'S ST.

HANOVER

SQ.

ST. GEORGE'S ST.

BROOK ST.

CONDUIT ST.

SAVILE ROW

ST.

NEW BURLINGTON ST.

OLD BURLINGTON ST.

CLIFFORD ST.

CORK ST.

BURLINGTON GDNS.

VIGO ST.

SACKVILLE ST.

PICCADILLY STREET

REGENT STREET

JERMYN

ARLINGTON ST.

BENNET ST.

ST. JAMES'S STREET

BURY ST.

DUKE ST.

RYDER ST.

ST. JAMES'S

CHARLES II ST.

ST. ALBANS

SUFFOLK ST.

HAYMARKET

END

ST.

PARK PLACE

KING ST.

SQ.

WATERLOO PL.

MALL

ST. JAMES'S PL.

LITTLE ST. JAMES

RUSS CT.

ST.

PALL

CLEVELAND ROW

CLEVELAND ROW

0   100   200
Yards

160

John Gay

Edward Gibbon

Richard Glover

R. B. Cunninghame Graham

Thomas Gray

George Grote

Nathaniel Hawthorne

Lord John Hervey

James Hogg

Theodore Hook

David Hume

Bishop Richard Hurd

Inigo Jones

Charles Kemble

George Granville,
   Lord Lansdowne

Sinclair Lewis

John G. Lockhart

David Mallet

Capt. Frederick Marryat

Edward Marsh

Harriet Martineau

William Mason

Prosper Merimée

Andrew Millar

Monckton Milnes

Lady Mary Wortley Montagu

Thomas Moore

William Morris

Sir Isaac Newton

Sir Gilbert Parker

Thomas Parnell

Ambrose Philips

Letitia Pilkington

Alexander Pope

Charles Reade

Samuel Rogers

Richard Savage

Sir Walter Scott

Joseph Severn

George Bernard Shaw

Percy Bysshe Shelley

William Shenstone

Caroline Sheridan

Richard Brinsley Sheridan

Clement K. Shorter

Charlotte Smith

James Smith

Sydney Smith

Mrs Germaine de Stael

Thomas Stanley

Sir Richard Steele

Laurence Sterne

Benjamin Stillingfleet

Jonathan Swift

John Taylor

Sir William Temple	**Sir John Vanbrugh**
William Makepeace Thackeray	**Edmund Waller**
Mrs Hester Lynch Thrale	**Horace Walpole**
Sir Herbert Beerbohm Tree	**Joseph Warton**
Edward J. Trelawny	**William Whitehead**
Anthony Trollope	**Oscar Wilde**
Martin Tupper	**Thomas Wolfe**

Leave the underground at the *Oxford Circus Station*. Without cross-ing Oxford Street, drop down Regent Street (to your left) one block, and cross over it into Prince's Street.

1. Follow Prince's Street one block to *Hanover Square*. CHARLES DICKENS (1812-70), the novelist, rented rooms at *No. 3* in 1861, and gave public readings here. The American novelist NATHANIEL HAW-THORNE (1804-64), on his first visit to London (1855) lodged with his family at *No. 24*; and another American novelist THOMAS WOLFE (1900-38) lodged at *No. 26* in the spring of 1935. This square (origin-ally laid out in 1717) was once a most fashionable place. Dr Johnson's friend MRS HESTER THRALE (1741-1821) lived here (1784-95) after Dr Johnson's death. Her house was at the extreme left (east) end of the lower (south) side of the square. AMBROSE PHILIPS (1675-1749), poet, dramatist, essayist, and judge, as well as victim of Alexander Pope's fiendishly clever malice, spent the last years of his life (and died) at a house on the far (western) side of the square. The house stood on the lower (southern) corner of Hanover Square and Brook Street. At about where *No. 20* now stands, the Scottish Lord Minto had a house, and there had for his secretary and close friend the poet THOMAS CAMPBELL (1777-1844), once regarded as one of the true greats of English literature. Among Campbell's more famous works were the long didactic poem *The Pleasures of Hope*, and the short 'Ye Mariners of England' and 'Lord Ullin's Daughter'.

2. At the lower end of Hanover Square, the statue of William Pitt the Younger looks down *St George Street*. The following literary figures have been associated with this street: MME. GERMAINE DE STAEL (1766-1817), French novelist and bluestocking, opponent of Napoleon, at *No. 3* in 1813, during part of her exile from France; DAVID MALLET (1705-65), Scottish poet and dramatist of dubious character and literary reputation, at *No. 7* from 1758 until his death here; RICHARD

BRINSLEY SHERIDAN (1751-1816), dramatist and politician, at *No. 9*, with his son Thomas, in 1803-5; the novelist ARNOLD BENNETT (1867-1931), with his wife, at *No. 12B*, from 1919 to 1924; LADY MARY WORTLEY MONTAGU (1689-1726), wit, letter-writer, first a friend and then an enemy of Alexander Pope (who satirized her in the 'Epistle to Dr Arbuthnot'), who died at *No. 44*.

A block down the street from Hanover Square stands *St George's Church*—with two large cast-iron hunting dogs guarding its porch, and a steeple described by Leigh Hunt as 'a horn growing out of the church's neck'. Since 1724, when it was built, this church has been famous for its weddings. Here were married *Topham Beauclerk*, Dr Johnson's dear friend and member of the Literary Club (to a daughter of the Churchill family, two days after her divorce from a previous husband); Sir William Hamilton to the little adventuress Emma Hart (eventually Lord Nelson's mistress), whom Sir William had just bought from his nephew; BENJAMIN DISRAELI (1804-81), novelist and Prime Minister (to Mrs Wyndham Lewis); GEORGE ELIOT (MARY ANN EVANS) (1819-81), novelist (to the American banker J. W. Cross); the poet PERCY BYSSHE SHELLEY (1792-1822) (to Harriet Westbrook, confirming an earlier irregular Scottish marriage); CAROLINE SHERIDAN (1808-77), poet, novelist, social reformer, granddaughter of Richard Brinsley Sheridan, and mistress of Lord Melbourne, later Prime Minister; *Herbert Asquith*, another Prime Minister, and his wife MARGOT ASQUITH (1865-1945), author of some gossipy memoirs, and the original of William Watson's poem 'Woman with a Serpent's Tongue'; LORD ALFRED DOUGLAS (1870-1945), poet whose relationship with Oscar Wilde led, indirectly, to the latter's imprisonment, and OLIVE CUSTANCE, also a poet; JOHN BUCHAN (1875-1940), diplomat and voluminous novelist; JOHN GALSWORTHY (1867-1933), novelist and dramatist, and Ada Cooper; and Theodore Roosevelt. EDWARD MARSH (1872-1953), editor of the famous *Georgian Poetry* series (1913-21), friends of many literary people of his time, as a boy attended services at this church twice each Sunday. Thackeray's Barnes Newcome (*The Newcomes*) married Lady Clara Pullyen here; and *Boswell* occasionally worshipped here.

3. At the next street, *Conduit*, beyond the church, turn sharp left. HARRIET MARTINEAU (1802-76), sociologist and fiction writer, lived at *No. 6* when she first came to London in 1832. JAMES BOSWELL (1740-95) lodged on this street in 1772-3, apparently at the first corner on your right, before you turn into Savile Row.

4. At the first street crossing Conduit, turn right into Savile Row.

Two short blocks down the latter street *New Burlington Street* opens to your left (opposite a police station). Here, at *No. 13*, MARTIN TUPPER (1810-89) lived before his family moved to *No. 5* in 1825. *No. 5* was Tupper's permanent address thereafter. His poems, ballads, and versified *Proverbial Philosophy* were very popular in Victorian England, and Tupper was seriously regarded in many quarters (including the royal palace) as a genius of major stature.

5. Continue down Savile Row, past the police station, and turn right, into *Clifford Street*. BISHOP RICHARD HURD (1720-1801) lived at *No. 5* in 1792. Today he is forgotten by everybody but specialists—yet his two essays on 'Imitation' (1751, 1757) and his *Letters on Chivalry and Romance* (1762) had a powerful influence in shaping the tendencies and tastes of the Romantic movement. The left-hand corner where this street ends in New Bond Street was the site of Long's Hotel, where LORD BYRON (1788-1824), the poet, lived occasionally during eight or ten years, and where he and *Sir Walter Scott* met for the last time (1815). On the right-hand corner stood Stevens's Hotel, where Byron and his friend THOMAS MOORE (1779-1852), the Irish poet and musician, dined regularly in the early days of their friendship.

6. But before you reach the end of Clifford Street, turn left, into *Cork Street*. Erasmus Lewis, lived at *No. 7* from 1724 to 1754, and was here visited by his good friend *Alexander Pope* on many occasions; he was also a friend of Swift, John Gay, and Matthew Prior. Another friend of Lewis, DR JOHN ARBUTHNOT (1667-1735), lived at *No. 11*, and died here. Court physician, satirist, creator of the name and character of 'John Bull', he is best remembered as the addressee in Pope's 'Epistle to Dr Arbuthnot'. GERTRUDE ATHERTON (1857-1948), American novelist, lived at Hall's Hotel, on this street, during her prolonged visits to London. *George Peabody* (1795-1869), American philanthropist, settled in London, and lived at *No. 15*.

7. At the lower (southern) end of Cork Street, turn left, into *Burlington Gardens*, and walk along it. On your left, as you reach Old Burlington Street, lived the stepson and widow of the poet-essayist-dramatist Joseph Addison; and, later on, JOSEPH SEVERN (1793-1879), mediocre artist but immortal as the devoted friend of John Keats. On your right stands a building (its façade with an army of statues) erected in 1869 for the University of London, but now headquarters of the *British Academy* 'for the promotion of historical, philosophical, and philological studies'. Its endowments provide for an annual

Shakespeare Lecture, the Raleigh Lectures on History, the Warton Lectures on English Poetry, the Italian Lecture, a lecture on English philosophy and literary history, and a biennial prize for English studies.

8. Just opposite the British Academy, turn into *Old Burlington Street*, entering from your left. At the corner on your right, just as you have turned into this street, stood the house of the Duchess of Queensberry. JOHN GAY (1685-1732), poet, friend of Pope, best known for his *Beggar's Opera*, was secretary to the Duchess, spent the last three years of his life here, and died here. Farther up the street, at *No. 12*, MARK AKENSIDE (1721-70), physician to the Queen, and author of the tremendously long, popular, and influential didactic poem *The Pleasures of the Imagination*, spent his last eight years, and died. At *No. 31* lived (1725-30) LORD JOHN HERVEY (1693-1743), courtier and politician, whose cynical memoirs reveal much about the corruption of himself and the court of George II, and who was attacked by Pope in several poems as 'Lord Fanny' or 'Sporus'.

9. At the end of Old Burlington Street, turn right, and reach *Savile Row* again. Turn right, and walk down it. Robert, brother of SYDNEY SMITH (1771-1845), wit and editor, lived at *No. 20* for many years, and here Sydney stayed for long visits, intermittently from 1818 to 1833. At *No. 17* stands the house to which RICHARD BRINSLEY SHERIDAN (see above) is said to have been taken to die. But most authorities think he died at *No. 14* (a house lent him by the Duke of Wellington), where he had been living for some years before his last illness. Until the mid-twentieth century, the Savile Club was located at *No. 15*. Its membership included *Andrew Lang, Robert Louis Stevenson, Sir Sidney Colvin, W. K. Clifford, William Butler Yeats, Edmund Gosse.* *No. 12* was for years the home of GEORGE GROTE (1794-1871), famous historian and liberal politician, who wrote a celebrated twelve-volume *History of Greece*.

10. At the end of Savile Row, turn left, into Vigo Street. Here (first building on your right) the Bodley Head publishing house was established by John Lane. It issued much of the *avant garde* literature of the late nineteenth and early twentieth centuries. Turn right into *Sackville Street*. Dr Johnson's Literary Club met at 'Prince's' (*No. 23*) for a while (1783-5). JOSEPH WARTON (1722-1800), poet and critic, early leader of the revolt against neo-classic rules, lived on this street in his later years. *Arthur Young* (1741-1820), early student of the

science of agriculture, lived and died at *No. 32*. Mary Evans, Coleridge's first love, lived at *No. 17*.

11. At the lower end of Sackville Street, cross over Piccadilly, and
visit *St James's Church*, which is almost opposite. Designed by Wren,
it was gutted by the bombings of 1940, but has been restored according to the original plan. However, the marble font at which Dr Johnson's LORD CHESTERFIELD (1694-1773) and (incongruous coupling!)
the mystic poet WILLIAM BLAKE (1757-1827) were baptized was pre-
served, and is still to be seen. SIR RICHARD STEELE'S daughter Elizabeth and son Richard were also baptized here. Among those buried
in the church or its churchyard are CHARLES COTTON (1630-87), author
of graceful and charming 'Cavalier' lyrics, a long satirical poem,
nature poems admired by Wordsworth and Coleridge a century later,
translations of Montaigne, and a treatise on fly-fishing that his friend
Izaak Walton added as Part II to *The Compleat Angler*; TOM
D'URFEY (1653-1723), writer of comedies, humorous poems, and
songs; DR JOHN ARBUTHNOT (see above); DR MARK AKENSIDE (see
above); JAMES DODSLEY (d. 1797), the bookseller, who was, with
his brother Robert, one of the most important publishers of the
eighteenth century; BENJAMIN STILLINGFLEET (1702-71), nature poet.
(*Incidental intelligence: Edward Gibbon*, the historian, while walking
in the churchyard one day, sprained his ankle badly by stumbling over
a gravestone.)

12. As you leave the church, and return to Piccadilly, turn right, walk
a few steps, and then turn right again, into little Church Place. The
next street you will reach is *Jermyn Street*. Turn right, along this
street. Dr Johnson's friend MRS HESTER LYNCH THRALE (1741-1821),
herself the author of a voluminous and highly readable collection of
memoirs, letters, and journals, spent much of her girlhood here;
BISHOP GEORGE BERKELEY (1685-1753), the idealist philosopher who
doubted the existence of matter, lodged, in 1725, at 'Mr Bindon's, at
the Golden Globe in Jermyn Street, near Piccadilly'; Colonel *John
Churchill*, later Duke of Marlborough ancestor of Sir Winston
Churchill, lived at the 'west end, south side, about five doors down',
which would be well to your right, at about where *No. 70* or *71* now
is, from 1675 to 1681. THOMAS GRAY (1716-71), author of 'An Elegy
Written in a Country Churchyard', had several lodgings, at different
times, to your left, near Regent Street, in the 1750's; and WILLIAM
SHENSTONE (1714-63), poet and landscapist, who was influential in
the growth of romanticism (through his interest in nature, ancient
ballads, Spenser, and sentiment rather than rationalism) lodged on

this street when he was in town. Tourists will be touched by his lines—

> *Whoever has travelled life's dull round,*
> *Where'er his stages may have been,*
> *May sigh to think he still has found*
> *The warmest welcome at an inn.*

Laura Seymour, an actress, was living at *No. 13* (to your left, near Regent Street) when the novelist CHARLES READE (1814-84) first began corresponding with her, in 1837. Shortly afterwards she became his mistress, and the two lived together with mutual devotion till her death many years later. WILLIAM MAKEPEACE THACKERAY (1811-63), novelist, author of *Vanity Fair* and *Henry Esmond*, lived at *No. 27* (just to your left as you emerge from Church Place) for over two years, 1843-5. LORD BYRON (see above) was staying at Cox's Hotel, *No. 55*, when he first read, in the *Edinburgh Review*, the vicious criticisms of his *Hours of Idleness*—criticisms to which he responded with his *English Bards and Scotch Reviewers. No. 58* was the home, in 1825, of THOMAS MOORE (see above) Irish poet and friend of Byron; and GEORGE BORROW (1803-81) novelist, wanderer, writer on gypsies, and author of *Lavengro*, stayed at the same place in 1840. SIR WALTER SCOTT (1771-1832) stayed at the Waterloo Hotel, *No. 85-6*, on several of his later visits to London; and he lodged at the St James's Hotel, *No. 76*, on his way home from his last trip to the Continent before going home to die. Here he stayed for three weeks (June and July, 1832) being, as someone said, 'half asleep, half dreaming, half dead', the entire time. SYDNEY SMITH (see above), who invariably crops up, stayed briefly at Miller's Hotel, *No. 74* (formerly *No. 81*) in 1811. SIR ISAAC NEWTON (1642-1727) lived (1696-1700) at *No. 88*, and then (1700-09) next door at *No. 87*.

13. Continue along Jermyn Street to where *Bury Street* enters from the left. Turn into the latter. SIR RICHARD STEELE (1672-1729), essayist, dramatist, politician, originator of the *Tatler*, and creator of Sir Roger de Coverley, lived at the third house on your right (about where *No. 21* or *No. 22* now stands) as you descend the street, from 1707 to 1712, just when he was producing the *Tatler* and helping with the *Spectator*. His daughter Elizabeth and his son Richard were born here (1709, 1710). Farther down the street, on the right-hand side, England's greatest satirist, JONATHAN SWIFT (1667-1745), lodged in 1710 and 1713; and he stayed on this street again when he made his last trip to England (from Dublin) in 1726. The poet THOMAS MOORE (see above) stayed on this street often during twenty-five

years: at *No. 19* in 1816, 1829, and 1830; at *No. 24* in 1824; at *No. 28* 'off and on for ten or twelve years' from 1805, and especially in 1810-12, when he brought his young wife here. Daniel O'Connell (1775-1847), Irish political leader whose work led to Catholic emancipation, lived at the same *No. 19* in 1829. In 1922-3 the American novelist SINCLAIR LEWIS (1885-1951) was working on what is probably his best novel, *Babbitt*, at *No. 10*; he worked on *Arrowsmith* in the same rooms in 1924, and occupied the rooms again in 1927 and 1930. GEORGE CRABBE (1754-1832), the harshly realistic poet of British rural life, lodged at *No. 37* in 1817, while arranging publication for his book of poems *Tales of the Hall*. *Joseph Haydn lodged at No. 1 in 1794-5.*

14. Follow Bury Street down to *King Street* (two blocks) and turn left. Immediately across the street, at *No. 23-4 King Street*, stood (1835-1957) *St James's Theatre*, which saw première productions of plays by *Arthur Wing Pinero* (especially the famous *The Second Mrs Tanqueray*), by *Henry Arthur Jones*, by the once-celebrated poet-playwright *Stephen Phillips*, by *A. A. Milne* (*Michael and Mary*), and by *Anthony Hope* (*The Prisoner of Zenda*)—as well as the premières of *Oscar Wilde's Lady Windermere's Fan* and *The Importance of Being Earnest*, and *George Bernard Shaw's Androcles and the Lion*. George Miller, *Laurence Olivier*, and Olivier's wife *Vivien Leigh* were the last managers of this theatre; and stone bas-reliefs depicting their heads, and also the head of *Oscar Wilde*, may be seen on the building now occupying the site of the old theatre.

At *No. 26*, just beyond the theatre site, the man who established Almack's Tavern on Pall Mall (see below) built his famous 'Assembly Rooms' (1765). Shrewdly, he turned over the direction of these rooms to a committee of aristocratic ladies—the result being an enormous popularity of the place from its inauguration until the late nineteenth century. In 1844 CHARLES KEMBLE (1757-1854), the actor, gave his 'Readings from Shakespeare' in the ballroom of this place; and in 1851 WILLIAM MAKEPEACE THACKERAY (see above), the novelist, delivered his *Lectures on the English Humorists* in May, June, and July. Among those attending these lectures were the historians *Henry Hallam* and *Thomas Babington Macaulay*, the sociologist *Harriet Martineau*, the actress *Fanny Kemble*, *Thomas Carlyle*, *Monckton Milnes*, *Charlotte Brontë*, and *Charles Dickens*. Dickens himself presided over two great public dinners here, 1866 and 1867.

Somewhere on this street JONATHAN SWIFT (see above) lived briefly; and Alexander Pope's friend Theresa Blount, who was always kind and considerate towards the hunch-backed, waspish little man, lived here in 1712. CHARLOTTE SMITH (1749-1806), poet who influenced Coleridge, and novelist who combined sentimentalism and Gothicism to become the most popular novelist of her time, was born somewhere on this street.

15. At the next corner, turn left, into *Duke Street*. At *No. 1*, on your right, EDWARD J. TRELAWNY (1792-1881), adventurer, friend and biographer of Byron and Shelley, lived in 1836-7. CAPTAIN FREDERICK MARRYAT (1792-1881), novelist, lived at *No. 8* (1837-9), and THOMAS CAMPBELL (see above) at *No. 10* (1830-40). THOMAS MOORE (see above) stayed at *No. 11* in 1817; at *No. 15* in 1829 and 1833; and at *No. 33* in 1814. EDMUND BURKE (1729-97), statesman and philosopher, had his last permanent lodgings at *No. 67* in 1790; but he returned for temporary visits to *No. 6* in 1793, and to *No. 25* in 1794.

16. When you reach *Ryder Street* (one block), turn left into it. *Hester Vanhomrigh* ('Vanessa'), who loved Swift, and whom he may have loved in his strange cat-and-mouse way, lived on this street—at or near the next corner (Bury Street), probably on the north-west (far right-hand corner as you walk along Ryder Street). She lived here from at least 1712 to 1714. SWIFT himself lodged a little farther along the street in 1712. By coincidence, *Mrs Rebecca Dingley*, later the companion of Swift's 'Stella' in Ireland, had lodged opposite Swift's lodgings, in earlier years.

17. Follow Ryder Street across St James's Street, and to the entrance of *Park Place*, a bit to your right. The philosopher DAVID HUME (1711-76) lived on the latter street, 1767-9. Earlier in the century, the notorious madam, Mother Needham, lived here. She appears in the first plate of Hogarth's *The Harlot's Progress*, figures in Pope's *Dunciad*, was pilloried (1731) here at the juncture of Park Place and St James's Street, and was so roughly handled by the crowds that she died of the experience—poor thing!

From this place continue on up St James's Street (towards Piccadilly), and turn left at the first corner, *Bennet Street*. On this street, at *No. 4*, the poet LORD BYRON (1788-1824) lived, 1813-14; and the much lesser, but once famous and respected, poet RICHARD GLOVER (1712-85), author of the epic poem *Leonidas* (twelve books) and the *Athenaid* (thirty books!) lived at *No. 9*. RICHARD STEELE (see above) also lived briefly on this street in 1705.

18. Walk along Bennet Street's one block, and reach *Arlington Street* —once an aristocratic residential street. In a house on the far side of

the street, and well to your left as you emerge from Bennet Street, lived LADY MARY WORTLEY MONTAGU (1689-1762) as a young woman before her marriage. She was a wit, letter-writer, bluestocking, victim of Pope's satire (after having been his friend). In another house on the far side, now replaced by *No. 22*, lived the Prime Minister *Sir Robert Walpole*; and here his son HORACE WALPOLE (1717-97), also a famous wit and letter-writer, as well as novelist, was born. Later on (1743) Sir Robert moved across the street to *No. 5*—and here Horace lived till 1779, and from here wrote many of his gossipy letters. The Earl of Tyrconel gave a home on this street to the tragic and misguided RICHARD SAVAGE (1697-1743), who at one time stood in the shadow of the gallows (on a murder charge). Behind *No. 16*, in the park, LORD JOHN HERVEY (see above), courtier, gallant, public official, author of some fascinating memoirs, and another victim of Pope's satire, fought a duel (1731) with William Pultney over a pamphlet that Hervey may have written, and was almost killed. DAVID MALLET (1705?-65), a Scottish poet of both fame and ill fame in his day, lived on the street, 1746-7. The French novelist PROSPER MÉRIMÉE (1803-70) stayed at *No. 18* in 1860. CLEMENT K. SHORTER (1857-1926), journalist, editor, author of solid and reliable biographies of the Brontës, Dr Johnson, and George Borrow, lived at *No. 7* in the 1920's.

19. Walk on up Arlington Street towards Piccadilly. When you reach the latter, turn right, and then right again, and double back down *St James's Street*. This is (and has been since the late seventeenth and early eighteenth centuries) a street renowned for its coffee houses and, later on, its clubs—many of which grew out of the original coffee houses. The buildings occupied by the famous ones are either gone, or no longer recognizable today.

  White's began (1693) as White's Chocolate House, on the east (left) side, down at *No. 28*; then (1697-1755) it was on the west side, at *Nos. 68-9*, two to four doors down from St James's Place; and then (from 1755) at *No. 38*, on the east side. Richard Steele mentions it in the first number of the *Tatler*: 'all accounts of gallantry, pleasure and entertainment shall be under the article of White's Chocolate House.' It is mentioned in over 60 subsequent numbers of the *Tatler*, in many plays and poems of the eighteenth century, and in many letters of the time. *Pope, Gay,* and *Swift* patronized it. It appears in Plate 4 of Hogarth's *The Rake's Progress*. After it became a private club (1736) its membership included, at one time or another, *Colley Cibber* (actor and dramatist, as well as Poet Laureate), *Horace Walpole, Richard Brinsley Sheridan,* and *Lord Chesterfield*. From the beginning, the club was famous (or notorious) as a gaming house where gentlemen of quality bet enormous sums on almost anything.

The *Cocoa Tree* was established, early in the eighteenth century, as a chocolate house on Pall Mall (see below); later (1745) it became a private club; and still later (1799) moved to *No. 64 St James's Street*. *Sheridan* and *Byron* frequented it.

Boodle's (established 1762) at *No. 28* had both men and women as members, and was patronized largely by country gentry. *Gibbon* was a member.

Brooks's (1764), at *No. 60*, was headquarters for Whigs and Liberals during many years—'the most famous political club that will ever have existed in England'. Members included *Edmund Burke, David Hume, Sir Joshua Reynolds, Richard Brinsley Sheridan, Horace Walpole, David Garrick, Charles Fox,* and *Edward Gibbon.* Gambling at cards was especially heavy here.

The *Thatched House Tavern* stood, early in the eighteenth century, or perhaps even earlier, until 1842, at about where *Nos. 74-6* are today. It was frequented by *Steele* and *Swift*; and the Literary Club of which *Dr Johnson* had been a member moved there in 1799. *Parsloe's Subscription Room*, at *No. 85*, was the home of the Literary Club just mentioned from 1792 to 1799.

Many other clubs and coffee houses have come, and many have gone, along St James's Street during the centuries. The most famous of the coffee houses was *St James's* (established 1705) which stood on the right-hand (west) side as you walk away from Piccadilly—at *No. 87*, which is three doors up from St James's Palace. (The site is now occupied by a post office.) It was a Whig resort, and Addison mentions it in *Spectator No. 1* (1711): 'Foreign and domestic news you will have from St James's Coffee-house.' *Swift* went there often, and had Stella address her letters to him there; *Sir Richard Steele* wrote many letters from here to his beloved Prue; and over 50 of the *Tatler* papers are dated from here. Dr Johnson's Literary Club had dinners at St James's occasionally. Here (or possibly at *Saunders's Chocolate House*, at *No. 85*, just above St James's Coffee House) *Oliver Goldsmith* was, as usual, late for one of the Literary Club's dinners. While the others were waiting for him, they made up some humorous verses about him. In answer, he wrote the poem 'Retaliation', in which he made exquisitely perceptive and witty thumbnail sketches of those who had versified about him.

In this same area (above St James's Coffee House) the *Smyrna Coffee House* was located after 1768. *Boswell* frequented it.

One of the earliest literary inhabitants of the street was EDMUND WALLER (1606-87), a poet once admired as the dawning light of Neoclassic poetry. He bought property, and lived, on the right-hand (west) side of the newly developing street, at about where *No. 64* is now located. He lived here from 1653 till his death. *Sir Christopher Wren*, the architect, lived and died at a house about where Waller's had stood. SIR RICHARD STEELE (see above) lived, 1714-16, in a house at *No. 26*. LETITIA PILKINGTON, poet and former wife of the poet Matthew Pilkington (both had been friends of Swift in Ireland) lived directly across the street from White's. She and her husband came to London, depending on Swift to help them; but desperate poverty and Swift's cruel undependability forced them to behaviour that made Swift say of the pair that 'he is the most arrant scoundrel and she the greatest whore in England'. She wrote *Memoirs* (1748) which were a bit scandalous, and in which Swift does not fare too well.

LORD BYRON was living at *No. 8* when the first two cantos of *Childe Harold's Pilgrimage* appeared (March 10, 1812) and Byron, as he said, 'awoke one morning and found myself famous'. His friend J. C. Hobhouse, with whom he had made the pilgrimage (into eastern Europe) lived at *No. 32*. And the inevitable THOMAS CAMPBELL (see above) lived for a time at *No. 41*. EDWARD GIBBON (see above), considered the greatest of English historians, took lodgings in November, 1793, above a bookseller's at *No. 74* (south corner of Little St James's and St James's Streets), a very sick man; and there he died in January, 1794. WILLIAM MAKEPEACE THACKERAY (1811-63), the novelist, lived at *No. 88* during 1845-6, and wrote *Barry Lyndon* here.

20. The next street opening on your right as you descend St James's Street from Piccadilly to the palace is *St James's Place*. JOSEPH ADDISON (1672-1719), poet, dramatist, essayist, government official, had lodgings on this street in 1710, together with his secretary (who was also his cousin) EUSTACE BUDGELL (1686-1737). The latter contributed nearly 40 essays to the *Spectator*, and conducted his own periodical, *The Bee*, 1733-5. Addison's friend AMBROSE PHILIPS (1674-1749), poet, dramatist, essayist, and victim of Pope's satire, often stayed here with his friend. MRS MARY (GRANVILLE) DELANEY (1700-88), bluestocking, and author of six volumes of gossipy letters, lived on the street in several different houses, and in one (*No. 33*) from 1771 to her death. Here she often entertained other literary ladies—including *Mrs Elizabeth Montagu, Mrs Hester Chapone, Mrs Elizabeth Carter*, and *Fanny Burney*, as well as literary men like *Horace Walpole* and *Soame Jenys*. The poet THOMAS PARNELL (1697-1781)—author of melancholy reflective poems such as 'Night-Piece on Death', that mark him as an early member of that 'Graveyard School' of poets of whom Thomas Gray is the most celebrated—lived in this street in 1710. And EDWARD GIBBON (see above) lodged at *No. 2* ('Miss Lake's') in 1766.

WILLIAM WHITEHEAD (1715-85), scholar, dramatist, and Poet Laureate, lodged (1768-72) at *No. 3*. In the next century the famous SAMUEL ROGERS (1763-1855), banker, philanthropist, poet, conversationalist, patron of letters, friend of everybody who was anybody during his lifetime, lived fifty-two years (1803-55) at *No. 22*—located around the corner of the street with its back to Green Park. The house of this 'wealthy, sardonic, but kindly man', says Miss Alice Acland, 'was renowned both in England and America' for its beautiful neo-classic interiors, exquisite furnishings, and priceless paintings by Raphael, Titian, Giorgione, and others. To Rogers's breakfasts here would come the most interesting and the wittiest men (and women) in London: the Duke of Wellington, the Irish patriot Henry Grattan, *Lord Byron, Madame de Staël, Sir Walter Scott, Thomas Campbell, Thomas Moore, Lord Macaulay, Charles Lamb, Sydney Smith, Washington Irving, William Wordsworth*, and many others. Rogers was actually offered the Poet Laureateship, but declined it in favour of Wordsworth. The dramatist RICHARD BRINSLEY SHERIDAN (see above) lived at *No. 37* in 1802; CAPTAIN FREDERICK MARRYAT (see above) occupied *No. 38* in 1832. The American novelist JAMES FENI-MORE COOPER (1789-1851) lodged, with his family, at *No. 33* from March to May of 1828; and another American novelist, NATHANIEL HAWTHORNE (1804-64) lodged at *No. 33* in the spring of 1856. A darker history hangs over *Nos. 10-11*, for it was here, in the early 1890's, that OSCAR WILDE (1854-1900), poet, dramatist, and novelist, kept rooms where he met the disreputable young men who testified against him at his trial in 1895. The artist (and writer) AUBREY BEARDSLEY (1872-98) stayed at the same place, 1895-6.

21. The next street entering from your right (as you walk down St James's Street) is Little St James's Street—but nothing of much literary significance seems to be associated with this street.

The *next* street, running along in front of St James's Palace, and off to the right, is *Cleveland Row*. CAPTAIN FREDERICK MARRYAT (see above), the adventure novelist, owned the lease at *No. 5*, and lived there, 1822-7. He sub-let the place to THEODORE HOOK (1788-1841) for a time (1827-31). Hook was a novelist, dramatist, biographer, writer of operas, and fashionable man-about-town. He had to borrow money to furnish the house here, and his ostentatious style of living while he was here left him bankrupt. WILLIAM MASON (1724-97), friend of Thomas Gray, and poet of some influence in turning his century's interest away from Greco-Latin topics and towards native historical themes, brought his new bride (1767) to a house on this street, 'the last door but one nearest Green Park wall'. At about where

173

little Cleveland Square is now located, at the far end of Cleveland Row, ALEXANDER POPE (1688-1744), satirical poet who established 'rules' for poetry that prevailed long after he was gone, took lessons in painting from Charles Jervais, who lived here. Pope studied assiduously during four or five years, and often lived at Jervais's place, wrote letters from here, and had letters delivered here.

22. Return to the foot of Cleveland Row, past the gyrating redcoats guarding the palace, and continue straight ahead along *Pall Mall.* (St James's Palace itself has few literary associations. Odes of the Poets Laureate in the eighteenth century used to be recited at the Great Council Chamber before the king and queen; and the great scholar RICHARD BENTLEY (1662-1742) lodged here as Royal Librarian, 1696-1700. Once a week he met here with the diarist *John Evelyn*, the architect *Christopher Wren*, the philosopher *John Locke*, and the mathematician *Isaac Newton*.) Just beyond the palace stands the Queen's Chapel, designed by INIGO JONES (1573-1652), the architect who was also a stage designer and writer of masques. (Farther back stands the red-brick Marlborough House, designed by Christopher Wren for the Duke of Marlborough.) In the eighteenth century, the first building beyond the palace, and facing Pall Mall, was the *King's Head Tavern*, frequented and written about (in the *Tatler*) by *Sir Richard Steele*. At about where *No. 79* now stands, Nell Gwynn, mistress of King Charles II, lived (1671-87) in a house the king had given her, and here she died. Two doors beyond Nell's place, still on Pall Mall, SIR WILLIAM TEMPLE (1628-99), statesman, essayist, historian, social philosopher, and relative and benefactor of Swift, had a house after 1680. Next beyond Temple lived (1680-91) Robert Boyle, the chemist, who first distinguished between a chemical element and a chemical compound. He died here. A century later, the painter *Thomas Gainsborough* (1727-88) moved into a house located at *Nos. 80-81*, lived here the last fourteen years of his life, and died here. Across the street (at *No. 29*) EDWARD GIBBON (see above) lodged, 1769-70, at 'Mr Taylor's Grocers'. About six doors beyond the Gainsborough place (premises occupied by the Royal Automobile Club when this book was being written) the *Cocoa Tree Chocolate House* was first established, before 1698. In 1757 it moved to *No. 46*; in 1787 to *No. 64*; and in 1799 to *No. 64 St James's Street*. It is mentioned in *Spectator No. 1*. The dramatist *Nicholas Rowe* came here regularly; and *Jonathan Swift* always repaired to it immediately on his arrival in London. In 1745 it became a private club, whose membership later included *Edward Gibbon, Richard Brinsley Sheridan*, and *Lord Byron.* (Byron's great-uncle killed his neighbour, 'Mr

Chaworth', in a duel at a tavern located at *Nos. 94-5*, in 1765.)

The *Smyrna Coffee House* was the seventh house (*Nos. 58-59*) on your left (north side) from the corner of St James's Street. It remained here from 1707 to 1772. Swift refers to it in his *Journal to Stella*; it is mentioned several times in both the *Tatler* and the *Spectator*; subscriptions for James Thomson's great pioneering nature poem *The Seasons* were taken here; *Boswell* called it 'one of my first resorts in London'; and *Dr Arbuthnot* (see above), friend of Pope, and the poet *Matthew Prior* frequented it.

At *Nos. 49-50* was *Almack's Tavern* (1762-78). Here several subsequently famous clubs were first established—including *Almack's* in 1762 (it was notorious for excessively extravagant gambling by young gentlemen of fortune); *Brooks's* in 1764; *Boodle's* in 1762; the *Macaroni* in 1764; the *Ladies Club* in 1769; and *Goostree's* in 1762. Edward Gibbon, the historian, said of Almack's, of which he was a member, that 'it attracted the flower of English youth'; and he added: 'The style of living though somewhat expensive, is exceedingly pleasant; and, notwithstanding the rage of play, I have found more entertainment and even rational society here than in any other club to which I belong.'

CAPTAIN FREDERICK MARRYAT (see above) stayed at *No. 120* in 1841 and 1844; GEORGE BORROW (1803-81), novelist of gypsies, lodged briefly at *No. 56A* in 1848, and *53A* in 1854. ROBERT DODSLEY (1703-64), bookseller, leading publisher of poetry in his time, and himself a poet and dramatist (though he began his career as a footman), had his headquarters at *No. 51*, from which he issued the works of Pope, Dr Johnson, Edward Young, Thomas Gray, Goldsmith, Akenside, Shenstone, Sterne, and various famous collections of poetry. ANDREW MILLAR (1707-68), another celebrated publisher and bookseller (he published, among others, James Thomson, Henry Fielding, and David Hume) lived for several years, and died, at *No. 25*. JOHN G. LOCKHART (1794-1854), editor, and biographer of his father-in-law *Sir Walter Scott*, lived at this same *No. 25* during the 1820's, and was visited here by Sir Walter in 1826-7. MONCKTON MILNES (1809-85), poet, philanthropist, and friend of writers, lived at *No. 26* for twenty-six years; and J. J. Stockdale published the anonymous *Original Poetry* (1810), which was Shelley's first published verse. (The volume was the work of Shelley and, apparently, his sister Elizabeth; it was withdrawn from sale when the publisher discovered that one of the poems in it was plagiarized from a poem by Matthew Gregory Lewis.)

23. About halfway down Pall Mall, *St James's Square* opens on your left. Turn into it. Dr Johnson's LORD CHESTERFIELD (see above) lived

at *No. 18* till he married. Pope's LORD JOHN HERVEY (see above) lived at *No. 6*; SIR PHILIP FRANCIS (1740-1818), reputed author of the *Letters of Junius*, lived at *No. 16-17* from 1791 till his death here; and EDWARD GIBBON (see above) lived for a time at *No. 76*. Byron's daughter Ada and her husband, the Earl of Lovelace, lived at *No. 12*. (Three Prime Ministers—William Pitt, the Earl of Derby, and Gladstone—have lived at *No. 10*.)

[23A. *Charles II Street* opens into St James's Square on the side to the right (east) of where you entered. EDMUND BURKE (see above) had lodgings here (1780), as did EDWARD GIBBON (see above) in 1758, and also HESTER LYNCH SALUSBURY (later MRS THRALE, Dr Johnson's friend) when she was a girl.]

24. Return to Pall Mall, and continue along it to *Waterloo Place*, with its many statues. Before this was built, the novelist LAURENCE STERNE (1713-68) lodged (1760) a little beyond the Crimean War monument, and on the left-hand (north) side of Pall Mall. Bubb Dodington (1691-1762), rich eccentric whose career touched those of Pope, James Thomson, Fielding, Richard Cumberland, Edward Young, and many other writers, had a fine house on the right-hand (south) side of Pall Mall, in the middle of today's Waterloo Place. On the right-hand corner where Pall Mall enters Waterloo Place stands the *Athenaeum Club*, to which many of England's men of letters have belonged, and still belong. Named almost at random, some of them have been *Matthew Arnold, James Barrie, G. K. Chesterton, Joseph Conrad, G. Lowes Dickinson, Conan Doyle, John Galsworthy, H. Rider Haggard, Rudyard Kipling, William Makepeace Thackeray*, and *W. B. Yeats*.

[24A. *Carlton House Terrace* crosses Waterloo Place to the right (south of Pall Mall. Here, at *No. 20*, lived SIR GILBERT PARKER (1862-1923), novelist, dramatist, journalist, and poet. Farther up Waterloo Place, to the left of Pall Mall, and behind the Crimea monument, JAMES HOGG (1770-1835), the 'Etterick Shepherd', uneducated Scottish poet who was discovered by Sir Walter Scott, stayed at *No. 11* on his only visit to London (1831-2). At *No. 13* were published Lamb's *Essays of Elia* and De Quincey's *Confessions of an English Opium Eater*.]

25. Continue along Pall Mall to *Haymarket*, entering from your left. Turn into it, and walk a block to the *Haymarket Theatre*, on your right, and *Her Majesty's Theatre*, on your left. The Haymarket was first opened in 1720, but was not very successful till the comedies of HENRY FIELDING (1707-54), who is better known as a novelist than as

a dramatist, were produced here in the 1730's. Fielding was manager of the theatre from 1735 to 1737. SAMUEL FOOTE (1720-77), dramatist, satirist, wit, was manager, 1747-76; the dramatist GEORGE COLMAN THE ELDER (1732-94) was manager, 1776-94; and his son GEORGE COLMAN THE YOUNGER (1762-1836) succeeded him, and was manager until 1803. The theatre was rebuilt, and given its present exterior in 1820; but its interior has been reconstructed several times. Her Majesty's Theatre opened as the Queen's Theatre in 1705, with the dramatist WILLIAM CONGREVE (1670-1729) as its first manager. The architect was SIR JOHN VANBRUGH, who was also a dramatist. It became the King's Theatre in 1714, with the death of Queen Anne and the accession of George I, but it has been Her Majesty's Theatre since the accession of Queen Victoria, 1837. It has been rebuilt several times. The present building dates from 1897, at which time SIR BEERBOHM TREE (1853-1917), in his day 'the leader of the English theatre', became the manager, and remained so until his death.

26. Return to the bottom of Haymarket, and continue along Pall Mall. The next street entering from your left is *Suffolk Street*. JONATHAN SWIFT (see above) had lodgings on this street from July to October, 1711. ANTHONY TROLLOPE (1815-82), the novelist, lived at *No. 15* (Garland's Hotel) during the last year of his life—though he died at a nursing home in the Marylebone area. JAMES BEATTIE (1735-1803), the Scottish poet, author of the long poem *The Minstrel*, which is extremely important in the development of Romanticism, lived at *No. 27* on his visit to London in 1773. (Dr Johnson said of him: 'We all love Beattie.') THOMAS STANLEY (1625-78), minor Renaissance poet and philosopher, translator of Aeschylus, also lived on this little street.

27. Continue along Pall Mall into Trafalgar Square, and straight on in front of the National Gallery (which, of course, you must visit sometime), till you reach *St Martin's-in-the-Fields Church* on the next corner. A church has stood here since 1222, though the present church dates only from 1726. In the older church SIR FRANCIS BACON (1561-1626), philosopher, essayist, scientist, jurist, was baptized. The Irish poet THOMAS MOORE (see above) was married here in 1811. In the church, or in the extensive churchyard that once adjoined the church, were buried THOMAS STANLEY (see above); SIR JOHN DAVIES (1589-1626), poet and jurist; JOHN TAYLOR (1580-1653), the 'Water Poet' and realistic prose writer; GEORGE FARQUHAR (1678-1707), dramatist; JAMES SMITH (1775-1839), who, with his brother, wrote the tremendously clever *Rejected Addresses* as parodies on the Romantic poets.

THOMAS HOLCROFT (1745-1809), 'cautiously radical' novelist, dramatist, and actor, was baptised here. One of the most dramatic episodes of Dickens's *David Copperfield* occurred on the steps of this church when, on a snowy night, David happened to meet Mr. Peggotty searching for Emily.

Turn right, at the corner of St Martin's-in-the-Fields, and walk along the eastern side of Trafalgar Square to the *Trafalgar Square Underground Station.* Here this tour ends. But from here you may begin *Tour No. 1* or *Tour No. 6.*

Tour 11
Piccadilly

Joseph Addison

Harrison Ainsworth

Dr John Arbuthnot

James Barrie

Aubrey Beardsley

William Beckford

Arnold Bennett

Bishop George Berkeley

James Boswell

Edward Bulwer-Lytton

Frances ('Fanny') Burney

Lord Byron

Thomas Campbell

Mrs Elizabeth Carter

Wilkie Collins

Sir John Denham

Charles Dickens

John Evelyn

Ronald Firbank

Gilbert Frankau

John Galt

Richard Glover

William Hazlitt

Oliver Wendell Holmes

W. D. Howells

Sir Henry Irving

Henry James

Francis Jeffrey

Douglas Jerrold

Edmund Kean

Rudyard Kipling

Sir George Lewis

Matthew ('Monk') Lewis

Amy Lowell

Thomas Babington Macaulay

Monckton Milnes

Thomas Moore

John Murray

Mrs Caroline Norton

E. Phillips Oppenheim

Alexander Pope

Charles Reade

Sir Walter Scott

Percy Bysshe Shelley

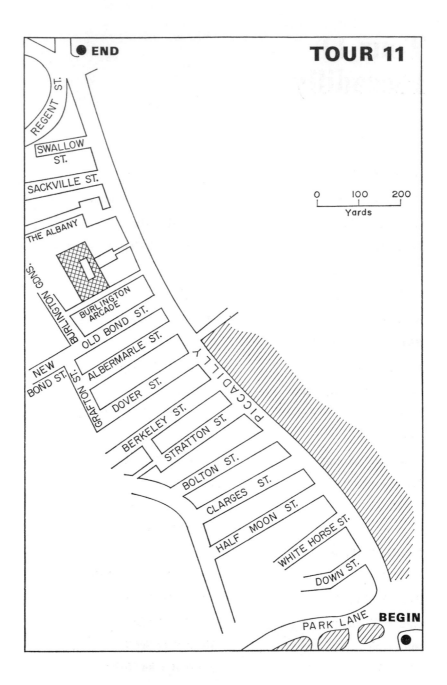

TOUR 11

END

REGENT ST.

SWALLOW ST.

SACKVILLE ST.

THE ALBANY

BURLINGTON GDNS.

BURLINGTON ARCADE

OLD BOND ST.

NEW BOND ST.

GRAFTON ST.

ALBERMARLE ST.

DOVER ST.

BERKELEY ST.

STRATTON ST.

BOLTON ST.

CLARGES ST.

HALF MOON ST.

WHITE HORSE ST.

DOWN ST.

PICCADILLY

PARK LANE

BEGIN

0   100   200
Yards

Richard Brinsley Sheridan	**Algernon Charles Swinburne**
Leonard Smithers	**John Addington Symonds**
Sir Richard Steele	**John Tenniel**
Laurence Sterne	**Mrs Hester Lynch Thrale**
Sir John Suckling	**Horace Walpole**
Jonathan Swift	**Oscar Wilde**

See also the list of 'Albany' residents in Section 13.

Leave the underground at the *Hyde Park Corner Station*, and find your way over to Piccadilly, left-hand (north) side.

> *Note:* In walking up Piccadilly, you will be exploring almost every side-street entering from the left. After each side excursion, you may return to Piccadilly—or you may find it simpler to walk on to the top of the street you are exploring, turn right, and descend the next street into Piccadilly.

1. Because of the many side-streets off Piccadilly, you may find it less confusing to have sites on *Piccadilly* itself mentioned now.

At *No. 139* stood the house where LORD BYRON (1788-1824) and his incompatible wife lived, and here their daughter Augusta was born. From here Lady Byron left her husband forever. At *Nos. 137-8* Lord Elgin first exhibited the Elgin Marbles; and here *John Keats* saw them, and found inspiration for one of the greatest poems in English, 'Ode on a Grecian Urn'. The novelist SIR WALTER SCOTT (1771-1832) visited at *No. 96* (corner of White Horse Street); the novelist and busy letter-writer HORACE WALPOLE (1717-97) lived for a time at *No. 90*; and the novelist ARNOLD BENNETT (1867-1932) lived at *No. 80* (Royal Yacht Club), without his wife, during the First World War. *No. 74* was the publishing address of J. C. Hotten (d. 1873), who published books that the Victorians considered pornographic—among them Swinburne's *Poems and Ballads* (1866) after a previous publisher had withdrawn it from circulation. *No. 193* was the later headquarters of Chapman and Hall, who published here Charles Dickens's *A Tale of Two Cities, Great Expectations, The Uncommercial Traveller, Our Mutual Friend*, and *The Mystery of Edwin Drood*. George Meredith, Anthony Trollope, and both the Brownings were also published here.

As you ascend Piccadilly, you might recall that OSCAR WILDE (1854-1900), poet and self-proclaimed prophet of aestheticism, used to walk down this street (in the opposite direction from yours) on his visits to the 'professional beauty' Lillie Langtry, then living in Belgravia. Being at that time an impoverished young man, Wilde could not afford to take many flowers to the lady—but each day he would take her a single lily—as a symbol both of the Aesthetic movement and of the lady named Lillie. W. S. Gilbert, in satirizing the Aesthetic movement as a whole, and Wilde in particular under the character of 'Reginald Bunthorne', in the light opera *Patience*, referred to this bit of literary history:

> *Though Philistines may jostle,*
> *You will rank as an apostle*
> *In the high aesthetic band*
> *If you walk down Piccadilly*
> *With a poppy or a lily*
> *In your medieval hand.*

2. The third street from Hyde Park corner is *Down Street*, where, at *No. 10*, WILLIAM HAZLITT (1778-1830), critic who revolutionized literary criticism, lived (1823-7). The American poet JAMES RUSSELL LOWELL (1819-91) stayed at *No. 11* on a visit to England in 1872.

3. Return from Down Street, and walk along Piccadilly for three blocks, to *Half Moon Street*. JAMES BOSWELL (1740-95), Dr Johnson's biographer, and author (among other works not discovered till the twentieth century) of the best-selling *London Journal* (1950), lived on this street in 1768. He had as guests here *Benjamin Franklin, David Garrick, David Hume, George Oglethorpe*, and *Dr Johnson*. FRANCES ('FANNY') BURNEY (1752-1840) lived at *No. 1*, corner of Half Moon Street and Piccadilly, 1828-36. She was one of the earliest authors (in the line of Samuel Richardson and Jane Austen) of novels dealing with everyday social and domestic life, instead of melodramatic adventure. JOHN ADDINGTON SYMONDS (1840-93), poet, critic, literary biographer, historian, lived at *No. 7* in 1854. HENRY JAMES (1843-1916), American-born novelist, who has become a kind of deity to critics, lived at the same house, *No. 7*, in 1878. Another American novelist, WILLIAM DEAN HOWELLS (1837-1920), stayed at *No. 18* for a month or so in 1910. JOHN GALT (1779-1839), Scots novelist, lived briefly at *No. 29*. WILLIAM HAZLITT (see above) moved to *No. 40* in 1827, and remained more than two years. *Lola Montez* (1818-61), the Irish-born adventuress who became the mistress of Louis I of Bavaria, as well as celebrated actress and lover throughout Europe and America, lived at *No. 27*.

4. Perhaps you should walk through to Curzon Street, at the top of Half Moon Street, and turn right, and then right again, into *Clarges Street*. The American poet JAMES RUSSELL LOWELL (1819-91) lodged at *No. 40* in 1886; and RONALD FIRBANK (1886-1926), novelist, was born at the same place the same year. *No. 32* was the home of Douglas Kinnaird, banker and friend of Lord Byron. Here he often entertained at dinner *Byron, Thomas Moore, Richard Brinsley Sheridan,* and the actor *Edmund Kean.* ELIZABETH CARTER (1717-1806), poet, translator from the Greek, contributor to the *Gentleman's Magazine,* friend of Dr Johnson and most of his Club, lived for many years at *No. 20,* and died at *No. 21.* The popular novelist E. PHILLIPS OPPENHEIM (1866-1946) lived at *No. 13* in the 1920's. FRANCIS JEFFREY (1773-1850), essayist, critic, editor of the *Edinburgh Review* had lived at the same address for a time. (Violently anti-romantic, he began a famous essay about Wordsworth with the sentence, 'This will never do'.) EDMUND KEAN (1787?-1833), one of the greatest Shakespearean actors of all time, lived at *No. 12* from 1816 to 1824. At *No. 11* lived Lord Nelson's Lady Hamilton, 1804-6; and, many years later, the parents of the novelist, poet, and dramatist GILBERT FRANKAU (1884-1952) lived at the same number. The poet and historian THOMAS BABINGTON MACAULAY (1800-59) lived at *No. 3* from 1838 to 1840.

5. Turn left on Piccadilly, and then left again on *Bolton Street.* Martha and Theresa Blount, the friends of ALEXANDER POPE (1688-1744), who was probably in love with Martha, were living on this street in 1715. HENRY JAMES (see above) lived at *No. 3* from 1876 to 1885. The novelist FRANCES BURNEY (see above) moved to *No. 11* in 1818, and continued there till 1828. Here she was visited by *Sir Walter Scott* in 1824. MRS CAROLINE NORTON (1808-77) lived at *No. 24* in the late 1830's. She was a novelist, poet, feminist, advocate of humanitarian social reforms, granddaughter of the dramatist Richard Brinsley Sheridan, and (probably) mistress of Lord Melbourne (later Prime Minister). At the very end of Bolton Street there was formerly a set-back line of houses known as 'Bolton Row'. Here, in *No. 6* (long since gone) lived, 1855-65, CHARLES READE (1814-84), novelist, whose greatest work was *The Cloister and the Hearth.* His nominal landlady was a Mrs Seymour, who stayed with him the rest of his life as his mistress.

6. Turning right on Curzon Street, you can find (almost opposite Fitzmaurice Place) a narrow passage on your right, leading down to *Stratton Street.* The mobile poet THOMAS CAMPBELL (1777-1844) was staying at *No. 2* in 1802. SIR HENRY IRVING (1838-1905), great actor,

the first of his profession to be knighted, lived at *No. 17* in 1900; and JAMES BARRIE (1860-1937), dramatist and novelist, lived at the same address in 1908. At the foot of the street, and on your left as you reach Piccadilly, stood *Devonshire House*, originally built in 1735, and not torn down till the twentieth century. Here, in 1857, EDWARD BULWER-LYTTON's play *Not so Bad as We Seem* was given an amateur production with the chief parts being played by the novelists CHARLES DICKENS and WILKIE COLLINS, the dramatist DOUGLAS JERROLD, and the artist JOHN TENNIEL (original illustrator of *Alice in Wonderland*).

7. Turn left on Piccadilly, and reach *Berkeley Street*. At the juncture of the two streets (far, or east, corner) was the *Berkeley Hotel*, which was the regular residence of the American poet AMY LOWELL (1874-1925) when she was in London. Up this street, where *No. 9* now stands, the poet ALEXANDER POPE (1688-1744) bought a house as his London residence, and willed it to Martha Blount. She died here in 1763.

8. The next street for you to ascend is *Dover Street*. DR JOHN ARBUTHNOT (1677-1735) (to whom was addressed Pope's poem 'Epistle to Dr Arbuthnot') lived (1714-21) at the second door on the left as you leave Piccadilly—though, of course, his house is not there now. Arbuthnot was the official court physician, as well as a sharp satirical poet. His five anti-Whig pamphlets (called collectively *The History of John Bull*, 1712) invented the character of John Bull as the representative Englishman. JOHN EVELYN (1620-1706), famous for his diary, but also a writer on science, politics, forestry, art, and many other subjects, spent the last seven years of his life at a house 'nine doors up, on the east side' (that is, on your right) of the street, and died there. Beyond this, on the same side of the street, WILLIAM BECKFORD (1760-1844) was living at *No. 16* in 1801. In addition to travel books, Beckford wrote two burlesque novels and one real novel, *Vathek*. This last made him as famous as his scandalous life had made him infamous. At *No. 17*, then a small hotel, the American poet, novelist, and essayist OLIVER WENDELL HOLMES (1809-94) stayed on his visit to London in 1886. Beyond this, at about *Nos. 21-4*, was one entrance to *Brown's Hotel*, where RUDYARD KIPLING stayed often, and MARK TWAIN was a guest.

Somewhere on this street lived the sister of the painter Sir Joshua Reynolds—who was herself an artist. Here *Dr Johnson* sat ten times, several hours at a time, for a portrait by her—with, as he said, 'the patience of mortal born to bear'.

9. At the top of Dover Street, turn right, into *Grafton Street*. Americans will be interested in the fact that *Lord Cornwallis*, who surrendered to Washington at Yorktown, lived at *No. 16*, and that *Charles James Fox* (liberal statesman who opposed George III's policy with the American colonies, opposed intervention in the French Revolution, and supported greater independence for Ireland and abolition of slavery) lived on this street when he was Foreign Secretary in the 1780's. SIR GEORGE C. LEWIS (1806-63), statesman, historian, philologist, and editor of the *Edinburgh Review*, lived at *No. 21*. And *No. 15A* was the home, for nearly 30 years, of SIR HENRY IRVING (see above), the actor.

10. After one block on Grafton Street, turn right, into *Albemarle Street*. Some former literary inhabitants of this street whose addresses are unknown to the present writer include the following: JOSEPH ADDISON (1672-1719), poet, essayist, critic, dramatist, member of parliament, and government official, who established a residence here in order to be near the seat of government in St James's Palace; BISHOP GEORGE BERKELEY (1685-1753), philosopher who maintained that material things exist only in the minds of man and of God; RICHARD GLOVER (1712-85), author of the endless and once enormously celebrated epic *Leonidas* (1737), who died here; and the dramatist RICHARD BRINSLEY SHERIDAN (see above), who lodged here with his family in the winter of 1783-4.

At *No. 13* was the *Albemarle Club*. Here the Marquis of Queensberry (1844-1900), originator of the rules of modern boxing, left the fateful note for OSCAR WILDE (1854-1900), then a famous dramatist, implying that the latter was having a homosexual affair with Queensberry's son Lord Alfred Douglas, himself a poet. Wilde (probably at the urging of Douglas, who hated his father) brought suit for libel against Queensberry—who undertook to prove that his allegations were true. As a result, Wilde was tried on a morals charge, found guilty, and imprisoned for two years. By a kind of coincidence, *No. 12*, next door, is the *Royal Arcade*, where (at Nos. 4 and 5) the publisher LEONARD SMITHERS established himself in 1896, and began publishing works that other publishers (frightened by the fall of Wilde) would not touch. Here Wilde's own *Ballad of Reading Gaol* and *The Harlot's House* were published, as well as works by Ernest Dowson, Aubrey Beardsley, Sir Richard Burton, and others of the post-Wilde 'aesthetic' group. Smithers also published the *avant garde* periodical *The Savoy*.

At the end of this street, on your right, is *No. 50*. Here the publisher JOHN MURRAY (1776-1843) lived, as did his son later. Murray founded the *Quarterly Review* (1809), and appointed the harsh critic and satirist *William Gifford* editor. The *Review* is infamous for its savage personal and critical attacks on the poet *Keats*. Murray was a friend of Byron and of Thomas Moore, and published their works, as well as the works of Sir Charles Lyell, Washington Irving, Thomas Campbell, George Crabbe, Robert Southey, and Sir Walter Scott. It was in Murray's drawing-room that *Byron* and *Scott* first met, and often met later at the same place. It was also in this drawing-room, on a sad day for English literature, that Murray, on the insistence of William Gifford, burnt the manuscript of Byron's memoirs that had been handed over to him by Thomas Moore. Murray and Gifford had persuaded Moore that the memoirs were too indecent and revelatory for publication. Under the son, the Murray firm (now removed to *No. 50A Albemarle Street*) published Charles Darwin's work. MONCKTON MILNES (1809-85), poet, patron of letters, friend of Thackeray and Tennyson, lived for a while around 1835 next door to the Murrays, at *No. 49*.

Across the street, at *No. 1*, stood a hotel where BYRON lived for a time. He is said to have composed most of *The Corsair* while walking up and down this street.

11. When you reach Piccadilly, turn left, and (after one block) left again, into *Old Bond Street*. Today this street is famous for its men's fashions, as well as for picture galleries and jewellery shops. JAMES BOSWELL (see above) had lodgings on the street for a short time in 1769; he once had as dinner guests here *Dr Johnson*, the painter *Sir Joshua Reynolds*, the poet-dramatist-novelist *Oliver Goldsmith*, and the actor-dramatist *David Garrick*. At what was the third house on your left as you ascend the street, LAURENCE STERNE (1713-68), the novelist, lived his last two years, and died. The poet PERCY BYSSHE SHELLEY (1792-1822) stayed at *No. 15* (on your right, opposite Stafford Street) in 1814, when he was having troubles with his wife, his father, and his finances. *No. 28* is the other entrance of the *Royal Arcade*, already noted on Albemarle Street. At *No. 27* the novelist HARRISON AINSWORTH (1805-52), had a publishing office and bookshop.

[11A. Old Bond Street leads straight ahead into *New Bond Street*. Here, 'over against the Crown and Cushion', JONATHAN SWIFT (1667-1745), one of the giants of English literature, author of *Gulliver's Travels*, lodged briefly (1727) before leaving England forever—to return to Ireland and watch over the death of his beloved Stella. At the nearer corner of Clifford Street, entering from the right a bit farther along New Bond Street, stood *Long's Hotel*, where the poet LORD BYRON (see above) lived periodically during seven or eight years, and where he and *Sir Walter Scott* met for the last time (1815). On the farther corner stood *Stevens's Hotel* and *Coffee House*, where Byron and his friend THOMAS MOORE (1779-1852), the Irish poet, dined regularly in the early days of their friendship.]

12. To return to Piccadilly, you may either retrace your steps down Old Bond Street, or (at the juncture of Old and New Bond Streets) turn off into Burlington Gardens (to your right), walk a few steps along it, and turn right, into the Burlington Arcade (closed on Sundays). Built in 1819, it is still an alley of exclusive shops, and is worth visiting. At Piccadilly, turn left. Just beyond Burlington Arcade you will see, on your left, an archway opening back into a quadrangle with a huge and forbidding building behind it. This is *Burlington House*. The first house built here (in the 1660's) was designed by SIR JOHN DENHAM (1615-69), gentleman, soldier, amateur architect, amateur poet. The house was rebuilt and enlarged in 1715—and this is the house you see now. In the later eighteenth century, it was the unofficial headquarters of the Whig party—with *Edmund Burke* and *Richard Brinsley Sheridan*, the dramatist, often attending meetings here. Since 1869, the place has been the home of the Royal Academy of Arts, which holds annual exhibitions of current British painting here.

13. Return to Piccadilly, and go to the next little 'street' leading in from your left. This is *The Albany*—which is generally closed to all but residents. It has long been a fashionable address for those who would be considered fashionable; and the number of literary persons who have lived here has been lengthy. Here is a (certainly incomplete) roster:

RODNEY ACKLAND (b. 1908), playwright.

CLIFFORD BAX (1886-1962), highly successful dramatist.

ARNOLD BENNETT (1867-1931), major novelist who, having been born poor, loved the swank of living here.

DION BOUCICAULT (1822?-1890), actor and playwright.

EDWARD BULWER-LYTTON (1803-73), novelist and dramatist.

LORD BYRON (1788-1824), poet.

MRS PEARL CRAIGIE ('JOHN OLIVER HOBBES') (1867-1906), American-born novelist and playwright.

GRAHAM GREENE (b. 1904), novelist.

COSMO HAMILTON (d. 1942), author of 30 plays and 40 novels.

PATRICK HAMILTON (b. 1904), novelist and playwright.

ALDOUS HUXLEY (1894-1963), novelist, poet, essayist.

HENRY ARTHUR JONES (1851-1929), dramatist.

RICHARD JONES (1779-1851), actor and dramatist.

EDWARD KNOBLOCK (1874-1945), prolific novelist and dramatist.

JOHN LANE (1854-1925), *avant garde* publisher of the 1890's. He lived here the last 30 years of his life.

MATTHEW ('MONK') LEWIS (1775-1818), author of *The Monk* and other horror novels. He lived here the last eight years of his life.

THOMAS BABINGTON MACAULAY (1800-59), historian. He lived here 15 years.

MALCOLM MUGGERIDGE (b. 1903), humourist and satirist.

HAROLD NICOLSON (1886-1969), historian, diplomat, biographer, diarist.

J. B. PRIESTLEY (b. 1894), novelist, dramatist, social critic.

TERENCE RATTIGAN (b. 1911), 'England's most successful modern playwright'.

WILLIAM S. ROSE (1775-1843), poet, translator, friend of Byron.

MRS G. B. STERN (b. 1890), novelist. She lived here 16 years.

SIR HERBERT BEERBOHM TREE (1853-1917), actor and producer.

SIR WILLIAM WATSON (1858-1935), Victorian poet who kept writing in the Victorian manner long after Victoria and Victorianism were dead.

Just across the street from the Albany, JAMES BOSWELL (see above) took lodgings in 1773.

14. The next street leading off to the left is *Swallow Street*, once much longer than it is now. Somewhere on it, in the first years of the eighteenth century, lived Sir Richard Steele's 'dear Prue' before her marriage to Steele.

15. Continue along Piccadilly into *Piccadilly Circus*—the hub of London's twentieth-century theatre life. At its far (eastern) side, about where Coventry Street opens, there stood, in the seventeenth century, Piccadilly Hall—with gardens, trees, walks, and bowling greens. Tradition has it that the Cavalier poet SIR JOHN SUCKLING (1609-42) habitually frequented the gambling rooms of the place, and made so many reckless wagers with his and his two sisters' patrimony, that the girls once followed him here, and with tears in their eyes pleaded with him not to lose the money that was theirs, and leave them destitute.

On the lower (right-hand) side of the Circus stands the *Criterion Theatre* (opened in 1874, with *Topsy-Turveydom*, a short musical by W. S. Gilbert). The theatre has been mostly devoted to comedy and farce (including the first production of W. S. Gilbert's *On Bail*, 1877) —but in the 1890's it gave premières of several of the serious social plays of Henry Arthur Jones.

It is characteristic of this gaudy and glittering centre of illusion that the winged archer standing tiptoe on the pyramidal monument in the centre of the Circus was meant to represent the 'Angel of Christian Charity'—but has been so long mistaken for, and called, 'Eros' (God of Love) that its original name has been all but forgotten. (The archer is directing his shaft into the ground as a typically eccentric English pun on the name of the donor of the statue, the Earl of Shaftesbury!) In the 1960's and 1970's for the base of the statue was a favourite gathering place, on Sundays, for 'hippie' groups.

You are now near the entrance of the *Piccadilly Circus Underground Station*—the busiest in London—and here you end this tour.

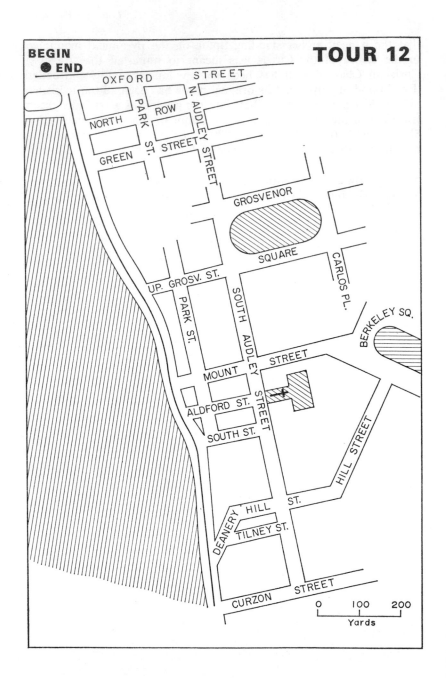

BEGIN
● END

TOUR 12

OXFORD STREET

NORTH

PARK ST.

ROW

N. AUDLEY STREET

GREEN

STREET

GROSVENOR

SQUARE

CARLOS PL.

UP. GROSV. ST.

PARK ST.

SOUTH AUDLEY STREET

BERKELEY SQ.

MOUNT STREET

ALDFORD ST.

SOUTH ST.

STREET

HILL STREET

DEANERY HILL

TILNEY ST.

ST.

CURZON STREET

0   100   200
Yards

190

Tour 12
Grosvenor Square

William Beckford

Bishop George Berkeley

James Boswell

Wilfred Scawen Blunt

Edward Bulwer-Lytton

Frances ('Fanny') Burney

Mrs Patrick Campbell

Elizabeth Carter

Lord Chesterfield

Winston Churchill

Benjamin Disraeli

Maria Edgeworth

'Ian Hay' (John Hay Beith)

Thomas Holcroft

John Home

Thomas Hughes

Washington Irving

Soame Jenys

Edward Jerningham

Dr Samuel Johnson

Matthew ('Monk') Lewis

David Mallet

Somerset Maugham

Lady Mary Wortley Montagu

Mrs Caroline Norton

John Osborne

John Payne

Ambrose Philips

Franklin Delano Roosevelt

John Ruskin

Mary Godwin Shelley

Percy Bysshe Shelley

Sydney Smith

Tobias Smollett

Algernon C. Swinburne

Mrs Hester Lynch Thrale

Kenneth Tynan

William Whitehead

Lady Jane Wilde ('Speranza')

Oscar Wilde

John Wilkes

John Wolcot ('Peter Pindar')

William Wordsworth

Leave the underground at the *Marble Arch Station*. Turn left, and go to the second street, which is Portman Street. Here, cross over Oxford Street, enter Park Street, and descend it.

1. Almost immediately you will cross *North Row*, and may wish to turn aside to *No. 20*, which was the home, in the 1870's, of the Pre-Raphaelite poet JOHN PAYNE (1842-1916)—who was also a translator of the Persian poets Omar and Hafiz, of the *Arabian Nights*, and of Villon, Boccaccio, and Heine.

2. Continue down *Park Street*. (But, before you have reached the end of the street, read Section 3, below.) (Note also that the numerical order of houses is adhered to in the following list.) JOHN RUSKIN (1819-96), social essayist and art critic, brought his bride to *No. 31*, and there lived most unhappily with her—since Ruskin never con-summated the marriage. MARY GODWIN SHELLEY (1797-1851), daughter of the novelist William Godwin, second wife of the poet Shelley, and author of *Frankenstein*, lived for two years (1837-9) at *No. 41*D. THOMAS HUGHES (1822-96), author of *Tom Brown's School Days* (a novel about Rugby) lived successively at *Nos. 113, 33*, and *80*. Hughes joined F. D. Maurice in the Christian Socialist movement, visited America several times, and founded a cooperative colony, called 'Rugby', in the Tennessee mountains. And LADY JANE WILDE ('SPERANZA') (1824-96), poet, Irish patriot, and mother of Oscar Wilde, lived at *No. 116* from 1883 to 1886.

3. As you descend Park Street, you will cross *Upper Grosvenor Street*. You may wish to turn aside here (to your right), and walk a block to Park Lane. On the corner here is *No. 93*, where BENJAMIN DISRAELI (1804-81), novelist and Prime Minister, lived for thirty-three years, 1839-72.... But return to Park Street.

4. Near the end of Park Street, you will reach *Aldford Street*. Turn left here. JOHN WOLCOT ('PETER PINDAR') (1738-1819), the satirical poet, once lived at *No. 1*. TOBIAS SMOLLETT (1721-71), the novelist, lived at *No. 11* from 1746 to 1748. The home of Harriet Westbrook, first wife of the poet PERCY BYSSHE SHELLEY (1792-1822), was at *No. 23*, and from here she and Shelley eloped. The first edition of Shelley's *Queen Mab* has the following imprint: 'London, printed by P. B. Shelley, 23 Chapel Street [the former name of this street], Grosvenor Square, 1813.'

5. At the end of Aldford Street, and facing down it, stands *Grosvenor*

Chapel, built in 1730. Here are buried LADY MARY WORTLEY MON-
TAGU (1689-1762), wit and letter writer, once a friend of Alexander
Pope, later his enemy, and caustically satirized by him in the 'Epistle
to Dr Arbuthnot'; AMBROSE PHILIPS (1675?-1749), poet, essayist,
journalist, and later a judge—who also quarrelled with the jealous and
spiteful Pope, and was also satirized by the latter; DAVID MALLET
(1705?-65), Scottish poet, friend of Pope and of James Thomson (of
the *Seasons*); ELIZABETH CARTER (1717-1806), poet, lady of letters,
friend of Dr Johnson; the famous LORD CHESTERFIELD (1694-1773),
though his body was subsequently removed and buried elsewhere;
WILLIAM WHITEHEAD (1715-85), dramatist, poet, and Poet Laureate;
and JOHN WILKES (1727-97), stormy politician, journalist, and satirical writer. He had private vices no worse than the generality of his
contemporaries—except that he was honest enough to admit (or
even flaunt) them. He was twice imprisoned for his liberal views on
freedom of the press and for his opposition to the tyranny of George
III. Boswell arranged a dinner between him and Dr Johnson, and
tells about it in one of the most entertaining parts of the *Life*. Wilkes
wrote his own epitaph, which may be seen here, on the balcony, at the
far left: 'The Remains of John Wilkes, a Friend of Liberty'.

6. When you leave the chapel, turn left, down *South Audley Street*.
This street has had some celebrated literary inhabitants, though the
precise address of most of them is unknown to the present writer.
General Pasquale Paoli (1725-1807), the Corsican patriot whom Boswell had visited and championed, fled to England in 1769, and lived
on this street. JAMES BOSWELL (1740-95), Dr Johnson's biographer,
often stayed with Paoli when he made trips to town. Once, when
Boswell fell ill here, he was visited by *Dr Johnson* and the painter
Sir Joshua Reynolds. JOHN HOME (1722-1808), the 'Scottish Shakespeare', who was famous for more than a century as author of the
play *Douglas* (1756), lodged here in 1758. And THOMAS HOLCROFT
(1745-1809), dramatist and novelist, worked as a boy at his father's
cobbler's shop on this street. Holcroft, who was a friend of Coleridge,
Lamb, and William Godwin, had some revolutionary humanitarian
ideals that he put into his writing. He was also the author of the first
'melo-drama' (1802), or melody drama, or what would today be called
a 'musical'.

At the very end of South Audley Street, on the left-hand corner,
stood *Chesterfield House*, built by LORD CHESTERFIELD (see above).
It was a 'magnificent mansion', fitted out with all the luxury and
taste that money could buy—filled with paintings, statuary, books,
objets d'art, and masterpieces of classical interior decoration. Chester-

field's only memorable literary production was his *Letters to his Son* (an illegitimate son), which, Dr Johnson said, 'taught the manners of a dancing master and the morals of a whore.'

7. On *Curzon Street*, almost opposite the end of South Audley Street, is *No. 19*, the house where BENJAMIN DISRAELI (see above) died. *No. 11A* was the home (1960's of JOHN OSBORNE (b. 1929), one of the 'Angry Young Men' of the 1950's. *No. 22* was the house of Becky Sharp in Thackeray's *Vanity Fair*.

8. Turn right, on Curzon Street, walk one block, to Park Lane. Here, turn right again, and walk up one block to where *Deanery Street* slants away to the right. At *No. 3* MRS PATRICK CAMPBELL (1865-1940), who was a friend and correspondent of Bernard Shaw, an actress for whom Shaw wrote some of his plays, and a woman for love of whom Shaw made something of a fool of himself, lived in the early 1920's.
[8A. Can anyone be interested in SOAMES JENYS (1704-87), poet, writer on religion, politician, and victim of a savage review by Dr Johnson? If anyone *is* interested—Jenys lived and died on little *Tilney Street*, which leads off from the right of Deanery Street.]

9. Follow Deanery Street back to South Audley Street once more, turn left, go a few steps, and turn left again, into *South Street*. George Bryan Brummell (1778-1840) (called 'Beau Brummell') lived at *No. 24*, and later at *No. 22*, for a time after 1809; and Florence Nightingale, pioneer nurse, lived at *No. 10*. Lord William Melbourne (1779-1848) lived at *No. 39* while he was Prime Minister, 1835-41. He is of literary interest once or twice removed. His wife, LADY CAROLINE LAMB (1785-1828), who is described as 'clever, beautiful, impulsive, and indiscreet', was a writer of novels, but is remembered mostly for the mad passion she conceived for Byron, and her affair with him. Lord Melbourne himself, after his separation from Lady Caroline, had an affair with MRS CAROLINE NORTON (1808-77), novelist, poet, feminist, and granddaughter of Richard Brinsley Sheridan.

10. At the end of South Street, turn right, into Park Lane again. Walk two blocks, and turn right, into *Mount Street*. The American man-of-letters WASHINGTON IRVING (1783-1859) lodged with his friend William Spencer at *No. 4* in 1824. FRANCES ('FANNY') BURNEY (1752-1840) lived at *No. 22* from 1838 till shortly before her death, and at *No. 112* from 1837 to 1838. SOMERSET MAUGHAM (1874-1965), novel-

ist and dramatist, was living at *No. 23* around 1910; WINSTON CHURCHILL (1874-1965), historian and Prime Minister, at *No. 105* in 1906; WILFRED SCAWEN BLUNT (1840-1922), who married Byron's granddaughter, raised Arabian horses, was an activist in seeking the independence of Ireland, India, and Egypt, and wrote poetry that was shockingly outspoken for its time, at *No. 100* around 1900; KENNETH TYNAN (b. 1927), journalist, critic, historian, dramatist, at *No. 120* in the 1960's; and ALGERNON CHARLES SWINBURNE (1837-1909), poet of complex melodies and sensual decadence, at *No. 124*, off the street, in the 1860's.

11. Turn back a few steps, cross the street, and ascend *Carlos Place*. OSCAR WILDE (1854-1900), poet and dramatist, lodged at *No. 9* on his return from his American lecture tour in 1883.

12. Continue to *Grosvenor Square*. The statue of FRANKLIN DELANO ROOSEVELT (1882-1945) stands in the square as a part of a memorial to the Four Freedoms; since Freedom of Expression is one of the Four Freedoms, the memorial deserves to be noticed in a book like this. The American Embassy (with its semi-detached and outsize eagle) occupies the left-hand (western) side of the square; and behind the Roosevelt statue is a building, marked by a plaque, where General Eisenhower planned the North African invasion. It was in a house on this square that DR SAMUEL JOHNSON, 'retired and uncourtly scholar', waited repeatedly and vainly in the ante-room for the elegant LORD CHESTERFIELD (see above) to take some notice of him and his projected *Dictionary*. In another house here Dr Johnson often visited his dear friends the Henry Thrales; MRS HESTER LYNCH THRALE (1741-1821) wrote voluminous diaries, and a valuable memoir of Dr Johnson. The novelist EDWARD BULWER-LYTTON (1803-73) spent his last five years at *No. 12*; and the dissolute WILLIAM BECKFORD (1760-84), author of the famous Gothic novel *Vathek*, lived at *No. 22*, where he often had Lady Emma Hamilton and her husband as house guests, while Horatio Nelson (Beckford's friend and Lady Hamilton's lover) was also a constant guest. (But since Sir William Hamilton had originally bought the lady from his nephew, who had found her God knows where, and was now approaching 70 years of age, while his lady was just a bit over 30, Sir William's husbandly compliance is understandable.) WILLIAM WORDSWORTH, the poet, visited with his friends the Beaumonts at *No. 29* in 1806. And JOHN WILKES (see above) lived and died at *No. 30*.

13. At the north-west corner of Grosvenor Square (between the Ameri-

can Embassy and the Eisenhower building) enter *North Audley Street*. The sister of MARIA EDGEWORTH (1767-1849), Irish novelist who wrote realistically about Ireland, wrote Gothic novels, and influenced Sir Walter Scott, lived at *No. 1*. Here the novelist made many prolonged visits, 1830-31 and 1841-4.

14. Near the upper end of North Audley Street, you will reach *Green Street*. Turn left into it. Somewhere on this street BISHOP GEORGE BERKELEY (1685-1753), the idealistic philosopher, and his family lived, 1731-4, on their return from America. EDWARD JERNINGHAM (1727-1812), poet and dramatist, also lived and died on this street. At *No. 56* died SYDNEY SMITH (1771-1845)—after having lived, it seems in every part of London (where we have, not tirelessly, traced him in this book). He was a clergyman, but wittier than any clergyman has a right to be, and a vigorous liberal who fought for the emancipation of Catholics, defended Ireland against English misrule, opposed slavery, and dedicated himself to the reforms that were finally incorporated in the Reform Bill of 1832. He helped found the *Edinburgh Review*, contributed to it, and published several volumes of sermons and essays. MATTHEW ('MONK') LEWIS (1775-1818), early 'horror' novelist, stayed at *No. 16* in 1812.

15. Green Street runs into Park Lane. Here you will find a pedestrians' subway leading under Park Lane to *Hyde Park*. You should certainly pass through this subway, ascend at the *Speakers' Corner* of the park, and listen to some of the speakers who appear there on Saturday and Sunday evenings, and often on other evenings as well. This particular spot (patrolled by London bobbies walking about calmly to see that everybody has his say without violence to anybody) is sacred to Anglo-Saxon traditions of free speech. It has been a model (too often ignored, alas!) for freedom of speech the world over. One feels like bowing in silent tribute.

Now return through the subway to the other side of Park Lane once more, and so, turning to your left, attain the *Marble Arch Underground Station* once more. If you are not tired (and you shouldn't be after this rather short trip), you may easily and quickly take the underground to the beginnings of the following tours, which are all on this same Central Line of the underground: *Tours Nos. 7, 8, 9, 17, 23, 28, 32, 33.*

Tour 13
Campden Hill Area

Joseph Addison

Richard Aldington

James Barrie

Max Beerbohm

Pamela Brown

G. K. Chesterton

Agatha Christie

George Colman The Elder

George Colman The Younger

Sidney Colvin

Joseph Conrad

Walter Crane

Edward de Vere

Hilda Doolittle

Ford Madox Ford

W. S. Gilbert

John Galsworthy

Lord Ronald Gorell

Kenneth Grahame

Thomas Anstey Guthrie
('F. Anstey')

Radclyffe Hall

Violet Hunt

Mrs Elizabeth Inchbald

Charles Kent

Thomas Killigrew

Rudyard Kipling

Richard le Gallienne

Wyndham Lewis

Thomas Babington Macaulay

Martin Madan

Alice Meynell

Wilfred Meynell

James Mill

Charles Morgan

Sir Henry Newbolt

Sir Isaac Newton

Ezra Pound

Anne Thackeray Ritchie

Arthur Reed Ropes

William Rothenstein

Olivia Shakespear

Sir Osbert Sitwell

L. A. G. Strong

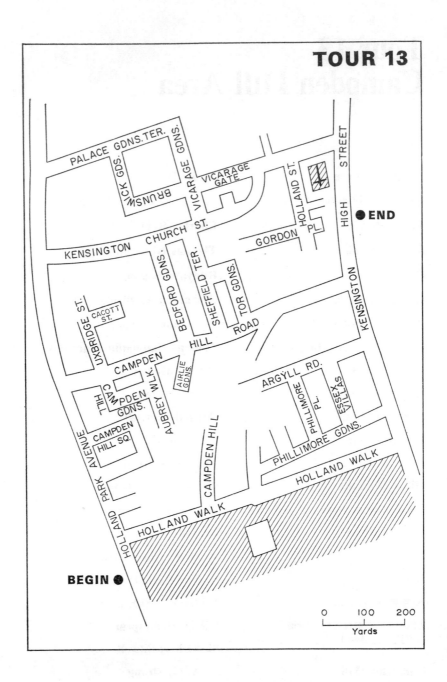

TOUR 13

PALACE GDNS. TER.

BRUNSWICK GDS.

VICARAGE GDNS.

VICARAGE GATE

HOLLAND ST.

HIGH STREET

● END

KENSINGTON CHURCH ST.

GORDON

PL.

KENSINGTON

BEDFORD GDNS.

SHEFFIELD TER.

TOR GDNS.

HILL

ROAD

UXBRIDGE ST.

CACOTT ST.

CAMPDEN

AIRLIE GDNS.

ARGYLL RD.

PHILLIMORE PL.

ESSEX VILLAS

CAMPDEN HILL

CAMPDEN GDNS.

AUBREY WLK.

PHILLIMORE GDNS.

PARK AVENUE

CAMPDEN HILL SQ.

CAMPDEN HILL

HOLLAND WALK

HOLLAND PARK

HOLLAND WALK

HOLLAND WALK

BEGIN ●

0   100   200
Yards

198

William Makepeace Thackeray **Hilda Vaughan**

Evelyn Underhill **Filson Young**

Leave the underground at the *Holland Park Station.*

1. On leaving the station, turn right, on *Holland Park Avenue*, and find *No. 84*, where the novelist, poet, and editor FORD MADOX FORD (1873-1939) lived from 1908 to 1919, and here had the editorial office of his *English Review*, a journal of considerable significance in the history of twentieth-century English literature.

2. Turn around, and go back down Holland Park Avenue the way you came, till you reach, on your right, *Campden Hill Square*. A number of literary notables have lived here: At *No. 16*, CHARLES MORGAN (b. 1894), novelist, critic, and semi-mystic (*The Fountain* is his best-known work); Morgan's wife HILDA VAUGHAN (b. 1892), novelist of the Welsh country folk; at *No. 20*, EVELYN UNDERHILL (1875-1941), poet, novelist, mystical writer. At *No. 23* lived the Davies family, whose children the novelist and dramatist JAMES BARRIE (1860-1937) adopted in all but name. With and for these children he composed many of the plots of his fairy stories and plays—including *Peter Pan.*

3. Return to Holland Park Avenue, and double back in the direction from which you came—till you reach little Holland Walk, a matter of a short block. Turn left into Holland Walk, and ascend it till you reach the first intersecting 'street' on your left, which is plain *Campden Hill*—here a narrow passage between brick walls. Down this street, on your right was *Holly Lodge*, where THOMAS BABINGTON MACAULAY (1800-59), historian, political writer, and even poet, spent his last years, and died. The place has been absorbed by buildings associated with a college; in his time it was only a small bachelor cottage with extensive grounds. Macaulay wrote the last volume of his great *History of England* here at Holly Lodge.

4. Return to Holland Walk, and continue along it till you reach an opening on your right, with a large, imposing building just inside. This is *Holland House*—or what is left of it. Built in 1607, it was for more than two centuries the resort of 'wits and beauties, of painters and poets, of scholars, philosophers, and statesmen' (Macaulay). Dramas were staged privately here during the Commonwealth period (1642-60) when public theatres were illegal. JOSEPH ADDISON (1672-1719), poet, dramatist, and essayist, married the widow of the sixth

Earl of Holland, moved here in 1716, and here died. After that, it became a kind of social headquarters and informal assembly place for prominent Whig politicians and writers until well into the nineteenth century. Some of those who came here for long or short visits, regularly or occasionally, were *Edward Bulwer-Lytton, Edmund Burke, Lord Byron, Thomas Campbell, Charles Dickens, George Grote, Washington Irving, Matthew ('Monk') Lewis, Monckton Milnes, Thomas Moore, Samuel Rogers, Sir Walter Scott, Richard Brinsley Sheridan, Sydney Smith, Madame de Stael, Blanco White,* and the actors *Edmund Kean* and *John Kemble.* The view nearest the gate where you enter shows a fine scalloped façade; but the grand and ornate front of the house is to your left, facing a road leading off at right angles to Holland Walk. The entire Holland estate here was owned, till the time of James I, by the De Veres, Earls of Oxford, who had a manor house at this place. It will be remembered that some people have attributed the works of Shakespeare to EDWARD DE VERE (1550-1604), the seventeenth earl, who was a lyric poet of much ability, and a patron of many contemporary men of letters, including John Lyly and Edmund Spenser.

5. Return to Holland Walk, cross it, and find, just opposite the place where you entered the park, the entrance to the Duchess of Bedford's Walk. Enter it, and turn immediately to your right, into *Phillimore Gardens.* Farther down, at *No. 6,* 'F. ANSTEY' (THOMAS ANSTEY GUTHRIE, 1856-1934), writer of humorous fiction and drama, and long-time contributor to *Punch,* lived during his early childhood.

6. Turn left, at the second street, into *Phillimore Place.* WILFRID MEYNELL (1848-1952), editor and 'discoverer' of the poet Francis Thompson, and his wife ALICE MEYNELL (1847-1922), the poet, lived on this street in the 1880's. And at *No. 16* KENNETH GRAHAME (1859-1931) lived during the first decade of the twentieth century. He was the author of several elaborately fanciful children's books—of which the most famous is *The Wind in the Willows* (1908), written at this place.

7. Continue to the end of the block, and turn right, on Argyll Road. Follow this for one block, and turn right, into *Essex Villas.* At *No. 8* W. S. GILBERT (1836-1911) lived, 1868-76.

> W. S. GILBERT wrote the librettos of the Gilbert and Sullivan comic operas to which Sir Arthur Sullivan composed the music. Called the 'Savoy Operas' because most of them were first produced in the Savoy Theatre, they include *The Mikado, The Pirates of Penzance, Iolanthe, H.M.S. Pinafore,* etc.

8. Return to Argyll Road, and continue along it (to your right) till it ends in Kensington High Street. Turn left here, walk one block, and then left again into *Campden Hill Road. No. 29* is the painfully ordinary house which was the London address of SIR HENRY NEWBOLT (1862-1938) during the last 20 years of his life, and here he died. Novelist, historian, government official, and poet, he tried to do (in his verse) for the British Navy what Kipling had tried to do for the British Army. Much farther up, at *No. 80*, lived VIOLET HUNT (d. 1942), novelist and for many years mistress of the novelist Ford Madox Ford.

9. Continue straight along Campden Hill Road (being careful not to branch off to your left along plain Campden Hill). For a while now you will be turning off to left or to right into several short streets— and then returning immediately to Campden Hill Road.

The first turn-off is to the right, into *Tor Gardens*—where JOHN GALSWORTHY (1867-1933), novelist and dramatist, stayed at *No. 10* in 1903.

The next turn-off, also to the right, is into *Sheffield Terrace*. GILBERT K. CHESTERTON (1874-1936), essayist, historian, wit, poet, critic, short-story writer, and apologist for Roman Catholicism, was born on this street in a house no longer standing. WILLIAM ROTHENSTEIN (1872-1945), artist and writer, lived at *No. 18* in the 1920's. And AGATHA CHRISTIE, mystery writer, lived at *No. 58*.

Return to Campden Hill Road, continue along it, and find, on your left, *Airlie Gardens* where, at *No. 10* FORD MADOX FORD (see above) lived, most unhappily, with his wife around 1904. WILLIAM ROTHENSTEIN (see above) lived at *No. 13* in the 1930's.

On your right, opposite the entrance of Airlie Gardens, is *Bedford Gardens*. The poet and literary historian RICHARD LE GALLIENNE (1866-1947) lived here, at *No. 5*, early in the twentieth century. His daughter Eva Le Gallienne became famous in America as an actress and producer.

Still farther along Campden Hill Road, *Peel Street* opens on your right. *No. 73* was the home, during the 1960's, of the children's novelist and television producer PAMELA BROWN (b. 1924).

Beyond Peel Street, *Aubrey Walk* enters Campden Hill Road from your left. The novelist-dramatist JOHN GALSWORTHY (see above) lived at *No. 16A* (off the street) in the early twentieth century.

Just as you enter Aubrey Walk, you will see (to your right) the entrance of a little street called Campden Hill Gardens. Walk up this street. FORD MADOX FORD (see above) lived at *No. 20A* for a few poverty-stricken months early in 1919; and he was succeeded here by

WYNDHAM LEWIS (1886-1957), an early 'modernistic' painter in England, and author of satirical, sometimes savage, novels and essays showing his fascist and anti-democratic sympathies.

[9A. This street debouches into Campden Hill Road once more, with the entrance of Uxbridge Street just opposite. Two blocks along the latter, and to your right, lies *Calcott Street*, where, at *No. 15*, the poet LORD RONALD GORELL (1884-1963) lived from the 1950's. His sensitive, pessimistic, and low-keyed verse has never attracted much attention.]

10. When you have again reached Campden Hill Road, turn left, and reach *Notting Hill Gate*. Turn right, and find where *No. 29* used to be. Here WYNDHAM LEWIS (see above) lived from 1945 till his death; and here *Ezra Pound*, after his release from confinement in America, sat for a well-known portrait by Lewis.

11. A little farther on, *Palace Gardens Terrace* enters from your right. Turn into it. *No. 35* was the long-time home of SIR SIDNEY COLVIN (1845-1927), man of letters, and friend and editor of Robert Louis Stevenson. Colvin died here. *No. 57* is the birthplace of MAX BEER-BOHM (1872-1956), essayist and caricaturist. At *No. 61* WYNDHAM LEWIS (see above) lived in the 1920's.

12. Follow Palace Gardens Terrace to the place where *Brunswick Gardens* enters on your right. Turn into this street. At *No. 42* lived the poet, novelist, and critic L. A. G. STRONG (1896-1958) in the 1930's. And at *No. 12* lived the novelist OLIVIA SHAKESPEAR (1866?-1938). She (with Maud Gonne and Lady Augusta Gregory) was one of the three women who profoundly influenced the life and work of the poet William Butler Yeats. Married to a man much older than herself, who would not give her a divorce, she became the short-time mistress (as 'Diana Vernon') and the long-time friend of Yeats. She is referred to indirectly in many of his poems—especially some of the early 'rose' poems, and poems in 'Words for Music, Perhaps'. In the poem 'Memory' she is meant in the first line of 'One had a lovely face,/And two or three had charm'. She was the mother of Dorothy Shakespear, who became the wife of the American poet EZRA POUND (1885-1972), who first met his bride-to-be here, and often visited here. Through the Shakespears, Pound met and became friends with Yeats, and was influential in helping the latter make the famous transition from his early lilting, dreamy poetry to his later close-knit, tough-fibred intellectual poetry.

13. Go on to the end of Brunswick Gardens. [Somewhere just ahead of you the Utilitarian philosopher JAMES MILL (1775-1836) lived 'in fame and opulence', during his last six years, and died.] Turn right, on Vicarage Gardens, and reach Kensington Church Street. Across it, and a bit to your left, is the entrance of *Gloucester Walk*, where JAMES BARRIE (see above) lived, at *No. 14*, in 1892.

14. Return to Kensington Church Street, and descend it. *Campden Grove* soon opens on your right. *No. 1* was the home of CHARLES KENT (1823-1902), well-known in the mid-Victorian period as a literary biographer and critic, journalist, editor, and even poet. *No. 2* was the last home of FILSON YOUNG (1876-1938), historian, journalist, and man of letters. And *No. 13* was the home, in the early 1920's, of ARTHUR REED ROPES ('ADRIAN ROSS') (1859-1933), who wrote the lyrics and librettos of dozens of famous musicals and light operas, as well as poems, literary history, and literary criticism in French.

15. Continue down Kensington Church Street. On your right, in the curve of the street, was the house where SIR ISAAC NEWTON (1642-1727), mathematician and physicist, spent his last three years, and died.

16. Farther down the street, on the left, is the opening to *York House Place*, with *York House* itself on the right of it. OSBERT SITWELL (1892-1969), poet and fascinating autobiographer, brother of Edith and Sacheverell Sitwell, lived at *No. 5 York House* in the early 1960's.

17. A little farther down Kensington Church Street, and on your right, find the entrance of *Holland Street*. Here, at *No. 13*, lived the poet and artist WALTER CRANE (1845-1915). Closely associated with the Pre-Raphaelites, he wrote three books of poems, and illustrated many romantic tales and poems; he collaborated with William Morris in the work of the celebrated Kelmscott Press; and he participated in the socialist movement, along with Morris, in the 1880's and 1890's. At *No. 37* RADCLYFFE HALL (188?-1943), novelist, bought a house, and lived for four years. Her novel *The Well of Loneliness* (1928), about lesbianism, made a literary, legal, and moral sensation at the time of its publication. She wrote seven other novels, four books of poetry, and short stories.

18. The first street opening into Holland Street from the left is the narrow little *Kensington Church Walk*. Here, at *No. 10*, EZRA POUND (see above) lived during his first London years, and from here in-

fluenced and dominated most of the 'new' poetry of his time. He lived on the first floor, facing the court. Across the court the young RICHARD ALDINGTON (1892-1962), poet, novelist, critic, and translator, lived briefly with the American Imagist poet HILDA DOOLITTLE ('H.D.') (1886-1961) before they were married.

19. A little farther along Holland Street, *Gordon Place* leads off to the right. Here, at *No. 17*, lived JOSEPH CONRAD (1857-1924), the Polish-born novelist, around 1904. He had moved to this place in order to be near his collaborator Ford Madox Ford (see above), who lived a short distance away on Airlie Gardens.

20. Return to Church Street, and continue along it till you reach the corner of Kensington High Street. Here, on your right, you will find the old *St Mary Abbots Church*. Though a church has stood on this spot since before 1100, the present building dates only from 1872. Either this or the previous church witnessed the following events of literary interest: *Church attendance* by JOSEPH ADDISON (see above); the novelist WILLIAM MAKEPEACE THACKERAY (1811-63); JAMES MILL (1773-1836), the Utilitarian philosopher THOMAS BABINGTON MACAULAY (see above). *Marriages* of Thackeray's daughter ANNE, who became LADY RITCHIE (1837-1919), herself a novelist, in 1887; of John Lockwood Kipling and Alice Macdonald, who became the parents of RUDYARD KIPLING, in 1865; of W. S. GILBERT (see above) in 1867; of GILBERT K. CHESTERTON (see above), in 1901; and of EZRA POUND (see above), in 1914. *Burials* of THOMAS KILLIGREW (1612-93), dramatist and theatre manager; the REVEREND MARTIN MADAN (1729-90), poet, musician, and pamphleteer, but most renowned for his *Thelyphthora* (1780), in which he advocates polygamy as a remedy for prostitution; the dramatists and theatre managers GEORGE COLMAN THE ELDER (1732-94) and his son GEORGE COLMAN THE YOUNGER (1762-1836); MRS ELIZABETH INCHBALD (1753-1821), actress, dramatist, and novelist; and JAMES MILL (see above).

You are now just across the street from the *Kensington High Street Underground Station*, and here you end this tour. But here also, if you wish, you may begin either *Tour No. 14* or *Tour No. 29*.

Tour 14
Soho

Dr John Armstrong

William Beckford

Arnold Bennett

William Blake

Henry St John, Viscount
   Bolingbroke

Mrs Golding Bright
   ('George Egerton')

Robert Williams Buchanan

Edmund Burke

Frances ('Fanny') Burney

Giovanni Casanova

Mrs Hester Chapone

Samuel Taylor Coleridge

William Collins

George Colman The Elder

Charles Darwin

W. H. Davies

Thomas De Quincey

Charles Dickens

Ernest Dowson

John Dryden

David Garnett

Stephen Graham

William Hazlitt

William Ernest Henley

William Hogarth

Thomas Jefferson Hogg

Theodore Hook

T. E. Hulme

David Hume

Mrs Elizabeth Inchbald

Douglas Jerrold

Dr Samuel Johnson

Edmund Kean

Charles Kemble

Frances ('Fanny') Kemble

John Logan

George, Lord Lyttleton

Thomas Babington Macaulay

Charles Macready

Edmund Malone

Karl Marx

Francis Meynell

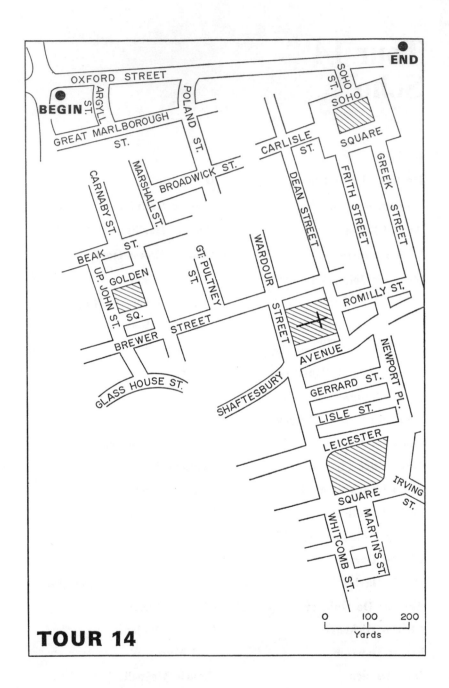

TOUR 14

Mary Russell Mitford	Percy Bysshe Shelley
Charles Molloy	Richard Brinsley Sheridan
Lady Mary Wortley Montagu	Thomas Sheridan
Hannah More	Mrs Sarah Siddons
Arthur Murphy	Tobias Smollett
Sir Isaac Newton	Mrs Germaine De Stael
James Northcote	Lytton Strachey
Coventry Patmore	Jonathan Swift
Matthew Prior	Mrs Germaine de Stael
Sir Joshua Reynolds	George Walker
Dante Gabriel Rossetti	William Wordsworth

Leave the underground at the *Oxford Circus Station.*

1. Double back to the right (eastward) on Oxford Street, and turn to your right, into *Argyll Street.* At *No. 30* MRS GERMAINE DE STAEL (1766-1817), the French novelist and bluestocking, lived in 1813-14, as an exile from Napoleon's France. The gentle and gentlemanly GEORGE LYTTLETON (1709-73), essayist and poet, friend of Pope, Fielding, and Thomson, lived (1743-9) at *No. 31.*

2. *Great Marlborough Street* crosses the bottom of Argyll Street. In a house just to the left of the end of Argyll Street, and on the far side of Great Marlborough Street, lived (1782-3) MRS HESTER LYNCH THRALE (1741-1821), diarist and letter-writer, friend of Dr Johnson until she offended him by re-marrying after her first husband's death. Dr Johnson did not like re-marriage, the new husband (he was, unforgivably, a foreigner), and the fact that the new husband was a musician. Two houses to the left of Mrs Thrale's place lived and died JAMES NORTHCOTE (1746-1831), a painter who wrote the lives of Reynolds and Titian, two series of *Fables*, and valuable memoirs (*Conversations*) telling of his acquaintanceship with Johnson, Burke, Reynolds, Goldsmith, Hazlitt, and other literary men. *Sir Walter Scott* sat for a portrait here in 1728. Northcote lived at this place for forty-one years (1790-1831).
    Continue on eastward along this street. CHARLES DARWIN (1809-82), father of the doctrine of evolution, lodged at *No. 41* from 1836

to 1838. The painter *Benjamin Haydon* (1786-1846), friend of Keats, Leigh Hunt, and many other writers of his time, lived (1808-17) also at *No. 41*. MRS SARAH (KEMBLE) SIDDONS (1755-1831), greatest actress of her time, lived with her husband, at *No. 54* for nearly thirteen years (1790-1802). JOHN LOGAN (1748-88), a Scottish poet who was writing with passionate and uninstructed innocence about nature (*e.g.*, 'Ode to the Cuckoo', 'Ode Written on a Visit to the Country in Autumn') before anybody might have been expected to do such things, died in lodgings somewhere on this street.

3. When you reach *Poland Street*, turn left. WILLIAM BLAKE (1757-1827), mystic poet and artist whose reputation both as poet and artist seems to grow with every passing year, lodged at *No. 28* from 1785 to 1791. Here he wrote *Songs of Innocence, Book of Thel, Tiriel, Marriage of Heaven and Hell, Ghost of Abel.* (If you care to walk on to the end of Poland Street, and turn the corner, you will find *No. 173 Oxford Street*, where, at a chemist's shop, *Thomas de Quincey*, author of *Confessions of an English Opium-Eater*, bought his first opium.) Turn around, and walk down Poland Street away from Oxford Street. On the left, at *No. 15*, lower corner of Poland and Great Marlborough Streets, PERCY BYSSHE SHELLEY (1792-1822) and his friend THOMAS JEFFERSON HOGG (1792-1862) lodged, in 1811, after they had been kicked out of Oxford—Shelley for writing a pamphlet on *The Necessity of Atheism*, and Hogg for defending him. Hogg later wrote a biography of his friend. FRANCES ('FANNY') BURNEY (1752-1840), the novelist, lived on this street as a child, at *No. 50*, on your right. And J. H. Reynolds, called 'Keats's dearest friend', and himself a poet stayed with friends at this *No. 50* around 1820.

4. You will soon reach *Broadwick Street* (formerly Broad Street). Turn right. In the 1960's a great modern building was erected at *No. 74* (formerly *No. 28*), where the poet and artist WILLIAM BLAKE (see above) was born. Next door (at what was *No. 27*) Blake, when he was 27 years old, set up an engraving and print shop, and did some of his earliest art work.

5. Follow Broadwick to its end, and turn left into Marshall Street. At the end of the latter, turn right into Beak Street. (At *No. 41 Beak Street* the great Italian painter *Antonio Canaletto* had lodgings, 1749-52.)
[5A. Opening from your right is *Carnaby Street*. In the seventeenth century the humanitarian Earl of Craven built 36 small houses, to your right on this street, for the reception of victims of the plague.

But in the 1960's this street became world famous for its youthful clothing styles.]

Turn left, into Upper John Street, and reach *Golden Square*. Matthew Bramble, in Smollett's novel *Humphry Clinker*, lodged here, with his entourage, on his visit to London; Ralph Nickleby (of Dickens's *Nicholas Nickleby*) lived at *No. 6* on this square; and Thackeray's Henry Esmond visited General Webb here, at *No. 22*. LADY MARY WORTLEY MONTAGU (1689-1762), wit, letter-writer, and bluestocking, lived with her cousin for a while on this square, at *No. 19*. And HENRY ST JOHN, VISCOUNT BOLINGBROKE (1678-1751), statesman, political philosopher, essayist, and profligate (to whom Alexander Pope dedicated the *Essay on Man*) lived on this square, at about where *No. 21* now stands, near the bottom (south) end of the square, and on this (western) side. Jonathan Swift records having dined with Bolingbroke here on several occasions.

6. From the corner of the square, continue along lower John Street to *Brewer Street*, and turn left on the latter.

[6A. If you are a very specialized scholar, you may wish to cross Brewer Street, and explore *Glasshouse Street* beyond. On this street lived (1722) Charles Boyle, Earl of Orrery, who, 30 years previously, had implicated himself in a literary quarrel out of which grew Swift's magnificent satire *The Battle of the Books*. Also on this street, at *No. 22*, lived the great Shakespearean scholar EDMUND MALONE (1741-1812), when he first came to London in 1777.]

DAVID HUME (1711-76), Scottish sceptical philosopher and historian, lived at 'Miss Elliott's' (*No. 67*) on Brewer Street in 1765 and 1767. His brother Scotsman TOBIAS SMOLLETT (1721-71), the novelist, lived on this street just below Golden Square, in 1765. (As you walk along Brewer Street, you will see *Sherwood Street* opening from your right. ERNEST DOWSON (1867-1900), finest lyricist of the Aesthetic Movement of the 1890's, frequented an inn at *No. 19*. A bit farther on, *Great Pultney Street* opens from the left. Up this street, at *No. 18*, *Joseph Haydn*, the Austrian musician, lived on his visit to England in 1791-2. At *No. 33* on this street the harpsichord maker Tschudi had his place of business, and both *Handel* and *Haydn* were often here. At about the place where Great Pultney runs into Brewer Street, or a little beyond, the ancient Britons had a large temple during the Roman occupation.)

7. When you reach the end of Brewer Street (at Wardour Street), turn right. *St Anne's Church* now stands immediately to your left. Horne Tooke, radical politician, philologist, friend of the American colonists

(he was tried for treason—but acquitted—because of his American sympathies), was baptized in this church, 1736. HESTER LYNCH SALUSBURY (see above) married HENRY THRALE here in 1763. The exiled Theodore, King of Corsica (he was a German adventurer who had got himself elected king), died in dire poverty in Soho, and is buried at St. Anne's—with a tombstone paid for by *Horace Walpole*, and bearing a poetic inscription by Walpole. WILLIAM HAZLITT (1778-1830), the essayist and critic, is also buried here.

8. Wardour Street runs directly in front of St Anne's. Follow this street across Shaftesbury Avenue, and one block beyond. Then turn left, into *Gerrard Street*. THOMAS SHERIDAN (1719-88), father of the dramatist Richard Brinsley Sheridan, gave 'Lectures on Elocution and Declamation' at a public hall on this street; the actor CHARLES KEMBLE (1757-1854) and his daughter, the even more famous FANNY KEMBLE (1809-93), lived at *No. 35*; and HANNAH MORE (1745-1833), once famous dramatist and novelist, lived on this street for many years after 1778. JAMES BOSWELL (1740-95), Dr Johnson's biographer, lodged at *No. 22* in 1775 and 1776. The dramatist and Poet Laureate JOHN DRYDEN (1631-1700) had his home at *No. 44* for years, and died there. In the 1780's *No. 37* was the town house of the statesman-philosopher EDMUND BURKE (1729-87). And ROBERT WILLIAMS BUCHANAN (1841-1901), poet, novelist, dramatist, and unfortunate author of 'The Fleshly School of Poetry', lived at *No. 36* around 1900. DAVID GARNETT (b. 1892), novelist, and FRANCIS MEYNELL (b. 1891), typographer, both of them members of famous literary families, established the celebrated Nonesuch Press at *No. 30*. Mr Jaggers, the lawyer in Dickens's *Great Expectations*, had his office at *No. 10*. Before the First World War a tavern at *No. 16* was the meeting place of a group including the critic *Edward Garnett*, the poet *Edward Thomas* (killed in the war) the poet *John Masefield*, the novelist *Norman Douglas*, the novelist and essayist *H. M. Tomlinson*, the novelist and poet *Ford Madox Ford*, the poet *W. H. Davies*, the critic and dramatist *William Archer*, the novelist and naturalist *W. H. Hudson*, the two Roman Catholic writers *Hilaire Belloc* and *G. K. Chesterton* (who first met each other here, and became fast friends), and sometimes the novelists *John Galsworthy* and *Joseph Conrad*. At *No. 9*, the Turk's Head Tavern, DR JOHNSON'S 'Literary Club' was founded, and met regularly, 1764 to 1783. (The original members of the club were *Sir Joshua Reynolds, Edmund Burke, Oliver Goldsmith, Topham Beauclerk, Bennet Langdon, Sir John Hawkins, Anthony Chamier*, and *Dr Robert Nugent*. Beauclerk was an amateur scholar; Hawkins wrote essays, and Nugent some conventional poems.) At

No. 4 the left-wing '1917 Club' met regularly. Many members of the Bloomsbury Group (see Tour No. 8), as well as (strange company!) Ramsay MacDonald, who became the first Labour Party Prime Minister, were members of this club.

9. At the end of Gerrard Street, turn right, on Newport Place, and then, after a short block, turn right again—on *Lisle Street*. DAVID HUME (see above), the philosopher, had lodgings here in 1758, 1763, and 1768. The orphaned EDMUND KEAN (1787-1833), the great Shakespearean actor, who became famous in England and America, and whose portrayals had 'such intensity, force, and insight' that they were 'a landmark in the history of the theatre', passed his boyhood with his uncle at *No. 9*. The uncle fastened about the boy's neck a brass collar with the inscription: 'This boy belongs at No. 9 Lisle Street, Leicester Square, please bring him home.' *No. 12* was the headquarters (from 1738) of the Royal Society of Musicians—to which often came *Johann Christian Bach, George Frideric Handel,* and *Dr Thomas Arne.*

[9A. You will pass, on your left, the entrance to *Leicester Place,* where, at *No. 10* (Prince of Wales Coffee House) CHARLES DICKENS presided at a dinner celebrating the completion of the *Pickwick Papers* (1837).

[9B. Next you will pass, on your left, the entrance of *Leicester Street.* KARL MARX (1818-83), the socialist philosopher, stayed at the German Hotel, *Nos. 1-2,* at the nearer corner with Lisle Street, in 1850, soon after his arrival in England.]

10. At the end of Lisle Street, turn left, into Wardour Street, and follow it straight on, across Coventry Street, till it becomes *Whitcomb Street.* About the only literary association this street seems to have is the fact that W. H. DAVIES (1871-1940) the 'Hobo Poet', who was a kind of modern William Blake in his simple and sincere humanitarianism, lived for a while (1914) at *No. 18.*

11. At the second street (Orange Street) beyond Coventry Street, turn left, walk one block, and reach *St Martin's Street.* Turn left into this street. To your right, on the upper corner of the far side of this intersection (north-east corner) there once stood a chapel. Beyond it, facing into St Martin's Street, at *No. 35,* was the house that the physicist ISAAC NEWTON (1642-1727) occupied from 1710 to 1727. He had an observatory atop it. Some of his regular visitors here included *Joseph Addison, Dr John Arbuthnot,* the classical scholar *Richard Bentley,* the historian *Bishop Burnet,* the playwright *William Congreve,* the poets *John Gay* and *Matthew Prior,* and *Jonathan Swift.*

Later on, *Dr Charles Burney*, the musician, rented the house, and here his daughter FRANCES BURNEY (see above) lived from 1774 to 1789, and here wrote her most celebrated novel, *Evelina*.

12. Just ahead of you lies *Leicester Square*. [To your right, *Irving Street* leads away from the corner of the square. At *No. 20* lived 'GEORGE EGERTON' (MRS GOLDING BRIGHT) (1860-1945), Australian-born dramatist and novelist.] In the middle of the square stands a silly and much-copied statue of Shakespeare: and, at each corner of the square, a statue of some former notable inhabitant. One statue represents SIR ISAAC NEWTON (who, as you have seen, lived a bit off the square). Another represents SIR JOSHUA REYNOLDS (1723-92), painter and member of Dr Johnson's Literary Club, who lived (1761-92) at *No. 47* (middle of left-hand, or west, side of the square). Another represents the artist WILLIAM HOGARTH (1697-1764)—who lived at the second house from the bottom of the square, right-hand (east) side, as you enter from St Martin's Street; he lived here from 1733, and died here. And the fourth statue represents Dr John Hunter (1728-93), anatomist and surgeon, who lived in the next house up from Hogarth's. In the tenth house up from the bottom on this same (east) side, lived the poet MATTHEW PRIOR (1664-1721), who was also a politician and ambassador to France. Dr Johnson's friend MRS HESTER LYNCH THRALE PIOZZI (see above) lived, in the 1790's, at a hotel that had been formed by throwing together the Hogarth and Hunter houses with two more here. MRS ELIZABETH INCHBALD (1753-1821), actress, dramatist, and novelist, lived in this hotel for five years (1798-1803); and the peripatetic JONATHAN SWIFT (1667-1745), satirist and statesman, lived for a while (1711) in lodgings here. Dr William Cruikshank, who attended Dr Johnson in his last illness, lived (1789-98) in the seventh house from the bottom, left-hand (west) side, as you enter from St Martin's Street.

[12A. *Cranbourne Street* leads away from the upper right-hand (north-east) corner of the square. The far end of the street once narrowed into what was called Cranbourne Alley. Here, in a milliner's shop, DANTE GABRIEL ROSSETTI found *Elizabeth Siddal*, who became his wife.]

13. Leave Leicester Square at its upper left-hand (north-west) corner. Walk a block along New Coventry Street, and then turn right, into Wardour Street. Reach *Shaftesbury Avenue*, and turn right. The next street-crossing will be Macclesfield on the right and Dean Street on the left. At the far corner of the former (*No. 90*) were the editorial

offices of the magazine *Woman* when it was edited by ARNOLD
BENNETT (1867-1931), the novelist.

14. Turn left, off Shaftesbury Avenue, into *Dean Street.*
[14A. After you turn, the first street on your right is *Romilly,* in which
Jean Paul Marat, the French revolutionary, lived in 1776. The
caricaturist *Thomas Rowlandson* (1756-1827), who illustrated the
works of Goldsmith, Smollett, and Sterne, lived at *No. 4* in the late
1770's.]

Somewhere near here, on *Dean Street,* lived HESTER LYNCH
SALUSBURY (see above), and from here she married Mr Thrale. The
actress *Peg Woffington* (famous for her beauty, talent, and immorality) lived (1740-8) at *No. 78.* Halfway up the street, on your
left, at *No. 73* (opposite Bateman's Street) there once stood (1834-
1953) a small theatre known originally as Miss Kelly's Theatre, but
later as the Royalty. In 1845 Ben Jonson's *Every Man in his Humour*
was presented here with the novelist CHARLES DICKENS and his friend
the dramatist DOUGLAS JERROLD in leading parts. Gilbert and Sullivan's
Trial by Jury was first produced here (1875)—the initial step in a
fabulous career of the collaborators. This theatre saw also the first
public performances in England of Ibsen's *Ghosts* and *The Wild
Duck,* and Bernard Shaw's *Widowers' Houses.* The first London performance of the (apparently) immortal *Charley's Aunt* was here (1892).
Joseph Nollekens (1737-1823), most admired and sought-after portrait sculptor of his day, was born at *No. 28*—though this may not
have been located precisely at today's *No. 28.* Today's *No. 28* was the
home of KARL MARX (1818-83), socialist philosopher, from 1851 to
1856; he and his family lived on the top floor of the building. He had
moved here from   *No. 64.* At *No. 33* stood Walker's Hotel, where
members of Dr Johnson's Literary Club used to meet informally; and
here Lord Nelson spent his last night in England. MRS HESTER
CHAPONE (1721-1801), good friend of Dr Johnson and of Fanny
Burney, and voluminous letter-writer and commentator on the society
of her time, lived at *No. 7* or *No. 8.* The Lamberts, of Thackeray's
The Virginians came to live on Dean Street.

15. Until shortly after the mid-eighteenth century, Dean Street ended
at *Carlisle Street.* The part of the latter that lies to the left of Dean
Street was called 'King's Square Court'—and the poet WILLIAM
COLLINS (1721-59), one of the purest geniuses in English literature,
author of 'Ode to Evening', 'lodged in a little house with a Miss
Bundy, at the corner of King's Square Court ... for a long time
together'. The place would be at the left-hand, nearer (south-west)

corner of the present crossing. MRS HESTER CHAPONE (see above) lived at *No. 17* in 1791. And Dr Manette, of Dickens's *A Tale of Two Cities,* lived at *No. 10.*

16. Turn right, on Carlisle Street, and reach *Soho Square.* THOMAS DE QUINCEY (see above) met the prostitute Anne, who befriended him, on this square; and *Sir Roger de Coverley,* of the *Spectator* papers, lived here when he was in London. The fountain in the middle of the square is by Caius Cibber, father of the dramatist, producer, Poet Laureate, and hero of Pope's *Dunciad*—Colley Cibber.

Turn left along the square, and circle it. Turn right at the top of the square (north side). At the second house on this side (the site later occupied by a church) was the Soho Academy for boys, 'one of the most celebrated and successful of private boarding schools'. It was attended by the sons of *Edmund Burke* and *James Boswell,* by the future novelist THEODORE HOOK (1788-1841), and by the painters *Thomas Rowlandson* and *J. M. W. Turner.* At the third house (*No. 10*) on this side of the square, LADY MARY WORTLEY MONTAGU (see above) lived in 1734. At the last house (*No. 17*) along this side, the novelist and publisher GEORGE WALKER (1772-1847) lived from 1820, and here died. Turn right, along the east side of the square. At the first house here the dramatist CHARLES MOLLOY (d. 1767) lived during the last thirteen years of his life and here died. Later on, the painter *W. H. Pickergill* did here a famous portrait of WILLIAM WORDSWORTH, the poet, and here *Charles Lamb* and his sister *Mary* came to see the portrait. Continue straight ahead, crossing the entrance of Sutton Street. At the first house on the lower corner Madame Teresa Cornelys had a famous salon for the gay and the fashionable in the late eighteenth century, and was here visited (1764) by the international adventurer and writer of scandalous *Memoirs* GIOVANNI CASANOVA. He had been her lover in Europe, and claimed to be the father of her beautiful daughter Sophia. Ironically, the site is now occupied by a church. Two doors farther on lived William Beckford, famous Lord Mayor of London, during the last eighteen years of his life, and here died; and here his son, the eccentric and dissolute novelist WILLIAM BECKFORD (1760-1844) was born. From 1772 to 1780 DR JOHN ARM-STRONG (1709-79), blank-verse poet at a time when blank verse was not popular, lived in the same house. Two doors beyond this house lived (1776-87) GEORGE COLMAN THE ELDER (1732-91) theatre mana-ger and prolific dramatist. Turn right, along the bottom of the square. About midway along this side of the square (*No. 29*) CHARLES KEMBLE and his daughter FANNY (see above), actor and actress, lived, 1822-5). A small passageway called *Bateman Buildings* leads off from this side of the square. The poet and editor WILLIAM ERNEST HENLEY (1849-1903), lodged at *No. 11 Bateman Buildings* when he first came to London as a youth on his own resources.

17. By now you will have found *Greek Street*. Its most notable literary inhabitant was THOMAS DE QUINCEY (see above), who came to *No. 61* when he ran away from a school in Wales in 1802, at the age of seventeen. Here he almost starved, and might have done so except for the help given by the prostitute Anne, mentioned above. COVENTRY PATMORE (1823-96), Catholic poet associated with the Pre-Raphaelite movement, lived as a child at *No. 12*. The Wedgwoods, of pottery fame, had a showroom back from the street between *Nos. 12* and *13*. DOUGLAS JERROLD (1803-57), dramatist and humorous writer, was born somewhere on this street. Thackeray's Becky Sharp (of *Vanity Fair*) lived here; and the original of Gainsborough's 'Blue Boy' lived at the bottom of the street. *Sir Thomas Lawrence* (1769-1830), 'the most successful English portrait painter of his day', lived and worked at *No. 60* for 25 years, 1790-1814.

18. Follow Greek Street to Shaftesbury Avenue, turn right, on the latter, and then right again, into *Frith Street*. At *No. 28* on this street lived (1801) ARTHUR MURPHY (1727-1805), actor, journalist, essayist, critic, and author of a large number of highly successful satirical comedies. At *No. 22* television was first (it is said) successfully demonstrated (1926), by John L. Baird. CHARLES MACREADY (1793-1873), actor, and manager of Covent Garden and Drury Lane Theatres, lived at *No. 64*. STEPHEN GRAHAM (b. 1884), author of many books of travel in eastern Europe, as well as of valuable political studies of that region, lived from the 1930's to the late 1960's at *No. 60*. In July, 1917, LYTTON STRACHEY (1880-1932), who revolutionized the art of biography, spent a week at *No. 60* with Dora Carrington (who, if she was not his mistress, wanted to be. She introduced him to her landlady as an uncle from the country!) The poet SAMUEL TAYLOR COLERIDGE (1772-1834) once lodged with a friend, Basil Montagu, at *No. 55*—but had a disagreement with his host after four days, and departed. MARY RUSSELL MITFORD (1787-1855), once a famous novelist, was living at *No. 49* in the mid-1820's; and the painter *John Constable* was living in this same house in 1811. As a boy, the musician *Wolfgang Mozart* (1756-91) lodged with his family at *No. 20*. WILLIAM HAZLITT (see above), essayist and critic, died at *No. 6*, with *Charles Lamb* in attendance. A café at *No. 67* was the scene, before the First World War, of regular weekly meetings (dominated by the critic-philosopher T. E. HULME, who was killed in the war) of artists and

writers—including Hulme, the sculptors *Jacob Epstein* and *Gaudier-Brzeska*; the miscellaneous writers *Middleton Murry, J. C. Squire,* and *Edward Marsh*; and the poets *Ezra Pound, W. W. Gibson, F. S. Flint,* and sometimes *Rupert Brooke*. EDMUND KEAN (see above), the actor, passed his infancy with a poor couple on this street; THOMAS SHERIDAN (1719-88), teacher of elocution, lived here, in the 1760's, with his family, including the boy RICHARD BRINSLEY SHERIDAN (1751-1816), who became a famous dramatist; MRS ELIZABETH INCHBALD (see above) wrote her novel *A Simple Story* (1790) while living here; and THOMAS BABINGTON MACAULAY (1800-59), historian, biographer, and essayist, had lodgings here when he first came up from Cambridge.

When you reach the upper end of this street, you will be back in Soho Square. Cross the square to little Soho Street, which opens directly opposite Frith and Greek Streets. Follow Soho Street into Oxford Street. Here turn right, and go one block to St Giles Circus—where you will find the *Tottenham Court Road Underground Station*, and the end of this tour. But you may wish to start from here on *Tour No. 9*—into Covent Garden; or on *Tour No. 28*—to Fitzroy Square.

Tour 15
Chelsea West

Dr John Arbuthnot

Dr Thomas Arne

Bishop Francis Atterbury

Maurice Baring

Hilaire Belloc

Arnold Bennett

Phyllis Bentley

Augustine Birrell

Vera Brittain

Thomas Carlyle

Jane Welsh Carlyle

George Colman The Younger

Richard Harding Davis

William de Morgan

T. S. Eliot

John Fletcher

John Galsworthy

Mrs Elizabeth Gaskell

John Gay

W. S. Gilbert

Cicely Hamilton

Leigh Hunt

William Holman Hunt

Laurence Irving

Henry James

Pamela Hansford Johnson

Charles Kingsley

Henry Kingsley

James Laver

Laurie Lee

Benn W. Levy

Sinclair Lewis

Wyndham Lewis

Katherine Mansfield

Somerset Maugham

George Meredith

Andrew Millar

A. A. Milne

Sir Thomas More

Charles Morgan

John Middleton Murry

Kathleen Raine

Ernest Rhys

Samuel Richardson

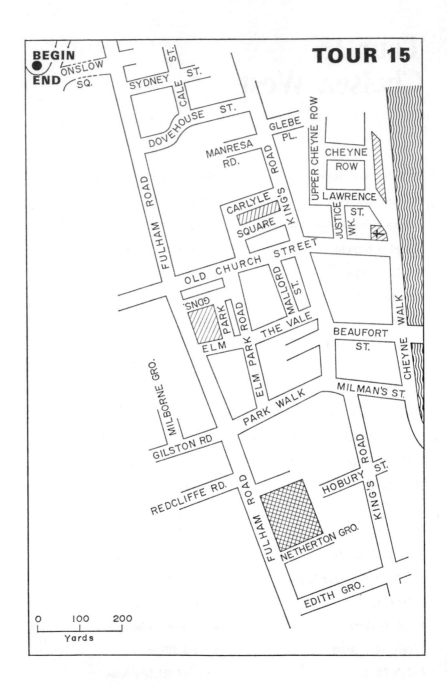

BEGIN
END
ONSLOW
SQ.

TOUR 15

SYDNEY ST.
CALE ST.
DOVEHOUSE ST.
GLEBE PL.
MANRESA RD.
UPPER CHEYNE ROW
CHEYNE ROW
LAWRENCE
FULHAM ROAD
CARLYLE SQUARE
KING'S ROAD
JUSTICE WK. ST.
OLD CHURCH STREET
GDNS.
ELM PARK
THE MALLORD ST.
THE VALE
BEAUFORT ST.
WALK
CHEYNE
ELM
MILBORNE GRO.
ELM PARK ROAD
PARK WALK
MILMAN'S ST.
GILSTON RD
REDCLIFFE RD.
FULHAM ROAD
HOBURY ST.
KING'S ROAD
NETHERTON GRO.
KING'S ST.
EDITH GRO.

0   100   200
Yards

Arthur Reed Ropes	**Ellen Terry**
William Rothenstein	**Dylan Thomas**
Bertrand Russell	**Arnold Toynbee**
William Bell Scott	**Peter Ustinov**
Thomas Shadwell	**George Villiers**
Sir Osbert Sitwell	**James McNeill Whistler**
Tobias Smollett	**Alfred North Whitehead**
J. C. Squire	**Emlyn Williams**
Jonathan Swift	

Leave the underground at the *South Kensington Station*. You may have some difficulty orienting yourself in the complex of streets before you as you emerge from the station. But by bearing somewhat to your left, you will eventually hit upon a street called Onslow Square. Descend it, away from the station, and go straight on through its continuation as Sydney Place till you reach Fulham Road (about three blocks).

1. Turn right, on Fulham Road, and then immediately cross it, and enter *Sydney Street. No. 31* was the residence of BERTRAND RUSSELL (1872-1969), philosopher, mathematician, logician, essayist, social and political reformer, and even novelist.

2. Turn right, off Sydney Street, into Gale Street; go one block, and reach *Dovehouse Street*. Here, in the mid-1960's, *No. 123* (just to your right, across the street) was the home of EMLYN WILLIAMS (b. 1905). Williams first became famous for his impersonations of Charles Dickens; but he has been also a highly successful actor on stage and screen, the author of many 'hit' plays for stage and screen, a producer of plays, and a charming autobiographer.

3. Turn left along Dovehouse Street, and follow it to where it ends in King's Road. At the corner here, on the left, is a recreation ground which was once a cemetery. Here was buried ANDREW MILLAR (d. 1768), prominent eighteenth-century publisher and bookseller, who first printed Thomson's *Seasons*, Johnson's *Dictionary*, Collins's *Odes*, Fielding's *Tom Jones*, and Hume's *History of England*.

4. Turn right, on King's Road, and then, after one block, right again into *Manresa Road*. Up this road, on the right, stands (or stood) the

'Wentworth Studios'—where DYLAN THOMAS (1914-53), the Welsh poet whose short life was so fevered and tragic, and whose poetry was certainly the finest written in England during the 1940's and 1950's, lived with his family (Flat No. 3) from 1942 to 1944.

5. Return to *King's Road*. Just across it, on the left-hand (eastern) corner, stands a group of three old buildings. *No. 213* was the home, in the later 1920's, of SOMERSET MAUGHAM (1874-1965), novelist, dramatist, short-story writer. At *No. 215*, in a house built in 1720, lived DR THOMAS ARNE (1710-78) in the early 1770's. He wrote various operas and operettas and composed music for them, wrote music for Milton's *Comus* and for many of Shakespeare's songs, and was in charge of the music at various London theatres. In this same *No. 215*, from 1904 to 1920, lived ELLEN TERRY (1848-1928), the great actress, friend and correspondent of Bernard Shaw, and first wife of the pre-Raphaelite painter G. F. Watts. PETER USTINOV (b. 1921), the actor-writer, lived in the same *No. 215* in the 1950's.... Farther along *King's Road*, at a house that occupied the present site of *No. 247*, SAMUEL RICHARDSON (1689-1761), 'Father of the English novel', lived many years, and died. He did more than anybody else to make the novel something more than a tale of adventure, and to give it psychological appeal rather than mere melodramatic suspense.

6. The Arne-Terry-Ustinov place stands at the entrance to *Glebe Place*. Down this short street, in a group of flats called 'Cedar Studios', lived the young JOHN GALSWORTHY (1867-1933), future novelist, dramatist, and Nobel Prize winner; his life here in Chelsea is reflected in the story of young Jolyon in *The Forsyte Saga*. PHYLLIS BENTLEY (b. 1894) and her friend VERA BRITTAIN (b. 1896?), both of them well-known novelists, lived together at *No. 19*. CICELY HAMILTON (1872-1952), novelist, playwright, and actress, was living at *No. 44* in the early 1920's; and somewhat later, the prolific novelist JAMES LAVER (b. 1899) lived at *Nos. 4-10*. Laver was also a poet and a successful dramatist. WILLIAM ROTHENSTEIN (1872-1945), artist and biographer, lived at *No. 53* in the 1880's. *No. 60* was the home of REGINALD BLUNT (1857-1944), historian of Chelsea.

7. Return to King's Road, and turn left. Almost immediately you will reach *Carlyle Square*, on your right. SIR OSBERT SITWELL (1892-1969), poet, novelist, autobiographer, and brother of Edith and Sacheverell Sitwell lived, through most of the 1960's, at *No. 2*; and the philosopher ALFRED NORTH WHITEHEAD (1861-1947) was living at *No. 14* in the 1920's.

8. Continue down King's Road for one block, and turn right, into Old Church Street.
[8A. WILLIAM DE MORGAN (1839-1917), artist, ceramist, socialist, friend of William Morris, and (in the last years of his life) successful novelist, lived, during his last seven years, at *No. 127 Old Church Street*; and KATHERINE MANSFIELD (1888-1923) lived at *No. 141A*, in 1917.]
Turn immediately left into Mallord Street. A. A. MILNE (1882-1956), poet, novelist, dramatist, creator of the immortal Christopher Robin and Winnie-the-Pooh, lived at *No. 11* in the early 1920's, and at *No. 13* from 1925 to the end of the 1930's. All of his most memorable works were written in these two places.

9. At the end of Mallord Street, turn right, on *The Vale*. But to your left, in houses now gone, the painter J. M. WHISTLER (1834-1903) lived (1886-90) at *No. 2*; and WILLIAM DE MORGAN (see above) lived at *No. 1* for 22 years.

10. Walk two blocks along The Vale to *Elm Park Road*. AUGUSTINE BIRRELL (1850-1933), critical essayist, biographer of authors, and public official, lived at *No. 70* during the last ten years of his life.

11. Continue straight on in line with The Vale into *Elm Park Gardens*. The American novelist SINCLAIR LEWIS (1886-1957) and his wife stayed in a hotel at *No. 58* in 1923-4. LAURIE LEE (b. 1914), poet and dramatist, lived at *No. 49* during most of the 1950's and 1960's.

Note: Sections 12-16 that follow require a rather long walk that you may not wish to undertake. In that case, turn left on Fulham Road, walk a block to Beaufort Street, and turn left into the latter. Descend this street to its end, turn right, and take up the tour at Section 17.

12A. Turn left on Fulham Road, and walk along till you reach *Gilston Road*, entering from your right. Turn into it, and find *No. 27*, where the actor and dramatist LAURENCE IRVING (1871-1914) lived.
12B. Turn right, off Gilston Road, into *Milborne Grove*, where, at *No. 12*, the poet, essayist, and editor J. C. SQUIRE (1884-1958) lived in the early 1900's.
12C. Continue straight on up Gilston Road, a considerable distance, to *The Boltons*. W. S. GILBERT (1836-1911), the librettist of Savoy Opera fame, lived here (1878-81), and here wrote *The Pirates of Penzance, Patience*, and *Iolanthe*.... Now return to Fulham Road.

13. Continue westward on Fulham Road till you reach *Redcliffe Road*, entering from your right. Here, at *No. 47*, JOHN MIDDLETON MURRY (1889-1957), critic, essayist, editor, and literary biographer, took lodgings; and soon afterward KATHERINE MANSFIELD (see above), the short-story writer, moved to the same place. WYNDHAM LEWIS (1884-1957), artist and controversial political philosopher, lodged at *No. 37* in 1920.

14. Return to Fulham Road, and continue along it. You will pass (on your left) *St Stephen's Hospital.* Here DYLAN THOMAS (see above) was once brought from his home on Manresa Road (see above), suffering from alcoholic gastritis. Just beyond the hospital, *Netherton Grove* enters Fulham Road from your left. Enter it, and find *No. 6.* Here ARNOLD BENNETT (1867-1931), the novelist, lived from 1891 to 1897, as a paying guest of his friends Mr and Mrs Frederick Marriott. His host taught art at the University of London—and his cultured and intellectual friends were an important influence on the young Bennett, who had just come up to London from the Midlands.

15. Return to Fulham Road, and walk one block farther along it. Then turn left, into *Edith Grove.* JOHN MIDDLETON MURRY (see above) and KATHERINE MANSFIELD (see above) were living at *No. 102* in 1914. They were so poor that they were for ever seeking better quarters at a cheaper rent, and so were continually moving about.

16. Walk on down Edith Grove, and turn left into King's Road once more. After a longish walk (four blocks), you will reach *Hobury Street*, entering from your left. GEORGE MEREDITH (1828-1909), novelist and poet, lived at *No. 8*, immediately after he and his wife separated. (His sequence of poems *Modern Love* record his reactions to his difficulties with his wife.) Here he wrote his novel *The Ordeal of Richard Feverel.*

17. Continue along King's Road for two blocks, and then turn right, into Milmans Street. Descend the latter to *Cheyne Walk*, paralleling the river. Turn right on Cheyne Walk, and trudge along till you find *No. 131-2*, where KATHERINE MANSFIELD (see above) lived in 1910-11. Then turn around and come back along Cheyne Walk, and follow it down to Cheyne Row (see below).

Just this side of the Mansfield house at No. 131-2, you will find *No. 118-9 Cheyne Walk*, the house where England's greatest landscape painter, *J. M. W. Turner* (1775-1851) lived as a recluse from about 1846 until he died here. The same house was occupied, in the winter of 1907-8, by the American reporter and fiction-writer RICHARD HARDING DAVIS (1864-1916) and his family. HILAIRE BELLOC (1870-1953), poet, essayist, historian, biographer, lived with his wife at *No. 104* from about 1900 to 1906. *No. 101* was the first London home (1863-6) of JAMES McNEILL WHISTLER (1834-1903), leader of the revolt against Victorianism that affected literature as well as painting, and author of the redoubtable *The Gentle Art of Making Enemies.* He left this place for *No. 96*, where he lived from 1866 to 1878. He lived at *No. 21* from 1890 to 1892; and he died at *No. 72*. He liked to paint the old Battersea Bridge (replaced by a new one) which was near here. ELIZABETH CLEGHORN STEVENSON, who became the novelist MRS GASKELL (1810-65), was born at what is now *No. 93*; WILLIAM BELL SCOTT (1812-90), Pre-Raphaelite artist and poet, lived at *No. 92*; and *Charles Conder* (1868-1909), decorative artist of the 1890's, and significant contributor to the Aesthetic movement, lived at *No. 91* from 1901 until his death here. At the far (east) corner of Church Street stands a famous old church (to be mentioned again presently); and just beyond it, facing Cheyne Walk, lived JOHN FLETCHER (1579-1625), collaborator with Francis Beaumont, as a boy and youth. Just beyond this place (at *No. 63*) lived BISHOP FRANCIS ATTERBURY, in 1708. An able controversialist of the time, he figures in Swift's *Battle of the Books*, and is praised highly in Steele's *Tatler No. 66*; and he was a friend of Swift, Pope, Prior, Gay, and Dr Arbuthnot. *No. 60*, near the corner of Cheyne Walk and Lawrence Street, marks the site of the home of THOMAS SHADWELL (1642?-92), Poet Laureate, dramatist and burlesque 'hero' of Dryden's *MacFlecknoe*; he died here and was buried in the nearby church; *No. 59*, on the corner, was the home of WILLIAM HOLMAN HUNT (1827-1910), one of the original members of the Pre-Raphaelite Brotherhood; here he painted his most famous picture, *The Light of the World*. Later on, ERNEST RHYS (1859-1946), the Welsh poet, lived in the same house. *Don Saltero's Coffee House*, which contained a museum of curios, and was famous among literary men of its time, occupied this corner from about 1690 to 1707.

18. Meanwhile, you will have reached the entrance of *Beaufort Street*, on your left. Turn into this street and ascend it. The manor house, with extensive gardens, of SIR THOMAS MORE (1478-1535) was located about where you are walking up the street. More was one of the leaders of the 'New Learning', and one of the earliest and most influential figures in bringing about the Renaissance in England. His chief literary work was *Utopia*. He lived here from about 1520 till he was arrested, and taken away to the Tower and his death.

Here he was visited by *Erasmus*, the great humanist, and by Henry VIII himself. In 1679, the place was in the hands of GEORGE VILLIERS, DUKE OF BUCKINGHAM (1628-87), poet, critic and playwright, who was here visited by *John Evelyn*, the diarist. MRS GASKELL (see above) often visited her father and her step-mother at *No. 3*; and CHARLES MORGAN (1894-1958), the novelist and critic, lived at *No. 20*.

19. Continue along Cheyne Walk to *Danvers Street*. About here stood Danvers House, a gift of *Sir Thomas More* to his daughter, Margaret Roper, and her husband, William Roper, as dowry. The house was demolished in 1720. Farther up, on the left, at the place now occupied by the transported Crosby House, JONATHAN SWIFT (1667-1745), the great satirist, lived in 1711. At that time, BISHOP FRANCIS ATTERBURY (see above) lived across the street from him.

20. Continue along Cheyne Walk to *Old Church Street*. On the far corner stands the *Chelsea Old Church*. Though a church has stood here since the twelfth century, the building occupying this spot before the Second World War dated, mostly, from the sixteenth and seventeenth centuries. Most of the church was destroyed by the bombings of 1941—though the south chapel (rebuilt by Sir Thomas More in 1528), an arch or two, and a good many old monuments survived. *Sir Thomas More* attended services here; the mother of the dramatist *John Fletcher* (see above) was buried here; and so was the mother of *George Herbert* (1593-1683), the mystically religious poet. *John Donne* (1752-1631), the poet, preached the funeral service of Herbert's mother; and Donne's friend *Izaak Walton* (1593-1683), author of *The Compleat Angler*, attended the funeral. THOMAS SHADWELL (see above) was buried here, as was Sir John Fielding, half-brother of the novelist *Henry Fielding*, in 1780. GEORGE COLMAN THE YOUNGER (1762-1836), manager of the Haymarket Theatre and prolific dramatist, was re-married here in a ceremony which made official a more irregular and romantic marriage at Gretna Green. Under the heading 'Baptized' the church register contained the following entry for February 13, 1597: 'Charles, a boy, by estimacon x or xii yers olde, brought by Sir Walter Rawlie from Guiana.'

Farther up the street (in a house whose location is unknown—at least to the present writer) lived DR JOHN ARBUTHNOT (1667-1735), satirist, court physician, friend of Swift and Alexander Pope, originator of the character 'John Bull' to represent the typical Englishman, and the person addressed in one of Pope's best, and best-known, poems, 'Epistle to Dr Arbuthnot'. The popular dramatist BENN W. LEVY (b. 1923) lived at *No. 66* for over 20 years: from the 1940's to the late 1960's. On the right-hand side of the street, just before you reach King's Road, is the rectory where the father of the novelists CHARLES KINGSLEY (1819-75) and HENRY KINGSLEY (1830-76), lived from 1836 to 1860—and where his two sons spent much of their youth. ARTHUR REED ROPES ('ADRIAN ROSS') (see above) lived at *No. 68* during the last ten years of his life.

21. Return to Cheyne Walk, and continue along it till you pass the next street (Lawrence Street). You will then see, on your left, a large and rather pretentious apartment complex called 'Carlyle Mansions'. Here HENRY JAMES (1843-1916), spent his last years, and died. He was the American novelist who became a British subject, and who has had such an enormously successful revival among professional literary critics in the mid-twentieth century—though there is not much chance of his ever becoming very popular with the general public. T. S. ELIOT (1888-1965), the Nobel Prize-winning poet, who also was an American who became a British subject, lived in the same group of flats during and after the First World War. And the same place was home for the historian ARNOLD TOYNBEE (b. 1889) in the 1920's.

22. About now you will have reached a little green traffic island on your right, separating Cheyne Walk from the Embankment beyond. Look for a familiar and much-copied statue of Thomas Carlyle among the trees and shrubbery of the island. Just about here, but on your left, is the entrance to *Cheyne Row*. Turn into it. Not far up this narrow little street, at *No. 18*, MAURICE BARING (1874-1945), novelist, historian, poet, dramatist, diplomat, and charming autobiographer, lived throughout most of the 1930's. *No. 6* was the home of the novelist PAMELA HANSFORD JOHNSON (b. 1912) before she married the novelist C. P. SNOW. At *No. 24* is a house that THOMAS CARLYLE (1795-1881) occupied for 47 years before his death. His wife JANE WELSH CARLYLE (1801-66), no mean writer herself—of letters, mostly —lived here with him until her death. The house is now a museum, and should be visited. At the top of the house is a semi-soundproof room, with the desk on which Carlyle wrote *The French Revolution, Heroes and Hero Worship, Past and Present,* and biographies of Oliver Cromwell and of Frederick the Great.

23. When you have left the Carlyle house, continue on up Cheyne Row to its end. Turn right, on *Upper Cheyne Row*, for a few steps, and see *No. 22* (an early eighteenth-century house) where LEIGH HUNT (1784-

1859), poet, critic, editor, and friend of most of the great Romantic poets of his time, lived, 1833-40.

24. Now turn about, and walk in the other direction along Upper Cheyne Row till you reach *Lawrence Street. No. 16*, at the corner directly opposite Upper Cheyne Row, marks the site of Monmouth House, where JOHN GAY (1685-1732), poet, author of *The Beggar's Opera*, was secretary to the Duchess of Monmouth. A later occupant (of a part of the present house) was the novelist TOBIAS SMOLLETT (1721-71), who lived here from 1747 to 1762.

25. Turn left on Lawrence Street, walk a few steps down it, and turn right, into Justice Walk. This leads back to Old Church Street again. Turn right, and ascend the latter street a few steps till you find Paulton's Street entering from your left. Turn into this, and follow it to *Paulton's Square*. For many years during the 1950's, 1960's, and 1970's, KATHLEEN RAINE (b. 1908), poet, editor, and scholar, lived first at *No. 9* here, and then at *No. 47*.

Walk on through Paulton's Square to King's Road. Cross over this street, and catch a bus to the *Sloane Square Underground Station*. Here this tour ends. But *Tour No. 16* begins here—and you may have sufficient energy left to want to undertake that tour.

Tour 16
Chelsea East

Eric Ambler

Dr John Arbuthnot

Cecil Beaton

E. F. Benson

Laurence Binyon

Dion Boucicault

Dr Charles Burney

Frances ('Fanny') Burney

Egerton Castle

Charles Dickens

George Eliot

John Evelyn

Garnett Family

Sir Philip Gibbs

George Gissing

Harley Granville-Barker

Radclyffe Hall

Thomas Hardy

William Dean Howells

Pamela Hansford Johnson

James Laver

Charles Kingsley

Sir Sidney Low

Sir Desmond MacCarthy

George Meredith

A. A. Milne

John Osborne

Arthur Wing Pinero

Anne (Thackeray) Ritchie

Dante Gabriel Rossetti

Bertrand Russell

Olive Schreiner

George Bernard Shaw

Logan Pearsall Smith

Bram Stoker

John Strachey

Algernon Charles Swinburne

James Thomson ('B.V.')

Edward Trelawny

Mark Twain

Peter Ustinov

Horace Walpole

James M. Whistler

Lady Jane Wilde ('Speranza')

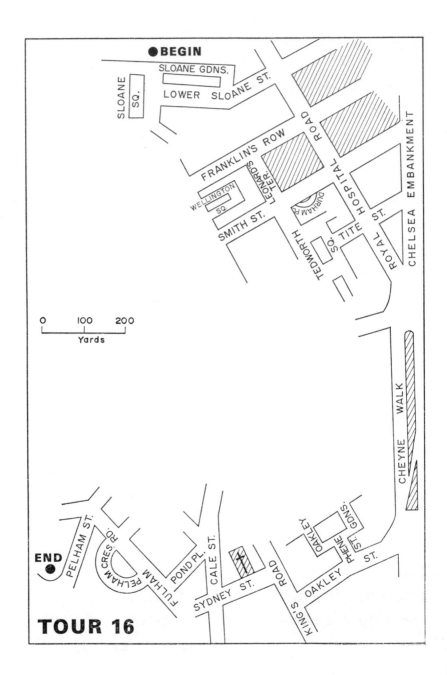

BEGIN

SLOANE GDNS.

SLOANE SQ.

LOWER SLOANE ST.

FRANKLIN'S ROW

WELLINGTON SQ.

SMITH ST.

LEONARD'S TER.

TEDWORTH SQ.

DURHAM PL.

TITE ST.

HOSPITAL ROAD

ROYAL ST.

CHELSEA EMBANKMENT

O   100   200
Yards

CHEYNE WALK

PELHAM ST.

END

PELHAM CRES.

FULHAM RD.

POND PL.

CALE ST.

SYDNEY ST.

KING'S ROAD

OAKLEY ST.

PHENE ST.

OAKLEY GDNS.

ST. GDNS.

OAKLEY ST.

TOUR 16

Oscar Wilde   **Thomas Wolfe**

Emlyn Williams

Leave the underground at the *Sloane Square Station.*

1. Emerging from the underground, you will see, just to your right, and facing *Sloane Square*, the red-brick *Royal Court Theatre*—its front covered with a complex and ugly network of blatant electric signs. This theatre, built in 1888, succeeds a previous theatre that stood on the south side of the square. The present theatre is famous for having produced many *avant-garde* plays—including many by ARTHUR WING PINERO (1855-1934) in the 1890's, and by GEORGE BERNARD SHAW (1856-1950) in the first decade of the twentieth century. The actor-producer-dramatist DION BOUCICAULT (1822-90) was manager just before his death; and another actor-producer-dramatist, HARLEY GRANVILLE-BARKER (1877-1946) was manager in the early years of the twentieth century. Some of Somerset Maugham's and John Galsworthy's first plays were produced here, as well as English versions of Maurice Maeterlinck's plays.

2. Turn back from the theatre, pass in front of the underground station again, and descend *Sloane Gardens. No. 8* was the home, in the 1920's and 1930's of SIR PHILIP GIBBS (1877-1962), novelist, journalist, political analyst, and historian, during his most prolific period. EGERTON CASTLE (1858-1920), novelist and dramatist, lived at *No. 49* in his later years.

3. At the end of Sloane Gardens, turn right, and reach *Lower Sloane Street*. The complex of buildings just opposite you, across the street, was once the *Royal Military Asylum*, a school for the children of soldiers. Here JAMES THOMSON ('B. V.') (1834-82), poet, essayist, critic (author of the deeply pessimistic poem *City of Dreadful Night*) went to school (1850-4), and trained as a teacher. FRANCES ('FANNY') BURNEY (1752-1840), the novelist, lived at *No. 63* on this street, 1814-16.

4. Turn left on Lower Sloane Street, and walk on to where Pimlico Road enters from your left, and the *Royal Hospital Road* from your right. Turn into the latter. On your left is the *Old Burial Ground* where is buried DR CHARLES BURNEY (1726-1814), musician, author of many books on music, and a volume on the history of comets. He was a member of Dr Johnson's circle, and the father of Frances ('Fanny') Burney, the novelist (see above).

5. Turn left at the next street, and walk down it till you find the entrance to *Ranelagh Gardens* (an open park-like area) on your left. Here stood (1742-1805) the great Rotunda which was the late eighteenth century's favourite amusement place. 'The chief amusement was promenading round and round the circular area' below tiers of boxes where patrons looked down on the circling crowd, ate, and took refreshments, and listened to an orchestra. Everybody who was anybody frequented the place. Dr Johnson said it was, in some ways, 'the finest thing he had ever seen'; Horace Walpole wrote: 'Every night constantly I go to Ranelagh.... My Lord Chesterfield is so fond of it that he says he has ordered all his letters to be directed thither'; and Tobias Smollett, in *Humphry Clinker*, has Matthew Bramble and his family visit and comment on the place.

6. Return to the Royal Hospital Road, and turn left along it. On your left is the *Royal Hospital* for old and disabled soldiers. It is said that Nell Gwynn put the idea for the hospital into the head of her lover Charles II. But the influence of JOHN EVELYN (1620-1706), the great diarist, who was interested in several such projects, was most important in the establishment of the hospital—in 1682. DR JOHN ARBUTHNOT (1667-1735), satirical writer, and friend of Pope, Swift, and Gay—to whom Pope addressed one of his most famous poems, 'Epistle to Dr Arbuthnot'—was chief physician at the hospital. DR CHARLES BURNEY (see above) was organist for the hospital chapel, and for 30 years had living quarters in the uppermost floor of the hospital, looking out on the cemetery where he is now buried. The novelist and poet THOMAS HARDY (1840-1928) came here repeatedly to see the military museum in the hospital, and to talk to the old pensioners, in order to get authentic material for his drama of the Napoleonic Wars, *The Dynasts*. The museum is still open to the public; and the chapel, great hall, and grounds are open at certain times. The entrance is not far from the corner where you just turned into Royal Hospital Road.

7. Double back towards the cemetery, and turn left, up Franklin's Row. Follow this alongside the green cricket-field on your left, till you reach the corner of the latter. Here turn left, into *St Leonard's Terrace*. LADY ANNE (THACKERAY) RITCHIE (1837-1919), a novelist of some repute, and a daughter of the novelist William Makepeace Thackeray, lived the last six years of her life at *No. 9*, and died there. The celebrated literary critic LOGAN PEARSALL SMITH (1865-1946) lived at *No. 11* through the 1930's.

8. At the end of St. Leonard's Terrace (at the next corner of the cricket-field) turn right, into Smith Street. A few steps up it, on your right, is *Woodfall Street*, where, at *No. 15*, lived JOHN OSBORNE (b. 1929), dramatist, author of *Look Back in Anger*.

9. Continue to the end of Smith Street, turn right (on King's Road), and then right again, into *Wellington Square*. A. A. MILNE (1882-1956), dramatist and poet, creator of Christopher Robin and Winnie-the-Pooh, lived here (1904-6). JAMES LAVER (b. 1899), incredibly prolific novelist, dramatist, and poet, lived at *No. 11* in the 1940's and 1950's; JOHN STRACHEY (b. 1901), the socialist writer, lived at *No. 12*; and SIR DESMOND MACCARTHY (1878-1952), critic and journalist, lived at *No. 25* in the 1920's. THOMAS WOLFE (1900-38), American novelist, worked on his *Look Homeward, Angel* while staying at *No. 32* in 1926. *Mabel Beardsley*, once-celebrated actress, sister of the artist Aubrey Beardsley, lived at *No. 24* in the late 1890's. Yeats admired her, and addressed a series of poems (*Upon a Dying Lady*) to her.... Turn back, and reach again the corner of Smith Street and St Leonard's Terrace.

10. Just past this corner, on your right, is a row of handsome old houses set back from the street—*Durham Place*. SIR SIDNEY LOW (1857-1932), journalist and historian, lived at *No. 2*; and BRAM STOKER (1847-1912), author of *Dracula*, lived at *No. 4*.

11. Return to the corner of Smith Street and St Leonard's Terrace, and turn left around it. Walk a block to *Tedworth Square*. MARK TWAIN (1835-1910) stayed at *No. 23* on his long visit to London in 1896-7.

12. On the other side of the square (nearest the river) two streets open.
[10A. On the one to your left, *Ralston Street*, the philosopher BERTRAND RUSSELL (1872-1969) lived at *No. 4*, in 1905.]
   The street on your right is *Tite Street*. JAMES MCNEILL WHISTLER (1834-1903), the painter who helped slay Victorianism, lived (1881-5), at *No. 13*, and later (1888) at *No. 46*. LAURENCE BINYON (1869-1943), poet and art authority, lived at *No. 8*. Walking on down Tite Street, you will reach the Royal Hospital Road again. On the far left (southeast) corner stood *Walpole House*, summer home of Prime Minister Sir Robert Walpole—and of his son HORACE WALPOLE (1717-97), novelist and letter-writer. Continue down Tite Street, and find, on your right, *No. 34*, where OSCAR WILDE (1854-1900) lived (1884-95); all of his greatest works were written while he lived here. At *No. 31*

lived (for 24 years) and died the fashionable American portrait painter *John Singer Sargent* (1856-1925). Continue on down Tite Street to Chelsea Embankment. OSCAR WILDE had rooms at the last house on your left in 1880, when he was finishing his book of poems.

13. Turn right on *Chelsea Embankment*. At *No. 14* PETER USTINOV (b. 1921) lived (1949-53). At *No. 1 Swan Walk*, at the corner of Chelsea Embankment, the novelist RADCLYFFE HALL (188?-1943) lived for a while with her cousin.

14. Two blocks farther along the Embankment, at a three-way juncture of streets, cross over, and walk behind an island of trees parallel with the river. You will be on *Cheyne Walk*. At *No. 4* the novelist GEORGE ELIOT (1810-80) died, after having lived there less than three weeks—with her new (and legally first) husband, the American banker John Cross. (The famous painter *Daniel Maclise* had died in the same house ten years earlier.) *No. 6* was the home of PAMELA HANSFORD JOHNSON (b. 1912), the novelist, who later married the other novelist C. P. Snow. Farther on, *No. 14* was the home of the philosopher-mathematician BERTRAND RUSSELL (see above) during the early years of the twentieth century. At *No. 16* lived the painter-poet DANTE GABRIEL ROSSETTI (1828-82) during the last 20 years of his life. Here he was visited by most of his contemporary artists and writers—including *Whistler, Burne-Jones, Millais, Holman Hunt, Browning, William Morris, Wilde, Swinburne,* and many more. A. C. SWINBURNE (1837-1909), the poet, lived here with Rossetti for a time (1864-5); and GEORGE MEREDITH (1828-1909), novelist and poet, stayed here overnight once a week for years, when he came to town on business for the publisher who employed him as a reader. At *No. 18* stood (1718-1867) *Don Saltero's Coffee House*, with its museum of curios, visited and mentioned often by many eighteenth-century writers.

(From about here to *No. 26* stood *Henry* VIII's manor house. Here, *Catherine Parr*, Henry VIII's widow, lived till her death, and here—good woman that she was—cared for the small orphan who became *Queen Elizabeth* I. *Anne of Cleves*, divorced wife of Henry VIII, died here.)

15. Continue along Cheyne Walk till you reach busy *Oakley Street*. Turn right, into this street. Just around the corner is *No. 56*, which was the home of *Captain R. F. Scott*, Antarctic explorer, and second man to reach the South Pole; he died on his way back from the Pole. (Now read Section 16, just below.) Farther up on *Oakley Street*, at *No. 87*, LADY JANE WILDE ('SPERANZA') (1824-96), poetess, pam-

phleteer, Irish patriot, and mother of Oscar Wilde, lived from 1886 until her death. Her home here became a kind of literary salon, especially for Irish men of letters in London. Visitors here included *Robert Browning, Edmund Gosse, Ouida*, and Justice *Oliver Wendell Holmes*. At *No. 102* lived E. F. BENSON (1867-1940), popular novelist, autobiographer, and member of the remarkable family that included his father, who was an archbishop; his brother *Arthur Christopher Benson*, poet, critic, and master of Magdalen College, Cambridge; and another brother, *Robert Hugh Benson*, writer and Roman Catholic priest.

16. In walking up Oakley Street, you may wish to make a quick sally to your right, along Phene Street, to *Oakley Gardens*. Here, at *No. 17*, lived GEORGE GISSING (1857-1903), author of some bitter naturalistic novels.... Now return to Oakley Street, and continue walking up it.

17. When you have reached the end of Oakley Street, turn right, on King's Road, walk a block, cross over King's Road, and ascend *Sydney Street*. After one block, you will come to *Saint Luke's Church*, on your right. Built in 1820-4, this church is an early example of the Gothic revival in architecture that came with the Romantic Movement, and in particular with the passion for things medieval that was engendered by the novels and poems of Sir Walter Scott. CHARLES KINGSLEY (1819-75), clergyman, novelist, and social reformer, was curate here for a time, under the rectorship of his father. The novelist CHARLES DICKENS (1812-70) was married here, in 1836, to Catherine Hogarth—a marriage that proved fruitful both in children and in acute unhappiness for the two principals.

18. Pass the church, and turn to the right (on Cale Street) at the corner of the playground adjoining the church. This playground was once a part of the church burial grounds; its displaced tombstones now form a fence about the church—a true example of the old dead making way for the living young. After two short blocks along Cale Street, turn left, beyond the school, where there is a three-way juncture of streets, and ascend *Pond Place. No. 19* was the home, from 1913 to the end of his life, of EDWARD GARNETT (1867-1937), critic, publishers' reader, discoverer of Galsworthy and Conrad, encourager of literature and literary men for many decades. (His father, Richard Garnett, was a librarian at the British Museum, and wrote—among other works—biographies of Milton, Coleridge, Carlyle, and Emerson.) Edward's wife, CONSTANCE (BLACK) GARNETT (1862-1946), made

many well-known translations of Russian novelists. And their son, DAVID GARNETT (b. 1892), who lived here with his parents as a young man, is a novelist—whose multi-volume autobiography is more interesting than his novels.

19. Continue along Pond Place till you reach Fulham Road. Cross over the latter, turn right, walk a block, and turn into *Pelham Crescent*, on your left. *No. 7* was the intermittent home (from 1857 till his death) of the fabulous EDWARD J. TRELAWNY (1792-1881), adventurer in many parts of the world, friend of Byron and Shelley, author of an autobiographical novel and of memoirs of his two great poetic friends. He helped to burn Shelley's body on the seashore where it washed up after the poet had drowned; and he served with Byron in the Greek war of independence. The American novelist WILLIAM DEAN HOWELLS (1837-1920) spent the summer of 1882 at *No. 18. No. 15* was the home of EMLYN WILLIAMS (b. 1905), actor and playwright from 1955 to 1960. And ERIC AMBLER (b. 1909), the novelist, was living at *No. 16* in the 1960's. *Francois Guizot* (1787-84), former French Premier and historian, lived at *No. 20* in 1848-9, after he was driven out of France by a revolution.

20. At the end of Pelham Crescent, turn left, and then left again, into *Pelham Street*. (But read the following section before you walk farther.) OLIVE SCHREINER (1855-1920), author of the still viable novel *The Story of an African Farm* (1883), and an early champion of women's legal and personal rights, lived at *No. 7* in 1884.

21. Before you reach the end of Pelham Street, turn aside into *Pelham Place*, where, at *No. 8*, lived CECIL BEATON (b. 1904) the photographer. He is famous not only for his fashionable portraits of nobility and royalty, but also for the rich and original imagination which brought 'modernism' into the art of photography. He wrote and illustrated many books.... Return to Pelham Street.

Walk straight ahead to the end of Pelham Street, and find *South Kensington Underground Station*, where this tour ends. But you may prefer to continue, from here, either *Tour No. 15* or *Tour No. 27*.

Tour 17
Buckingham Area

Topham Beauclerk

Mackenzie Bell

Christopher Benson

Jeremy Bentham

Dr Richard Bentley

Thomas Betterton

James Bryce

Edmund Burke

Dr Charles Burney

Lord Byron

Thomas Campbell

William Caxton

George Chalmers

John Cleland

William Davenant

Havelock Ellis

Ian Fleming

John Galsworthy

William Gifford

Richard Glover

Lord Ronald Gorell

George Grote

Arthur Henry Hallam

Henry Hallam

Sir John Hawkins

William Hazlitt

Lord John Hervey

Aaron Hill

Henry Hyndman

Dr Samuel Johnson

Edward Knoblock

Letitia Elizabeth Landon

Frederick Locker-Lampson

Richard Lovelace

Thomas Babington Macaulay

Capt. Frederick Marryat

Somerset Maugham

James Mill

A. A. Milne

John Milton

George Moore

Mrs Caroline Norton

Mrs Margaret Oliphant

Matthew Prior

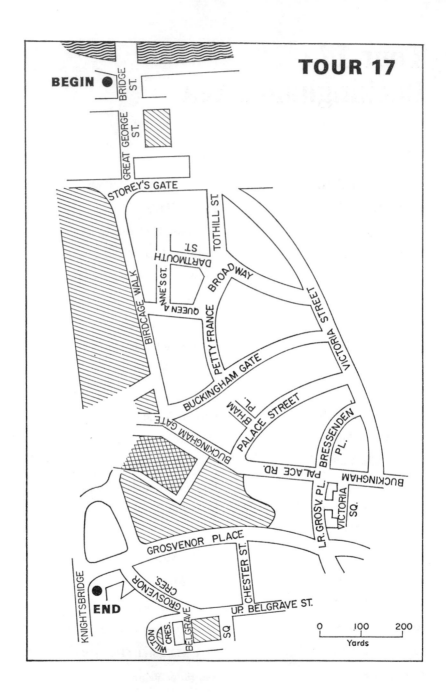

TOUR 17

BEGIN

END

Henry J. Pye	John St Loe Strachey
Mrs Ann Radcliffe	Sir Arthur Sullivan
Sir Walter Raleigh	Algernon C. Swinburne
John Sheffield, Duke of	Thomas Tyrwhitt
Buckingham	Mrs Humphry Ward
Mary Godwin Shelley	H. G. Wells
Percy Bysshe Shelley	John Wilkes
Thomas Southerne	William Wordsworth
Herbert Spencer	Peg Woffington
Edward Stillingfleet	Leonard Woolf

Leave the underground at the *Westminster Station.*

1. *Westminster Bridge* is just to your left as you leave the station, and should be visited. The present bridge was built (1852-62) on the site of the former stone bridge where *William Wordsworth* stood, in 1802, and had a view of the city that inspired the sonnet, 'Earth hath not anything to show more fair'. It was also on this older bridge that the poet *George Crabbe* walked back and forth all night long, in March, 1781, contemplating suicide; and here young *James Boswell*, to satisfy a fancy of his, had intercourse with a street girl in May, 1763. On the far side of the river, just to the right of the bridge, you can see the imposing long façade of *St Thomas's Hospital*, where the novelist SOMERSET MAUGHAM (1874-1965) studied and practised medicine, and which figures in his novel *Of Human Bondage*. The psychologist HAVELOCK ELLIS (1859-1939), who first informed the English that sex is important, also studied (for seven years) at this hospital.

2. Turn back from the bridge, and (keeping in a straight line with it) walk away from it. Cross busy Parliament Street, and continue straight along *Great George Street*—with government office buildings on your right, and a green square on your left. Nothing remains here of buildings having historic literary associations—but perhaps imagination can partly reconstruct what once was here. At *No. 5*, near Parliament Street, THOMAS TYRWHITT (1730-86), famous scholar who issued the first really scholarly edition of Chaucer, lived from 1758 to 1762. THOMAS BABINGTON MACAULAY (1790-1859), historian, poet, government official, lived at *No. 12* briefly, (1839-40) when he was

Secretary for War; and TOPHAM BEAUCLERK (1739-80), amateur scholar, dear friend of Dr Johnson, and member of the latter's Literary Club, lived (1797-8) at *No. 14.* The body of the poet *Lord Byron* (1788-1824) lay in state for two days in what was then *No. 25* while a controversy raged as to whether it should be buried in Westminster Abbey. (The final decision went against the poet.) And the body of the dramatist *Richard Brinsley Sheridan* (1751-1816) also lay in state for two days, at the home of a friend (Peter Moore, M.P.) on this street while a similar, but milder, controversy went on. (This time the decision was in favour of the deceased.) CAPTAIN FREDERICK MARRYAT (1792-1848), author of many novels of sea adventure that were once popular with boys (and that Joseph Conrad considered almost the greatest novels in English!), was born in a house on this street. The last house on the right was the home of JOHN WILKES (1727-97), stormy and scandalous politician, editor of the *North Briton*, author of what was once considered an obscene *Essay on Women*, friend of Edmund Burke, and subject of one of the most entertaining episodes in Boswell's *Life of Johnson*. But for all his personal weaknesses (which he did not deign to hide) he was a powerful influence for individual freedom, and was willing to fight and suffer for his opposition to the tyranny of George III.

Around the corner to the right once stood a row of buildings, with their backs to St James's Park, extending up to King Charles Street. THOMAS CAMPBELL (1777-1844), once-famous poet, lived here in 1802; and, farther up, near King Charles Street MATTHEW PRIOR (1664-1721), diplomat and poet, lived for more than ten years, (1706-17).

3. Just beyond the end of Great George Street is a portion of *Storey's Gate.* To the left, at *No. 2*, lived MRS CAROLINE NORTON (1808-77), poet, novelist, pamphleteer in favour of women's rights and against child labour. She was the granddaughter of the dramatist Sheridan, more-than-friend to Lord Melbourne (Prime Minister), original of George Meredith's *Diana of the Crossways*, and good friend of Bulwer-Lytton, Disraeli, Thomas Moore, Edward J. Trelawny, Harrison Ainsworth, and Samuel Rogers—all of whom visited her here.

4. Turn left at the end of Great George Street, and descend Storey's Gate till you reach *Tothill Street*, opening directly opposite the main door of Westminster Abbey. Just to your left, *before* you turn into Tothill Street, stood the *Gatehouse Prison*, where SIR WALTER RALEIGH (1552?-1618) was confined the night before his execution, and where the poet RICHARD LOVELACE (1618-58), also a prisoner, is supposed to have written his famous poem 'To Althea, from Prison'.

The diarist *Samuel Pepys* and the controversial clergyman *Jeremy Collier* were also confined here briefly, for political reasons.... Just to your left *after* you turn into Tothill Street, and on beyond, WILLIAM CAXTON (1421-91), England's first printer, set up his printing press in 1482-3—about five years after he had established England's very first printing press within the Abbey precincts. Here he printed the second edition of Chaucer's *Canterbury Tales*, and Malory's *Morte d'Arthur*. Centuries later, EDMUND BURKE (1729-97), statesman and philosopher, lived for many years in a house on about the same spot.

On *Tothill Street* itself THOMAS BETTERTON (1635-1710) was born. Adapter of Shakespeare's plays, celebrated actor, theatre manager (he opened the Haymarket Theatre in 1705), friend of Dryden, and husband of the first woman ever to play the parts of Shakespeare's heroines, Betterton wrote several successful plays, and was a major influence in the introduction of scenery to the English stage. SIR WILLIAM DAVENANT (1606-68), also a dramatist and theatre manager, as well as poet and Poet Laureate, lived on this street. And THOMAS SOUTHERNE (1660-1746) Irish-born dramatist and friend of Dryden lived for years at about where *No. 4* is today.

5. Near the far end of Tothill Street, turn sharp right, into *Dartmouth Street*. As late as the 1960's the main office of the Fabian Society was at *No. 11*. This society played a significant part in the early careers of George Bernard Shaw, H. G. Wells, Sidney and Beatrice Webb, and many other writers and reformers from the 1880's to the present.

6. Walk up Dartmouth Street a block, to where *Queen Anne's Gate* intersects. Turn left, into the latter, and keep following this street to the left as it circles what was once called Queen Square. PEG WOFFINGTON (1714?-60), the actress, died in lodgings on this square. Peg, David Garrick and the actor Charles Macklin, set up for a time a *menage-à-trois* that, apparently, made all three of them happy. Peg played the part of an effeminate young beau (in one of Congreve's plays) so often that she once remarked peevishly, 'I think half London believes I am a man.' To which a dissolute young gentleman standing by answered, 'Yes, madam, and the other half knows that you are a woman!' A very different kind of character, the sternly orthodox BISHOP EDWARD STILLINGFLEET (1635-99), author of some narrowly theological books, also died here. Stillingfleet's chaplain, DR RICHARD BENTLEY (1662-1742), one of the greatest of all classical scholars, lived here with the bishop; Pope satirized him in the *Dunciad* because Bentley denied that Pope's translation of Homer was really Homer. TOPHAM BEAUCLERK (see above) lived at what is now *No. 15*, in the

239

late 1780's; and Frances Reynolds, sister of the painter Sir Joshua Reynolds, and herself a painter, lived (1792-8) at this same *No. 15*. SIR JOHN HAWKINS (1719-89) (who drew up Dr Johnson's will, wrote his life, was one of his executors, and edited his works, as well as the works of Izaak Walton) lived (1778-83) at *No. 46*. The celebrated bluestocking *Miss Lydia White* (d. 1827) had her salon about where *No. 16* stands; and the poet WILLIAM WORDSWORTH (see above) was a more-or-less permanent guest of Joshua Watson at *No. 16* around the year 1835. JAMES MILL (1773-1836), Utilitarian philosopher, and father of *John Stuart Mill* (who stayed here as a child) lived at *No. 40* for many years (1814-31). HENRY HYNDMAN (1842-1921), the 'father' of socialism in England, author of *England for All* (1881), and founder of the Social Democratic Federation, lived at *No. 9* in 1900, and for many years thereafter. JOHN ST LOE STRACHEY (1860-1927), editor of *Cornhill Magazine* and of the *Spectator*, father of the Labour politician John Strachey, and author of several sociological books, lived at *No. 14* in the 1920's.

7. Just after you have made your second left turn in circling the square, and have St James's Park at your back, note the huge and ugly *Queen Anne's Mansions* on your right. Where it stands was the site of the home of JEREMY BENTHAM (1748-1832), the Utilitarian philosopher, and here he died. MRS LETITIA ELIZABETH LANDON (1802-38), once a celebrated and popular novelist and poet (who died in Africa through either suicide or murder) lived for a time in Queen Anne's Mansions; and SIR ARTHUR SULLIVAN (1842-1900) who composed the music for 'Onward Christian Soldiers' and 'The Lost Chord', as well as for the Gilbert and Sullivan light operas, lived here.

8. At the next corner, turn right, into *Petty France*. JOHN MILTON (1608-74) lived (1652-60) just down from the corner where you turned —on the right-hand side of the street, with a garden reaching back to St. James's Park. Here both his first and his second wife died; here he wrote his *Second Defence of the English People* as well as his defence of himself; here he wrote some of his most famous sonnets ('On the Late Massacre in Piedmont', 'On His Deceased Wife', 'On His Blindness'); and here he started *Paradise Lost*. Jeremy Bentham (see above) bought the property (then *No. 19*), and rented it successively to JAMES MILL (see above), the philosopher and historian, and to WILLIAM HAZLITT (1778-1830), essayist and literary critic, who lived here seven years, 1812-19. AARON HILL (1685-1750), journalist and essayist, dramatist, epic poet, disciple of Pope, friend of the poets John Gay and John Dyer, had a house, also on your right in this

street, and also with a garden (containing an artificial grotto!) reaching back to St James's Park. JOHN CLELAND (d. 1789), author of the justly celebrated *Fanny Hill*, lived and died on this street.

9. Now about-face, and walk back to the corner of Queen Anne's Gate and Petty France. Immediately before you, and also turning off to your right, is the street called *Broadway*. *No. 31* was the later residence of A. A. MILNE (1882-1956), dramatist and creator of Christopher Robin and Winnie-the-Pooh.

10. As you follow Broadway down, you will reach *Caxton Street*. Just around its corner, on your right, is *St Ermin's Hotel*, where H. G. WELLS (1855-1946), novelist, social critic, scientist, and reformer, lived from 1928 to 1930.

11. When you reach the end of Broadway, turn right, on Victoria Street. Walk along the latter for about two blocks, and then turn right again, into *Buckingham Gate*. The house-numbering begins at the far end of the street, after you have turned a corner facing Buckingham Palace. *Joseph Severn* (1793-1879), an artist, lived at *No. 21*. With great hardship to himself, he accompanied the poet John Keats to Rome, and stayed with him till Keats died. RICHARD GLOVER (1712-85), the poet, lived at *No. 11*. He was famous in his time for his long epic *Leonidas* (1737)—which had Whiggish overtones. Originally, the poem had nine books, but was enlarged to twelve. It was immensely popular in England, and was translated into French and German. Much later, MACKENZIE BELL (1856-1930), poet, literary historian, critic, lived at the same number from about 1904 to 1914. WILLIAM GIFFORD (1756-1826), editor of the *Quarterly Review*, harsh satirical poet, and editor of Ben Jonson and John Ford, lived and died at *No. 6*. Scotsmen will be interested in *No. 3*, which was for many years the home of GEORGE CHALMERS (1742-1825), antiquarian, historian of Scotland, and biographer of literary men. Also at *No. 3* lived JAMES BRYCE (1838-1922), long-time Ambassador to the United States, sympathetic commentator on American life, historian, statesman, jurist. HENRY J. PYE (1745-1813), poet, lived at *No. 2*. Baugh's *Literary History of England*, though 1600 pages long, spares only the following space (in a footnote) to Pye: 'Author of *Alfred*, an epic (1801) and many other volumes of worthless verse; poet laureate, 1790-1813.'

12. By this time you will be in full sight of *Buckingham Palace*— which would seem to have few literary associations. However, Buck-

ingham House (which preceded the Palace here) was built by JOHN
SHEFFIELD, DUKE OF BUCKINGHAM (1648-1721), poet and patron of
Dryden. The Duke's widow left the house to JOHN, LORD HERVEY
(1696-1743), immortalized as 'Sporus' in Pope's *Epistle to Dr Arbuthnot*: 'this bug with gilded wings,/This painted child of dirt, that
stinks and sings.' Hervey not only composed satirical poems, but also
wrote his *Memoirs of the Reign of George the Second*, a brilliantly
witty and scathing account of his years as a courtier. George III
bought the house in 1762, and established the King's Library there.
It was in this library that Dr Samuel Johnson had his famous inter-
view with the king. (In the reign of George IV Parliament gave permission, and granted sums, for the enlargement and restoration of
the old house. But the project ended in a complete replacement of
the old house by the present palace—a kind of royal con game that
completely deceived the Parliament. George IV, who loved fat women
better than he loved fat books, got his father's library out of the way
by giving it to the nation. It is now in the British Museum.)

13. You will have turned left in following Buckingham Gate towards
Buckingham Palace Road. Now turn left again, into *Palace Street*.
[13A. The first street on your left here is *Stafford Place*, where, at
No. 64, the philosopher of the theory of evolution, HERBERT SPENCER
(1820-1903) lodged (1845) during his early days in London.]
    JOHN GALSWORTHY (1867-1933), novelist and dramatist, lived at
No. 3 Palace Street as a young man.

14. Turn left into *Catherine Place*—the second street leading off from
Palace Street. The poet LORD RONALD GORELL (1884-1963), who was
also a busy public figure and prolific man of letters, lived at *No. 11*
in the 1920's. Follow this small street as it turns right; then turn right
again, into *Buckingham Place*. Here, at *No. 8*, lived for a time *S. F.
B. Morse* (1791-1872), inventor of the telegraph.

15. Reach Palace Street again, and follow it on down to *Victoria
Street*.
[15A. Just across the street here you will see the entrance to *Ashley
Place*. EDWARD KNOBLOCK (1874-1945), immensely prolific novelist,
dramatist, and even poet, and collaborator with Arnold Bennett and
J. B. Priestley, lived at *No. 21* during his last ten years.]
    Turn right, on *Victoria Street*. In a lodging place located at *No.
92* lived the Irish novelist GEORGE MOORE (1852-1933) in the late
1890's. Here he was visited by William Butler Yeats and Edward
Martyn, who persuaded Moore to return to Ireland with them, and

there initiate what became the brilliant Irish Literary Renaissance.

16. Beyond Moore's place, turn right, into Bressenden Place, which leads back to *Buckingham Palace Road* at about where a Stafford Row used to be, before 'improvements' cleared it out. MRS ANN RADCLIFFE (1764-1823), author of *The Mysteries of Udolpho* and other Gothic novels, lived the last eight years of her life at *No. 5 Stafford Row*, and there died. GEORGE GROTE (1794-1871), historian of classical Greece, lived at *No. 3*.

17. Cross Buckingham Palace Road into Lower Grosvenor Place, which extends directly in line with Bressenden Place. After a few steps, turn left, into *Victoria Square*. At *No. 8* THOMAS CAMPBELL (see above), poet, editor, and public man, lived the last four years of his life, and died. At *No. 14* the immensely prolific novelist MRS MARGARET OLIPHANT (1828-97), a kind of lesser George Eliot, lived around 1880. IAN FLEMING (1908-64), author of fabulously popular spy-novels, spent the last ten years of his life at *No. 16*. And at *No. 24* LEONARD WOOLF (1880-1969), literary critic, writer on economics, and husband of Virginia Woolf, the novelist, lived after 1944.

18. Now return to *Lower Grosvenor Place*. When it was named Arabella Road, the poet PERCY BYSSHE SHELLEY (1792-1822) and his wife MARY GODWIN SHELLEY (1797-1851), author of *Frankenstein*, lived at *No. 13* in 1815, after she had had a stillborn child at Hans Place. *No. 4* was the home of John Jackson, pugilist, from whom LORD BYRON (1788-1824) took lessons in fisticuffs, and who became the poet's good friend. Byron often visited him here.

19. At the end of Lower Grosvenor Place, turn right, on broad *Grosvenor Place*. A block or two up this street is *No. 25*, which was the home, from 1891 to 1911, of MRS HUMPHRY WARD (1851-1920), niece of Matthew Arnold, novelist who wrote about characters involved in the 'conflict between science and religion' (she gave preference to the former), and who participated more directly, through essays and articles, in the science-versus-religion controversies of her earlier years. At *No. 18* the poet of beautiful and decadent paganism, ALGERNON CHARLES SWINBURNE (1837-1909), lived in the early 1860's just when he was writing those magnificently resounding poems that first made him famous—to the surprise of all his acquaintances, who had not dreamed that the odd and excitable little redhead was a genius.

20. Turn left, off Grosvenor Place, into *Chester Street*. SWINBURNE (see above) was born on this street, probably at *No. 7*. FREDERICK LOCKER-LAMPSON (1821-97), the poet of pleasantly light verse that is still readable, and father-in-law of the critic Augustine Birrell, lived at *No. 19* in 1850, immediately after his marriage.

21. At the far end of Chester Street, turn right, into Upper Belgrave Street, and reach (one block) fashionable Belgrave Square. Though many lords, generals, admirals, and the like have lived on this square, no really prominent literary person is known (by the present author) to have been drawn hither.
[21A. You may turn left when you reach the square, and walk along its (south) side to the next corner. *Belgrave Place* now opens on your left. A few steps down this street, at *No. 3*, lived the famous historian GEORGE GROTE (1794-1871) from 1836 to 1848; here he wrote the first two volumes of his monumental *History of Greece.*]

22. Turn right, along the far (western) side of the square, and walk straight on till you reach *Wilton Crescent* curving away to your right. Follow this curve, and find *No. 36*, where ALGERNON CHARLES SWINBURNE (see above) was living in 1865, while he was correcting proofs on his *Atalanta in Calydon*, the poem that made him famous. At *No. 24* lived and died HENRY HALLAM (1777-1859), historian, whose 'knowledge of original sources was unequalled before his day'. Of more interest to poetry-readers, this Henry Hallam was father of ARTHUR HENRY HALLAM (1811-33), brilliant young poet, friend of Tennyson, and subject of the latter's greatest poem, the elegaic *In Memoriam*.

23. At the end of Wilton Crescent, walk back towards Belgrave Square; but before reaching the latter, turn sharp left into Grosvenor Crescent. Follow this to its end in Grosvenor Place. You will note *St George's Hospital* off to your left. In the eighteenth century a *St George's Chapel* was associated with the hospital—and here, in 1749, was married DR CHARLES BURNEY (1726-1814), musician, composer, musical historian, and father of the celebrated Frances ('Fanny') Burney. The marriage occurred about a month after the first child of Dr Burney and his bride was born.

Just beyond the hospital is the *Hyde Park Corner Underground Station*, where you will end this tour. But two other tours into a fashionable section of London begin here, and you may wish to undertake them. They are *Tours No. 11* and *19*.

Tour 18
Coram's Fields Area

William Archer

Martin Armstrong

James Barrie

George Borrow

Robert Bridges

Dr Charles Burney

Frances ('Fanny') Burney

Dr John Campbell

Thomas Carlyle

Thomas Chatterton

Charles Churchill

William Cowper

E. M. Delafield

Charles Dickens

Benjamin Disraeli

Havelock Ellis

Edward Fitzgerald

E. M. Forster

Robert Frost

Roger Fry

John Galt

David Garnett

Douglas Goldring

Aldous Huxley

John Maynard Keynes

Henry Kingsley

D. H. Lawrence

Wyndham Lewis

Eva Le Gallienne

Richard Le Gallienne

E. V. Lucas

Thomas Babington Macaulay

Edward Marsh

John Masefield

F. D. Maurice

George Meredith

Charlotte Mew

Harold Monro

William Morris

John Payne

Bryan Waller Procter
   ('Barry Cornwall')

W. R. Rodgers

Peter Mark Roget

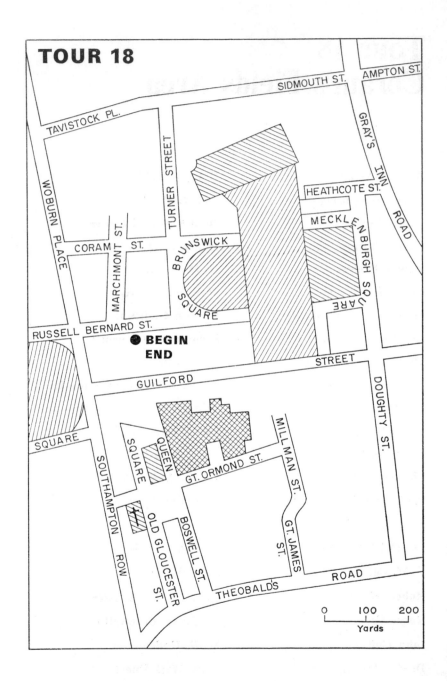

TOUR 18

SIDMOUTH ST.

AMPTON ST.

TAVISTOCK PL.

TURNER STREET

GRAY'S INN

HEATHCOTE ST.

WOBURN PLACE

MECKLENBURGH SQUARE

CORAM ST.

MARCHMONT ST.

BRUNSWICK SQUARE

ROAD

RUSSELL BERNARD ST.

● **BEGIN**
END

STREET

GUILFORD

DOUGHTY ST.

SQUARE

SQUARE

QUEEN

MILLMAN ST.

GT. ORMOND ST.

SOUTHAMPTON ROW

OLD GLOUCESTER ST.

BOSWELL ST.

GT. JAMES ST.

ROAD

THEOBALD'S

0   100   200
Yards

246

John Ruskin	Frank Swinnerton
George William Russell ('A.E.')	William Makepeace Thackeray
George Augustus Sala	Arthur Waley
Dorothy Sayers	Theodore Watts-Dunton
Olive Schreiner	Richard Whiteing
Percy Bysshe Shelley	Leonard Woolf
Sydney Smith	Virginia Woolf
Algernon C. Swinburne	Edmund Yates

Leave the underground at the *Russell Square Station.*

1. Emerging from the underground, turn left, walk a block to Woburn Place, and turn right. After a block along Woburn Place, turn right again, into *Coram Street.* At *No. 13* WILLIAM MAKEPEACE THACKERAY (1811-63), the greatest of the Victorian novelists except Dickens, lived in relative poverty, 1837-43. EDWARD FITZGERALD (1809-93), translator of the *Rubaiyat* of Omar Khayyam, lived with Thackeray for a time in 1843. RICHARD LE GALLIENNE (1866-1947), poet and critic of the Aesthetic movement, father of the actress and producer Eva Le Gallienne, lived at *No. 49* in 1889.

[1A. You will cross *Marchmont Street.* The poet PERCY BYSSHE SHELLEY (1792-1822) lodged briefly at *No. 26* in 1816.]

2. Continue down Coram Street to its end in Brunswick Square, and turn left, into *Hunter Street.* JOHN RUSKIN (1819-1900), art critic, social philosopher, one of the 'greats' of Victorian literature, was born a few houses along this street, at *No. 54.*

[2A. Continue along Hunter Street to *Tavistock Place,* and turn left. JOHN GALT (1779-1839), Scottish novelist who was a friend and travelling companion of Byron around the Mediterranean, a road-builder in Canada, and an accomplished realistic novelist, lived at *No. 31.*

[2B. Where Marchmont Street crosses Tavistock Place, turn right on the former, and reach *Cartwright Gardens.* JOHN GALT (see above) lived at *No. 9* during 1813 and 1814. The REV SYDNEY SMITH (1771-1845), philosopher, wit, essayist, espouser of all liberal causes, letter-writer, speech-maker, lived at *No. 26* in 1835 and 1836, and at *No. 34* from 1836 to 1839. 'His sayings are among the most brilliant attributed to any person in English history.' ... Now return to Tavistock Place, turn left, and reach the corner of Hunter Street again.]

3. At the juncture of Hunter Street and Tavistock Place, turn right. You will reach *Regent Square* immediately. The novelist, poet, and essayist ALDOUS HUXLEY (1894-1963) lived at *No. 36* in 1921.

4. Sidmouth Street leads on out of Regent Square—in direct line with Tavistock Place. After crossing Gray's Inn Road, the street changes names again, and becomes *Ampton Street*. Here, a few doors down from Gray's Inn Road, at *No. 33*, THOMAS CARLYLE (1795-1881) and his wife Jane lived for a few months (1831-2) when they first came to London.

5. Return to Gray's Inn Road and turn left. A long block down this dreary street, Heathcote Street opens on your right. Enter it, turn left at the first corner, and explore *Mecklenburgh Square*. Some writers who have lived here are the following: JOHN MASEFIELD (1878-1967), Poet Laureate, at *No. 18*, from 1932 to 1935; W. R. RODGERS (b. 1909), Irish-born poet, and script-writer for the BBC, who has been extravagantly praised and extravagantly criticized; the novelist VIRGINIA WOOLF (1882-1941) and her husband LEONARD WOOLF (1880-1969), at *No. 37*—she from 1939 till her death (by suicide), and he from 1939 to 1942; D. H. LAWRENCE (1885-1930), poet and novelist who first brought the psychology of sex openly into English literature, at *No. 44* briefly (he never stayed long anywhere) in November, 1917; RICHARD WHITEING (1840-1928), journalist and novelist, who wrote realistically about London's poor, at *No. 45*, from 1895 to 1903; and GEORGE AUGUSTUS SALA (1828-96), famous and flamboyant journalist, as well as editor and essayist, at *No. 46*.

6. The side of Mecklenburgh Square nearest Gray's Inn Road leads down to Guilford Street, with Doughty Street opening beyond.
[6A. At Guilford Street you may wish to turn left, reach Gray's Inn Road again, and then turn left again till you reach *St Andrew's Gardens* on the far (right-hand, or western) side of Gray's Inn Road. Here are deposited the bones of THOMAS CHATTERTON (1752-70), young poet (the 'marvellous boy' of Wordsworth) who committed suicide at the age of seventeen.... Now return to the juncture of Guilford and Doughty Streets.]
    Enter *Doughty Street*. *No. 10* was the birthplace of the slight, but very real, poet CHARLOTTE MEW (1869-1928). *No. 14* was one of the innumerable places where SIDNEY SMITH (see above) lived in London. Just across the street, at *No. 48*, the novelist CHARLES DICKENS (1812-70) lived 1837-9. In this house he completed writing the *Pickwick Papers* (begun at Furnivall's Inn); *Oliver Twist* and *Nicholas Nickleby*

were written; and here *Barnaby Rudge* was begun. The house is now a Dickens museum, open to the public for a small fee, filled with memorabilia, manuscripts, pictures, and so on, associated with Dickens. You should visit it. *No. 49* was, in the late 1880's and early 1890's, a cooperative residence of the 'Fellowship of the New Life', of which HAVELOCK ELLIS (1859-1939), poet, essayist, social critic, and author of the monumental *Studies in the Psychology of Sex*, was the the prime mover. (By the way, it was out of this organization that the powerful Fabian Society rose as one of the most effective advocates of socialism in England.) The poet RICHARD LE GALLIENNE (see above) lived at *No. 42* in 1899; and here his daughter EVA LE GALLIENNE, the actress and producer who played such an important part in the American theatre in the pre-World War II days, was born. *No. 43* was the home (1854-60) of the novelist EDMUND YATES (1831-94); and *No. 57* was the home of the novelist E. M. DELAFIELD (real name, ELIZABETH E. DASHWOOD) (1890-1943) in the 1930's.

6. From here it is a rather lengthy trek down to *Theobald's Road*; but when you have reached the latter, you should turn aside, to your left, for two or three steps, to see *No. 22*, where the novelist and Prime Minister BENJAMIN DISRAELI (1804-81) was born.

7. Do not explore farther in this leftward direction. Instead, turn about and follow Theobald's Road in the opposite direction. After one long block, turn right, on *Great James Street*. ALGERNON CHARLES SWINBURNE (see above), the poet of paganism and decadence in a language more lushly beautiful than ever heard before in English verse, lived at *No. 3* from 1872 to 1875, and again in 1877-8. FRANK SWINNERTON (b. 1884), realistic novelist and literary historian and critic, lived with his mother at *No. 4*, and wrote here his first novel, *The Merry Heart*, as well as several other novels. *No. 5* was the home of E. V. LUCAS (1868-1938), novelist, essayist, literary biographer, in the late 1890's. THEODORE WATTS-DUNTON (1832-1914), critic, poet, and novelist, who befriended Swinburne when Swinburne needed a friend, was living at *No. 15* in 1872-3. It was here that the acquaintanceship of Swinburne and Watts-Dunton ripened into a friendship. ARTHUR WALEY (1889-1966), whose translations of Oriental poetry gave most English-speaking readers their first knowledge of Eastern (especially Chinese) poetry, was living at *No. 22* in the 1960's. *No. 24* was the home of DOROTHY SAYERS (1893-1957), novelist, thought by many to be the finest writer of detective stories in modern times. Finally, GEORGE MEREDITH (1828-1909), novelist and poet, lived with his father at *No. 26* in the 1840's.

Great James Street leads without warning into *Milman Street*. When the young GEORGE BORROW (1803-81), novelist of Gypsy life, first came to London (1824) he lodged here, at *No. 16*.

8. You will see *Great Ormond Street* entering from your left. Turn into it.

[8A. A bit farther along this street, you will cross *Lamb's Conduit Street*, and may wish to turn aside to the site of *No. 19*, where 'Keats's dearest friend', *John Hamilton Reynolds* lived with his family, and where *Keats*, the poet, often visited. By the way, one of the Reynolds girls (Jane) became the wife of the poet *Thomas Hood*.]

Though *John Howard* (1726?- 90) is hardly a literary figure (even if he did write several books on English and European prisons), this great and good man, who, almost single-handedly, brought about prison reforms in England and America, insisted on regarding convicts as human, and who helped abolish some of the worst savageries of the old prisons, should be mentioned here. He lived at *No. 23 Great Ormond Street*. The world has need of him again today. WILLIAM ARCHER (1856-1924), dramatist and critic, who was largely instrumental in introducing the plays of Ibsen to England, lived at *No. 34* in the 1890's. At *No. 38* WYNDHAM LEWIS (1884-1957), highly 'advanced' painter, novelist, and political thinker, who followed nobody and was followed by nobody, established his *Rebel Art Centre* in 1914. WILLIAM MORRIS (1834-96), poet, artist, social reformer and designer of furniture, wallpaper, tapestries, stained glass, and fine books—an English Leonardo—brought his new wife to live with him at *No. 41*, during 1859-60. MARTIN ARMSTRONG (b. 1882) one of the original 'Georgian Poets' who appeared in the volumes of *Georgian Poetry*, edited by *Edward Marsh*, lived for a long time (1920's and 1930's) at *No. 37*. Farther along the street, on your right, stands the Hospital for Sick Children. ROBERT BRIDGES (1844-1930), Poet Laureate and physician, last of the major Victorian poets, was 'assistant physician' here. JAMES BARRIE (1860-1937), dramatist and novelist, willed all the proceeds of his play *Peter Pan* to this hospital —a bequest that has brought much benefit to the hospital. (The hospital contains a 'Barrie Wing' and a 'Peter Pan Ward'.) On the site now occupied by the Homeopathic Hospital (beyond the Hospital for Sick Children), THOMAS BABINGTON MACAULAY (1800-59), historian, biographer, poet, and politician, lived with his family (1823-31), and was their chief support.

9. Just after you pass the Homeopathic Hospital, turn left, down *Boswell Street* (formerly Devonshire Street). The famous Poetry

Bookshop, established by the poet HAROLD MONRO (1879-1932) stood at *No. 35* (1913-26). It published and sold books of contemporary poetry and drama; and here most of the significant poets of the time held public readings. The American poet ROBERT FROST (1874-1963) and his wife took rooms over the Bookshop in 1913 ('by pure accident', Frost says), and soon began to meet British poets in the Bookshop—among them F. S. Flint, who recognized Frost as an American by his shoes, and who advised him to look up the other American poet *Ezra Pound*. Frost followed the advice; and the results are part of the history of American literature.

10. If you are particularly interested in EDWARD FITZGERALD (1809)-93), translator of the *Rubaiyat of Omar Khayyam*, continue along Boswell Street to Theobald's Road, turn right, then right again, up *Old Gloucester Street*. FitzGerald stayed at *No. 17* in 1854.

11. If you are not interested in the FitzGerald place, turn back up Boswell Street, the way you came. (In either event, you will end at *Queen Square*.) Just to your right, as you emerge from Boswell Street, lived (1771-4) DR CHARLES BURNEY (1726-1814), musician and musicologist, with his daughter FRANCES ('FANNY') BURNEY (1752-1840), who became a novelist. At the diagonally opposite corner of the square (just beyond the end of the square itself, and, next a tiny garden) lived (1757-75) DR JOHN CAMPBELL (1708-75), historian and biographer, immensely respected in his time. Boswell records that Campbell once drank 18 bottles of port at a sitting; he never went to church, but always removed his hat when passing a church. *Dr Johnson* often visited Campbell here till it occurred to him that 'the shoals of Scotchmen who flocked about him might probably say, when anything of mine was well done, "Ay, ay, he has learnt this of Cawmell"'. At *No. 21* (just opposite Campbell's house) lived the social reformer *F. D. Maurice* (1805-72). The Homeopathic Hospital on this (eastern) side of the square has wiped out the site (near the middle) of a young ladies' boarding school where CHARLES CHURCHILL (1731-64), disreputable satiric poet, was a teacher—though he behaved here with perfect decorum. Also on this side (*No. 26*) WILLIAM MORRIS (1834-96), poet, artist, and socialist, lived and had his decorator's shop (1865-71). WILLIAM COWPER (1731-1800), the poet, went to services regularly at *St George the Martyr Church* at the lower (south-west) corner of the square when he was a law student living nearby.

12. Leave the square by the little passageway (Cosmo Place) next to the church. When (after a few steps) you reach *Southampton Row*,

251

turn right. At the ninth door from your turning stood the house where lived the girl cousins of WILLIAM COWPER, the poet (see above). As he said, in one of his letters years later, he spent most of his time here 'giggling and making giggle' with his cousins (he was in love with one of them) instead of reading law.

13. After a longish block, turn right, into *Guilford Street*. The poet ALGERNON CHARLES SWINBURNE (see above) was living at *No. 25*, in 1879, when he was rescued, by Theodore Watts-Dunton (see above), from the debauchery that was killing him. After his rescue, Swinburne never again wrote any significant poetry. EDWARD MARSH (1872-1952), editor of *Georgian Poetry* (1913-21) was born at *No. 38*; SYDNEY SMITH (see above) lodged at *No. 77* in 1803; and OLIVE SCHREINER (1855-1920), novelist and feminist, lodged at *No. 81* in 1882, while being treated at a nearby hospital. JAMES BARRIE (see above) had his first London lodgings on this street. J. H. Reynolds, 'Keats's dearest friend', lived at *No. 88* in the 1840's.

14. Turn left, into *Grenville Street*. JAMES BARRIE (see above) moved from his Guilford Street lodgings to *No. 8* here, in 1885.

15. At the end of the street is *Brunswick Square*. BRYAN WALLER PROCTER ('BARRY CORNWALL') (1787-1864), poet, friend of poets and literary biographer, as well as father of the once-famous poet Adelaide Procter, lived somewhere on this square in 1816. GEORGE WILLIAM RUSSELL ('A. E.') (1867-1935), poet and wise man of many abilities, Ireland's own candidate for the Leonardo da Vinci Prize, lived at *No. 1* in 1934, self-exiled from his country, and dying of cancer. The novelist DOUGLAS GOLDRING (1887-1960) lived at *No. 12* many years (1922-49); he was an editor, a discoverer of poets, a biographer and historian, and an autobiographer. *No. 26* was the home of the novelist E. M. FORSTER (1879-1968), best known for his *A Passage to India*, for ten years, 1929-39. DAVID GARNETT (b. 1892), novelist, auto-biographer, publisher, and member of the Bloomsbury group (see Tour No. 8) lived at *No. 27* after his marriage. VIRGINIA STEPHEN (1882-1941), who became the novelist VIRGINIA WOOLF, lived at *No. 38* before her marriage; and her husband LEONARD WOOLF, historian and diarist, and their friends JOHN MAYNARD KEYNES (1883-1946) (the economist) and *Duncan Grant* (b. 1885) (the painter) also lived here.

16. You may wish to find *Lansdowne Terrace*, paralleling Grenville Street, at the south-east corner of Brunswick Square. JOHN PAYNE

(1842-1916), poet, Pre-Raphaelite, and translator of classics from French, German, Italian, and Persian literature, lived (1884-6) at *No. 5.*

17. Return to *Bernard Street,* which leads off the south-west corner of Brunswick Square, and walk along it. HENRY KINGSLEY (1830-76), novelist, brother of Charles Kingsley, lived at *No. 24* from 1871 to 1873, and here wrote two of his best-known novels, *Oakshott Castle* and *Reginald Heatheredge.* PETER MARK ROGET (1779-1869), physician and lexicographer, who compiled the celebrated and (to authors) invaluable *Thesaurus of English Words and Phrases* (1852) lived at *No. 39.* ROGER FRY (1866-1934), controversial painter and even more controversial art critic, member of the Bloomsbury group (Virginia Woolf wrote his biography), and at one time (1905-10) director of the Metropolitan Museum of Art in New York, lived at *No. 48.*

You are now right at the *Russell Square Underground Station*—where this tour began, and where it ends.

Part Two

Excellent Tours

Tour 19
Berkeley Square

John Hay Beith ('Ian Hay')

William Blake

James Boswell

Edward Bulwer-Lytton

General John Burgoyne

Edmund Burke

Frances ('Fanny') Burney

Colley Cibber

George Colman The Younger

R. B. Cunninghame Graham

W. H. Davies

George du Maurier

Gilbert Frankau

Mrs Elizabeth Gaskell

Edward Gibbon

George Frideric Handel

Dr Samuel Johnson

Earl of Lytton ('Owen Meredith')

Edward Marsh

Somerset Maugham

Henry Milman

Thomas Moore

Mrs Caroline Norton

Joseph Priestley

Edwin Arlington Robinson

John Ruskin

Richard Brinsley Sheridan

Edith Sitwell

Sydney Smith

Horace Walpole

Leave the underground at the *Hyde Park Corner Station.* You will probably be utterly lost when you emerge; but by availing yourself of various underpasses and some calculations by dead reckoning, you will eventually find the bottom of Park Lane. (Or will you?)

1. Ascend Park Lane on the side opposite Hyde Park—the right-hand side to you. (The novelist and dramatist EDWARD BULWER-LYTTON lived briefly in a house at the very foot of Park Lane. But the street now covers the place.)

257

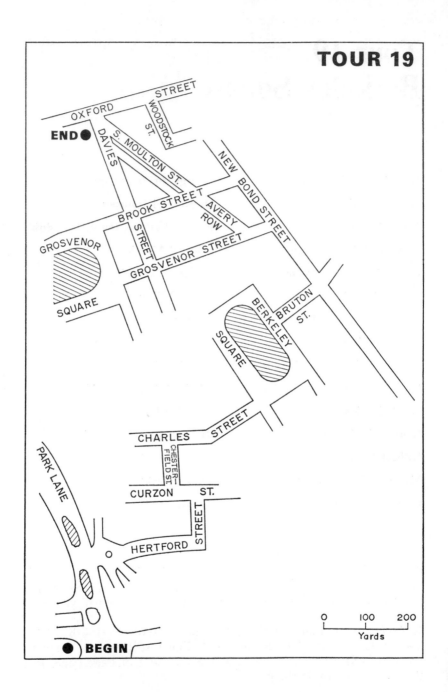

TOUR 19

STREET

OXFORD

WOODSTOCK ST.

END●

DAVIES

S. MOULTON ST.

NEW BOND STREET

BROOK STREET

AVERY ROW

GROSVENOR

STREET

GROSVENOR STREET

SQUARE

BERKELEY

BRUTON ST.

SQUARE

CHARLES STREET

CHESTER-FIELD ST.

PARK LANE

CURZON ST.

STREET

HERTFORD STREET

0   100   200
Yards

●) **BEGIN**

After one block, you will reach a confluence of streets on your right. Brave this as best you can, and cross over to *Hertford Street*. The house numbers are arranged crazily here; I give them in reverse numerical order. At *No. 47* the inevitable SYDNEY SMITH (see above) lodged in 1824. *No. 36* was the home of the novelist EDWARD BUL-WER-LYTTON (1803-73), from 1831 to 1834. Here he wrote his formerly celebrated novels *Rienzi* and *The Last Days of Pompeii*. His son EDWARD ROBERT LYTTON (1831-91), who became an earl and Viceroy of India, as well as a poet writing under the name of 'OWEN MEREDITH', was born here. *Edward Jenner, originator of vaccination for smallpox, lived at* No. 14 *for some years after 1803*. At *No. 10*, on the other side of the street from the Lytton house, and a little farther along, RICHARD BRINSLEY SHERIDAN (1751-1816), the dramatist and politician, lived from 1795 to 1802. In the same house had lived GENERAL JOHN BURGOYNE (1722-92), who lost the Battle of Saratoga, in America, to Benedict Arnold, and then returned home and won acclaim as the author of several successful plays. He died here. The American poet EDWIN ARLINGTON ROBINSON (1869-1935) stayed at *No. 3* on his visit to London in 1923.

2. Beyond the Sheridan-Burgoyne house, Hertford Street turns abruptly to your left. Follow it on to Curzon Street. Cross the latter, turn left for a few steps, and then right, into *Chesterfield Street*. MRS CAROLINE NORTON (1808-77), poet, novelist, reformer, granddaughter of Richard Brinsley Sheridan (see above), lover (no doubt) of Lord Melbourne, the Prime Minister, lived for 30 years (1845-75) at *No. 3*. *George (Beau) Brummell* (1776-1840), arbiter of taste, came to *No. 4* in 1799, and immediately commenced his reign over London society. SOMERSET MAUGHAM (1874-1965), novelist and dramatist, bought a house at *No. 6* in 1911, and lived there; but the house has since been replaced.

3. At the end of Chesterfield Street, turn right, on *Charles Street*. Beau Brummell (see above) lived as a boy at *No. 42*. SYDNEY SMITH (again!) (see above) lived (1836-9) at *No. 33*. JOHN RUSKIN (1819-1900), social essayist and art critic, one of the really major figures of English literature, lived at *No. 6* early in his unfortunate married life.

4. Charles Street ends in *Berkeley Square*. This is the 'Gaunt Square' figuring so prominently in Thackeray's *Vanity Fair*, and the 'Buckley Square' of the *Yellowplush Papers*. At the lower end of the square (to your right as you enter from Charles Street) stood Lansdowne House (*No. 54*), where JOSEPH PRIESTLEY (1733-1804), the chemist, was

librarian, and where he discovered oxygen. He wrote a book on government, and several books on liberal religion. To your left, as you enter the square, at *No. 45*, Lord Clive (1725-74), conqueror of India, lived and committed suicide.

[4A. Just beyond the Clive house, *Hill Street* enters from your left. Down this street, at *No. 49*, lived IAN HAY (real name JOHN HAY BEITH) (1876-1952), journalist, novelist, and playwright, immensely popular during and just after the First World War, from 1945 till his death.]

On the opposite side of the square, on the lower (southern) corner where Bruton Street enters the square, at *No. 19*, COLLEY CIBBER (1671-1757), actor, dramatist, producer, and Poet Laureate, lived during his last years, and there died. HORACE WALPOLE (1717-97), novelist, letter-writer, critic, gossip, moved to *No. 11* in 1779, and died there eighteen years later. (The house, now gone, was the eighth house beyond Cibber's; the entire area is now occupied by a large modern building.)

> COLLEY CIBBER was a remarkable man. The most celebrated comic actor of his day, he became manager of the Drury Lane Theatre, and wrote over 30 plays. He was the first to write a 'sentimental comedy' in 1696, and with it started a vogue that lasted almost a century. (Sentimental comedy assumes that man is essentially good, and usually involves some exhibition of generosity that recalls an erring villain to his essential nobleness.) Cibber became Poet Laureate, incurred Alexander Pope's jealousy as a result, and was made the hero of the second edition of Pope's *Dunciad*.

5. Enter *Bruton Street*, and walk away from the square. RICHARD BRINSLEY SHERIDAN (see above) lived on this street briefly in 1784-5. Queen Elizabeth II was born (1926) at *No. 17*—now replaced by a bank. 'IAN HAY' (JOHN HAY BEITH) (see above), journalist of the First World War, and novelist, lived at *No. 21* from 1921 to 1930. EDWARD MARSH (1872-1953), editor, biographer, critic, and friend of many literary people, spent his early childhood at *No. 36*, and his young manhood at *No. 30*. You will see also on this street the *Time and Life Building* (1952), with carvings by the great sculptor Henry Moore.

> EDWARD MARSH edited the five volumes of *Georgian Poetry* (1913-21) that introduced the public to many contemporary poets who later became famous—including Rupert Brooke, D. H. Lawrence, Walter de la Mare, and others. He was a friend of Brooke, and wrote a memoir of him; he was a friend and secretary of Winston Churchill; he advised Somerset Maugham and many other people about their writing.

6. When you reach *New Bond Street*, turn left on it. JAMES BOSWELL,

Dr Johnson's biographer, lodged somewhere on this street for a short time; and EDWARD GIBBON (1737-94), historian of *The Decline and Fall of the Roman Empire*, lived at what would now be *No. 127-8*. Lord Nelson lived at *No. 147*, and his Lady Hamilton at *Nos. 150*.

7. Walk a couple of longish blocks up New Bond Street, and turn left into Grosvenor Street. But, almost immediately, turn right, into *Avery Row*, where W. H. DAVIES (1871-1940), the charmingly naïve and movingly humanitarian 'Hobo Poet', lived at *No. 13* in the 1920's.

8. Return to *Grosvenor Street*, and continue along it. GEORGE COLMAN THE YOUNGER (1762-1836), manager of the Haymarket Theatre, and author of many popular dramas, lived at *No. 94* in the 1790's. In his plays he combined a popular taste for shivery and mysterious 'Gothic' romance with an equally popular taste for sentimental morality. GEORGE DU MAURIER (1834-95), artist and novelist (he wrote the once celebrated *Trilby*), lived at *No. 82* in the 1860's. John Westbrook, father of Harriet, first wife of the poet Shelley, kept the Mount Coffee House at *No. 78*, and made a small fortune from it. The novelist *Laurence Sterne* came often to this place, and dated some of his love-letters from here. The harum-scarum Tory and soldier GILBERT FRANKAU (1884-1952), novelist, dramatist, and poet, lived at the house of his mother, *No. 64*, between marriages and other such adventures. EDITH SITWELL (1887-1964), whom many critics consider the greatest poetess whom England has produced, lived for years at the Sesame Club, *No. 49*. And FRANCES ('FANNY') BURNEY (1752-1840), the novelist, moved to *No. 29* in 1839, not long before her death.
[8A. When you reach *Davies Street*, crossing Grosvenor Street, you may wish to turn off, and find *No. 44*, where THOMAS MOORE (1779-1852), the Irish poet, friend of Byron, lived in 1817, and where his oldest daughter, Barbara, died.... Return to Grosvenor Street.]

9. Follow Grosvenor Street to Grosvenor Square (see Tour No. 12), turn right, along the nearer side of the square, and reach its (northeastern) corner. Here turn right again, into *Brook Street*. The town house of EDMUND BURKE (1729-97), statesman, philosopher, member of Dr Johnson's Literary Club, and strange combination of liberal and conservative, was for many years at *No. 72*. R. B. CUNNINGHAME GRAHAM (1852-1936), traveller, writer, adventurer, and activist liberal, was living at *No. 52* in the late 1880's. HENRY MILMAN (1791-1868), clergyman, historian, dramatist, poet, influential figure in the early days of the 'Higher Criticism' of the Bible, eventually Dean of St Paul's, 'one of the forgotten intellectual giants of the nineteenth

century', was born at *No. 40.* GEORGE FRIDERIC HANDEL (1685-1759), the musician, lived from about 1720 till his death at *No. 25*, and here composed the *Messiah*. The unbelievably peripatetic SYDNEY SMITH (see above) occupied the same house in 1835. The novelist MRS GASKELL (1810-65) often visited with an uncle at *No. 25*.

10. When you have found the places just mentioned, find also (opposite Avery Row) the place where *South Moulton Street* slants away, to your left, from Brook Street. At *No. 17* the artist and mystic poet WILLIAM BLAKE (1757-1827), whose reputation grows larger every year, lived from 1803 to 1821—and here wrote, among other poems, his 'Milton' and 'Jerusalem'.

11. Follow South Moulton Street till it joins Davies and Oxford Streets. If you think it worth while, turn right, on Oxford Street, go a block, and turn right again, into *Woodstock Street*. You will be walking the same street that DR SAMUEL JOHNSON (1709-84) walked when he lodged in this street in 1737.

Now return to Davies Street and the *Bond Street Underground Station*, where this tour ends. But if you wish, you may start here on another tour—*No. 23.*

Tour 20
Brompton

Effie Albanesi

Lady Cynthia Asquith

Jane Austen

Arnold Bennett

John Hay Beith ('Ian Hay')

E. F. Benson

Lord Byron

Mrs Patrick Campbell

George Colman The Younger

R. B. Cunninghame Graham

Lord Edward Dunsany

T. S. Eliot

Frederick W. Faber

W. S. Gilbert

Mary Godwin

Radclyffe Hall

Letitia Elizabeth Landon

Lillie Langtry

James Russell Lowell

Stephane Mallarmé

Edward Marsh

Somerset Maugham

Mary Russell Mitford

Alfred Noyes

Mrs Margaret Oliphant

Edgar Allan Poe

Alan Ross

Rafael Sabatini

Percy Bysshe Shelley

Edward J. Trelawny

Dennis Yates Wheatley

Lady Jane Wilde ('Speranza')

Cecil Woodham-Smith

Leave the underground at the *Knightsbridge Station.*

1. From the station, turn to your right, on *Sloane Street,* and find *No. 7,* a few doors down. Here R. B. CUNNINGHAME GRAHAM (1852-1936) lived around 1906. An aristocrat, he helped found the Labour Party in Britain, travelled in Spain and Morocco, ranched in Texas and Argentina, and wrote tales reflecting his adventurous life.

263

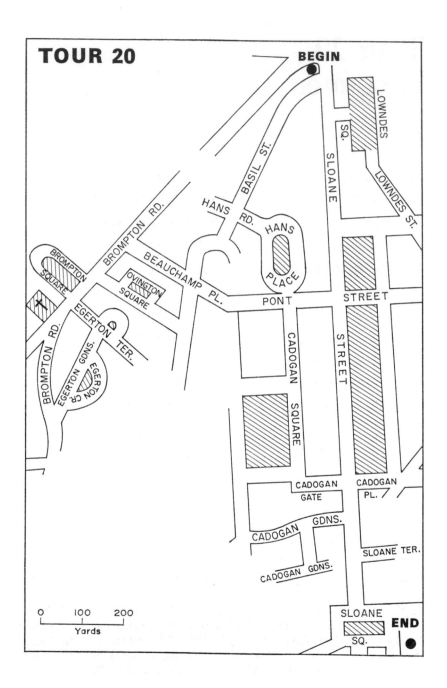

TOUR 20

BEGIN

LOWNDES

SQ.

LOWNDES ST.

SLOANE

BASIL ST.

HANS RD.

HANS PLACE

BROMPTON RD.

BEAUCHAMP PL.

PONT

STREET

STREET

BROMPTON SQUARE

OVINGTON SQUARE

EGERTON TER.

BROMPTON RD.

EGERTON GDNS.

EGERTON CR.

CADOGAN SQUARE

CADOGAN GATE

CADOGAN PL.

CADOGAN GDNS.

SLOANE TER.

CADOGAN GDNS.

0   100   200
Yards

SLOANE

SQ.

END

2. A little farther along Sloane Street, turn left, into Harriet Street, and reach *Lowndes Square.* At *No. 10,* and then at *No. 31,* the American poet JAMES RUSSELL LOWELL (1819-91), lived (1881-5) while he was American minister to the British Court of St James.

3. Go to the far right-hand corner of the square, and *Lowndes Street.* JAMES RUSSELL LOWELL (see above) lived at *No. 37* in 1880.

4. Follow Lowndes Street to its end, and turn sharp right on *Pont Street.* MRS PATRICK CAMPBELL (1865-1940), actress, who achieved incomparable success in her time in roles from Pinero, Ibsen, Shaw, Maeterlinck, and many others, lived at *No. 64* from 1928 to her death. Shaw was in love with her; she created the part of Eliza Doolittle in Shaw's play *Pygmalion*; and Aubrey Beardsley drew her picture. Years later, the popular novelist EFFIE ALBANESI (d. 1936) lived at this number. W. S. GILBERT (1836-1911), who wrote the librettos of the Gilbert-and-Sullivan light operas, lived at *No. 52* around 1909. RAFAEL SABATINI (1875-1950), author of many popular novels of romantic adventure, lived at *No. 22* in the 1930's. LILLIE LANGTRY (1852-1929), actress, mistress of princes, and favourite of poets, lived for a time at *No. 18.* *Oscar Wilde* visited her here, wrote his poem 'The New Helen' for her, and is said to have written his much later *Lady Windermere's Fan* for her to play in. She eventually wrote her memoirs—which are disappointingly discreet.

5. In walking along Pont Street, you will soon cross *Cadogan Place.* If you wish, you may turn aside, and find *No. 85,* where MRS MARGARET OLIPHANT (1828-97), enormously prolific and popular novelist, lived during the last few years of her life; and *No. 48,* where lived CECIL WOODHAM-SMITH (b. 1896), one of the most successful of women historians, as well as playwright, biographer, and fiction-writer.

6. Return to Pont Street, and continue along it till you reach Sloane Street once more. (Up Sloane Street, at *No. 62,* was the first brief London lodging place of the American painter *James M. Whistler,* in 1848.) Cross Sloane Street, and continue a couple of blocks till you see a narrow opening between buildings on your right, and greenery beyond. This is *Hans Place.* Enter between the buildings, and walk around the interior oval. *No. 23,* on your left, occupies the site of the house where a brother of JANE AUSTEN (1775-1817) once lived, and where the novelist paid him long visits annually from 1811 to 1816. At *No. 25* was born LETITIA ELIZABETH LANDON ('L. E. L.')

(1802-38), poet and novelist, of whom the literary historian Samuel Chew writes: 'Her life—gay in its promise, tragic in its ending—has an abiding interest not found in her poetry. She supplied her public with sentiment and prettiness.' The last statement is not altogether true of her novels. She committed suicide (or was murdered) in South Africa. In the far left-hand corner of the 'square' (*No. 41*) the poet PERCY BYSSHE SHELLEY (1792-1822) lived with MARY GODWIN (1797-1851) for a short time. Either in this house or in another (not identified) in Hans Place, the first child of the two was born dead. MRS MARGARET OLIPHANT (see above) lived at *No. 44*, the house of a friend, in the mid-1880's. In her realistic portrayals of provincial life she was a lesser George Eliot. She also wrote histories and biographies. At *No. 22* two French ladies kept a girls' school that was attended by as remarkable a group of young ladies as can be imagined in one place: MISS LANDON (see above); FANNY KEMBLE (1809-93), the great actress who belonged to a British 'royal family' of actors and actresses; MARY RUSSELL MITFORD (1787-1855), dramatist, who was taken very seriously by the critics of her time; and the girls who became Lady Caroline Lamb (famous for her infatuation with the poet Byron), and Lady Rosina Bulwer-Lytton, wife of the novelist Edward Bulwer-Lytton. (Lady Rosina had mother-in-law trouble, and separated from her husband after nine years of marriage. Her son—who adopted the pen-name 'Owen Meredith'—became a poet, and Viceroy of India.)

7. Return to Pont Street by the way you left it, turn right, and continue along it till it crosses Walton Street, and you find yourself in *Beauchamp Place*. At a pub called 'The Grove' on this street, the poet T. S. ELIOT (1888-1965) used to meet regularly with the critic and philosopher *Herbert Read*, the poet *F. S. Flint*, the scholar *Bonamy Dobrée*, the critic and miscellaneous writer *Frank Morley*, and others who contributed regularly to Eliot's journal the *Criterion*.

8. At the end of Beauchamp Place, turn left, on Brompton Road, and walk along it till you find *Brompton Square*, on your right. This square, with its surrounding streets, was long a favourite residence of actors, dramatists, and musicians—as well as a few other types of writers. GEORGE COLMAN THE YOUNGER (1762-1836), prolific dramatist and manager of the Haymarket Theatre, lived and died at *No. 22*, STEPHANE MALLARMÉ (1842-98), French poet, leader of the Symbolist group in France, one of the first 'modern' poets, lived at *No. 6* in 1863. E. F. BENSON (1867-1940), author of innumerable novels and autobiographical works, lived at *No. 25* from about 1920 till his death.

9. A little farther along *Brompton Road*, on your right, stands the *Brompton Oratory*, where ALFRED NOYES (1880-1958), almost the last of the true poets who tried to see the world through romantic eyes, was married to his second wife (1927). FREDERICK W. FABER (1814-63), poet in the romantic tradition, and hymn-writer, was head of the Oratory during the later years of his life.

10. Now turn back up Brompton Road the way you came, but on the side of the street opposite the Oratory. You will find Egerton Terrace entering from your right. Walk down it to *Egerton Place*, on your left. At *No. 16* EDWARD J. TRELAWNY (1792-1881), adventurer, novelist, friend of Byron and Shelley, and biographer of his two great friends, lived in the late 1830's.

11. Return to Brompton Road, turn right, and continue back up it till you find Ovington Gardens entering from your right. Follow this little street down to *Ovington Square*, where, at *No. 1*, Oscar Wilde's mother, LADY JANE WILDE ('SPERANZA') (1824-96), poet, pamphleteer, and miscellaneous writer, lived around 1880.

12. Continue through Ovington Square to *Walton Street*. At *No. 86* EDWARD MARSH (see above) spent his last seven years. The poet and novelist ALAN ROSS (b. 1922) was living at *No. 2* in the 1960's.

13. Turn left on Walton Street, go one block, and find yourself at Pont Street once more. Turn right, into Pont Street, and walk a block, to where *Cadogan Square* enters from your right. Explore this complex street (and square). At *No. 60* lived DENNIS YATES WHEATLEY (b. 1897), prolific writer of mystery novels. At *No. 62* Lord and Lady Elcho lived with their daughter Cynthia when she was a child. She became LADY CYNTHIA ASQUITH (d. 1947), great beauty, friend of J. M. Barrie, D. H. Lawrence, Edward Marsh, and most other prominent literary, social, and aristocratic figures of her time—and author of a life of Barrie, and memoirs and diaries in which she told much about the people she knew. LORD EDWARD DUNSANY (1878-1957), poet and master of fantasy in drama and story, lived from about 1925 to 1940 at *No. 66*. The Lord Chancellor Frederick Maugham, brother of the novelist SOMERSET MAUGHAM (1874-1965), lived for years at *No. 73*, and here the novelist often visited. (The two brothers detested one another; but Somerset was fond of his sister-in-law and her children.) ARNOLD BENNETT (1867-1931), the novelist, lived at *No. 75* from 1922 to 1930—when he left the house and his wife together. (Bennett having risen from poverty, was always very proud of his

literary and monetary successes. His friend H. G. Wells, visiting him in this rather ornately decorated place, noted the many mirrors all about the room, and asked Bennett if they did not bother him. 'Do they disturb you?' Bennett answered placidly. 'They don't bother me at all.') RADCLYFFE HALL (188?-1943), whose novel, *The Well of Lonliness*, about lesbianism, made a sensation in the 1920's, lived for some years, before 1915, with a woman friend at *No. 59*.

14. To your right, as you stand facing the Bennett house, a street leaves the corner of the square. Enter it, and follow it till it becomes *Cadogan Gardens*. This is a wildly sprangling street that would be confusing to describe; therefore you had best look for the house numbers on your own. The poet ALFRED NOYES (see above) lived at *No. 85* during the 1920's; it is across the street from the Roman Catholic Chapel—Noyes having become a convert to Roman Catholicism. 'IAN HAY' (JOHN HAY BEITH) (1876-1952), once a popular novelist and journalist, lived at *No. 21* in the 1920's, when he was at the height of his career. LILLIE LANGTRY (see above) once lived at *No. 2*.

15. Find your way over to nearby Sloane Street, cross it, and find *Sloane Terrace*—one block above Sloane Square. Somewhere on this short street the mother of the poet LORD BYRON (1788-1824) had lodgings with her son when he was about ten years old; and here the boy came for holidays and week-ends from school during two years.

16. Return to *Sloane Street*, and turn left, towards Sloane Square. At *No. 138* LETITIA ELIZABETH LANDON (see above) lived with her family when she was a child and a young woman. At *No. 146* (the last number on your left) the child who became the poet EDGAR ALLAN POE (1809-1849) attended a boarding school in 1816-17.

17. *Sloane Square* and its literary associations are described in *Tour No. 24* of this book. If you do not plan to come this way again, you should refer now to that tour.

When you reach the square, turn left, and find, at the end of the square, *Sloane Square Underground Station*, where this tour ends. From here, however, you may begin *Tour No. 24*.

Tour 21
Portland Place

James Boswell

James Bryce

John Buchan

Lord Byron

Thomas Campbell

Hilda Doolittle ('H. D.')

Edward FitzGerald

Gilbert Frankau

William Gerhardi

Thomas Hardy

Leigh Hunt

Washington Irving

Dr Samuel Johnson

Charles Kingsley

Sir Charles Lyell

Edmund Malone

Katherine Mansfield

Frederick D. Maurice

Arthur Wing Pinero

Ezra Pound

Bryan Waller Procter
   ('Barry Cornwall')

Adelaide Procter

Louise de la Ramée ('Ouida')

Samuel Rogers

Christina Rossetti

Dante Gabriel Rossetti

Mrs Hester Thrale

Edgar Wallace

Horace Walpole

John Wolcot ('Peter Pindar')

Leave the underground at the *Regent's Park Station*. (If you wish to look about the attractive Park Crescent, you may find *No. 23*, where Joseph Bonaparte, ex-king of Spain, lived in 1833; and *No. 12*, where the great surgeon Lord Joseph Lister (1827-1912), father of aseptic surgery, lived. He was the physician of the poet W. E. Henley, who wrote a fine sonnet in tribute to him.) Turn to your left on Marylebone Road, and walk two blocks beyond Crescent Gardens, till you reach Harley Street, entering from your left.

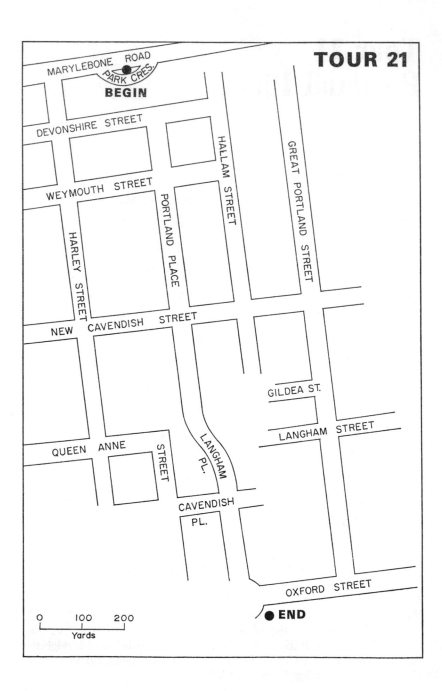

TOUR 21

MARYLEBONE ROAD
PARK CRES.
BEGIN

DEVONSHIRE STREET

WEYMOUTH STREET

HALLAM STREET

GREAT PORTLAND STREET

HARLEY STREET

PORTLAND PLACE

NEW CAVENDISH STREET

GILDEA ST.

LANGHAM STREET

QUEEN ANNE STREET

LANGHAM PL.

CAVENDISH PL.

OXFORD STREET

0   100   200
Yards

● END

1. Turn into *Harley Street*, and walk down it. MRS HESTER THRALE (1741-1821), diarist, letter-writer, and good friend of Dr Johnson, took a house on this street for the winter season of 1782; Arthur Wellesley, later Duke of Wellington, lived on it, as did the widow of Lord Nelson. *Allan Ramsay* (1713-84), highly successful painter of royal portraits, and son of the Scottish poet of the same name (whose poems about the common man were influential in the early stages of the Romantic Movement), lived on the right-hand side of the street, not far from where you entered it. ARTHUR WING PINERO (1855-1934), dramatist, lived at *No. 115A* from about 1910 into the 1920's. He was a significant figure in the 1890's, when (in such plays as *The Second Mrs Tanqueray*) he brought a new kind of thoughtfulness and realism into drama. The poet and novelist THOMAS HARDY (1840-1928) used to visit with his friends the Jeunes at *No. 79*. At *No. 73* the geologist SIR CHARLES LYELL (1797-1875) lived from 1854 till his death. W. E. Gladstone (1809-98), four times Prime Minister, moved into this same house in 1876, and stayed there till 1882. *J. M. W. Turner*, the landscape painter, lived at *No. 45* from 1803 to 1812. And KATHERINE MANSFIELD (born KATHLEEN BEAUCHAMP, in New Zealand) (1888-1923) lived at *No. 41* when she and her sisters were attending Queen's College, 1901-6. Queen's College itself, one of the earliest colleges for women, is just to your right now. It was founded in 1848 by the great liberal humanitarian F. D. MAURICE (1805-72), whose friend CHARLES KINGSLEY (1819-75), poet and novelist, became Professor of English Literature at the college. The college occupies the site of the old home of Florence Nightingale. BARRY CORNWALL (real name BRYAN WALLER PROCTER) (1787-1874), poet and song-writer, lived with his more celebrated daughter, the poet ADELAIDE PROCTER (1825-64) at *No. 38* in the 1840's and 1850's.

> SIR CHARLES LYELL, in his *Principles of Geology* (1830-3), was the first Englishman to demonstrate beyond popular question that the world had existed considerably longer than from the generally accepted date of 4004 B.C.

> KATHERINE MANSFIELD, whose real name was Kathleen Beauchamp, may have found the name 'Mansfield' in the nearby Mansfield Street and Mansfield Mews, which her apartment overlooked when she was a student at Queen's College—though she did have a distant relative of that name.

2. Continue to the next cross-street (Queen Anne Street), and turn left on it. Follow it till it ends in *Chandos Street*, and turn right on the latter. Farther down this street, at *No. 8*, the American man-of-

letters WASHINGTON IRVING (1783-1859) lived (1829-32). while he was assistant to the American ambassador, whose offices were just across the street.

3. At the lower end of Chandos Street, turn left, on Cavendish Place, and reach *Langham Place*. Turn left here, and you will soon see on your left an 'immense and ugly building' which, at the present writing, is a part of the BBC properties. It was once the very fashionable *Langham Hotel*—just across the street from All Souls' Church. Many notable American writers visiting London have stayed here—among them the poet *Henry Wadsworth Longfellow* (1868), the fiction writer *Bret Harte, Mark Twain* on several occasions, and the novelist *Ellen Glasgow* (1927). The popular novelist 'OUIDA' (LOUISE DE LA RAMÉE) (1839-1908) had apartments here in the 1860's and 1870's, and again in the mid-1880's, and presided here over a kind of literary salon to which came such figures as J. E. Millais (the Pre-Raphaelite painter), *Robert Browning*, the novelist *Lord Lytton, Oscar Wilde*, and many others.

4. Continue along Langham Place till it becomes *Portland Place*, one of London's widest streets, laid out by the famous Adam brothers in 1774. The headquarters of the BBC is immediately to your right, at the foot of the street—identified by the sculptured group of Prospero and Ariel over the entrance. Continue on up this street. The site that was once *No. 5* was occupied briefly by the novelist and letter-writer, friend of *Thomas Gray* and son of a Prime Minister, HORACE WALPOLE (1717-97). His 'Gothic' novel *The Castle of Otranto* (1764) is significant in the romantic movement because of its interest in matters medieval, matters supernatural, and emotion for its own sake. *John Holroyd, Lord Sheffield*, friend and editor of Edward Gibbon, died at *No. 20* in 1821. James Monroe (1758-1831), later President of the United States, lived at *No. 23* when he was Ambassador to England, in 1807. EDGAR WALLACE (1875-1932) author of over 150 novels, thousands of stories, and numerous plays, lived, around 1930, at *No. 31*. EDWARD FITZGERALD (1809-83), poet and 'translator' of the *Rubaiyat* of the Persian poet Omar Khayyam, lived with his parents at *No. 39*. Talleyrand (1754-1838), the French statesman and diplomat, lived at *No. 51*. JAMES BRYCE (1838-1922), historian, diplomat, statesman, jurist, Ambassador to the United States, especially well known in America for his *The American Commonwealth* (1888), lived at *No. 54*. Sir Ralph Milbanke, father of Anne Isabella Milbanke whom LORD BYRON (1788-1824) married (to his and her everlasting sorrow), lived at *No. 63*; and here Byron wooed and won her: a demonstration of

the physical law that fire can melt an icicle. JOHN BUCHAN (1875-1940), Scottish novelist, diplomat, and politician, bought the house at *No. 76* and lived there with his family, 1912-19.

[4A. In walking up Portland Place, you may wish to turn aside, to your left, on *Weymouth Street*. At *No. 32* BRYAN WALLER PROCTER ('BARRY CORNWALL') (see above), poet, dramatist, song-writer, friend and biographer of Charles Lamb, lived for many years after 1861. With him lived his more famous daughter, the sentimental poet ADELAIDE PROCTER (see above). At *No. 32A* GILBERT FRANKAU (1884-1952), novelist, dramatist, and (by courtesy) poet, passed his infancy. The principal character in George Moore's novel *Esther Waters* (almost the first truly 'naturalistic' novel in English) was drawn from Frankau's wet nurse.]

5. When you reach Devonshire Street, turn right, and go one block, to *Hallam Street*. Turn right again, and descend Hallam Street till you find *No. 110*—a large group of flats occupying the site of the house in which the poets DANTE GABRIEL ROSSETTI (1828-82) and his sister CHRISTINA ROSSETTI (1830-94) were born. The novelist WILLIAM GERHARDI (b. 1895) lived here from the early 1930's into the late 1960's. At about the place now occupied by *No. 95* SAMUEL ROGERS (1753-1855) wealthy poet and friend of poets, was born.

6. Continue down Hallam Street till you reach *Duchess Street*, entering from your right. The American poet EZRA POUND (1895-1972) stayed at *No. 8* on his first visit to London, 1906, and lodged there again in 1908. Another American poet, HILDA DOOLITTLE ('H. D.') (1886-1961) lodged at the same place in 1911.

7. Farther down Hallam Street, little *Gildea Street* enters from your left. At *No. 1* lived (1800-3) JOHN WOLCOT ('PETER PINDAR'), almost too-clever and too-malicious verse satirist.

8. Hallam Street ends in *Langham Street*. EZRA POUND (see above) moved to *No. 48* from his more expensive Duchess Street lodgings. The once-famous poet THOMAS CAMPBELL (1774-1844), who wrote the long didactic poem *The Pleasures of Hope*, lived for a time at *No. 30*; and EDMUND MALONE (1741-1812) (famous Shakespearean scholar who, knowing a good thing when he saw it, helped Boswell make the greatest of biographies thorough and scholarly without suppressing the vivacity and bounce of the author) lived at *No. 58* from 1779 until his death there.

9. Move over, by Langham Street, to *Great Portland Street*. You may wish to ascend it (to your left) a short distance to *No. 122*, where JAMES BOSWELL (1740-95), Dr Johnson's biographer, died—after having failed to reconcile himself to living in his native Scotland. Farther down Great Portland Street, LEIGH HUNT (1784-1859), a mediocre poet who was a friend of Keats, Shelley, and Byron, and also a courageous editor, sprightly essayist, and sound biographer, lived at *No. 35* in 1812. The poet EDWARD FITZGERALD (see above) lived (1856-7) at *No. 31*.

Continue to the bottom of the street, turn right, on Oxford Street, and reach the *Oxford Circus Underground Station*—where this tour ends. But from here you may start out on either *Tour No. 10* or *Tour No. 17*.

Tour 22
Marylebone

Margot Asquith

Sir Francis Bacon

James Barrie

Arnold Bennett

Elizabeth Barrett Browning

Robert Browning

Samuel Butler

Lord Byron

Thomas Campbell

Anthony Collins

Wilkie Collins

Thomas de Quincey

Charles Dickens

George du Maurier

Maria Edgeworth

Ford Madox Ford

Gilbert Frankau

John R. Green

William Heinemann

Thomas Holcroft

Washington Irving

Walter Savage Landor

Rose Macaulay

Macdonald Sisters

Arthur Machen

Frederick D. Maurice

Lady Mary Wortley Montagu

Arthur Morrison

Bryan Waller Procter
('Barry Cornwall')

Adelaide Procter

Louise de la Ramée ('Ouida')

Richard Brinsley Sheridan

Sydney Smith

John Addington Symonds

Mrs Hester Lynch Thrale

Anthony Trollope

Thomas Tyrwhitt

H. G. Wells

Charles Wesley

Thomas Woolner

Leave the underground at the *Bond Street Station.* Turn left as you

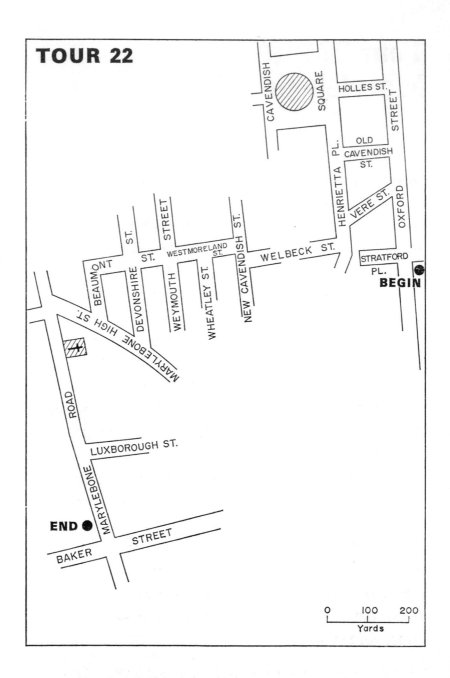

TOUR 22

CAVENDISH SQUARE

HOLLES ST.

OLD CAVENDISH ST.

HENRIETTA PL.

VERE ST.

OXFORD STREET

STRATFORD PL.

BEGIN

BEAUMONT ST.

STREET

WESTMORELAND ST.

DEVONSHIRE ST.

WEYMOUTH ST.

WHEATLEY ST.

NEW CAVENDISH ST.

WELBECK ST.

MARYLEBONE HIGH ST.

ROAD

LUXBOROUGH ST.

MARYLEBONE

END

BAKER STREET

0   100   200
Yards

leave the station, and cross over Oxford Street. Now turn right. For the next few blocks you will be turning left into small streets every few minutes, and then returning to Oxford Street.

1. Turn left, into *Stratford Place*. The ubiquitous SYDNEY SMITH (1771-1845), wit, editor, writer, reformer, clergyman, lived at *No. 18* in 1835.

2. Return to Oxford Street, continue on it for two blocks, and turn left, into *Vere Street*. The great comic actor Edward Askew Sothern (1826-81) had his home at *No. 1*, and died there. Farther up the street is a chapel where FREDERICK D. MAURICE (1805-72) was pastor from 1860 till his death. Though Maurice did write one novel and many books of philosophy-theology, he is best remembered as the principal founder of 'Christian Socialism' in 1848. This was one of the first English movements to recognize that society, rather than erring individuals, needed some drastic changes. The movement was directly responsible for Charles Kingsley's *Alton Locke* and Mrs Gaskell's *Mary Barton*; and it was the ancestor of the Fabian Society, in which George Bernard Shaw and H. G. Wells were active.

3. Return to Oxford Street, and walk two more short blocks, to *Old Cavendish Street*. *No. 15* was the home of JAMES BARRIE (1860-1937), novelist and dramatist, in 1890. THOMAS CAMPBELL (1777-1844), a poet once enormously respected, lived at *No. 18* immediately after his wife died and his only living child went mad. As some indication of the respect in which Campbell was formerly held, it may be noted that Francis Palgrave, in his great anthology *The Golden Treasury* (1861), included more poems by Campbell than by any other poets, except Shakespeare, Scott, and Shelley.

4. Return to Oxford Street, continue one block, and turn left, into *Holles Street*. At *No. 3* ANTHONY TROLLOPE (1815-82), author of more than 50 novels (including the *Barchester* series), plus other books, lived for a short time in 1872-3. At *No. 8* MARIA EDGEWORTH (1767-1849), the Irish novelist, author of *Castle Rackrent*, lived for a while in 1821-2. And at *No. 24* LORD BYRON (1788-1824), was born.

5. Continue to the end of Holles Street, and reach *Cavendish Square*. LADY MARY WORTLEY MONTAGU (1689-1762), minor poet, celebrated wit and letter-writer, made immortal (as such things go) by Alexander Pope's merciless satire of her in several of his poems, lived (1731-43) on this square, in the second house to the left of Holles Street—though her residence here was not altogether continuous. From 1749 to 1761 her official home was in the fourth house, on the square, directly to

the left of Holles Street. *George Romney* (1734-1802), the painter, lived 25 years (1773-98) on this square, in the fifth house (*No. 32*) to the right of Holles Street. In the same house had lived and died ANTHONY COLLINS (1676-1729), rationalist, deist, freethinker, tough-minded necessitarian, and author of several books stating his philoso-phical-theological position. He was a friend of the philosopher John Locke, and was satirized by Swift. In a large apartment complex, 'York Mansions', on the left-hand (western) side of this square (as you enter it from Holles Street) ARTHUR MORRISON (1863-1945) the fiction writer, playwright, and critic of Oriental art, lived in the 1920's and 1930's. His short stories written in the 1890's are almost the first truly naturalistic short stories written in England. The then Captain Horatio Nelson and his wife lived at *No. 5* in 1787. The peripatetic SYDNEY SMITH (see above) lived at *No. 8* in 1803. WILLIAM HEINE-MANN (1865-1929), the publisher, lived at *No. 19*. By publishing trans-lations of Ibsen, Bjornson, Turgenev, and Dostoevsky, as well as then-controversial items from the pens of Whistler, Wells, Maugham, and D. H. Lawrence—he helped put an end to the insularity and stodginess of England's reading. Herbert Henry Asquith (1853-1928), Prime Minister, and his wife MARGOT ASQUITH (1864-1945) lived at *No. 20* for many years. Both of them wrote memoirs and autobio-graphical works (hers were excessively frank and gossipy), and she wrote a novel. Sir William Watson wrote a poem about her: 'The Woman with a Serpent's Tongue'. (Unluckily for him the Poet Laureateship fell vacant soon afterwards—at a time when the serpent-tongued woman's husband was Prime Minister. Sir William hadn't a chance!)

6. Having circled the square, find *Henrietta Place* at its lower corner —to your left as you emerged from Holles Street. *No. 22* here was the lodging house of the American WASHINGTON IRVING (1783-1859) when he came to London in May, 1824). He wrote that he had 'a room that a cat could not turn in'. He moved soon afterwards.

7. Follow Henrietta Place two blocks to *Welbeck Street*. Turn right, into the latter. In the days before house-numbering had become man-datory, the following persons lived on this street: *Edmund Hoyle* (1672-1769), the writer on whist and other games, from whose rules is derived the now proverbial saying, 'according to Hoyle'; Martha Blount, who was probably beloved of *Alexander Pope*; James Mac-lean, the highwayman who held up and robbed *Horace Walpole*; and THOMAS TYRWHITT (1730-86), who is responsible for the first truly scholarly edition of Chaucer (1775-8). MARIA EDGEWORTH (see above),

the novelist, stayed briefly with relatives at *No. 69* in 1830. The poets ROBERT BROWNING and his wife ELIZABETH BARRETT BROWNING stayed at *No. 58* in 1852, on one of their visits home from Italy. 'OUIDA' (see above) lived with her mother at *No. 51* from 1867 to 1883. ANTHONY TROLLOPE (see above) died in a nursing home at *No. 34* in 1882. Dr Johnson's friend MRS HESTER LYNCH THRALE (1741-1821), no mean writer of letters and of a famous diary, lived at *No. 33* after her second marriage—with Gabriel Piozzi, a marriage that estranged her from Dr Johnson. JOHN ADDINGTON SYMONDS (1840-93), historian of the Italian Renaissance, lived at *No. 29* in 1865; and THOMAS WOOLNER (1825-92), Pre-Raphaelite sculptor and poet lived earlier at the same address. *John Keats*'s first volume of *Poems* (1817) was published at *No. 3*; and, in Dickens's *Barnaby Rudge*, Lord George Gordon addressed the mob from the balcony of *No. 64*.

8. Welbeck Street ends where *New Cavendish Street* crosses it. Near the intersection, you will find *No. 11,* where the novelist WILKIE COLLINS (1824-89) was born. In *The Moonstone* (which T. S. Eliot called 'the first and the greatest of English detective novels') he created Sergeant Cuff, the first detective in English literature.

9. Almost opposite the end of Welbeck Street, though a bit to the right, Westmoreland Street opens. Enter it, walk two short blocks, and find *Wheatley Street* opening on your left. At *No. 1* CHARLES WESLEY (1703-88), hymn-writer and brother of John Wesley lived and died. He had his share of the incredible energy of the Wesley family: while actively engaged on evangelical missions all about England and America, he composed over 6,000 hymns—of which the best known are 'Jesus, Lover of my Soul' and 'Hark! the Herald Angels Sing'. His son Charles and nephew Samuel Wesley, musicians and composers, also lived here at *No. 1*.

10. Follow Westmoreland Street on across Weymouth Street.
[10A. At *No. 32 Weymouth Street* lived, for many years after 1861, BRYAN WALLER PROCTER ('BARRY CORNWALL') (1787-1874), poet, songwriter, dramatist, friend and biographer of Charles Lamb. With him lived his daughter ADELAIDE PROCTER (1825-64), famous and much-respected poet in her time, and author of 'The Lost Chord'. At *No. 32A.* GILBERT FRANKAU (see above), passed his infancy.]
Beaumont Street opens opposite the end of Westmoreland Street; Enter it. The area about here was once occupied (late seventeenth to late eighteenth century) by a public pleasure garden, with orchards, gravelled walks, lawns, a bowling green, a fashionable dining place,

orchestras, and places for the performance of dramatic recitals and juggling exhibitions. *Samuel Pepys, John Locke,* and many other celebrated men frequented, or at least visited, the place. At *No. 4* lived JOHN R. GREEN (1837-83) one of the first historians to stress social change, rather than political shiftings, as a significant element in history. At *No. 17* the remarkable MACDONALD SISTERS lived with their parents towards the middle of the nineteenth century. One sister married the famous Pre-Raphaelite painter *Sir Edward Burne-Jones*; a second sister married *Sir Edward Poynter,* another celebrated painter, President of the Royal Academy; a third became the mother of *Rudyard Kipling*; and a fourth became the mother of Stanley Baldwin, Prime Minister of England during the 1930's. Eliza Mary Ann Savage—longtime friend and correspondent of SAMUEL BUTLER (1835-1902), and original of Alathea Pontifex in *The Way of All Flesh*—lived at *No. 22*. Butler called her 'the best, kindest, wittiest, most lovable, and, to my mind, handsomest woman I had ever seen'. At *No. 38* the poet WALTER SAVAGE LANDOR (1775-1864) had lodgings in 1794, after he was expelled from Oxford for having fired a pistol at the window of a Tory whom he disliked. (As you cross *Devonshire Street* you may look at a few doors to your left and find *No. 19* where the future wife of the novelist FORD MADOX FORD (1873-1939) lived, and where he courted her. They were later divorced.)

11. Follow Beaumont Street on to the place where it ends in *Marylebone High Street*. Across the street here you will see a garden. Cross over to it. The place marks the site of a church which had stood there from the early fifteenth century to 1741, when a new church was built. This church (which became a chapel after a new, larger church was built around the corner in 1813-17) was bombed out during the last war, and was not rebuilt. In the original church SIR FRANCIS BACON (1615-1626), the philosopher, essayist, author of the utopian *New Atlantis*, and father of the modern scientific method, was married in 1606. CHARLES WESLEY (see above) was buried in the churchyard here (find his grave), as was his nephew *Samuel Wesley*, the composer. THOMAS HOLCROFT (1745-1809), skilful dramatist of the 'sentimental' school, author of the first English play called a 'melo-drama' (that is, a melody-drama, ancestor of the modern 'musical'), and friend of Coleridge, Charles Lamb, and William Godwin, is also buried here. He was imprisoned briefly (1794) for having espoused the principles of the French Revolution. William Hogarth, the artist, showed his Rake (of *The Rake's Progress*, 1734) being married in this church.

In the new church that succeeded the old one, (1741) RICHARD BRINSLEY SHERIDAN (1751-1816), the dramatist, was married to his romantic Miss Linley, in 1788; LORD BYRON (1788-1824) was baptized in the same church in the same year. Later on, Horatia Nelson, daughter of Lord Nelson and Lady Hamilton, was baptized in this church.

12. Continue on around the left-hand corner into *Marylebone Road.* Just as you turn the corner you will find a small porch in an ugly yellow building that occupies the site of the house where CHARLES DICKENS (1812-70) lived from 1839 to 1851. The porch has an attractive bas-relief showing Dickens and some of the characters from the novels he wrote here: *Barnaby Rudge, The Old Curiosity Shop, Martin Chuzzlewit,* the *Christmas Carol, David Copperfield,* and part of *Dombey and Son.* Many scenes from the last-mentioned work are laid in this part of London, and the church where Mr Dombey was married and Paul Dombey christened and buried is the *St Marylebone Parish Church* next door. GEORGE DU MAURIER (1834-96), artist and novelist, lived with his parents in the Dickens house immediately before Dickens moved there. In Marylebone Church the poets ROBERT BROWNING and ELIZABETH BARRETT were married after their elopement, in 1846. Here, in 1903, ARTHUR MACHEN (1863-1947), author of fantastic romances notable for their elegant style, and translator of Casanova, was married for the second time.

13. Continue along Marylebone Road, on the side where the church stands, till you reach *Luxborough Street*—opening to your left, just opposite Madame Tussaud's (which contains effigies of many authors). Down this street, at *No. 5,* THOMAS DE QUINCEY (1785-1859), essayist and literary critic, noted for his autobiographic *Confessions of an English Opium Eater,* lived in 1806-7. (The street was called Northumberland Street in his time.) At *No. 7-8* ROSE MACAULAY (d. 1958), poet and novelist, lived during most of the 1930's.

14. Return to Marylebone Road, continue along it for a block, and look across the street at the massively ornate building surmounting the railway and the underground station opposite you. In this building (called Chiltern Court) the novelist ARNOLD BENNETT (1867-1931) lived during the last year of his life, and died attended by his mistress. He lived in flat *No. 97.* Just above him, in *No. 47* in the same building, lived his longtime friend H. G. WELLS. He had moved here in September, 1930, just two months before Bennett came.

Now cross over Marylebone Road, and end this tour at the *Baker Street Underground Station*—or set out on *Tour No. 23* or *No. 34.*

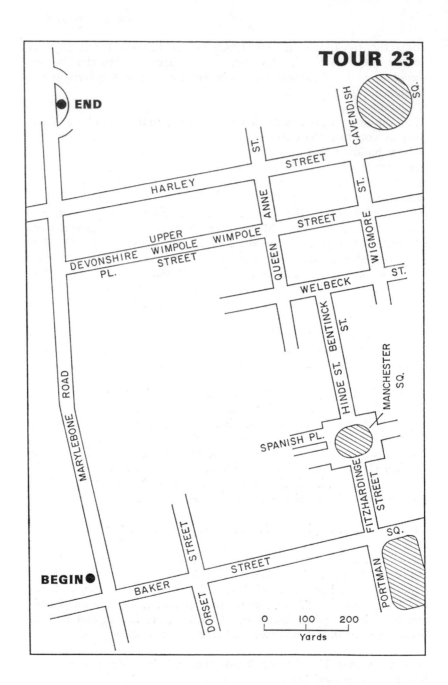

TOUR 23

END

CAVENDISH SQ.

ST.

STREET

HARLEY

ANNE

ST.

UPPER
DEVONSHIRE   WIMPOLE   WIMPOLE
PL.   STREET

STREET

QUEEN

WIGMORE

WELBECK

ST.

MARYLEBONE ROAD

HINDE ST.   BENTINCK   ST.

MANCHESTER SQ.

SPANISH PL.

FITZHARDINGE   STREET

STREET

BEGIN

BAKER

DORSET

STREET

SQ.

PORTMAN

0   100   200
Yards

Tour 23
Wimpole Street Area

William Beckford	George Grossmith, Jr
Sir Alexander Boswell	Arthur Henry Hallam
James Boswell	Henry Hallam
Stopford Brooke	Thomas Hardy
Elizabeth Barrett Browning	Matthew ('Monk') Lewis
Robert Browning	Rose Macaulay
Edward Bulwer-Lytton	Capt. Frederick Marryat
Edmund Burke	Bryan Waller Procter
Wilkie Collins	Adelaide Procter
Richard Cumberland	William Rothenstein
Charles Dickens	Herbert Spencer
Conan Doyle	Algernon C. Swinburne
Maria Edgeworth	Martin Tupper
Edward Gibbon	

Leave the underground at the *Baker Street Station.* On emerging into Marylebone Road, turn right, walk a few steps to the corner, cross over Marylebone Road, and take off down Baker Street.

1. SIR ARTHUR CONAN DOYLE's immortal Sherlock Holmes was supposed to have rooms at *No. 221B Baker Street*—which is behind you; but Doyle's descriptions of the place correspond more closely with *No. 109* or *111*. (Some Holmes experts have placed the rooms at *No. 61*.) The novelist and playwright EDWARD BULWER-LYTTON (1803-73) was born at *No. 68* (formerly *No. 31*). He was born plain Bulwer, but changed his name when he inherited the Lytton estates in 1843. A prolific and popular writer, his pen made him wealthy; and his novel *The Last Days of Pompeii* (1834) is still very readable.

2. As you descend Baker Street, you will cross *Dorset Street*. This extends about two blocks on either side of Baker Street, and should be explored now. ROBERT BROWNING (1812-89), the poet, and his wife ELIZABETH BARRETT BROWNING (1806-61), who was considered, in her lifetime, a better poet than her husband, stayed at *No. 13* in 1855. Here Mrs Browning wrote *Aurora Leigh*, a realistic sociological novel in blank verse. This place was her last residence in England before she went back to Italy, and died. The poet ALGERNON CHARLES SWINBURNE (1837-1909) lived more than five years (1865-70) at *No. 22*, where many of his most famous poems were written. In a large apartment complex called *St Andrew's Mansions*, on this street, ROSE MACAULAY (1889-1959), poet, novelist, critic, essayist, author of at least 30 books, lived for many years after 1926.

3. Continue down Baker Street till you reach the corner of Portman Square. Here turn left, into Fitzhardinge Street, and reach *Manchester Square*. At *No. 1* on this square lived the Irish-born STOPFORD BROOKE (1832-1916), essayist, critic, scholar, biographer, and dramatist, lecturer at University College, London. In earlier years he was Queen Victoria's chaplain; but later he became a Unitarian minister. At *No. 2* Sir Julius Benedict (1804-85), musical composer and orchestra director, lived and died. His best-known opera was *The Lily of Killarney*. The *Wallace Collection* of art is housed in an imposing building at the north (left-hand) end of the square, and should be visited. Though not so celebrated nor so extensive as either the National Gallery or the Tate Gallery, the collection here is still one of the finest assemblages of art and *objets d'art* ever put together. The building occupies the site of what was the French ambassador's house; and here the French statesman and historian *François Guizot* (1787-1874) lived as ambassador in 1840.

4. At the far upper (north-east) corner of the square, the street called *Spanish Place* enters. At *No. 3* lived CAPTAIN FREDERICK MARRYAT (1792-1848), old seaman and novelist of adventure at sea, who was once the favourite writer of all boys who read anything at all, and was greatly admired by Joseph Conrad. Later on, GEORGE GROSSMITH, JR. (1847-1912), comic actor and theatre manager, lived at the same address.

5. Continue around the square till you reach *Hinde Street*—just opposite *Fitzhardinge Street*, where you entered. At *No. 20, Hinde House*, on this short street, ROSE MACAULAY (see above) lived from

1941 till her death. The philosopher HERBERT SPENCER (1820-1903) lodged at *No. 6* in 1862-3.

6. Hinde Street is continued into *Bentinck Street*. Here the family of CHARLES DICKENS (1812-70), the novelist, lived at *No. 18* in 1833-4, when Charles was 21 years old, and when his *Sketches by Boz* first began to appear in periodicals. EDWARD GIBBON (1737-94), the historian, lived at *No. 7* from 1772 to 1783. He loved this place, and wrote here the first half of *The Decline and Fall of the Roman Empire*.

7. At the end of Bentinck Street, turn left, on Welbeck Street, and then, after a few steps, turn right, on *Queen Anne Street*. This was a fashionable residential street in the eighteenth century, though the precise locations of some of the older literary sites along the street are lost. Erasmus Darwin, brother of *Charles Darwin* and friend of Carlyle, lived at *No. 6*, and was often visited here by his famous brother. *J. M. W. Turner* lived at *No. 23* for many years, and did most of his finest work here. He lived also at *Nos. 22* and *45*. RICHARD CUMBERLAND (1732-1811), the dramatist, lived at one of the corners (which one is not known to the present writer) of Queen Anne and Wimpole Streets. Though Cumberland is largely forgotten today, he was a distinguished man in his time: Ambassador to Spain, friend of Byron, Scott, and Thomas Moore, author of 40 plays and two novels, besides many poems, essays and religious tracts. He was one of the last to practise the 'sentimental comedy', and one of the first to write a play (*The Jew*, 1794) combating anti-Semitism. His best play (*The West Indian*, 1771) was written here on Queen Anne Street.

8. Follow Queen Anne Street to *Harley Street*. Here turn right, and descend one block, to Cavendish Square. You will pass *No. 12*, where WILKIE COLLINS (see above) lived with a mistress (1859-64).

9. At the corner of Cavendish Square, turn right. (If you wish to explore this interesting square at this time, see Tour No. 22, Section 5.) You will regain *Wimpole Street* immediately. Turn right, and ascend it. The poet-novelist THOMAS HARDY (1840-1928) was a very frequent visitor to his friends the Jeunes, who lived at *No. 39* before they moved over to nearby Harley Street. At *No. 50* a modern house partly replaces the one in which the poet ELIZABETH BARRETT (1806-61) lived with her jealous and tyrannical father, and from which she eloped with the poet ROBERT BROWNING. At *No. 57* lived the distinguished historian HENRY HALLAM (1777-1859) father of ARTHUR

HENRY HALLAM (1811-33), memorialized in Tennyson's *In Memoriam.* At *No. 82* WILKIE COLLINS (see above) spent his last years, and died.

10. Wimpole Street leads on into *Upper Wimpole Street*, where a Mrs Davis kept a school for girls and young women, attended by MARIA EDGEWORTH (1767-1849), novelist, writer of children's stories, friend of Sir Walter Scott, and propagandist for the higher education of women.

11. Upper Wimpole Street leads on into *Devonshire Place.* At *No. 2* CONAN DOYLE (1859-1930), who was a medical doctor as well as a creator of Sherlock Holmes, had his first doctor's office. He was notably unsuccessful in attracting patients—to which fact we may attribute his resort to writing. WILLIAM BECKFORD (1760-1844), author of a celebrated Gothic novel *Vathek* (1784), and dissolute friend of Lord Nelson, lived at *No. 4.* MATTHEW ('MONK') LEWIS (1775-1818), author of the early 'horror' novel *The Monk* (1796) that partly inspired (shall we say?) Mary Shelley's *Frankenstein,* had a home at *No. 9.* And at *No. 10* lived, in the 1940's, WILLIAM ROTHENSTEIN (1872-1945), the artist and writer.

12. At the end of Devonshire Place, turn right, on *Marylebone Road.* The place on your right, on the corner (the London Clinic at the present writing), was once occupied by the house where MARTIN TUPPER (1810-89) was born. A moralist in verse, he was immensely popular in Victorian England and America, was admired by Queen Victoria, and was almost appointed Poet Laureate.

13. Continue along Marylebone Road. The first street on your left is *Upper Harley Street*, where, at *No. 13,* lived 'BARRY CORNWALL', friend of Shelley, Lamb, Hazlitt, Browning, Tennyson, and Swinburne.

At this point, if you wish to end this tour, walk on another block to the *Regent's Park Underground Station.* Or, if you wish to do another tour, turn into Harley Street, opening opposite Upper Harley Street, and begin *Tour No. 21.*

Tour 24
Kensington East

Joseph Addison

Enid Bagnold

Richard Blackmore

Rupert Brooke

Robert Browning

Sir Edward Burne-Jones

Mrs Patrick Campbell

Winston Churchill

Mary E. Coleridge

Lady Mary Montgomerie Currie
('Violet Fane')

Charles Dickens

Jacob Epstein

Sir Francis Galton

W. S. Gilbert

Lord Ronald Gorell

Henry Harland

Aldous Huxley

Thomas Henry Huxley

Mrs Elizabeth Inchbald

Henry James

John Stuart Mill

Sir John E. Millais

William Morris

Charles Hubert Perry

Lady Anne Ritchie

Dante Gabriel Rossetti

Sir Richard Steele

Sir Leslie Stephen

William Makepeace Thackeray

H. G. Wells

Virginia Woolf

Leave the underground at the *Kensington High Street Station.*

1. As you leave the station, you will pass through a small shopping arcade before emerging on Kensington High Street itself. Once outside, turn sharp to your right, pass quickly by the temptations of a plush department store, and then turn sharp right again into Derry Street. Follow this a short block to *Kensington Square,* a charming green area encircled by the neat, narrow little streets of the seventeenth century, when this square was laid out. Both JOSEPH ADDISON

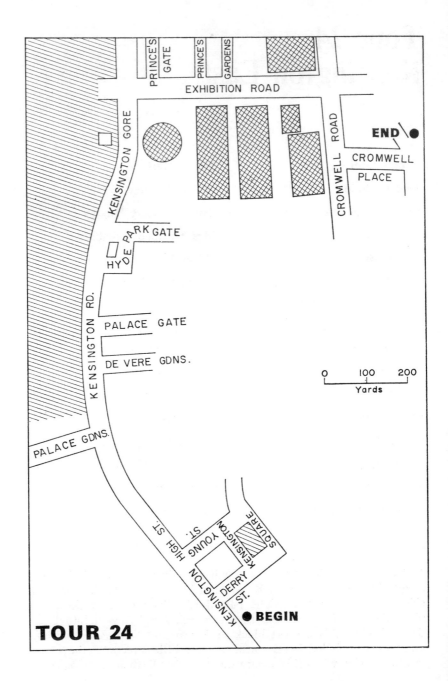

PRINCE'S GATE
PRINCE'S GARDENS

EXHIBITION ROAD

KENSINGTON GORE

CROMWELL ROAD

END

CROMWELL PLACE

HYDE PARK GATE

KENSINGTON RD.

PALACE GATE

DE VERE GDNS.

0   100   200
Yards

PALACE GDNS.

KENSINGTON HIGH ST.

YOUNG ST.

DERRY ST.

KENSINGTON SQUARE

BEGIN

TOUR 24

(1672-1719) and his good friend SIR RICHARD STEELE (1672-1729) lived at different times on this square, in houses that have disappeared. Addison is best remembered for his periodical essays published in the *Spectator*, rather than for his more pretentious poetry and drama: and Steele is remembered for his essays, his comedies in the new 'sentimental' manner, and, most of all, for his warm and engaging character. SIR RICHARD BLACKMORE (1655-1721), epic poet, essayist, critic, and physician to William III, lived at the corner of the square just ahead of you (south-west) as you enter it. At *No. 35* LORD RONALD GORELL (1884-1963), a poet who should be better known than he is, lived from the early 1920's to the late 1950's. MRS PATRICK CAMPBELL (1865-1940), the actress, lived at *No. 33* for more than twenty years (1900-21). She was all the rage with the young rebels and aesthetes of the 1890's. Aubrey Beardsley drew her picture (which was published in the *Yellow Book*); she acted in the plays of George Bernard Shaw (some of his plays were written especially for her); and Shaw was so in love with her that he made something of a fool of himself about her. The Pre-Raphaelite painter SIR EDWARD BURNE-JONES (1833-98) lived at *No. 41* in the latter half of the 1860's. His wife was the sister of Rudyard Kipling's mother; and the marriage of the elder Kiplings took place from this house.

Continue walking around the square, keeping to your left. JOHN STUART MILL (1806-73), the Utilitarian philosopher, lived at *No. 18* from 1837 to 1851. Mill's thought has had a tremendous influence on the thought of Britain and America; pragmatic, empirical, common sensible, it is at the same time profoundly humanitarian, liberal in politics, and socialistic in economics. Next door, at *No. 17*, lived the musician SIR CHARLES HUBERT PARRY (1848-1919) who wrote several books on the history of music, and who has some association with literature by having written incidental music for Aristophanes's *The Frogs* and *The Birds*, and made the musical arrangement for William Blake's poem *Milton* that is well known under the title *Jerusalem*. Circling on around the square, you will come to *No. 7*, which was the residence of Lady Castlewood, in Thackeray's *Henry Esmond*.

2. Keep walking straight ahead, towards Kensington High Street once more, until you suddenly find yourself (at the corner of the square) on *Young Street*. A few doors along it, on your left, is *No. 16*, a quiet dark-brick house where WILLIAM MAKEPEACE THACKERAY (1811-63) was living (1846-54) when he wrote his two greatest novels: *Vanity Fair* and *Henry Esmond*. Later on (1878-83) his daughter, LADY ANNE RITCHIE (1837-1918), also a novelist, lived at *No. 27*—which has disappeared. Thackeray was, of course, along with Dickens and George

Eliot, one of the 'Big Three' of Victorian fiction. His work, rich with character and incident, reveals an extraordinary combination of cynicism and tenderness, satire and sentimentality.

3. Follow Young Street one block to Kensington High Street. Turn right on the latter, walk along it one block, and then cross to the other side. Here is the entrance to *Kensington Palace Gardens*—a quiet, tree-lined, impressive street, free of all but pedestrian or authorized traffic. A few yards up the street, on the left, is *No. 2*, an orange-brick house designed by WILLIAM MAKEPEACE THACKERAY (see above), and his home during the last two years of his life. He died in the left-hand (to you) front corner room, second storey.

(Off to your right, and open to the public, is Kensington Palace, once the principal residence of British sovereigns, but part of it now a museum of the history of London. Both Queen Victoria and Queen Mary, wife of George v, were born here; William III and his Queen Mary, as well as Queen Anne and George II, lived and died here. It saw the goings and comings of many literary figures; *Sir William Temple*, essayist and statesman; *Jonathan Swift*, England's greatest satirist, and also at one time a behind-the-scenes power in British politics; *Sir John Vanbrugh*, dramatist and royal architect; Pope's *Dr Arbuthnot*, political writer, satirist, and court physician to Queen Anne; Pope's *Bolingbroke*, historian, political writer, and disreputable politician; Pope's bitterly satirized *Lord John Hervey*, courtier, memoirist, and minor poet; *Lady Mary Wortley Montagu*, letter writer, wife of an ambassador, first a friend and then an enemy of Pope, who satirized her in verse; *Colley Cibber*, actor, theatre manager, dramatist, Poet Laureate, victim of Pope in the *Dunciad*; *Matthew Prior*, poet and diplomat; *William Congreve*, dramatist and government employee; *Joseph Addison*, essayist, poet, dramatist, government official; *William Mason*, poet, dramatist, and court chaplain; *Lord Chesterfield*, of the *Letters*; *Horace Walpole*, novelist, son of a Prime Minister; *Voltaire*, French satirist, who visited here.)

4. Return to Kensington High Street, cross back over it, and continue along it to your left (eastward). A group of buildings called *Kensington House* once faced the street here, on your right. Here lived, at different times, *James Elphinstone* (friend of Dr Johnson, translator, teacher, reformer of spelling), and MRS ELIZABETH INCHBALD (1753-1821) (actress, dramatist, novelist), who died here. Soon you will reach *De Vere Gardens*, entering from your right. At the nearer corner, in residential apartments, lived HENRY HARLAND (1861-1905), American-born novelist and story writer, but best known as editor

of the *Yellow Book* in the 1890's. *No. 29 De Vere Gardens* was the last home (1888-9) in England of ROBERT BROWNING (1812-89), the great Victorian poet, who left here for Italy, where he soon died. Just across the street, at *No. 34*, HENRY JAMES (1843-1916) lived and worked on *What Maisie Knew*, *The Awkward Age*, *The Wings of the Dove*, and *The Ambassadors*. MARY KEEGAN ('Mary Heathcott' or 'Mary Raymond') (b. 1914), popular novelist, was living at *No. 44* in the 1960's.

5. Return to Kensington High Street, and continue along it till you reach, entering from your right, the street called *Palace Gate*. A few steps down it stands *No. 2*, where the popular and successful painter SIR JOHN E. MILLAIS (1829-96) lived and died. He helped found the literary-artistic Pre-Raphaelite Brotherhood, was a friend of many poets (including Rossetti, Swinburne, and Browning), illustrated the poems of Tennyson and the novels of Trollope, and married the erstwhile wife of the writer John Ruskin.

6. Return to Kensington High Street, and continue along it to your right. You will soon reach a street called *Hyde Park Gate*, and then what looks like another one of the same name. When you have finally reached a place that extends off to your right as a real street, turn into it, and walk on past a modern apartment development on your left. This development occupies the site of *No. 16*, where CHARLES DICKENS (1812-70) had lodgings in 1862, when he had come up to London from Gad's Hill. At *No. 18* (an ancient and lugubrious-looking place, on last inspection) the sculptor JACOB EPSTEIN (1880-1959) lived and died. He is of literary interest because of his many literary friendships, and his magnificent bronze busts of Joseph Conrad, Bernard Shaw, W. H. Davies, R. Cunninghame Graham, and W. B. Yeats (among others). He sculpted the memorial monument to W. H. Hudson that is in Hyde Park, and the monument on Oscar Wilde's grave in Paris. Farther on is *No. 22*, where SIR LESLIE STEPHEN (1832-1904), scholar, originator and editor of the *Dictionary of National Biography*, and a friend and benefactor of R. L. Stevenson and W. E. Henley, lived during the last 25 years of his life, and where he died. His daughter, who became the novelist VIRGINIA WOOLF (1882-1941), was born here. WINSTON CHURCHILL (1874-1965) had *No. 28* as his private home before, during, and after his second term as Prime Minister, in the 1950's and here he died. ENID BAGNOLD, novelist and poet, author of *National Velvet* (1937) lived at *No. 29* for more than 30 years, from the 1930's to the 1960's.

7. Return to Kensington High Street, and continue along it to your right. Presently you will see the incredible Albert Memorial on your left, and the Royal Albert Hall on your right. On the site of the latter once stood Lady Blessington's famous Gore House, where the poets *Walter Savage Landor* and *Thomas Moore* were frequent guests. Turn right, into broad *Exhibition Road*.

[7A. Just after you have turned, *Prince's Gate* opens on your left. Here lived, early in the twentieth century, a minor but very interesting poet, 'VIOLET FANE' (LADY MONTGOMERIE CURRIE).

[7B. One block down Exhibition Road, you may wish to turn left, into *Prince's Gardens*. W. S. GILBERT (1836-1911), author of the librettos of the Gilbert and Sullivan light operas, lived at *No. 36* from 1894 to 1898. And ALDOUS HUXLEY (1894-1963), novelist, poet, and essayist, lived at *No. 44* in the 1920's. ... Return to Exhibition Road.]

On the right of Exhibition Road stand relatively new buildings housing colleges of the University of London. At one of these colleges THOMAS HENRY HUXLEY (1825-95), the biologist who did so much to defend Darwin's theories of evolution, lectured for many years. H. G. WELLS (1866-1946), novelist and social philosopher, was one of Huxley's students here.

Farther on, to your right, are the Geological and Science Museums. On your left is an entrance to the enormous *Victoria and Albert Museum* of the fine arts—which you *must* see. Its treasures are inconceivable, both in quantity and in quality. A visitor with literary interests will visit the *Green Dining Room* (take the first corridor to the left after you enter, walk to its end, and then take a turn to the right), which was decorated and furnished by the artisan-painter-poet WILLIAM MORRIS (1834-96) and his friends the painter SIR EDWARD BURNE-JONES (1833-98) and the architect Philip Webb (1830-1915), together with others of the Pre-Raphaelite group. Inquire as to the location of a painting by another friend of Morris and Burne-Jones, DANTE GABRIEL ROSSETTI (1828-82), of his wife Elizabeth Siddal, together with a poem by Rossetti incorporated into the frame of the picture. On the second floor of the museum is *Room 74*, devoted to the Art of the Book—with exhibits including early illuminated manuscripts and other examples of book-making right down to the present. Here also are exhibited many manuscripts of literary interest, including the complete manuscript of Dickens's *A Tale of Two Cities*. The Library (adjoining Room 74) exhibits many other manuscripts; and *Room 132*, directly above Room 74, has exhibits illustrating the Art of the Theatre.

WILLIAM MORRIS was a kind of modern Leonardo—a poet, painter, worker in stained glass and tapestries, designer of furniture and wallpaper, translator, book-designer, and active figure in the socialist movement of the 1880's.

DANTE GABRIEL ROSSETTI was the greatest and most tragic of the Pre-Raphaelite Brotherhood. He wrote a collection of sonnets to his wife Elizabeth (mentioned above); and when she died, he laid the manuscript of the sonnets on her breast, and had them buried with her. But, some years later, he was persuaded by his friends to allow the body to be exhumed, and the sonnets retrieved and published.

8. Emerge from the museum at its front entrance, on Cromwell Road. Just across the latter lies *Thurloe Square*. Here, at *No. 5*, the poet RUPERT BROOKE (1888-1915) lived in 1913.

9. Just across from the side of the Victoria and Albert Museum where you entered (that is, at the corner of Exhibition and Cromwell Roads) stands the Natural History Museum—a monument (1873-80) to the Victorian love of vastness, pretension, and over-elaboration in architecture. Much of the early biological and paleontological material on which the doctrine of evolution was based is housed here; and monumental statues of the two chief figures in the early history of that doctrine—CHARLES DARWIN (1809-92) and THOMAS HENRY HUXLEY (see above)—are at either side of the great Central Hall opposite the entrance of the museum.

10. Almost directly in front of the Museum of Natural History, *Cromwell Place* opens, and extends southward towards the underground station. Enter this street. *No. 12* was the home of MARY E. COLERIDGE (1861-1907), the poet, in 1905-6. She was the grand-niece of Samuel Taylor Coleridge. SIR JOHN E. MILLAIS (see above) lived at *No. 8* from 1868 to 1872.

Continue on down Cromwell Place to *South Kensington Underground Station*. Here you may end this tour—or you may wish to launch yourself on either *Tour No. 15* or *Tour No. 27*.

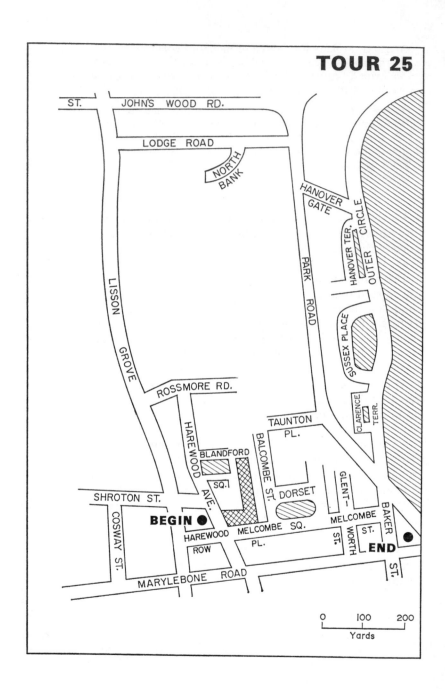

TOUR 25

ST. JOHN'S WOOD RD.

LODGE ROAD

NORTH BANK

HANOVER GATE

HANOVER TER.

OUTER CIRCLE

PARK ROAD

LISSON GROVE

SUSSEX PLACE

CLARENCE TERR.

ROSSMORE RD.

TAUNTON PL.

HAREWOOD AVE.

BLANDFORD

SQ.

BALCOMBE ST.

DORSET

GLENT-

SHROTON ST.

COSWAY ST.

BEGIN ●

HAREWOOD ROW

MELCOMBE SQ.

PL.

MELCOMBE

ST.

WORTH ST.

BAKER ST.

END ●

MARYLEBONE ROAD

0   100   200
Yards

294

Tour 25
Regent's Park West

Harrison Ainsworth	George Henry Lewes
Herbert Asquith	Elizabeth Linton
Elizabeth Bowen	John Lockhart
Wilkie Collins	Arthur Machen
Cyril Connolly	Louis Macneice
Charles Dickens	Alfred Noyes
G. Lowes Dickinson	Harold Pinter
George Eliot	Adelaide Procter
T. S. Eliot	Bryan Waller Procter
Gilbert Frankau	Olive Schreiner
Edmund Gosse	Mary Shelley
George Grossmith	Mrs Sarah Siddons
Benjamin Haydon	George Robert Sims
'Sherlock Holmes'	Charlotte Smith
Leigh Hunt	H. G. Wells
Thomas Henry Huxley	William Hale White
Walter Leaf	('Mark Rutherford')

Leave the underground at the *Marylebone Station*. Turn right, on Harewood Avenue, and reach (one block) Marylebone Road.

1. Turn right, on *Marylebone Road*, and find *No. 69* where lived WILLIAM HALE WHITE ('MARK RUTHERFORD') (1831-1913), realistic novelist concerned with the science-religion conflict. MRS ELIZABETH LINTON (1822-98), popular novelist, lived at *No. 238*.

2. After two blocks, turn right, into *Cosway Street. No. 5* was the home of ARTHUR MACHEN (1863-1920), novelist of fantasy, critical essayist, and translator of Casanova's *Memoirs*.

3. At the end of Cosway Street, turn right (Shroton Street), and walk straight on to Harewood Avenue. Turn left, to *Blandford Square.* At *No. 9* OLIVE SCHREINER (1855-1920), novelist, author of *The Story of an African Farm,* lived in 1885-6. At *No. 16* the critic, biographer, and editor GEORGE HENRY LEWES (1817-78) lived with the novelist GEORGE ELIOT (MARY ANN EVANS) (1819-80), from 1860 to 1863. It was here that she wrote *Romola* and *Felix Holt.* And at *No. 38* WILKIE COLLINS (1824-89), novelist and friend of Dickens, lived with his widowed mother in the late 1840's.

> GEORGE HENRY LEWES believed in the freedom of women to love when and whom they chose; therefore, when his wife fell in love with the son of Leigh Hunt, Lewes made no serious objection. Later on, he met George Eliot, and he and she began living together as man and wife. This relationship continued, most happily for both of them, until his death 24 years later.

> WILKIE COLLINS wrote more than two dozen novels, including the famous *The Woman in White* and *The Moonstone*—the latter being the first genuine detective novel in English. He never married; but he was faithful to several mistresses at the same time, had children by them, and supported them and the children.

4. You have already crossed *Lisson Grove*; return to it now, and walk on up it. Find Church Street, entering from your left. Beyond this, in a house that was *No. 13,* and has long since disappeared, LEIGH HUNT (1784-1859), the poet, and friend of Keats, lived after his release from prison (for having libelled the Prince Regent) in 1815. Here he was often visited by *Byron*; here Byron rode gleefully on the rocking-horse of Hunt's small son; here the poet Wordsworth visited Hunt; and here *Shelley* stayed with Hunt in 1817. At *No. 22* lived BENJAMIN HAYDON (1786-1846), the painter, who was also a friend of Keats, and who, though famous, lived an unfortunate life, and eventually committed suicide. At this house *Keats* met *William Wordsworth* at a dinner where *Charles Lamb* was also a guest. *Sir Walter Scott,* and many another 'royal, noble, or famous personage' visited Haydon here.

> LEIGH HUNT influenced Keats's early poems, to their detriment; and association with the liberal Hunt called down on Keats's head the scornful criticism of conservative reviewers. Hunt's poetry was sentimental, sometimes silly (e.g., 'Jenny Kissed Me'); but Hunt

was not a fool; a little of his poetry has endured, and his critical essays, political articles, and autobiography are still worth reading.

5. Lisson Grove becomes *Grove End Road* a few blocks farther on. Just beyond the junction, at *No. 5 Grove End Road*, lived BARRY CORNWALL (real name BRYAN WALLER PROCTER) (1787-1874), poet, friend of Lamb, Hazlitt, and Byron—and also the father of ADELAIDE PROCTER (1825-64), the sentimental and highly moral poet (author of 'The Lost Chord') who was idolized by the Victorians.

6. Just across the street from Barry Cornwall's place, but facing *St John's Wood Road*, was the house of *Sir Edwin Landseer* (1802-73), the celebrated painter and sculptor of animals, who, though not a writer, executed pictures that told stories. One work of his is known to most people in Britain: the lions at the base of the Nelson Monument in Trafalgar Square.

7. Retrace your route along Lisson Grove for one block, and find Lodge Road entering from your left. Turn into this road, and walk on past the huge and impressive Lodge Road Power Station. Just beyond this you will find *North Bank* curving off to your right. Enter it. MARY SHELLEY (1797-1851), wife of the poet Percy Shelley, and author of *Frankenstein*, lived at *No. 36* in 1836. From 1860 the critic and editor GEORGE HENRY LEWES (1817-78) and the novelist GEORGE ELIOT (1819-80) lived at *No. 21*—he till his death here, and she two years longer. Here she wrote her greatest novel, *Middlemarch*, and here the two were hosts at gatherings of the most famous literary people of England at that time. THOMAS HENRY HUXLEY (1825-95) lived briefly (1851) at *No. 41*.

8. Return to Lodge Road, and continue along it to the next street, Park Road. Turn right, and then take the first street to your left— which is Hanover Gate. At the far end of this short street, turn right, and then sharp right again, into *Hanover Terrace*. At *No. 17* the novelist WILKIE COLLINS (1824-89) was living with his widowed mother around 1850. EDMUND GOSSE (1849-1928), poet and famous literary historian and critic, lived at the same *No. 17* after 1901. At *No. 13*, ALFRED NOYES (1880-1958), the romantic poet, lived with his new wife in the late 1920's and early 1930's. G. LOWES DICKINSON (1852-1932), historian, critic, philosopher, was living at *No. 13A* at about the same time. H. G. WELLS (1866-1946) moved into *No. 13* in 1940, and died there. The dramatist HAROLD PINTER (b. 1930) was living in *No. 7* in the 1960's. And at *No. 3* CHARLES DICKENS (1812-70),

rented a furnished house, and wrote his novel *Great Expectations*.

9. Walk on to the end of Hanover Terrace, turn left, into the Outer Circle Road skirting Regent's Park—and then sharp right again, into *Sussex Place*. HARRISON AINSWORTH (1805-82), editor, and author of innumerable historical novels, lived at *No. 4* just after his marriage, in 1826. One WALTER LEAF (1852-1927), who managed to be a bank president, classical scholar, historian, and translator of Greek, Persian, and Russian masterpieces, lived at *No. 6* from 1911 till his death. HERBERT ASQUITH (1881-1947), son of the Prime Minister, and a novelist and poet, lived at *No. 8*. JOHN LOCKHART (1793-1854), son-in-law and biographer of Sir Walter Scott, editor of the *Quarterly Review*, and literary critic, lived for many years (after 1826) at *No. 24*. And CYRIL CONNOLLY (b. 1903), editor, critic, and novelist, was living at *No. 25* in the 1950's.

10. Walk to the end of Sussex Place, and into the Outer Circle once more. Turn sharp right, into *Clarence Terrace*. ELIZABETH BOWEN (b. 1899), the novelist and short-story writer, lived at *No. 2* from 1935 till her husband died in 1952. The poet LOUIS MACNEICE (1907-63) lived at the same address from 1955 to 1960. GEORGE ROBERT SIMS (1847-1922), a minor but once very popular dramatist and journalist, as well as novelist and poet, lived at *No. 12* from 1911 till his death.

11. Again walk on to the Outer Circle Road, and again turn sharply back to your right, through Clarence Gate, to Park Road. Walk back up the latter (to your right) for a block, cross over, and enter *Taunton Place*. At *No. 10* an illegitimate son was born to WILKIE COLLINS (see above) and one of his permanent mistresses, Martha Rudd.

12. Near the far end of Taunton Place, turn left (just before reaching the church) into Balcombe Street. (The musician *Richard Wagner*'s first London home, in 1855, was at *No. 65* on this street.) Continue down Balcombe Street till you reach *Dorset Square*. Here, at *No. 13*, lived, in 1905, a young lady with the impressive name Dorothea Frances Markham Drummond-Black, to whom, at this house, the incredible soldier-poet-novelist-traveller-film writer, GILBERT FRANKAU (1884-1952) proposed. He was accepted; the two were married a short time later in a fashionable wedding at St Margaret's Westminster; and they were divorced a few years later—after the wife had borne Pamela Frankau (b. 1908), who became a novelist of some reputation. At *No. 22* lived (around 1900) GEORGE GROSSMITH, JR (1847-1912),

actor, composer of many songs, creator of the chief roles in many Gilbert and Sullivan operas.

13. At the far side of Dorset Square, *Melcombe Place* leads in from your right. *No. 9* here was the home (1864-6) of WILKIE COLLINS (see above) and one of his string of mistresses.

14. Keep to the bottom of Dorset Square, and move away from Melcombe Place, along Melcombe Street, towards Regent's Park. The third cross-street you reach is now known as *Glentworth Street*—but was called Clarence Gate Gardens in the 1920's and 1930's. The poet T. S. ELIOT (1888-1965) lived here, at *No. 68* in the 1920's, and then at *No. 98* just before and just after 1930. Though American-born, Eliot became a British subject, won the Nobel Prize, and is buried in Westminster Abbey.... Return to Melcombe Street.

15. Continue on to *Baker Street*, and turn right. MRS SARAH SIDDONS (1755-1831), the actress (member of the celebrated Kemble family of actors), lived at *No. 226* for many years, though her cottage has, of course, long since disappeared. She acted for Garrick, had her portrait painted by *Reynolds*, was praised by Hazlitt and Byron, gained fame as a portrayer of Shakespeare's heroines, and is still the most famous actress England ever produced. *No. 221B* was, officially, the residence of *Sherlock Holmes*, Conan Doyle's immortal detective—but the actual site has been identified as a location farther down the street. OLIVE SCHREINER (see above) also lived on this street in 1885, at a house on your left, not far from where you entered Baker Street. Also on your left, four or five doors up from Marylebone Road (which you are approaching), was the home, late in life, of CHARLOTTE SMITH (1749-1806), 'probably the most popular novelist in the English-speaking world in the 1790's'.

Continue down Baker Street to the *Baker Street Underground Station.* Here you end this tour. Or here you may continue your walk with *Tour No. 23* or *No. 34.*

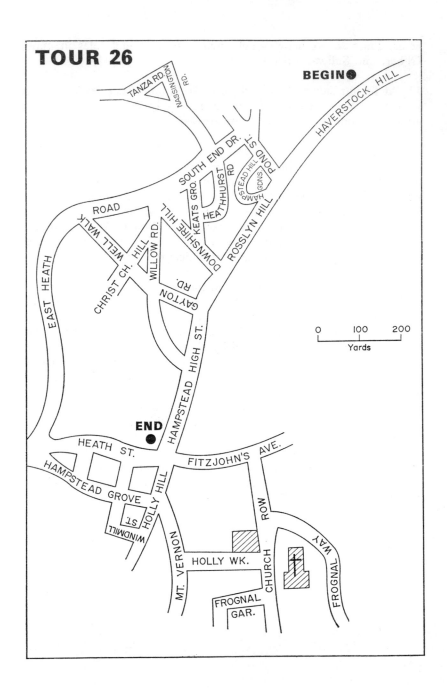

TOUR 26

BEGIN●

HAVERSTOCK HILL

TANZA RD.

NASSINGTON RD.

SOUTH END DR.

KEATS GRO.

HEATHHURST RD

HAMPSTEAD HILL GDNS

POND ST.

ROSSLYN HILL

ROAD

WELL WALK

EAST HEATH

CHRIST CH. HILL

WILLOW RD.

GAYTON RD.

DOWNSHIRE HILL

HAMPSTEAD HIGH ST.

0 100 200
Yards

END●

HEATH ST.

FITZJOHN'S AVE.

HAMPSTEAD GROVE

HOLLY HILL

WINDMILL ST.

MT. VERNON

HOLLY WK.

ROW

CHURCH

FROGNAL GAR.

FROGNAL WAY

300

Tour 26
Hampstead

Joanna Baillie	D. H. Lawrence
Mrs Laetitia Barbauld	Katherine Mansfield
Sir Walter Besant	John Masefield
Ivor Brown	T. Sturge Moore
George Calderón	Edwin Muir
Lord Alfred Douglas	Coventry Patmore
George du Maurier	J. B. Priestley
William Empson	Dollie Radford
Pamela Frankau	Sir William Rothenstein
John Galsworthy	Olive Schreiner
Richard Garnett	Percy Bysshe Shelley
W. W. Gibson	Sir Herbert Beerbohm Tree
Sir Julian Huxley	Arthur Waley
Henry Hyndman	H. G. Wells
John Keats	Anna Wickham

Leave the underground at the *Belsize Park Station.*

1. Turn right, on Haverstock Hill, and walk two or three blocks (first traffic light) to *Pond Street*, entering from your right. Turn into it. *No. 6* (now gone) was the home of *Dorothy Brett*, artist and friend of D. H. Lawrence, and many other literary people of importance during the 1910-30 period. KATHERINE MANSFIELD (1888-1923) stayed with Dorothy in 1922. *No. 31* was the home of SIR JULIAN HUXLEY (b. 1887), the biologist-philosopher.

2. You may wish to turn off to your left into *Hampstead Hill Gardens*, to *No. 1* the *Studio House*, where the critic WILLIAM EMPSON (b. 1906) was living in the 1960's. His most famous critical work is *Seven Types of Ambiguity*.... Return to Pond Street.

3. At the next crossing, where you will find a confusion of branching streets and traffic triangles, turn left, along South End Road. Walk a block—to the street-crossing with Heath Hurst Row on the left side, and South Hill Park on the right. Here you should glance over the rest of this Section 3, and decide whether you wish to turn to the right or to the left. If you turn to the right—

A. Keep to the right when the street forks, and then to the right again when it forks again. This will bring you to *Nassington Road*, where, at *No. 20*, lived W. W. GIBSON (1878-1962) in the 1930's. He was once famous as a poet of the labouring classes in England.

B. Continue along Nassington Road till you reach *Tanza Road*, intersecting from the left. Enter it. At *No. 27* lived, from 1900 to his death, RICHARD GARNETT (1835-1906), scholar, novelist, poet, biographer, essayist, father of Edward Garnett.

C. At the end of Tanza Road, turn back sharply to your left on *Parliament Hill*. *No. 68* was the home, in the 1920's of ANNA WICKHAM (b. 1883), who was a celebrated poet in the second and third decades of the twentieth century.... You will soon regain the corner where you began this side excursion.

4. When you have regained the corner just mentioned—or if you have decided at the beginning to turn left—continue on into Heath Hurst Road. It swings around and intersects *Keats Grove*. Three houses to the right of this intersection, and on your right, stands *Keats House*, where the poet JOHN KEATS (1795-1821) lived from December, 1818, to September, 1820. His *annus mirabilis* (1819), during which most of his supremely great poetry was produced, was passed here. He wrote the 'Ode to a Nightingale' in the garden. The house is a kind of Keats museum, and should be visited.

5. On leaving Keats House, turn left, along Keats Grove, and reach *Downshire Hill*. EDWIN MUIR (1889-1959), poet, novelist, critic lived at *No. 7*—a little to the left of the place where you entered the street. The novelist OLIVE SCHREINER (1863-1920) stayed at *No. 30* in 1885.

6. Turn right, on Devonshire Hill, and reach Willow Road, intersecting from the left. Turn into the latter, and walk straight up the hill to *Well Walk*.

[6A. As you climb Willow Road, you will see *Christchurch Hill* slanting off to your right. During the 1940's and 1950's the critic, novelist, and essayist IVOR BROWN (b. 1891) lived at *No. 20*. And at *No. 55* the novelist PAMELA FRANKAU (b. 1908) was living in the 1960's.]

When you reach *Well Walk*, turn right. At *No. 14* lived and died HENRY HYNDMAN (1842-1921), founder of British socialism, and author of many books on that topic. The poet JOHN MASEFIELD (1878-1967) had lived in the same house in 1912-14, when he was writing *The Widow in the Bye Street* and *Dauber*. The novelist, dramatist, and essayist J. B. PRIESTLEY (b. 1894) was living at *No. 27-8* in the 1940's; the poet JOHN KEATS lived (1816-17) in a house standing about where *No. 19* (a pub, at last inspection) now stands; DOLLIE RADFORD, poet and author of children's books, well known around 1895-1905, lived at *No. 32* in her later years; and the poet and artist T. STURGE MOORE (1870-1944) lived at *No. 40* during his last 20 years. The painter John Constable (1776-1837) had lived (1826-37) in the same house. GEORGE CALDERÓN (1868-1915), novelist and dramatist, lived and died at *No. 42*. MRS LAETITIA BARBAULD (1743-1825), poet and essayist, lived on this street in the 1780's.

7. At the end of Well Walk, turn left, on East Heath Road, and follow it (several blocks) till you reach a complex intersection of many streets. Off ahead of you, to the right, is *Whitestone Pond*, where the poet PERCY BYSSHE SHELLEY (1792-1822) (while visiting his friend Leigh Hunt, who lived in the Vale of Health, still farther to your right) sailed paper boats for children playing there. Turn left, into Heath Street. Just here, on your left (where a hospital stood in the 1960's), once stood the Upper Flask Inn—a regular meeting place of the famous Whig Kit-Kat Club, whose members included the poet and essayist *Joseph Addison*, dramatist and essayist *Sir Richard Steele*, poet and physician *Samuel Garth*, dramatist *William Congreve*, dramatist and architect *Sir John Vanbrugh*, and printer and publisher *Jacob Tonson*. Farther on, at *No. 110*, the poet and novelist D. H. LAWRENCE (1885-1930) lived, 1923-4. ARTHUR WALEY (1889-1966), translator of oriental poetry and fiction, lived in the same house a bit later.

8. When you have located the place just mentioned, cross over to the other (western) side of the street, and ascend a short flight of steps to The Mount. Turn right on this, and follow it around the corner to the street called *Hampstead Grove*. Emerging on the latter, you will see before you a small street called *Admiral's Walk*. At the far end of the latter is the house where JOHN GALSWORTHY (1867-1933), novelist and dramatist, lived the last 15 years of his life, and died. Just to your left, on *Hampstead Grove*, is *No. 28*, where GEORGE

DU MAURIER (1843-96), artist and novelist lived (1874-95). Continue down Hampstead Grove to its end, and there, to your right, around a corner, is the house (with plaque) where JOANNA BAILLIE (1762-1851), novelist, dramatist, poet, friend of the literary great, lived during her last fifty years. (Note also the house of the painter *George Romney*, to the left at the end of Hampstead Grove.)

9. Across the street from the Baillie House, you will see (on a wall behind an iron fence) a notice pointing 'To Mount Vernon'. Cross over, and follow the sign. At *No. 3 Mount Vernon* lived COVENTRY PATMORE (1823-96), Pre-Raphaelite and Roman Catholic poet.

10. A few houses beyond the Patmore house, turn left into a narrow street that leads straight ahead for some distance. (The street changes its name several times, but is unmistakable.) At the corner where you turn stood *Abernethy House*, where *Robert Louis Stevenson* and his friend *Sidney Colvin*, the critic, lodged briefly in 1874. The street leads on past a cemetery where are buried GEORGE DU MAURIER (see above); SIR HERBERT BEERBOHM TREE (1853-1917), famous theatre-manager; and SIR WALTER BESANT (1836-1901), novelist, antiquary, and author of a multi-volume history of London (frequently consulted by the author of the book you hold in your hand). The graves of du Maurier and Tree may be seen from the street (Church Row) at the lower side (south) of the cemetery.

11. Beyond the cemetery, you will see *St John's Church* just ahead of you, across Church Row. COVENTRY PATMORE (see above) was married here. JOANNA BAILLIE (see above) and the painter *John Constable* are buried here, in the south-east corner of the churchyard.

12. Turn right, along Church Row, walk a short block, and turn right again—into *Frognal Gardens*. Here, at *No. 18*, called 'Frognal End' (marked by a plaque), lived and died SIR WALTER BESANT (see above). The artist *Kate Greenaway* (1846-1901), popular illustrator of children's books, lived and died at *No. 39*.

13. Return to *Church Row*. Here *No. 26* was the home of SIR WILLIAM ROTHENSTEIN (1872-1945), artist and autobiographer, in 1903. In 1913-14 the same house was the home of LORD ALFRED DOUGLAS (1870-1945), the better-than-average poet who was Oscar Wilde's friend, and whose father, the Marquis of Queensberry, was instrumental in having Wilde imprisoned on a morals charge. H. G. WELLS lived at *No. 17* from 1909 to 1913. *No. 9* and *No. 2* were successively

the homes of MRS LAETITIA BARBAULD (see above), poet, editor, and literary biographer.

Follow Church Row on eastward (to your left, as you came down Holly Walk), and turn left at its end, on Fitzjohns Avenue. Follow about a block, and find the *Hampstead Underground Station*—where this tour ends.

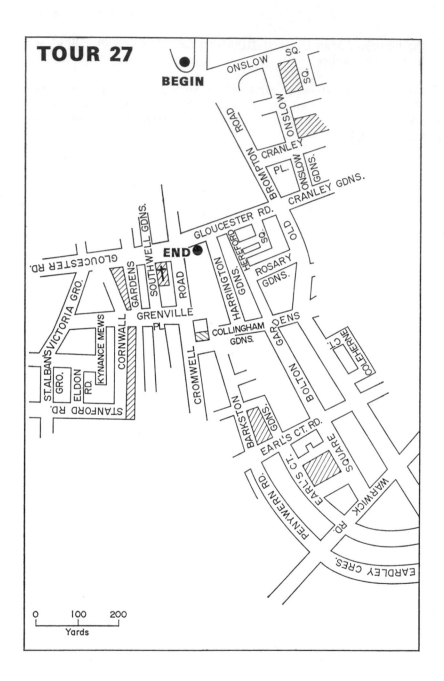

TOUR 27

BEGIN

ONSLOW SQ.
SQ.
ONSLOW
CRANLEY
ROAD
BROMPTON
PL.
ONSLOW GDNS.
CRANLEY GDNS.
GLOUCESTER RD.
OLD
CRANLEY GDNS.
GLOUCESTER RD.
SOUTHWELL GDNS.
END
HEREFORD SQ.
ROSARY GDNS.
GLOUCESTER RD.
VICTORIA GRO.
GARDENS
ST. ALBANS
GRO.
ELDON RD.
KYNANCE MEWS
CORNWALL GARDENS
GRENVILLE PL.
ROAD
HARRINGTON GDNS.
COLLINGHAM GDNS.
GARDENS
BOLTON
COLEHERNE CT.
STANFORD RD.
CROMWELL
BARKSTON GDNS.
EARL'S CT. RD.
SQUARE
WARWICK
EARL'S CT.
PENYWERN RD.
RD.
EARDLEY CRES.

0   100   200
Yards

306

Tour 27
South Kensington

Edwin Arnold	D. H. Lawrence
James Barrie	W. E. Lecky
Mackenzie Bell	John Lehmann
George Borrow	Doris Lessing
Brigid Brophy	H. B. Marriott-Watson
John Brophy	Rosamund Marriott-Watson
E. B. Chancellor	Harold Nicolson
Ivy Compton-Burnett	Francis Palgrave
A. J. Cronin	Sir Charles Petrie
Charles Dickens	Anne Thackeray Ritchie
John Drinkwater	Sir William Rothenstein
T. S. Eliot	Victoria Sackville-West
Gilbert Frankau	Sir Leslie Stephen
James Anthony Froude	Dame Ellen Terry
W. S. Gilbert	William Makepeace Thackeray
Thomas Anstey Guthrie	Sir Herbert Beerbohm Tree
Sir Rider Haggard	William Butler Yeats
James Laver	

Leave the underground at the *South Kensington Station*. Here you
will find yourself in a maze of underground corridors and above-
ground streets. But by reaching street-level, and keeping generally to
your left, you will eventually (after inquiries) find a street called
Onslow Square—though it is not a square here.

1. Descend this street (away from the underground station) till you reach *Onslow Square* itself—a distance of one block. Turn right, into the square, and walk along its nearer side till you find *No. 36* where the novelist WILLIAM MAKEPEACE THACKERAY (1811-63) lived from 1853 to 1861. Here he completed *The Newcomes,* wrote *The Virginians,* and worked on the *Roundabout Papers.*

2. The upper side of the square leads on (at the north-west corner) into a street still called Onslow Square. Enter this, and go one block to *Cranley Place,* opening on your right. At *No. 16* here lived FRANCIS PALGRAVE (1824-97), poet and anthologist. His *Golden Treasury (The Golden Treasury of the Best Songs and Lyrical Poems in the English Language,* 1861) was one of the most admirable and popular anthologies ever published.

3. Return to the street called Onslow Square, turn right, and continue along *Onslow Gardens.* This is an involved system of branching and circuitous streets lying ahead of you and on either side for some blocks. Doubtless it will be easier for you to find the following numbers on your own initiative than to try to read complex directions telling you where they are:
  No. 5 was the long-time home (1865-92) of the historian JAMES ANTHONY FROUDE (1818-94), who was also a biographer and novelist. ANNE (THACKERAY) RITCHIE (1837-1919), daughter of the novelist, and herself a novelist, lived at *No. 16* for nine years (1864-73); she also wrote literary reminiscences, literary criticism, and essays. SIR LESLIE STEPHEN (1832-1904) lived in this same house (1867-73). He had married another of Thackeray's daughters. At *No. 38* lived another celebrated historian, W. E. LECKY (1838-1903), whom many critics rank next to Gibbon as a historical writer in English. He also wrote poems, and histories of philosophy and morals. E. B. CHANCELLOR (1868-1937), historian of London, lived at *No. 65.*
  [3A. While exploring Onslow Gardens, you will see a street leading off from your left (towards the south) with the name *Neville Terrace* on the left, and *Selwood Terrace* opposite it. At *No. 10 Neville Terrace* lived (in the 1950's), SIR HAROLD NICOLSON (1886-1969) with his wife, the poet and novelist VICTORIA SACKVILLE-WEST (1892-1962). He was a historian, biographer, diarist, and diplomat; his works include the lives of Byron, Swinburne, Tennyson, Paul Verlaine, and George V. His extensive diaries, acutely self-critical, show how he happened to choose the wrong side politically on most occasions. His wife's best-known novels are *The Edwardians* (1930) and *All Passion Spent* (1931).... Across the street, at *No. 9 Selwood*

Terrace, D. H. LAWRENCE (1885-1930), the novelist and poet, stayed with his wife Frieda in the summer of 1914.

[3B. Leading off to the right (west) of Selwood Terrace, you may have noted *Selwood Place*. The novelist CHARLES DICKENS (1812-70) lived at *No. 18* in 1835-6, to be near his future wife, Catherine Hogarth, whose family lived just around the corner on what is now Fulham Road.... Return to Onslow Gardens.]

4. Continuing to the end of Onslow Gardens, you will reach the intersection with Cranley Gardens. Here turn right; go one block to Old Brompton Road; turn left on the latter. After one block along this street, turn right, into *Rosary Gardens. No. 31* was the home of SIR BEERBOHM TREE (1853-1917), born BEERBOHM, and half-brother of the essayist Max Beerbohm. He managed the Haymarket Theatre for ten years (1887-97), and Her Majesty's Theatre for 20 years (1897-1917).

5. Continue to the end of Rosary Gardens; then turn right, and right again, into *Hereford Square. No. 22* was the home of the traveller, novelist, Bible salesman, and companion of gypsy tribes, GEORGE BORROW (1803-81), for 14 years (1860-74). GILBERT FRANKAU (1884-1952) lived with his first wife on this square in 1915.

6. Make the circuit of Hereford Square back to *Gloucester Road*, and turn left on the latter. About here you will find *No. 133*, where JAMES BARRIE (1860-1937), novelist and dramatist, lived (1896-8), and wrote his last fictional works before turning altogether to drama.

7. Continue up Gloucester Road till you reach *Harrington Gardens*, entering from your left. Turn into this street. At *No. 39* is the fabulous house (an incredible combination of medieval Dutch and Victorian English styles) designed by and built for W. S. GILBERT (1836-1911), of light-opera fame. He lived here from 1883 to 1890.

8. Continue along Harrington Gardens till it intersects Collingham Gardens. Turn left on the latter, and walk one block to *Bolton Gardens*. Turn right, and find the home, at *No. 31*, of SIR EDWIN ARNOLD (1832-1904), poet, translator, and writer of travel books. Having spent some years in India, he wrote a long epic poem, *The Light of Asia* (1879), on the life of the Buddha. Buddhists attacked it for its alleged misconceptions about Buddhism, and Christians attacked it for its sympathetic portrayal of a 'heathen god'. To make amends, Arnold wrote an epic on the life of Christ, *The Light of the World*

(1891). The early book was extraordinarily successful, and went through many editions; the later one was a failure.

9. Continue along Bolton Gardens till you reach Earl's Court Road. [9A. You may wish to turn left on Earl's Court Road, go one block to Old Brompton Road, cross over the latter, turn left, and find *Colherne Court*, on your right. Here, in the 1960's, the novelist JOHN BROPHY (1899-1965) lived at *No. 59*; he was the father of the novelist BRIGID BROPHY (b. 1929)—whose home, in the 1960's and 1970's was farther east on *Old Brompton Road*, at *No. 185*. SIR CHARLES PETRIE (b. 1894), editor and voluminous historian, lived, in the 1960's and 1970's, at *No. 190 Colherne Court*. The novelist and playwright H. B. MARRIOTT-WATSON (1863-1921) and his wife, the poet ROSAMUND MARRIOTT-WATSON (d. 1911), lived for many years at *No. 201*.
[9B. If, on emerging from Colherne Court, you wish to expend a bit more energy, you may descend Redcliffe Road one block to *Redcliffe Square*. Here, at *No. 24*, lived SIR RIDER HAGGARD (1856-1925), highly romantic novelist, whose best-known works are the novels, *She, King Solomon's Mines*, and *Allan Quartermain.* . . . Now return to the juncture of Bolton Gardens and Earl's Court Road.]
   Follow the line of Bolton Gardens across Earl's Court Road into *Earl's Court Square*. At *No. 138* D. H. LAWRENCE (see above), novelist and poet, who first brought Freudian psychological truths openly into English fiction, lodged briefly (he seldom stayed long anywhere) with his wife Frieda in 1917.

10. Walk to the end of Earl's Court Square, reach Warwick Road, and turn right on it. Within a block or two you will reach *Eardley Crescent*, intersecting from your left. Enter it, and find *No. 58*, where WILLIAM BUTLER YEATS (1865-1939), the Irish poet, dramatist, and mystic (whom many critics regard as the greatest poet writing in English in the twentieth century) was living with his parents in the late 1880's. Here his mother had the stroke that left her mind impaired thereafter.

11. Return to Warwick Road.
[11A. A short distance up this road, to your left, was the home, in the 1960's and 1970's, of the novelist DORIS LESSING (b. 1919), at *No. 58*.]
   Cross over Warwick Road, and walk straight ahead into Penywern Road—and on till it becomes *Barkston Gardens*. DAME ELLEN TERRY (1847-1928), the great actress, and friend and correspondent of George Bernard Shaw, lived here, at *No. 22*. She was the first wife of the painter G. F. Watts, and the mother of Edith Craig (actress and producer) and of Gordon Craig (revolutionary theorist and writer about

the theatre). Ellen Terry (with her children) lived here during her long association with Sir Henry Irving at the Lyceum Theatre.

12. Continue straight along Barkston Gardens into Courtfield Gardens. But after two blocks on the latter, turn left, and reach Cromwell Road. There turn right, and then right again at the next street, into *Ashburn Gardens*. Here, at *No. 4*, lived JOHN DRINKWATER (1882-1937), author of many plays, some better-than-average poetry, several literary studies, and some fiction.

Return to Cromwell Road. One block to your right is the *Gloucester Road Underground Station*. Here you may end this tour. Or if you are not too tired after this unusually long walk, you may adventure a bit farther, as follows:

Addendum to Tour No. 27

13. Cross Cromwell Road opposite Ashburn Gardens, and ascend Grenville Place. (Charles Booth, 1840-1916, one of the first scientific sociologists, lived at *No. 6*.) You will soon reach *Cornwall Gardens*, where you will note a large apartment development called 'Braemar Mansions', where IVY COMPTON-BURNETT, the novelist, was living in *No. 5* in the 1960's and 1970's. The poet, critic, literary historian, and biographer JOHN LEHMANN (b. 1907) was living at *No. 85 Cornwall Gardens* in the same period.

14. Continue up Grenville Place to Kynance Mews, on your left. Turn here; go a block; turn right and then left, into *Eldon Road*. *No. 21* was the first home of W. S. GILBERT (see above) and his wife. *No. 3* was the home of the novelist A. J. CRONIN (b. 1896) (he wrote *The Citadel* and *The Keys of the Kingdom*) in the 1930's before he went to live in America.

15. At the far end of Eldon Road, turn right, on *Stanford Road*. SIR WILLIAM ROTHENSTEIN (1872-1945), the artist, lived for a time at *No. 24*. He is important as a voluminous biographer and autobiographer who knew most of the significant literary and artistic people of his day, wrote about them, and made portraits of them.

16. Keep ascending Stanford Road until you reach St Alban's Grove (which is a street, not a grove); turn right, and follow this street till you have passed through Victoria Grove, and have reached Gloucester Road. Turn right, and find on this street, just to your right, *St George's*

Court, where, at *No. 7*, was born THOMAS ANSTEY GUTHRIE ('F. ANSTEY') (1856-1934)—dramatist, humorous and satirical novelist, contributor to *Punch*.

17. Keep descending Gloucester Road (back towards Cromwell Road) till you reach *Southwell Gardens*. Turn aside here to *No. 8*, the home (1873-7) of LADY ANNE RITCHIE (1837-1919), daughter of the novelist Thackeray, and herself a novelist of some distinction. In the same house lived LESLIE STEPHEN (1832-1904), editor of the *Dictionary of National Biography*, father of the novelist Virginia Woolf, and husband of another of the Thackeray daughters. At the corner of Southwell Gardens and Gloucester Road stands *St Stephen's Church*, where the poet. T. S. ELIOT (1888-1965) was churchwarden for 25 years, and was on the Church Council till he died.

Now follow Gloucester Road on down a short distance to the *Gloucester Road Underground Station*—and end this tour.

Tour 28
Fitzroy Square

William Archer

James Beattie

Clive Bell

'Bloomsbury Group'

Thomas Campbell

Samuel Taylor Coleridge

Wilkie Collins

William Cowper

William de Morgan

Thomas de Quincey

Charles Dibdin

Charles Dickens

George du Maurier

Edward FitzGerald

Roger Fry

David Garnett

William Godwin

William Hazlitt

Thomas Holcroft

Theodore Hook

Selwyn Image

Anna Jameson

Lionel Johnson

Dr Samuel Johnson

Frances ('Fanny') Kemble

John Maynard Keynes

Rudyard Kipling

Wyndham Lewis

Charlotte Mew

Coventry Patmore

Victor Plarr

Arthur Rimbaud

Dante Gabriel Rossetti

Olive Schreiner

George Bernard Shaw

Percy Bysshe Shelley

Algernon C. Swinburne

Paul Verlaine

James McNeill Whistler

John Wolcot ('Peter Pindar')

Virginia Woolf

Leave the underground at the *Tottenham Court Road Station.*

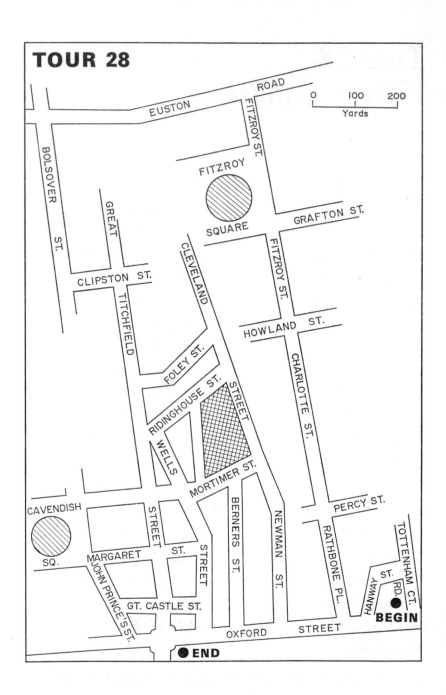

TOUR 28

EUSTON ROAD

FITZROY ST.

BOLSOVER ST.

GREAT

TITCHFIELD

CLIPSTON ST.

FITZROY SQUARE

GRAFTON ST.

CLEVELAND

FITZROY ST.

HOWLAND ST.

CHARLOTTE ST.

FOLEY ST.

RIDINGHOUSE ST.

STREET

WELLS

MORTIMER ST.

PERCY ST.

CAVENDISH

STREET

BERNERS ST.

NEWMAN ST.

RATHBONE PL.

TOTTENHAM CT.

SQ.

MARGARET

ST.

STREET

JOHN PRINCE'S ST.

GT. CASTLE ST.

HANWAY ST.

RD.

BEGIN

OXFORD STREET

END

0   100   200
Yards

1. Turn left, along Tottenham Court Road, and then, after one block, left again into *Hanway Street*. On this short street WILLIAM GODWIN (1756-1836), novelist, social philosopher, and father-in-law of Shelley, was in business as a bookseller. He opened his bookshop as an outlet for juvenile books that he himself wrote; but his reputation as a radical was such that he had to keep his ownership secret. (Children must never be corrupted by ideas.)

2. Follow Hanway on into Oxford Street, turn right, and then right again, into *Rathbone Place*. WILLIAM HAZLITT (1778-1830), essayist and literary critic, lived at *No. 12* from 1799 to 1803.

3. One very long block up Rathbone, turn right, into *Percy Street*. Accompanied by his good friend Mrs Unwin, the poet WILLIAM COWPER (1731-1800), author of many moving personal lyrics and long poems about English rural life, last visited London, at the house of a friend in *No. 23*, on September 19 1792. COVENTRY PATMORE (1823-96), Pre-Raphaelite and Catholic poet, lived at *No. 14*. And WYNDHAM LEWIS (1886-1957), painter, art critic, novelist, lived at *No. 4* in 1914, and at *No. 31* in the 1930's.

4. Return to Rathbone Place, and continue along it—but note that it has now become *Charlotte Street*. THEODORE HOOK (1788-1841), actor, singer, wit, editor, and novelist (he wrote 40 books), whose racy and scandalous realistic work, as well as racy and scandalous life, seems to have baffled modern criticism, was born at *No. 3*—the third house on your right. DAVID GARNETT (b. 1892), novelist, autobiographer, and general man of letters, lodged (1939-40) at *No. 15*. The poet CHARLOTTE MEW (1869-1928) spent part of her tragic life in lodgings next door to the Scala Theatre, about halfway up Charlotte Street. The eccentric Victorian poet EDWARD FITZGERALD (1809-83), apparently liked this street: he lived at *No. 18* in 1843; at *No. 19* in 1840, 1844-5, and 1848; and at *No. 60* in 1846-7. CHARLES DIBDIN (1745-1814), actor, singer, composer, novelist, poet, autobiographer, author of over 70 operas and musicals, lived for a while at *No. 30*.

5. Keep walking doggedly up Charlotte Street till you reach *Howland Street*, entering from the right. Turn into it. At *No. 35* lived the French poets PAUL VERLAINE (1844-96) and ARTHUR RIMBAUD (1854-91) when they were in London together in 1872-3. JOHN WOLCOT ('PETER PINDAR') (1738-1819), the satirist, lived on this street, near Tottenham Court Road, in 1810, when his house caught fire, and he

nearly lost his life trying (unsuccessfully) to save the life of a servant girl trapped in the house.

6. Return to Charlotte Street, and keep walking up it—except that now it has become *Fitzroy Street*. *Vanessa Bell* (daughter of Sir Leslie Stephen, and sister of Virginia Woolf), wife of CLIVE BELL (1881-1964), the art and literary critic, had a studio at *No. 8*; and *Duncan Grant* (b. 1885), the painter, occupied a studio behind that of Mrs Bell at the time of her occupancy. All three of these people were members of the 'Bloomsbury Group' (see Tour No. 8); and at this address the group often held parties between the two World Wars. The artist JAMES MCNEILL WHISTLER (1834-1903), who helped break up Victorianism in literature as well as in art, had a studio at the same place; and before him, the artist *Walter Sickert*. *Paul Nash* (1889-1946), another artist, stayed here in 1919. The artist *Simeon Solomon* (1840-1905), who was a significant and influential figure in the Aesthetic movement (which involved both literature and art), lived at *No. 12* in 1869. He was a weak and maladjusted character who later went to prison. The family of CHARLES DICKENS (1812-70) lived at *No. 25* when Charles was 20 years old; WYNDHAM LEWIS (see above), a peripheral member of the Bloomsbury Group, lived at *No. 18* in 1915-16; and LIONEL JOHNSON (1867-1902), whose poetry is so perfectly chiselled, and whose life was so tragic, lived at *No. 20*, about the year 1890, along with some bohemian friends who included VICTOR PLARR (1862-1929), poet, and friend and biographer of Ernest Dowson, and SELWYN IMAGE (1849-1930), poet. The novelist and feminist OLIVE SCHREINER (1855-1920), author of *The Story of an African Farm*, lived at *No. 32* in 1884.

7. When you reach *Grafton Way*, turn right, and find *No. 12*, where the poet ALGERNON C. SWINBURNE (1837-1909) lived in 1861-2.

8. Return to Fitzroy Street, which has now opened into *Fitzroy Square*. Here, at *No. 29*, GEORGE BERNARD SHAW (1856-1950), the dramatist, wit, and socialist, lived for 11 years (1887-98). Virginia Stephen (who became the novelist VIRGINIA WOOLF) (1882-1941) lived at the same *No. 29*, with her brother Adrian, from 1907 to 1911. Their house was a frequent meeting place of the Bloomsbury Group. At *No. 21* the painter *Duncan Grant* (see above) and the economist JOHN MAYNARD KEYNES (1883-1946), another member of the Bloomsbury Group, lived together. At *No. 33* ROGER FRY (1866-1934), painter, art critic, and member of the Group, opened the Omega Workshops (along with *Vanessa Bell* and *Duncan Grant*), in 1913. This venture

316

was intended to be something like the decorator shops that William Morris had established in the previous century; it produced pottery, textile designs, dress fashions, furniture, stained glass, carpets. WYNDHAM LEWIS (see above) and the sculptor *Henri Gaudier-Brzeska*, among others, were employed by the shop. The Pre-Raphaelite artist *Ford Madox Brown* (1821-93), grandfather of the novelist Ford Madox Ford, lived at *No. 37* in the 1870's—in a house that Thackeray had used for the home of Colonel Newcome, in *The Newcomes*. The famous ceramist WILLIAM DE MORGAN (1839-1917), who, in his old age, became even more famous as a novelist, lived at *No. 40*. The dramatist and dramatic critic WILLIAM ARCHER (1856-1924) lived at *No. 27* for many years; he wrote books on dramatic technique, and was the chief force introducing Ibsen to England.

9. Leave Fitzroy Square by Fitzroy Street at its upper corner (opposite the place where you entered the square); reach Euston Road; turn left; go two blocks; and turn left again, into *Bolsover Street*. Martha Rudd, mistress of the novelist WILKIE COLLINS (1824-89) lived at *No. 33*; and two of the three children she had by Collins were born here. The poet EDWARD FITZGERALD (see above) lived (1848-50) at *No. 39*.

10. Turn left, off Bolsover, on *Clipstone Street*. THOMAS HOLCROFT (1745-1809) dramatist, and friend of Coleridge, Lamb, and Godwin, died on this street.

11. Turn right, off Clipstone Street, on *Great Tichfield Street*. The critic and essayist THOMAS DE QUINCEY (1785-1859), whose best-known work is his autobiographical *Confessions of an English Opium Eater* (1821), lived at *No. 82* in 1809.

12. Turn left, off Great Tichfield Street, into *Riding House Street*. After a block or so, you will see the great *Middlesex Hospital* on your right. Here died RUDYARD KIPLING (1865-1936), poet and fiction writer.

13. Turn right, at the corner of the hospital, into *Cleveland Street*. The family of CHARLES DICKENS (1812-70) lived here, at *No. 22*, when the novelist was a child of two or three years; and he gave it as his address when he applied for book privileges at the British Museum in 1830. (The street was named Norfolk Street at that time.)

14. Continue along Cleveland Street till it leads into *Newman Street*.

GEORGE DU MAURIER (1834-96), artist and novelist (as well as grand-father of the novelist Daphne Du Maurier) lived at *No. 91* in 1861-2; at *No. 85* in 1860-1; and at *No. 70* in 1860. The last had been the studio of the painter JAMES MCNEILL WHISTLER (1834-1903), who had just moved out, leaving a good many household belongings to his friend and fellow artist. Whistler returned here periodically, and used the studio; and WILLIAM DE MORGAN (see above), designer of glass and tiles, and a highly successful novelist, had a studio in the same house while it was being used as a studio by Whistler and du Maurier. (By the way, the character of Little Billy, of du Maurier's *Trilby*, is based on Whistler.) ALGERNON CHARLES SWINBURNE (see above), who shocked the Victorian Age with his incredibly beautiful and passion-ately pagan poetry, lived at *No. 77* in 1860; and DANTE GABRIEL ROSSETTI (1828-82), Pre-Raphaelite painter and poet, lived at *No. 72* in 1850-1. *Benjamin West* (1738-1820), the American painter, lived at *No. 14* from 1777, and died here. FRANCES ('FANNY') KEMBLE (1809-93), the great Shakespearean actress, was born on this street. She was the author of some historically valuable memoirs. THOMAS HOLCRAFT (see above) lived, 1789-99, on this street.

15. Go to the end of Newman Street, turn right on Oxford Street, and then (after one block) right again, on *Berners Street*. GEORGE DU MAURIER (see above) lived for a while in 1860 at *No. 8*; and SAMUEL TAYLOR COLERIDGE (1772-1834) lived for 18 months (1812-13) at *No. 71*. At *No. 54* lived, in 1810, a Mrs. Tottenham, on whom the novelist THEODORE HOOK (see above) perpetrated the 'Berners Street Hoax'. In Mrs Tottenham's name Hook ordered hundreds of com-modities, all to be delivered to No. 54 at the same hour, and had requested, also for the same hour and place, the services of scores of ministers, lawyers, doctors, barbers, and other professionals. The confusion in the street, and the consternation of Mrs Tottenham, may be imagined.

16. At the upper end of Berners Street, turn left, into *Mortimer Street. Joseph Nollekens* (1737-1823), the most famous portrait sculp-tor of his day, lived for many years, and died, at *No. 44. Dr Johnson* sat here for a marble bust by Nollekens—a work that has been much admired. The Irish literary critic and lady-of-letters ANNA JAMESON (1794-1860) lived for many years at *No. 7*.

17. At *Wells Street*, turn left. JAMES BEATTIE (1735-1803), the Scottish poet and philosopher, lodged at *No. 64* when he visited London, in 1771.

JAMES BEATTIE attacked the scepticism of Hume, but is best re-membered for his long poem *The Minstrel*—a landmark in the development of romanticism, not only in that it is written in Spenserian stanzas, but also that it depicts the growth of a poet's mind under the influence of nature, and is thus a prelude (written 30 years earlier) to Wordsworth's *Prelude*.

18. Turn right, off Wells Street, into *Margaret Street*. As a youth, the novelist CHARLES DICKENS (see above) lived with his parents at *No. 70*, when his father was hiding from creditors. THOMAS CAMPBELL (1777-1844), the poet and public man, lived at *No. 62* in the early 1820's. And the poet PERCY BYSSHE SHELLEY (1792-1822) lived at *No. 56* in 1814, while arranging the separation from his first wife, Harriet.

19. Continue along Margaret Street to the corner of Cavendish Square, and here turn left into John Prince's Street. Descend it one block, and then turn left again, into *Great Castle Street*. Soon after DR SAMUEL JOHNSON came to London, he took permanent lodgings (1738) at *No. 6*—where he wrote (or finished) his poem *London*.

After finding Dr Johnson's place, turn right at the next corner, and immediately reach Oxford Street. Here you will be only a step from the *Oxford Circus Underground Station*, where this tour ends. But this is a convenient place from which you may continue your explorations, with *Tour No. 10* or *Tour No. 17*.

Part Three

Good
Tours

Tour 29
Kensington West

Clifford Bax

Stella Benson

Phyllis Bottome

Lord Byron

Gilbert K. Chesterton

Joseph Conrad

'Baron Corvo'
   (Frederick William Rolfe)

G. Lowes Dickinson

George du Maurier

John Galsworthy

George Arthur Greene

Thomas Anstey Guthrie

Laurence Housman

Leigh Hunt

Mrs Elizabeth Inchbald

Jean Ingelow

Christopher Isherwood

Pamela Hansford Johnson

Rudyard Kipling

Andrew Lang

Sir Sidney Lee

Alice Meynell

Wilfred Meynell

Sir Henry Newbolt

Walter Pater

Arthur Ropes ('Adrian Ross')

William Rothenstein

C. P. Snow

Frederick Tennyson

Angela Thirkell

Arnold Toynbee

Arthur Waley

Edmund Watson

Alec Waugh

Leave the underground at the *Kensington High Street Station.*

1. After you have left the shopping arcade into which you emerged from the train, turn sharp left on Kensington High Street, then sharp left again—and descend Wright's Lane. After two blocks, turn right, into *Cheniston Gardens*—which itself immediately bends to the left.

323

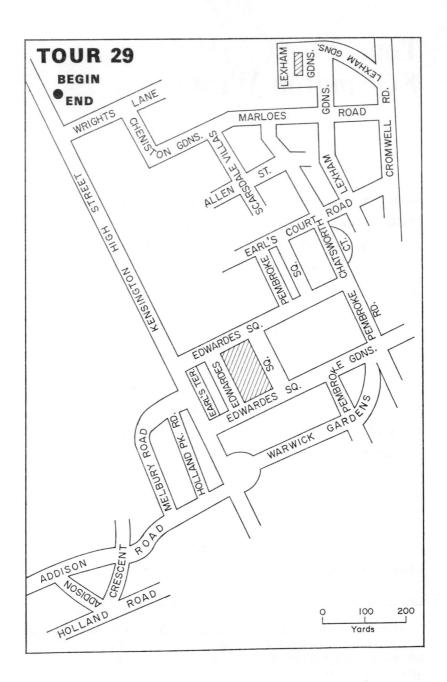

TOUR 29

BEGIN

● END

WRIGHTS LANE

CHENISTON GDNS.

MARLOES

LEXHAM GDNS.

GDNS.

LEXHAM GDNS.

GDNS. ROAD

CROMWELL RD.

ALLEN ST.

SCARSDALE VILLAS

LEXHAM ROAD

KENSINGTON HIGH STREET

EARL'S COURT

PEMBROKE

SQ.

CHATSWORTH ROAD

CHATSWORTH CT.

PEMBROKE RD.

EDWARDES SQ.

EARLS TER.

EDWARDES SQ.

EDWARDES SQ.

EDWARDES SQ.

PEMBROKE GDNS.

MELBURY ROAD

HOLLAND PK. RD.

WARWICK GARDENS

ADDISON ROAD

CRESCENT ROAD

ADDISON ROAD

HOLLAND ROAD

0   100   200
Yards

Here, at *No. 15*, lived the famous eccentric 'BARON CORVO' (FREDERICK WILLIAM ROLFE) (1860-1913), around 1904. He wrote 'decadent' stories and romances, and contributed to the *Yellow Book* (the organ of the Aesthetic movement in the 1890's).

[1A. At the end of Cheniston Gardens (where it becomes Marloes Road) *Scarsdale Villas* enters from the right. EDMUND WATSON (1865-1948), novelist, essayist, and literary critic, lived at *No. 19*.

[1B. One block along the street, you will find *Allen Street*, with a church at the intersection. Just opposite the church, on the Allen Street side, in a house no longer standing, the poet ALICE MEYNELL (1847-1922) and her husband, WILFRID MEYNELL (1852-1948) began their married life. He was the founder of the Catholic magazine *Merry England*, and 'discoverer' of the poet Francis Thompson, W. H. Hudson, and Hilaire Belloc.... Return to Cheniston Gardens.]

2. Cheniston Gardens leads into *Marloes Road*. LAURENCE HOUSMAN (1865-1959), poet, dramatist, artist, brother of the poet A. E. Housman, lived with his sister Clemence at *No. 43* for 14 years. At the far end of this street, at *No. 1*, ANDREW LANG (1844-1912) had his home (1876-1912). He was a scholar, historian, folklorist, poet—one of Scotland's most distinguished men of letters.

3. Marloes Road intersects *Lexham Gardens*. At the intersection you will find signs indicating which parts of this complex street contain the house numbers you may be seeking. PHYLLIS BOTTOME (1884-1963), autobiographer and writer of novels and stories having a psychological interest, lived at *No. 46*. And, in the early part of the twentieth century, SIR SIDNEY LEE (1859-1926) lived at *No. 108A*. He followed Leslie Stephen as editor of the *Dictionary of National Biography*, wrote many scholarly books on Shakespeare and the Elizabethan Age, and a biography of Queen Victoria.

4. At the end of Marloes Road you will reach *Cromwell Road*. Turn right, and find *No. 199*, where lived the novelist C. P. SNOW (b. 1905) and his wife, another novelist, PAMELA HANSFORD JOHNSON (b. 1912), during the 1950's and 1960's. Snow, a physicist by profession, became a best-selling novelist whose books dealt with the personal conflicts and jealousies among men of science.

5. Continue along Cromwell Road to the next street entering from the right—*Earl's Court Road*. Turn into it. At *No. 101* lived the parents of *Rudyard Kipling* after their retirement from their work in India. Their son often visited them here.

6. Continue on up Earl's Court Road.

[6A. At the second street-crossing, turn left, and find *Chatsworth Court* just around the corner, to your left. ARTHUR WALEY (born SCHLOSS) (1889-1966), the orientalist, whose many volumes of translations first acquainted many Western readers with Chinese and Japanese literature, lived at *No. 115*.]

Farther up Earl's Court Road you will find, on your left, *Pembroke Square*, where, at *No. 45*, the historian ARNOLD TOYNBEE (b. 1889) lived from the late 1940's to the late 1960's.

7. Walk on through Pembroke Square, and find *Pembroke Villas* beyond it. Turn left, down this street. At *No. 2* lived STELLA BENSON (1892-1933), poet, novelist, and short-story writer, who was much honoured and widely read in the post-World War I world.

8. When you reach Pembroke Road, turn right, walk a block, and then turn right again, into *Pembroke Gardens*. Ascend this street, being sure to follow its sharp turn to the left. GEORGE ARTHUR GREENE (1853-1921), poet, novelist, translator of Greek and Italian poetry, and editor of the two volumes of 'advanced' poetry issued by the Rhymers' Club in the 1890's, lived at *No. 23*. CHRISTOPHER ISHERWOOD (b. 1904), dramatist, novelist, and travel writer, lived at *No. 19*. ANGELA THIRKELL (1890-1961), popular author of light and urbane fiction portraying the English middle class, lived at *No. 6* during the 1930's and 1940's. She was the daughter of the Oxford poetry professor and literary critic J. W. Mackail, and cousin of the painter Sir Edward Burne-Jones.

9. At the end of Pembroke Gardens, turn right, into *Warwick Gardens*, and go on till you reach *No. 11* (on your right). Here GILBERT KEITH CHESTERTON (1874-1936), poet, critic, fiction writer, and essayist, spent the years of his youth (age five to 25). A Roman Catholic convert and apologist, he wrote almost every kind of literature, and wrote it well. He was popularly celebrated for his Father Brown detective stories, and for the paradoxes of his style.

10. Follow Warwick Gardens to Kensington High Street. Cross the latter, and find yourself at the foot of *Addison Road*. Several long blocks up this road is *No. 14*, which was the town house (1904-14) of JOHN GALSWORTHY (1867-1933), Nobel Prize-winning novelist and dramatist. JOSEPH CONRAD (1857-1924), the novelist, who was Galsworthy's friend and protégé, visited here often, and sometimes lived

in the house when the Galsworthys were away. *No. 31* was the home, around 1910, of ARTHUR ROPES ('ADRIAN ROSS') (1859-1933), who wrote the lyrics and librettos of numberless light operas and musicals. And *No. 72*, across the street from the Galsworthy house, was the home of CLIFFORD BAX (1886-1962) in the 1930's. He too wrote many musicals and dramas, fiction and poetry, and biographies of persons associated with the theatre—a highly successful man in his day.

[10A. If you think it worth while, cross over (via Addison Crescent, which enters Addison Road from your left) to Holland Road, and ascend it to where *Holland Villas Road* branches from it to your right. At *No. 6* lived JEAN INGELOW (1820-97), poet, novelist, and author of children's books. FREDERICK TENNYSON (1807-98), brother of Alfred, and collaborator with him and their brother Charles in Alfred's first book, *Poems by Two Brothers* (1827) lived at *No. 14*.]

11. If you ascend Addison Road to Galsworthy's place, you will have to retrace your steps to the junction of Addison Road and *Melbury Road*, on your left (east). This was a street where many artists once lived. Among these was *Holman Hunt* (1827-1910), one of the original Pre-Raphaelite Brotherhood, who lived at *No. 18* (plaque). His best-known painting is, probably, *The Light of the World*, one version now at Keble College, Oxford, and another (minutely different) in St Paul's Cathedral. *Lord Frederick Leighton* (1830-96), one of the most famous and revered painters of his day, and President of the Royal Academy, lived at *No. 12* (the place is gone, or altered unrecognizably). His work now seems grandiose rather than great, and unoriginal rather than inspiring. *Sir Luke Fildes* (1844-1927), another once-famous painter, lived at *No. 31* from 1878 till his death here. He began his artistic career depicting the life of the poor, but ended it as a portraitist of royalty. His best-known painting is *The Doctor*, depicting a physician sitting at the bedside of a sick child—a vastly sentimental work once regarded as one of the greatest paintings of all time. It is now in the Wallace Collection (see Tour No. 22). *G. F. Watts* (1817-1904) lived and worked for many years at *No. 6*. He was married for one year (1864-5) to the great actress *Ellen Terry*, and lived with her here, but at a previous house occupying the same site. *Sir William Hamo Thornycroft* (1850-1925), the sculptor, lived at *No. 2A*. He is responsible for many heroic statues in London and elsewhere—including the statue of General Gordon in Trafalgar Square, and of Oliver Cromwell outside Westminster Hall.

[11A. Follow the curve of Melbury Road almost to its end, and (if you wish) turn right, into *Holland Park Road*. THOMAS ANSTEY GUTHRIE ('F. ANSTEY') (1856-1934), satirical and humorous playwright and novelist, lived at *No. 24* from 1921 till his death; and SIR SIDNEY LEE (see above) lived at *No. 26* for the last five years of his life.... Return to Melbury Road.]

12. Follow Melbury Road on to its ending in Kensington High Street. Cross over the latter, and find (immediately in front of Melbury Road) *Earl's Terrace*, facing the High Street, and parallel to it. In the house of a family friend here LORD BYRON (1788-1824), as a boy, spent his first night in London—and threatened his host with violence. The actress and dramatist MRS ELIZABETH INCHBALD (1753-1821) lived at *No. 4*; the artist and novelist (*Trilby* and *Peter Ibbetsen*) GEORGE DU MAURIER (1834-96) lived at *No. 12* as a newly-married man in 1866; and WALTER PATER (1839-94), essayist, critic, philosopher of Aestheticism, and author of the philosophical novel *Marius the Epicurean*, lived at the same *No. 12* later on (1885-93). SIR HENRY NEWBOLT (1862-1923), poet, historian, novelist, and spokesman of British imperialism, occupied *No. 23* during the first decade of the twentieth century. *No. 24* was occupied by the novelist ALEC WAUGH (b. 1898), novelist and travel writer, after separating from his wife (who was the daughter of the poet W. W. Gibson).

13. At either end of Earl's Terrace, turn into a street called *Edwardes Square*, walk away from Kensington High Street, and find the square itself. GILBERT K. CHESTERTON (see above) and his wife spent the first months of their married life here in a house on the upper (north) side of the square, *No. 1*. SIR WILLIAM ROTHENSTEIN (1872-1945), artist, biographer, and autobiographer, lived on this square for a while, in a house (not identified by the present writer) later occupied by LAURENCE HOUSMAN (see above). G. LOWES DICKINSON (1862-1932), political theorist and writer on pacificism and internationalism, lived at *No. 11*. And LEIGH HUNT (1784-1859), the poet who was a friend of Keats, Shelley, Byron, Wordsworth, Southey, and others, lived at *No. 32* from 1840 to 1851. A liberal, he spent two years in jail for his outspoken criticism of the Prince Regent.

You have now finished this tour, and should return to Kensington High Street. (On the far side of this street, and a block or two to your right, is the modern building of the *Commonwealth Institute*— one of the very few London buildings in the 'modern' style that possesses any originality, distinctiveness, or beauty. It is worth a visit —even though the authorities in charge of the Commonwealth exhibits inside have not seen fit to include anything of literary interest or significance from the Commonwealth among their displays.)

Walk on (or take a bus) back towards the *Kensington High Street Underground Station*—where this tour began, and where it ends. Once there, you may, if you are not too tired, start out on *Tour No. 24.*

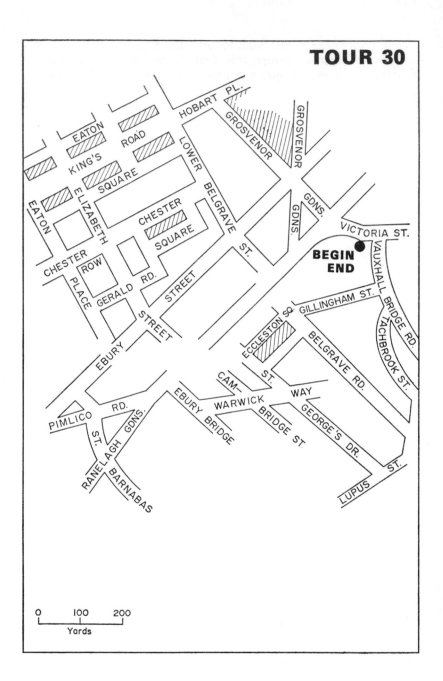

TOUR 30

EATON
KING'S
ROAD
SQUARE
LOWER
HOBART PL.
GROSVENOR
GROSVENOR
EATON
ELIZABETH
BELGRAVE
GDNS.
GDNS.
VICTORIA ST.
CHESTER
SQUARE
ST.
BEGIN
END
VAUXHALL BRIDGE RD.
CHESTER
ROW
PLACE
GERALD RD.
STREET
STREET
ECCLESTON SQ.
GILLINGHAM ST.
TACHBROOK ST.
EBURY
STREET
ST.
BELGRAVE RD.
CAM-
WAY
PIMLICO
RD.
GDNS.
EBURY
WARWICK
BRIDGE
BRIDGE ST.
GEORGE'S DR.
ST.
RANELAGH
BARNABAS
ST.
LUPUS

0   100   200
Yards

Tour 30
Belgravia-Pimlico

Arthur à Beckett

Matthew Arnold

Aubrey Beardsley

Laurence Binyon

Thomas Campbell

Winston Churchill

Joseph Conrad

Noel Coward

George Darley

Charles Dickens

George Eliot

T. S. Eliot

Martha Gellhorn

W. S. Gilbert

R. B. Cunninghame Graham

William Heinemann

Rosamund Lehmann

George Meredith

George Moore

Harold Nicolson

Mrs Margaret Oliphant

Charles Reade

Victoria Sackville-West

Mary Godwin Shelley

John Collings Squire

John St Loe Strachey

James Thomson ('B. V.')

Edward Trelawny

Mrs Lucy Walford

Thomas Wolfe

Leave the underground at the *Victoria Station.* Emerging on the street, you will find the directional situation bewildering. But eventually you will find your way across Buckingham Palace Road, and ascend Grosvenor Gardens.

1. *Grosvenor Gardens* is, in the quaint British fashion, an X-shaped street. You will be starting at the bottom of the X—and it makes no difference which of the lower legs you take. But at the crossing, take the left-hand leg (or arm) on upward. On this street, formerly called Upper Eaton Street, THOMAS CAMPBELL (1777-1844), poet, editor, and

public-spirited citizen, famous in his time, lived at *No. 25* (long since demolished) just after his marriage. GEORGE DARLEY (1795-1846), Irish poet, dramatist, critic, and writer of graceful songs, lived at *No. 5* (1827-30) and at *No. 27* (1839-42). Ironically, Campbell's most celebrated poem was *The Pleasures of Hope*, and Darley's *The Sorrows of Hope*. Darley 'anticipated the symbolist school of poetry'.

2. At the end of the arm that you have been following, turn left, into Hobart Place, and follow it straight on into *Eaton Square*. EDWARD J. TRELAWNY (1792-1881), soldier of fortune who was a friend of Byron and Shelley, and wrote his recollections of them, lived at *No. 17* in 1838. W. S. GILBERT (1836-1911), librettist of the immortal Gilbert and Sullivan light operas (and himself a kind of Colonel Blimp whom he should have satirized) had a town house at *No. 90* (1907-11). The novelist ROSAMUND LEHMANN (b. 1903) lived at *No. 70* during most of the 1950's and into the 1970's.

3. At the far end of Eaton Square, turn left, and walk straight ahead into South Eaton Place. Continue on till you find *Gerald Road* entering from the left. Turn into it. *No. 17* was the official residence of NOEL COWARD (b. 1899), actor and director, as well as author of sophisticated comedies and musicals, from about 1935 to 1955.
[3A. After one block, Gerald Road crosses *Elizabeth Street*. Down the latter, to your right, *No. 79A* was the home of R. B. CUNNINGHAME GRAHAM (1852-1936), traveller, adventurer, rebel, and author, in the 1920's and early 1930's.]

4. Turn left, on Elizabeth Street. The first street you will reach, on your left, is *Chester Row*. CHARLES DICKENS (1812-70), lived at *No. 1* in 1846; and at *No. 5* the American-born, Nobel Prize-winning poet T. S. ELIOT (1888-1965), who is buried in Westminster Abbey, lived in the 1920's with his first wife.

5. Turn back (to your right, off Elizabeth Street) into *Chester Square*. At *No. 76 Chester Square* lived JOHN ST LOE STRACHEY (1860-1927), editor of *Cornhill* and the *Spectator*, and writer on sociological and cultural topics. (He was father of John Strachey, prominent in the Labour Party, and author of several books on socialism. His cousin was the biographer Lytton Strachey.) In *No. 24* (another of the monotonously similar houses of this square) *Claire Clairmont* (sister-in-law of the poet Shelley, and mistress of Byron, to whom she bore the daughter Allegra) lived in 1846. She was succeeded here by her half-sister MARY GODWIN SHELLEY (1797-1851), second wife and

widow of Shelley, and author of the celebrated terror novel *Franken-stein*. Mary Shelley died in this house. MARTHA GELLHORN (b. 1908), journalist and novelist, and third wife of Ernest Hemingway, was living at *No. 20* in the 1960's. Farther along, at *No. 2*, MATTHEW ARNOLD (1822-88), poet, critic, and educator—one of the finest minds among the Victorians—lived for many years.

6. Chester Square ends in *Lower Belgrave Street*. Near the place where you enter the latter street, you will find *No. 32*, where lived in the 1920's, *William Heinemann* (1865-1929), a minor dramatist, but especially important as a publisher who first introduced the some-what provincial Victorian public to translations of foreign authors who were previously unknown in England: Ibsen, Tolstoi, Maeter-linck, Bjornson, and others. Farther down, at *No. 6*, GEORGE DARLEY (see above) lived, 1844-5.

7. Turn right, along Lower Belgrave Street, go one block, to *Ebury Street*, and turn right again—into this wide, uninteresting street of middle-class shops and flats without architectural distinction. The American novelist THOMAS WOLFE (1900-38) stayed at *No. 75* in 1930-1 while working on his novel *Of Time and the River*. NOEL COWARD (see above) lived at *No. 111* in the early 1930's. The novelist MARGARET OLIPHANT (1828-97) lived at *No. 112* in 1884. Farther on is *No. 121*, a small white house where lived GEORGE MOORE (1852-1933), poet, novelist, racy autobiographer, and prominent figure in the modern 'Literary Renaissance' of Ireland. He lived in this house for many years, and died here. Through his front door passed most of the notable literary men of his time: *Yeats, Wells, Bennett, Shaw*, and many others. GEORGE MEREDITH (1828-1909), poet and novelist, was living at what is now *No. 153* in 1849. At *No. 181 Wolfgang Mozart* (1756-91) was living when he composed his first symphony—he being a mere child at the time. HAROLD NICOLSON lived with his wife, VICTORIA SACKVILLE-WEST (1892-1962), at *No. 182* in the 1920's.

8. Walk on almost to the end of Ebury Street, turn left, and cross Pimlico Road into St Barnabas Street. At the next cross-street, *Rane-lagh Grove*, turn left, and find *No. 4*—the home, in the 1940's and 1950's, of SIR JOHN COLLINGS SQUIRE (1884-1958), poet, essayist, and editor.

9. Continue along Ranelagh Grove till you reach Pimlico Road again. Here things get a bit complicated. Turn right, across a busy inter-section of several streets, and then bear right again into Ebury Bridge

(*not* Ebury Bridge Road), and follow it to where Warwick Way enters from the left. Turn into the latter street, and walk a couple of blocks to *Cambridge Street*. The novelist GEORGE ELIOT (1819-80) lived at *No. 21* in 1853-4, just before she and George Henry Lewes, left for their German tour. AUBREY BEARDSLEY (1872-98), artist and writer, prolific and original genius, who fixed the stamp of his own satirical-decadent-aesthetic personality on much of the thought, art, and literature of the 1890's and after, lived at *No. 32* in 1889-90, and at *No. 114* from 1893 to 1895.

10. Continue down Cambridge Street till you reach *Charlwood Street*, and here turn left. AUBREY BEARDSLEY (see above) lived at *No. 59* from 1891 to 1893.
[10A. You will cross *St George's Drive*, and may wish to turn aside to *No. 92*, where the novelist CHARLES READE (1814-84), author of *The Cloister and the Hearth* (1861) and many other historical and reforming novels, lived with his mistress in the 1860's.... Return to Charlwood Street.]

11. Presently you will arrive at *Belgrave Road*. Almost at the intersection is *No. 118*, where the poet LAURENCE BINYON (1869-1943) lived during the second decade of the twentieth century. He was the author of many works on Oriental art, and was a poet of considerable power in the traditional school.

12. Turn left, on Belgrave Road, and soon reach *Warwick Square*, on your left. The once very well-known and prolific Scottish novelist MRS LUCY WALFORD (1845-1915) lived for many years at *No. 17*.

13. Return to Belgrave Road, and continue up it to *Eccleston Square*, again on your left. WINSTON CHURCHILL (1874-1965), historian and Prime Minister, lived at *No. 33* before the First World War. ARTHUR Á BECKETT (1844-1909), journalist, humourist, and dramatist, lived and died at *No. 87*. He was the son of the even more famous humorous writer (and lawyer) *Abbot à Beckett*.

14. Return to Belgrave Road, ascend it a few steps, and find *Gillingham Street* entering on your right. At *No. 16* the novelist JOSEPH CONRAD (1857-1924) lived from 1891 to 1895. Here he wrote most of his first-published book, *Almayer's Folly*, as well as *An Outcast of the Islands*. Polish-born, he learned English as a foreign language, deliberately chose it as his medium, and became one of England's greatest novelists.

15. At the end of Gillingham Street, turn left, on *Vauxhall Bridge Road*. Not far from where you turn is *No. 240,* where JAMES THOMSON ('B. V.') (1834-82), essayist, critic, and deeply pessimistic poet (author of *City of Dreadful Night*) lived (1872-4). (He moved from this place to *No. 60 Tachbrook Street*—which you could reach by turning back on Vauxhall Bridge Road, and finding Tachbrook Street branching off to your right.)

Continue up Vauxhall Bridge Road till you reach Victoria Street, with the *Victoria Underground Station* just to your left. Here this tour began, and here it ends.

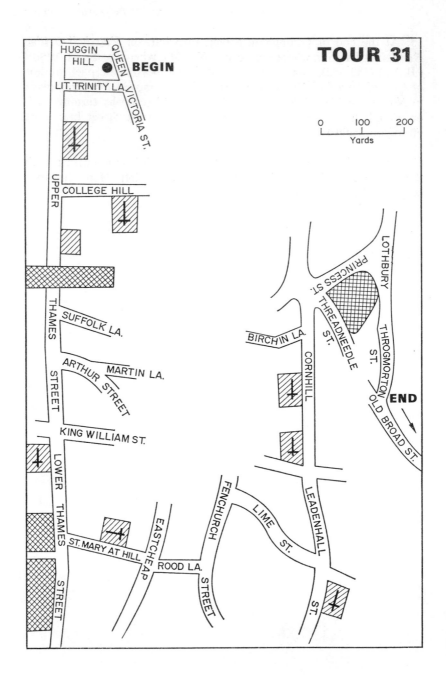

TOUR 31

BEGIN

HUGGIN HILL

LIT. TRINITY LA.

QUEEN VICTORIA ST.

UPPER

COLLEGE HILL

THAMES

SUFFOLK LA.

ARTHUR STREET

MARTIN LA.

STREET

KING WILLIAM ST.

LOWER

THAMES

ST. MARY AT HILL

EASTCHEAP

ROOD LA.

FENCHURCH

STREET

STREET

LIME ST.

BIRCHIN LA.

CORNHILL

THREADNEEDLE ST.

PRINCES ST.

LOTHBURY

THROGMORTON ST.

OLD BROAD ST.

END

LEADENHALL

ST.

0   100   200
Yards

336

Tour 31
North of London Bridge

George Borrow	Thomas Killigrew
Anne Brontë	Charles Lamb
Charlotte Brontë	William Langland
John Bunyan	Thomas Lodge
John Byrom	James Mill
Thomas Chatterton	John Stuart Mill
Geoffrey Chaucer	Thomas Love Peacock
Richard Church	George Peele
John Cleveland	Frederick Reynolds
Miles Coverdale	James Shirley
William Cowper	Edmund Spenser
Daniel Defoe	Sir Richard Steele
T. S. Eliot	John Stowe
Richard Glover	William Makepeace Thackeray
Kenneth Grahame	James Thomson
Thomas Gray	George Villiers
John Hawkesworth	Isaac Watts
Thomas Hood	Edward Young

Leave the underground at the *Mansion House Station*. Turn left, on either Little Trinity Lane or Huggin Hill, and descend (towards the river) to Upper Thames Street.

1. Turn left on Upper Thames Street. Almost immediately you will see, on your left, *St James's Church*, where GEORGE PEELE (1558?-97?),

dramatist and poet, was baptized. The original building, however, was destroyed in the Great Fire of 1666, and the present building (designed by Sir Christopher Wren) was finished in 1682. Walk on about a block, till you reach *College Hill*, on your left. Sir Richard Whittington (d. 1423), lived at the upper end of this street, and built a 'college' (houses for a community of clergymen) on the right-hand side of the street as you walk up it. Whittington was buried in the church which stood (till destroyed by the Great Fire) on the place where the present *Church of St Michael* stands. JOHN CLEVELAND (1613-58), the royalist poet, was buried in the former church. Immediately across the street from the church stood Buckingham House, the London home of GEORGE VILLIERS, DUKE OF BUCKINGHAM (1628-87), brilliant and dissolute poet and playwright.

2. Return to *Upper Thames Street*, and continue along it. At approximately the place where you will find (at last inspection) a little open space called *Whittington Gardens* (or, probably, a little farther along the street) on the left-hand side, stood the house in which England's first great poet GEOFFREY CHAUCER (1340?-1400), was born, and spent his boyhood.

3. Continue along Upper Thames Street to *Suffolk Lane*, entering from the left. Not far up this street, on the left-hand side, stood the *Merchant Taylors' School*, founded in 1561, but moved to Charterhouse in 1875. Some literary men who attended this school as boys were the poet EDMUND SPENSER (1552?-99), author of the *Faerie Queene*; the dramatist JAMES SHIRLEY (1596-1666), author of over 40 plays; THOMAS LODGE (1558?-1625), poet and fiction writer; and JOHN BYROM (1692-1763), poet and religious writer, contributor to the *Spectator*.

4. Return to Upper Thames Street, and continue along it till you find *Arthur Street*, entering from your left. If anyone is interested, this street was the birthplace of RICHARD GLOVER (1712-85), once highly respected and widely read poet, author of the immense epics *Leonidas* and *Atheniad*, to say nothing of three sombre classical tragedies and the blank verse *London: or, The Progress of Commerce*.

5. Return to Upper Thames Street, and continue along it past the approaches to London Bridge, and on into *Lower Thames Street*. On your left, at the nearer corner of Fish Street Hill, stood the *Church of St Mary Somerset*, where SIR RICHARD STEELE (1672-1729), poet and dramatist, was married (1707) to his beloved 'Prue'. The church was demolished in 1867.

In the next block, but on your right, still stands the *Church of St Magnus the Martyr*. In a previous church on this site (destroyed in the Great Fire) MILES COVERDALE (1488-1569), who made the first translation of the Bible to be printed in English, was rector, and was buried in the church. T. S. Eliot mentions it in *The Waste Land*: 'inexplicable splendour of Ionan white and gold.' Coverdale's grave may be seen near the altar.

A block or two beyond the church you will find, on your right, Billingsgate Market, for centuries the principal fish market of London, and origin of much picturesque language. Beyond this is the Customs House, to whose quay WILLIAM COWPER (1731-1800), the poet, once came with the intention of drowning himself. Here a much more recent poet, RICHARD CHURCH (1893-1972) worked as a boy and youth. Still farther along the street, between it and the river, was the Wool Quay, where GEOFFREY CHAUCER (see above) was Controller—though it is doubtful that he worked here regularly.

6. Immediately in front of the Billingsgate Market find a street called *St Mary at Hill*, and turn into it. In the church on your left, farther up the street, EDWARD YOUNG (1683-1765), author of the long blank verse poem *Night Thoughts* (1742-44), was married (1731). The poem was immensely popular, in many editions, to the mid-nineteenth century.

7. Continue along this street to *Eastcheap*. Here, about a block to your right, JAMES THOMSON (1700-48), greatest of England's nature poets, served as a tutor in a private academy for boys (1726-7), and here wrote (or worked on) his poem *Summer*.

8. Cross Eastcheap, and ascend Rood Lane to Fenchurch Street. Turn left on the latter, walk a block, and then turn right, into *Lime Street*. JOHN HAWKESWORTH (1715?-73), essayist, dramatist, editor, friend of Dr Johnson, died on this street; and the minor playwright FREDERICK REYNOLDS (1764-1841) was born here. On the left-hand corner, at the top of the street, where it runs into Leadenhall, the great *East India House* once stood. Here the essayist and friend of poets CHARLES LAMB (1775-1834) was a clerk for thirty years. *James Mill* (1773-1836), the Utilitarian philosopher, editor, and historian of India, was also a clerk and department chief here; and his more famous son JOHN STUART MILL (1806-73), also a Utilitarian philosopher with some elements of humanism and socialism intermingled, followed his father as a clerk for the East India Company, and became chief of the same department his father had headed. THOMAS LOVE PEACOCK (1785-1866), the

novelist, was a clerk here for many years, under the supervision of James Mill.

9. On the corner diagonally opposite the location of East India House (that is, at the corner of St Mary Axe and *Leadenhall*) stands *St Andrew Undershaft Church*, where JOHN STOWE (1525?-1605), historian of England, and of London in particular, was buried. [Two blocks to the right, along Leadenhall, in *St Katherine Cree Church, Hans Holbein*, the painter, is believed to have been buried. And at a bookseller's in the churchyard—a customary location for booksellers in former times—Milton's *Paradise Lost* was first offered for sale (1667).]

10. If you are standing at the door of St Andrew Undershaft, turn right, on Leadenhall Street, and follow it on into *Cornhill*. Just to your left, on the corner, as you cross over from Leadenhall, stands *St Peter's Church*. GEORGE BORROW (1803-81), the novelist, adventurer, and writer about gypsies, was married here in 1840. A little farther along Cornhill, and still on the left, is *St Michael's Church*, where the father of Thomas Gray, the poet, is buried; and farther still, at *No. 39*, stood the house in which THOMAS GRAY (1716-71) himself was born. Farther on, little *Change Alley* opens on your left. At *Nos. 3-4 Change Alley* stood the ancient Garroway's Coffee House, mentioned in Fielding's *Amelia*, and in several of Dickens's novels. Formerly, *Freeman's Court* opened just opposite Change Alley; here DANIEL DEFOE (1660-1731), father of the English novel, kept a hosiery shop before he turned to literature. A few yards on up Cornhill beyond this place Defoe, as a political offender, was exposed in the pillory (1703). At *No. 32*, in the offices of a publisher, occurred the memorable meeting between the novelists WILLIAM MAKEPEACE THACKERAY (1811-63) and the two BRONTË sisters, CHARLOTTE (1816-53), author of *Jane Eyre*, and ANNE (1820-59), author of the largely autobiographical novel *Agnes Gray*. A panel in the door of the present building commemorates the meeting. At *No. 31* stood *Tom's Coffee House*, from which the boy poet THOMAS CHATTERTON (1752-70) wrote to his sister shortly before he committed suicide. At about *No. 18*, on your left, was the entrance to *Pope's Head Alley*, where were printed Ben Jonson's *Every Woman in her Humour*, Thomas Middleton's *The Roaring Girl*, and John Webster's *The White Devil*. The American-born, Nobel-Prize-winning poet T. S. ELIOT (1888-1965), who is buried in Westminster Abbey, first started working for Lloyd's Bank at *No. 17*, in 1917. WILLIAM LANGLAND (1332?-1400?) author of *Piers Plowman*, is said to have resided in Cornhill.

11. At the end of Cornhill, turn right, across *Threadneedle Street,* and walk up Prince's Street, right beside the Bank of England. Here in the Bank KENNETH GRAHAME (1859-1931), author of the children's classics *Dream Days, The Golden Age,* and *The Wind in the Willows,* was a clerk, 1898 to 1908.

12. At the next corner, turn right, on *Lothbury.* THOMAS KILLIGREW (1612-93), Restoration dramatist and theatre manager, was born on this street, and THOMAS HOOD (1799-1845), the poet, went to school at *No. 45.*

13. Lothbury continues as Throgmorton Street. Almost at the beginning of the latter *Angel Court* leads off to the left. THOMAS LOVE PEACOCK (see above) was employed in a shop on this little street when he was fourteen years old.

14. Throgmorton leads on into *Old Broad Street.* On your right, at *No. 19,* once stood the offices of the South Sea Company, where CHARLES LAMB (see above), the essayist, was a clerk, 1789-92. A block or two up the street, the narrow lane called *Pinner's Hall* recalls a famous Independent meeting house that once stood facing Old Broad Street, between Pinner's Hall and the next corner. JOHN BUNYAN (1628-88), author of *Pilgrim's Progress,* preached in the hall; and ISAAC WATTS (1674-1728), the hymn-writer, who wrote 'O God Our Help in Ages Past' and 'Joy to the World', was a minister in charge. [In the next street on your left (Winchester Street) Edmund Halley (1646-1742), the astronomer, had his home. He was the first person who correctly predicted the return of a comet—which was named after him.]

Continue up Old Broad Street to the *Liverpool Street Underground Station,* where this tour ends.

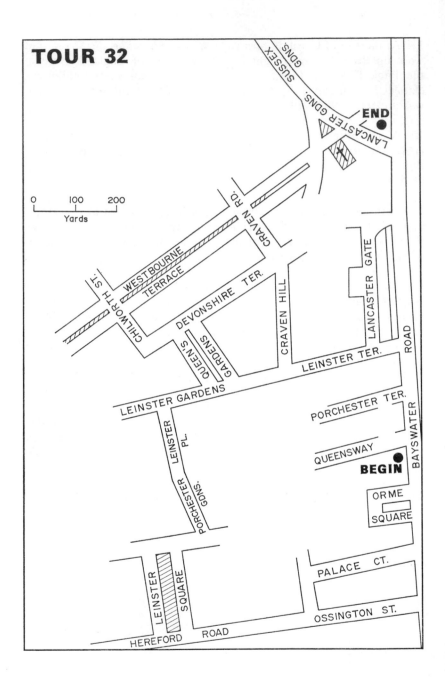

TOUR 32

0 100 200
Yards

SUSSEX GDNS.

LANCASTER GDNS.

END

CRAVEN RD.

WESTBOURNE TERRACE

CHILWORTH ST.

DEVONSHIRE TER.

QUEEN'S GARDENS

CRAVEN HILL

LANCASTER GATE

ROAD

LEINSTER TER.

LEINSTER GARDENS

PORCHESTER TER.

BAYSWATER

LEINSTER PL.

PORCHESTER GDNS.

QUEENSWAY

BEGIN

ORME

SQUARE

LEINSTER SQUARE

PALACE CT.

HEREFORD ROAD

OSSINGTON ST.

Tour 32
Bayswater

James Barrie

Mackenzie Bell

E. C. Bentley

Thomas Burke

Charles Cowden Clarke

Lady Elizabeth Clifford

Mrs Lucy Lane Clifford

Mrs R. E. Craigie

Gilbert Frankau

Rose Fyleman

Frederic Harrison

Bret Harte

John Lane

Shane Leslie

Wyndham Lewis

Mrs Elizabeth Lynn Linton

William James Linton

Meynell Family

Olive Schreiner

Edith Sitwell

Herbert Spencer

Lytton Strachey

Richard Wagner

Oscar Wilde

William Butler Yeats

Leave the underground at *Queensway Station.*
[1A. On emerging from the underground, you may wish to turn left, up *Queensway,* to *No. 66,* which was the home of THOMAS BURKE (1886-1945), novelist, author of *Limehouse Nights,* during the last five years of his life.]

1. On leaving the underground, turn right, and walk along Bayswater Road, with green Kensington Gardens on your left. You will soon reach *Orme Square. No. 8* here was the home of MACKENZIE BELL (1856-1930), poet, critic, and biographer, during his last years; and here he died. *No. 12* was the lodging place of RICHARD WAGNER (1813-83), German composer, during his London stay in 1877. From here he walked across Kensington Gardens to conduct concerts at the Albert Hall.

2. Continue along *Bayswater Road* till you find *No. 139*, where lived the novelist and dramatist LADY ELIZABETH CLIFFORD (1866-1945), who was the mother of the better-known novelist who wrote as *E. M. Delafield*. But about here find *Palace Court*, entering from your right. Turn into it. *No. 47* was the home (1889-1905) of the MEYNELL family —including WILFRID (1852-1948), editor, essayist, biographer; his wife ALICE (1847-1922), the poet; and several children, among them VIOLA and FRANCIS, who were minor literary figures. The house here was a kind of mecca for Roman Catholic writers and others: *Hilaire Belloc, Lionel Johnson, Coventry Patmore, Wilfred Blunt, Stephen Phillips, Katherine Hinkson,* and (regularly) *Francis Thompson*, who often baby-sat with the Meynell children in the neighbouring Kensington Gardens.

3. Return to Bayswater Road, and continue along it for one block, to *Ossington Street*. Turn into it and find *No. 33*, where WYNDHAM LEWIS (1886-1957) lived in the 1920's and 1930's. He was (in his own words) a 'novelist, painter, sculptor, philosopher, draughtsman, critic, politician, journalist, essayist, pamphleteer'—who (as someone else says) indulged in 'deadly, humourlessness, invective for its own sake'.

4. Continue up Ossington Street.
[4A. Just where it becomes Hereford Road, turn left, into *Moscow Road*. On this street, in a block of flats (called Pembridge Mansions) near Pembridge Square, the poet EDITH SITWELL (1887-1964) lived through the 1920's and most of the 1930's.]

   Return to Hereford Road, and keep ascending it till you reach *Leinster Square*, on your right. Here, at *No. 27* lived MRS ELIZABETH LYNN LINTON (1822-98), with her husband, the poet, journalist, biographer, WILLIAM JAMES LINTON (1812-97). Mrs Linton was one of the earliest of the nineteenth century's 'emancipated women': independent and unconventional. Yet, most curiously, she was a bitter anti-feminist!

5. Go on through Leinster Square to its eastern end; turn right briefly; and then turn left into *Porchester Gardens*. At *No. 11* OLIVE SCHREINER (1855-1920) lived briefly, 1882-3. At about this time appeared her novel *The Story of an African Farm*, the theme of which is religious questioning. The book was sensationally criticized at the time because it takes the part of science in its current controversy with Victorian religion. Miss Schreiner was another example of the 'new woman'—who lived independently, espoused radical political causes,

and had several love affairs, notably with Havelock Ellis, the psychologist.

6. Continue along Porchester Gardens into short *Leinster Place*, where the philosopher HERBERT SPENCER (see below) rented a study for many years at *No. 2*.

7. At the end of Leinster Place, turn right, and quickly reach *Queen's Gardens*. *No. 37* here was the home (1866-91) of the Darwinian philosopher HERBERT SPENCER (1820-1903). His work, immensely influential in its time, gave to evolutionary theory meanings and implications much wider and more profound than the anatomical-physiological studies of Darwin. Though Spencer's attempt to take Darwinism into the realms of politics and morality were not too successful, his fundamental ideas helped accomplish a revolution in the intellectual world.

8. Continue through Queen's Gardens to the east end.
[8A. If you care to turn left here, and then right, into *Chilworth Street*, you will find *No. 7*, which was the home, during the last twenty years of her life, of LUCY LANE CLIFFORD, novelist and dramatist. She was the wife of W. K. Clifford, mathematics professor and materialistic philosopher. WYNDHAM LEWIS (see above) lived (1935-6) at *No. 21....* Now return to the end of Queen's Gardens.]
    Turn right, along Devonshire Terrace till you reach *Craven Hill*, entering from your right. Turn into it. *No. 9* here was the home of CHARLES COWDEN CLARKE (1787-1877), scholar, editor, teacher, friend of many literary men—among them *John Keats* (whom he taught at this place), Leigh Hunt, William Hazlitt, Charles Lamb, Dickens, and Douglas Jerrold.

9. Walk on through Craven Hill and Craven Hill Gardens to Leinster Terrace. Turn left on the latter, and walk on to Bayswater Road once more. Just on the corner to your right, at *No. 100* Bayswater Road, JAMES M. BARRIE (1860-1937), novelist and dramatist, lived from 1903 to 1909. Here he wrote *Peter Pan*, *Alice Sit-by-the-Fire*, and *What Every Woman Knows*.

10. Go on along Bayswater Road beyond the Barrie place. You will find *Porchester Terrace* immediately, on your right. A few steps up this street is *No. 7*, where MRS R. W. CRAIGIE ('JOHN OLIVER HOBBES') (1867-1906), dramatist and novelist, lived as a child and (years later) as a divorced woman with her son. Mrs Craigie (born Richards), though a native of Boston, was brought to London at an

early age. Her novels were once highly popular. ROSE FYLEMAN (d. 1957), poet and writer of children's literature, lived at *No. 10*. E. C. BENTLEY (1875-1956) lived at the same *No. 10*.

11. Turn back around the Barrie corner, and into Leinster Terrace once more. Walk up it a few steps, and turn right, into *Lancaster Gate*. At *No. 56* MRS R. W. CRAIGIE (see above) had lived with her parents as a girl, here she spent the last ten years of her life, and here she died. At *No. 69* lived the parents of LYTTON STRACHEY (1880-1932), the biographer, from the time he was four years old, and this was his home until after he finished at Cambridge, years later. Strachey, with his *Eminent Victorians* and *Queen Victoria*, was the father of modern biography—which treats historical figures as if they were people, rather than public phenomena. *No. 74* was the place where BRET HARTE (1836-1902), novelist and short-story writer, settled in 1895, having previously lived for two years at *No. 109*. Harte, an American, spent much of his early life in the American West, and became the father of the 'local colour' school of fiction, from whom have descended the 'regional' writers of the twentieth century. His mistress and secretary, the widowed Mrs Marguerite Van Velde, lived with him here.

12. Pass on through Lancaster Gate, which turns to the right, and leads back to Bayswater Road.
[12A. Just before you reach Bayswater Road, turn right, into narrow *Lancaster Court*. JOHN LANE (1854-1925), founder of the Bodley Head Press, publisher of the *Yellow Book* in the 1890's, and bold publisher of other *avant garde* books of the *fin de siècle*, lived at *No. 8*.]
 Turn left on Bayswater Road, and continue along it, with the park on your right. Presently you will reach *Lancaster Gardens*, slanting away to your left, and filled with traffic. A short distance up it, at *No. 7*, GILBERT FRANKAU (see above) lived with his second wife, 1922-7. At *No. 17* WILLIAM BUTLER YEATS (1865-1939), stayed during the summer of 1935, on one of his last prolonged visits to London. A large and handsome church on your left, at the intersection of Lancaster Gardens with Sussex Gardens and Westbourne Terrace, is *St James's, Paddington*. Here the poet-novelist-dramatist-wit OSCAR WILDE (1854-1900) was married, improbably and incompatibly, to a handsome lady who was as prudish and conventional as Wilde was amoral and unconventional.
[12B. Up *Westbourne Terrace* (at right angles to Sussex Gardens) SIR SHANE LESLIE (b. 1885), poet, critic, biographer, lived at *No. 12*

in the 1920's and 1930's, when most of his major work was being written. *No. 38* was the home of FREDERIC HARRISON (1831-1923), jurist, professor, philosopher, and writer. He attempted most kinds of writing (biography, autobiography, history, criticism, philosophy, a verse tragedy, a novel), and did most of it well. Republican and humanitarian, he was the chief proponent of positivism in England in his time—this being the philosophy that rejects metaphysical speculation, and depends on experience and experiment for knowledge. He has been called 'the last of the great Victorians'. *No. 47* was the home, in his last years, of Sir John Hare (1844-1924), actor, as well as manager of the Garrick Theatre and of the Royal Court Theatre, on Sloane Square, where so many 'modern' plays have been produced.]

Return to Bayswater Road, and find the *Lancaster Gate Underground Station* just around the corner. Here this tour ends; but from this place you may take up *Tour No. 33.*

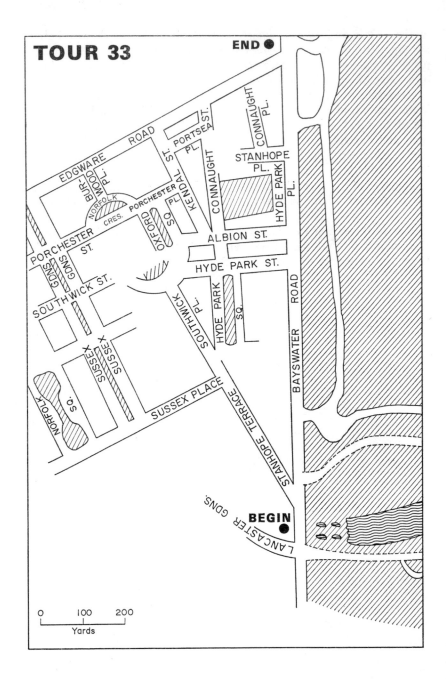

TOUR 33

END ●

BEGIN ●

```
0    100   200
      Yards
```

Tour 33
Hyde Park Area

Nigel Balchin	Richard Le Gallienne
James Barrie	Rose Macaulay
Max Beerbohm	Samuel Pepys
John Buchan	Ann Radcliffe
John Churton Collins	George William Russell ('A. E.')
Winston Churchill	Olive Schreiner
Charles Dickens	Percy Bysshe Shelley
George du Maurier	Richard Brinsley Sheridan
John Evelyn	Robert Southwell
Elinor Glyn	Laurence Sterne
Philip Guedalla	J. A. Symonds
Benjamin Haydon	William Makepeace Thackeray
W. H. Hudson	Horace Walpole
John Lane	

Leave the underground at the *Lancaster Gate Station*. When you reach the street (Bayswater Road), turn right, cross the next street, and then (if you can make it) cross over busy Bayswater to green Kensington Gardens.

1. Enter *Kensington Gardens* at the Marlborough Gate, and walk on into the park along a footpath that you will find. You cannot avoid seeing, to your left, The Fountain—an ornate paved garden with fountains, and with a sombre statue of Edward Jenner (1749-1823), discoverer of the principle of vaccination for smallpox (1706). A little farther on you will reach the statue of 'Peter Pan', the chief character in JAMES BARRIE's play of that name. The body of water on your left

is part of the Serpentine, but is known as the 'Long Water'. Harriet Westbrook Shelley, first wife of the poet PERCY BYSSHE SHELLEY (1792-1822), drowned herself here in 1816, after she had lost the poet to (if not a better) a much cleverer woman.

2. Continue along the path skirting the Long Water till you reach a bridge on your left, built in 1826. When you have crossed the bridge, you will be in *Hyde Park*. This has been the chief, and most celebrated, park in London since it was opened to the public by Charles I, in 1635. After crossing the bridge, do not continue along the waterside below the bridge—but follow a path on out in line with the bridge until you find yourself at a roadway. This is the Ring Road. Its predecessor, in earlier centuries, was considerably smaller, and lay farther ahead of you in what is now the main part of Hyde Park. JOHN EVELYN (1620-1706), the great diarist, mentions with resentment that he had to pay a small fee for driving his carriage in the Park in 1653, and that he witnessed a carriage-race here in 1657. SAMUEL PEPYS (1633-1703), the other great seventeenth-century diarist, saw a footrace around the Ring in 1660; and in 1669 he boasts that he here flaunted his first fine carriage, and also his pretty wife, in the faces of the fashionable. 'Everyone,' says De Gramont, the exiled French courtier, referring to the time of Evelyn and Pepys, 'who had either sparkling eyes or splendid equipage, constantly repaired thither.' The Ring was a promenade for beaux and belles in the daytime, and was often a duelling place at night. In *Henry Esmond* Thackeray describes a duel that occurred here; and RICHARD BRINSLEY SHERIDAN (1751-1816) duelled here. At night, however, it was a dangerous place through most of the eighteenth century. HORACE WALPOLE (1717-97), letter writer and author of the first 'Gothic' novel, was held up and robbed here in November, 1749.

At just about the place where your path approaches the Ring, cross over the latter, and find the monument (a large upright slab by a fountain) to W. H. HUDSON (1841-1922). The monument (which is by the sculptor *Jacob Epstein*) depicts Rima, heroine of Hudson's fantasy-novel *Green Mansions*. Beyond the monument is the Bird Sanctuary, established as another memorial to Hudson, an ornithologist.

3. Return to your former pathway, and follow it back to Bayswater Road. Leave the park through Westbourne Gate (almost opposite the underground station where this tour began), cross over Bayswater Road, and (if you have escaped the traffic unmaimed bear right, up Stanhope Terrace. [Lord Baden-Powell, founder of the Boy Scout movement, was born here, at *No. 11*.] On your left is *Sussex Square*,

where, at *No. 2*, WINSTON CHURCHILL (1874-1965), historian and statesman, lived in the 1920's.

4. Beyond Sussex Square, turn left on Sussex Place, and walk straight
ahead till you reach *Norfolk Square*, on your right. *No. 47* here was
the home (1865-7) of JOHN ADDINGTON SYMONDS (1840-93), eccentric
scholar and literary critic. He was the author of the seven-volume
classic *The Renaissance in Italy*, as well as volumes of poetry, literary
essays, literary biographies, translations from the Italian, and so on.
He lived here just before he left for Italy in 1866, and he returned
here (he had bought the house) the same year. JOHN CHURTON
COLLINS (1848-1908), incisive and controversial literary critic, essayist, and biographer, lived at *No. 51* for ten years (1896-1906).

5. Walk through Norfolk Square, reach Norfolk Place at its end, and
turn right. After one block, you will reach *Sussex Gardens*. Turn left.
[5A. After two blocks you will reach *Southwick Street*, crossing Sussex
Gardens. Just to your left, at *No. 37*, lived JOHN LANE (1854-1925),
publisher-to-be, who issued many works by the new Aesthetic and
naturalistic writers after more conventional publishers had refused
them. He founded the Bodley Head Press. With him here, during
1888-9, lived his friend the Aesthetic poet, critic, and literary historian
RICHARD LE GALLIENNE (1866-1947).... Return to Sussex Gardens.]
    Just beyond Southwick Street, at *No. 41 Sussex Gardens* (in a build-
ing replaced in the late 1960's) GEORGE WILLIAM RUSSELL ('A. E.')
(1867-1935) lived in 1933-4. An Irishman, and leader in the modern
Irish Literary Renaissance, he had left his own country because of
its oppressive censorship laws of the early 1930's.

6. The next street crossing Sussex Gardens is *Porchester Street*. Here
turn right. At *No. 7* (now gone) the poet RICHARD LE GALLIENNE (see
above) lived in the early 1900's.

7. At the end of Porchester Street, turn left, around Norfolk Crescent,
and on, after a few steps, left into Burwood Place. (On this little
street, in a house now vanished, the painter *Benjamin Haydon*, friend
of the poet John Keats, from whom he borrowed money at a time
when Keats could ill afford to lend, killed himself.) Continue to
Edgware Road, and turn right. *No. 63* was the home of ROSE
MACAULAY (d. 1958) in the early 1920's, just when she was becoming
famous as a poet, literary critic, and novelist.

8. After two blocks along Edgware Road, turn right, into Connaught

351

Street, and then right again, into *Portsea Place*. At *No. 16* lived (1885-7) OLIVE SCHREINER (1855-1920), whose novel *The Story of an African Farm* (1883) was famous in its day as a depiction of characters overcome by doubts in a scientific age. The book is still readable. Olive Schreiner was, for years, the mistress of the psychological writer Havelock Ellis.

9. At the upper end of Portsea Place, turn left into Kendal Street, and reach *Porchester Place*. At *No. 9* OLIVE SCHREINER (see above) spent her last two years, and here died.

10. Turn right, on Porchester Place, and reach *Oxford Square*. GEORGE DU MAURIER (1834-96), painter, cartoonist, and novelist, moved to *No. 17* in 1895, and here he died.

> GEORGE DU MAURIER is best remembered, perhaps as a cartoonist for *Punch*. He waged a sharp campaign of criticism and ridicule against the follies of the Aesthetic movement—but when he turned from cartoons to fiction, he treated the Aesthetic movement sympathetically in the best-known of his novels, *Trilby*. He was the father of the dramatist Guy du Maurier, and of the actor Gerald du Maurier. The latter was the father of Daphne du Maurier, well-known novelist.

11. At the other end of Oxford Square, bear slightly to your right, and find the entrance of *Southwick Place*. *No. 6* here was the home of the novelist CHARLES DICKENS (1812-70) in 1866.

12. At the end of Southwick Place, make a hairpin turn back to your left, into *Hyde Park Square*. JOHN BUCHAN, LORD TWEEDSMUIR (1875-1940), Scottish novelist and statesman, lived at *No. 40* from 1907 to 1910, immediately after his marriage.

13. Walk right through Hyde Park Square to *Hyde Park Street*. Turn right, and find *No. 5*, where the journalist, historian, and novelist PHILIP GUEDALLA (1889-1944) lived in the 1920's and 1930's—and *No. 15* where he lived in the 1940's.

14. Continue to Bayswater Road, and turn left, and then left again, into *Albion Street*. J. A. SYMONDS (see above) lived at *No. 13* in 1865; and the youthful WILLIAM MAKEPEACE THACKERAY (1811-63), was living with his mother at *No. 18* in the 1830's. In the 1920's W. L. GEORGE (1882-1926), in the first three decades of the twentieth century a prominent novelist, sociologist, and editor, lived at *No. 26*.

15. Return to Bayswater Road, and turn left along it. You will find that, suddenly, it has become *Hyde Park Place* along its left side. At *No. 5* CHARLES DICKENS (see above) had a home in the last year of his life. MAX BEERBOHM (1872-1956), essayist and cartoonist, lived with his parents at *No. 19*, 1892 to 1896. Along here you will see a ruined (bombed out) little church, with a park-like area behind it. This park-like area is an old cemetery; and here are buried the novelists LAURENCE STERNE (1713-68) and MRS ANN RADCLIFFE (1764-1832), author of *The Mysteries of Udolpho* (1794), one of the early 'Gothic' novels. (There is a Gothic story about Sterne: it is said that his corpse was dug up by body-snatchers, sold for dissecting purposes, recognized by the purchaser, and restored by him to its grave.) *Note:* The old cemetery is closed to the public; but, if you are lucky, you may attain entrance by application to the caretaker on the grounds.

> LAURENCE STERNE was one of the 'Big Five' of eighteenth-century fiction. (The other four were Defoe, Richardson, Fielding and Smollett.) His greatest work is *The Life and Opinions of Tristram Shandy* (1759-67), a long, rambling, eccentric, witty, and perverse novel that, as the years pass, ranks higher and higher in critical opinion.

16. Continue on the length of Hyde Park Place till you reach Stanhope Place, on your left. Turn into it. A few steps along it, and on your right, is the entrance to *Connaught Place*. It is said by some authorities that the Tyburn gallows (for centuries the public execution place of common criminals) stood, at one time, near what is now the corner of Stanhope Place and Connaught Place. Though the gallows was probably moved several times during the centuries, this was certainly not the spot that it occupied longest. At *No. 11 Connaught Place* MRS ELINOR GLYN (d. 1943) was living in the 1930's.

> MRS ELINOR GLYN's name will not be found in many histories of literature; but in the 1920's she was a celebrated popular novelist on whose books were based several films—in some of which the idolized Rudolph Valentino starred. She was also responsible for the once-widespread use of the phrase 'She has *it*' to describe the indescribable charm of some women.

17. Return to Stanhope Place, and follow it on till it ends, just ahead, in *Connaught Square*, where, at *No. 5*, the novelist NIGEL BALCHIN (1908-70) was living in the 1960's.

18. Return to Bayswater Road, turn left, and follow it on to its juncture with Edgware Road. Just opposite here, on the other side of

Bayswater Road, and near the Marble Arch, a tablet in the pavement marks the supposed site of Tyburn gallows. Actually, however, modern research has located the gallows site precisely at the corner of Edgware and Bayswater Roads. That is, if (as on this tour) you are walking eastward along the upper (northern) side of Bayswater Road, and pause to note the traffic situation before you step off the kerb into Edgware Road—you will be on the exact spot where the permanent gallows was located. During the last decade of its existence, however, it stood about 60-70 feet farther up Edgware Road. It was entirely removed from this general area in 1783, when the official execution place became Newgate. The since-beatified Jesuit priest ROBERT SOUTHWELL (1561?-95), Christian mystic poet, was hanged here. His crime was that he had stayed six years in England, serving his co-religionists, though by law his stay, if permitted at all, should have been limited to forty days. After the restoration of Charles II, Oliver Cromwell's body was disinterred from its resting place in Westminster Abbey, and hanged at Tyburn.

The long, straight (and therefore extremely un-British) stretch of road that slices northward here, and includes Edgware Road, Maida Vale, and Kilburn High Street, was a part of the Roman-built *Watling Street*. Originally, it extended straight on up through central England and to the north-western corner of the country. To your right, it extended to a crossing of the Thames at about where Vauxhall Bridge now stands.

Just ahead of you, about a block away, on the left, is the *Marble Arch Underground Station*. You may end this tour here; or you may take up *Tour No. 12* that begins at this station.

Tour 34
Bryanston Area

James Barrie	Shane Leslie
Max Beerbohm	Somerset Maugham
George Borrow	Meynell Family
Elizabeth Barrett Browning	Mrs Elizabeth Montagu
John Buchan	Thomas Moore
Edward Bulwer-Lytton	Robert Boyer Nichols
Thomas Campbell	Sir Gilbert Parker
Wilkie Collins	Olive Schreiner
Charles Dickens	Mary Godwin Shelley
Lovat Dickson	Richard Brinsley Sheridan
Conan Doyle	Sydney Smith
John Forster	Muriel Spark
John Fowler	Francis Thompson
Edward Knoblock	Anthony Trollope
Letitia Elizabeth Landon	Rebecca West
Edward Lear	

Leave the underground at the *Baker Street Station*. When you emerge from the station, turn to your right, and cross over Baker Street. Continue in the same direction for one block, and then turn left, cross Marylebone Road, and enter Gloucester Place.

1. Walk straight down *Gloucester Place*. At *No. 99* the Barrett family of whom ELIZABETH BARRETT (1806-61), the poet and wife, later on, of Robert Browning, was a member—lived for nearly four years (1835-8). At *No. 65* the novelist WILKIE COLLINS (1824-89) lived

355

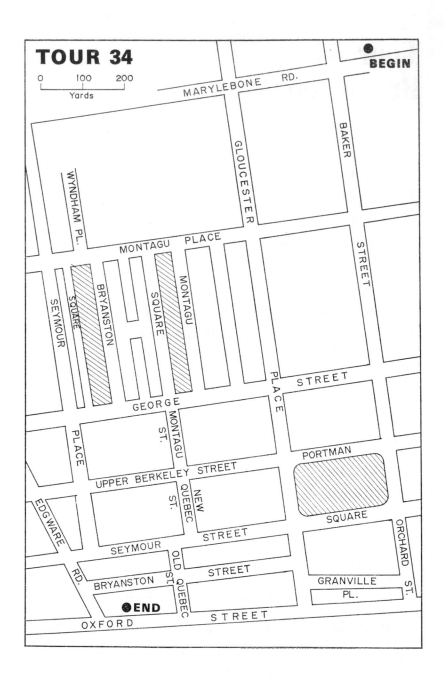

TOUR 34

0   100   200
Yards

BEGIN

MARYLEBONE RD.

GLOUCESTER

BAKER

WYNDHAM PL.

MONTAGU PLACE

SEYMOUR

SQUARE

BRYANSTON

SQUARE

MONTAGU

STREET

PLACE STREET

GEORGE

MONTAGU ST.

PLACE

PORTMAN

UPPER BERKELEY STREET

QUEBEC ST.

NEW

SQUARE

EDGWARE

SEYMOUR

STREET

ORCHARD ST.

OLD QUEBEC ST.

RD.

BRYANSTON

STREET

GRANVILLE
PL.

END

OXFORD STREET

356

(1866-80 and 1883-8), with one of his mistresses. At *No. 57* CHARLES DICKENS (1812-70) stayed in 1864. At *No. 34* lived *Thomas Monkhouse*, a member of Parliament and friend of literary men. Here, on April 4, 1823, he had for dinner guests *William Wordsworth, Samuel Taylor Coleridge, Thomas Moore, Charles Lamb, Mary Lamb*, and *Samuel Rogers*. Lamb wrote of the event the next day: 'I dined in Parnassus: half the poetry of England constellated in Gloucester Place. It was a delightful evening.'

2. Continue down Gloucester Place till it ends in *Portman Square*. Turn left along the square, and circle it till you find the following numbers: *No. 24*, where lived SIR GILBERT PARKER (1862-1923), Canadian-born novelist, dramatist, poet, journalist, and politician in the 1920's; *No. 33*, which was the address of the *Poetry Review* in the late 1940's when MURIEL SPARK (poet, novelist, playwright, literary biographer, and critic) was the editor; *No. 14*, 'in a magnificent block of family flats' known as 'Orchard Court', where lived DAME REBECCA WEST, novelist, critic, journalist, and political writer.

3. Continue straight down the eastern side of the square to *Orchard Street*. To *No. 22* on this short street RICHARD BRINSLEY SHERIDAN (1751-1816), dramatist and politician, brought his new wife (1774) after a remarkably romantic courtship and elopement; here their son Thomas was born; and here were written *The Rivals* and *The Duenna*. *No. 18* was the home (1804-8) of SYDNEY SMITH (1771-1845), liberal-minded clergyman, author, and wit, who had almost too many homes, at different times, for any of them to be a home.

4. Two blocks down Orchard Street, turn right, into *Granville Place*. At *No. 2A* (No. 4 Granville Place Mansions) lived the extraordinary MEYNELL family: WILFRID (1852-1948), founder and editor of the Roman Catholic literary magazine *Merry England*; his wife ALICE (1847-1922), a poet of great merit; their daughter VIOLA, poet and biographer. FRANCIS THOMPSON (1859-1907), the Roman Catholic poet, was such a frequent visitor here that he could almost have been counted a resident.

5. Walk the length of Granville Place, and at its end turn right, on Portman Street. Then, almost immediately, turn left into *Bryanston Street*. ROBERT BOYER NICHOLS (1893-1944), poet of the First World War, writer of philosophical novels, and dramatist, was living at *No. 7* around 1930. JOHN BUCHAN (1875-1940), Scottish novelist, politician, and diplomat, lived at *No. 13* in 1910-12, and here his first son was born. JAMES BARRIE (1860-1937), novelist and dramatist, lived

at *No. 14* in 1893. The novelist and friend of gypsies GEORGE BORROW (1803-81) lived briefly (1826) at *No. 26*.

6. At the end of Bryanston Street, turn right, on Edgware Road, and then double back on *Seymour Street*. At *No. 52* the poet, critic, and historian SHANE LESLIE (b. 1885) lived as a boy. EDWARD LEAR (1812-88), the artist and famous nonsense writer, lived at *No. 30*. At *No. 18* the Scottish poet THOMAS CAMPBELL (1777-1844) lived from 1820 to 1828; and the novelist EDWARD BULWER-LYTTON (1803-73) lived at *No. 10* as a boy.

> THOMAS CAMPBELL had a wide reputation during his lifetime as a distinguished public servant, editor for ten years of the *New Monthly Magazine*, one of the most active founders of the University of London, author of the long didactic poem *The Pleasures of Hope*, as well as of several long narrative poems, author of the song 'Ye Mariners of England' and the poem 'Lord Ullin's Daughter' (once widely quoted), and also a memorable phrase-maker (e.g., 'Coming events cast their shadows before'; 'Distance lends enchantment to the view'; 'Love lies bleeding'; and so on).

7. At the end of Seymour Street, turn left along Portman Square once more; then, at the next corner, turn left again, into *Upper Berkeley Street*. The corner house that stood on the right as you made the turn into this street was the home of MRS ELIZABETH MONTAGU (1720-1800), 'queen of the bluestockings', author of a book defending Shakespeare from the criticisms of Voltaire and other neo-classic literary theorists, and cousin by marriage of the more famous Lady Mary Wortley Montagu. To this house came *Dr Johnson, Boswell, Edmund Burke, Horace Walpole,* and many other literary personages. LETITIA ELIZABETH LANDON ('L. E. L.') (see above) lived at *No. 28*. And *No. 48* was the family home of the essayist MAX BEERBOHM (1872-1956) from the 1890's.

8. Continue to Seymour Place, turn right, and then (after one block) right again—on George Street. After a few steps, you will see *Bryanston Square* on your left. Turn into it. From 1923 to 1926 the novelist SOMERSET MAUGHAM (1874-1965) lived at *No. 43*.

9. Walk to the far end of Bryanston Square. Across the street, you will find the entrance to *Wyndham Place*. Here, at *No. 2*, SOMERSET MAUGHAM (see above) lived for three years before he moved to the Bryanston Square house. At the far end of this little street is the church in which LETITIA LANDON was married.

10. *Montagu Place* runs between Bryanston Square and Gloucester Place. Follow it in the direction of the latter street. In a house on the left-hand side ARTHUR CONAN DOYLE (1859-1930), creator of Sherlock Holmes, lived with his wife when he first came to London, with the intention of practising medicine. The prolific novelist-dramatist EDWARD KNOBLOCK (1874-1935) lived for many years at *No. 11*.

11. Turn right, into *Montagu Square*. *No. 5* was the home of HARRY GRAHAM (1874-1936), dramatist and humorous poet. At *No. 23* lived LOVAT DICKSON (b. 1902), publisher, novelist, autobiographer. ANTHONY TROLLOPE (1815-82), one of the major Victorian novelists, lived at *No. 39* from 1872 to 1880. JOHN FORSTER (1812-86), friend of Dickens and noted biographer of British literary and historical figures, lived, in the 1850's, at *No. 46*.

12. Walk on through the square till you reach *George Street* again. Here you will have to turn aside a few steps to find the location of *No. 44*. where THOMAS MOORE (1759-1852), the Irish poet and musician, and friend of Byron, lodged when he first arrived in London, 1799; and *No. 51*, where MARY GODWIN SHELLEY (1797-1851), widow of the poet Percy Bysshe Shelley, and author of the novel *Frankenstein*, lived for a while. Later on, MOORE moved to *No. 85* on this street.

13. As you left Montagu Square, and crossed George Street, *Montagu Street* opened in front of you. Enter it, walk down it. OLIVE SCHREINER (1855-1920)—early feminist, believer that women should be independent in sexual matters, and author of *The Story of an African Farm* (1883), which is a fictional study of the way in which the nineteenth-century religion-science controversy affected a character—lived at *No. 25* in 1888-9. GEORGE BORROW (see above) lived with his family at *No. 21* in 1860—before moving to a permanent home in Hereford Square.

14. Walk on through Montagu Street, and its extension as New Quebec Street. When the latter ends in Seymour Street, turn right a few steps, and then left, down *Old Quebec Street*. The novelist and dramatist JAMES BARRIE (see above) lived at *No. 14* in 1889.

Continue straight on till you reach Oxford Street. Then turn right, and walk half a block to the *Marble Arch Underground Station*, where this tour ends. But here also begins *Tour No. 12*.

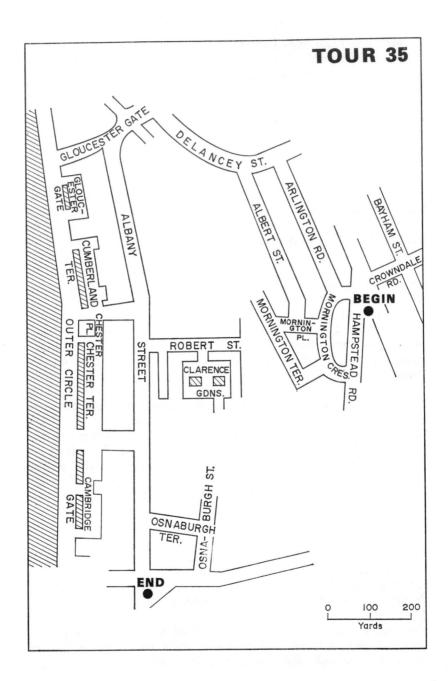

TOUR 35

GLOUCESTER GATE

DELANCEY ST.

GLOUC-ESTER GATE

ALBANY

CUMBERLAND TER.

ARLINGTON RD.

ALBERT ST.

BAYHAM ST.

CROWNDALE RD.

BEGIN

CHESTER PL.

CHESTER TER.

STREET

ROBERT ST.

CLARENCE GDNS.

MORNINGTON TER.

MORNINGTON PL.

MORNINGTON CRES.

HAMPSTEAD RD.

OUTER CIRCLE

CAMBRIDGE GATE

OSNABURGH ST.

OSNABURGH TER.

OSNA-BURGH

END

0   100   200
Yards

360

Tour 35
Regent's Park East

Sara Coleridge	Henry Mayhew
George Cruikshank	Charlotte Mew
W. H. Davies	Rossetti Family
Charles Dickens	William Sharp ('Fiona Macleod')
John Galsworthy	Alfred Sutro
Mrs Elizabeth Gaskell	Alfred Tennyson
W. W. Jacobs	Dylan Thomas
Edward Lear	H. G. Wells

Leave the underground at the *Mornington Crescent Station.*

1. This very first item may not be worth your while unless you are an ardent Dickensian.... Cross Camden High Street, and enter Crowndale Road, opposite the underground station. One block along this road, *Bayham Street* enters from your left. Turn into it. To *No. 141,* in a house long vanished, the father of CHARLES DICKENS (1812-70), the novelist, moved with his family on first coming to London, 1821. The father, a good but unfortunate man of weak will and drifting habits, soon landed in Marshalsea Prison for debt, while his wife and son Charles continued for some time to live here. Meanwhile Charles was working miserably in the shoe-blacking factory described in *David Copperfield.*

2. Return to your starting place, pass the underground station, and turn left into *Hampstead Road.* At *No. 263* GEORGE CRUIKSHANK (1792-1878), the caricaturist and illustrator, lived for many years, and here died. He illustrated some of Dickens's works, and Dickens's own concepts of the characters in his novels were certainly influenced by Cruikshank. DICKENS himself went to school (1824-6) a little farther down the road, at *No. 247.*

3. Turn right, off Hampstead Road, into Mornington Crescent. Follow this a short block to the entrance of *Mornington Terrace*, on your left. Turn here. *No. 12* was the home, for a time of H. G. WELLS. He lived here with his mistress after he and his wife had separated; and here he wrote *The Time Machine, The Wonderful Visit*, and *The Island of Dr Moreau.*

4. Turn right, into *Mornington Place*. H. G. WELLS lived at *No. 7* early in 1894, immediately after he had left his wife, and before he moved to Mornington Terrace. ALFRED TENNYSON (1809-92) lodged at *No. 25* on this little street in 1850. When he moved, he absent-mindedly left the manuscript of his greatest poem, *In Memoriam*, in a closet of his lodging house. Missing the manuscript some weeks later, he wrote asking his friend *Coventry Patmore* to go look for it. Patmore went, and after some difficulty with the landlady, retrieved the manuscript.

5. You may wish to turn off to the left, and make a short excursion up *Albert Street*. The poet WILLIAM SHARP (1855-1905) lived at *No. 19* in the 1870's and 1880's. He wrote poems, novels, and literary biographies under his own name. But he was a mystic who felt another personality within him—a woman named FIONA MACLEOD, under whose name he wrote (in the Gaelic tradition that was being revived in the 1890's) his best poems, as well as two plays. The identity of Fiona MacLeod was concealed from the public during Sharp's life.

6. Return to Mornington Place, follow it to its end in Mornington Crescent, and turn left. Then turn left again, into *Arlington Road*. On this street, at *No. 38*, the ROSSETTI FAMILY lived when DANTE GABRIEL ROSSETTI (painter-poet) was about 23 years old, WILLIAM MICHAEL (biographer, editor, poet) was 22, and CHRISTINA (religious poet) was 20.

7. Continue on Arlington Street till it is intersected by *Delancey Street*. Turn left on this street. The poet CHARLOTTE MEW (1869-1928) lived briefly somewhere on this street shortly before her death. The poet DYLAN THOMAS (1914-53) lived with his family at *No. 54*, in late 1951 and early 1952, before leaving for America, where he died. Though Thomas began publishing poems in the 1930's, he did not come into his own until after World War II. His powerful and beautiful readings of his own poems over BBC, and in public appearances, as well as his excesses in private life, made him a legend even before he died. No other post-war English poet has been so famous, or so much admired by ordinary readers and professional critics alike.

8. Delancey Street leads, at its left-hand (western) end, into Parkway. Turn left on the latter, and follow it on till it becomes *Gloucester Gate*, which then makes a turn alongside Regent's Park. At *No. 15A* W. W. JACOBS (1862-1943), author of many humorously realistic stories of the London waterfront, novels, dramas, and the superb horror story 'The Monkey's Paw', had his home in the 1930's.

9. Continue down the Outer Circle, skirting Regent's Park, till you reach *Cumberland Terrace*. MRS ELIZABETH GASKELL (1810-65), author of the early naturalistic novel of social protest, *Mary Barton* (1848), and of that pleasant novel of village life, *Cranford* (1853), stayed at *No. 17* in the late 1850's.

10. Abutting Cumberland Terrace at its far end is *Chester Place*. Here, at *No. 10*, lived (from 1837) and died SARA COLERIDGE (1802-52), daughter of the poet Samuel Taylor Coleridge, and wife of her cousin Henry Coleridge (who edited S. T. C.'s work). She was a literary figure in her own right: translator of Latin and Greek, writer of fairy tales, and editor of some of her father's work.
[10A. Beyond Chester Place, *Chester Terrace* stretches on alongside the Outer Circle of the Park. At *No. 31* lived ALFRED SUTRO (1863-1933) during his later years. He was a prodigiously prolific and successful dramatist almost up to his death, and a collaborator with *George Meredith* in dramatizing the latter's *The Egoist*.... Return to Chester Place.]

11. Find your way, between Cumberland Terrace and Chester Place, into *Albany Street*, and turn right. The poet, critic, editor, and biographer WILLIAM MICHAEL ROSSETTI (1829-1919) and his sister, the poet CHRISTINA ROSSETTI (1830-94), together with other members of their family, lived at *No. 166* from 1858 to 1865. EDWARD LEAR (1812-88), artist and humorous writer, lived at *No. 124* in the 1830's.

12. Continue down Albany Street till you find Robert Street intersecting from your left. Turn here, and then immediately right, into *Clarence Gardens*. The poet, W. H. DAVIES (1871-1940), who had been a beggar and a tramp in Britain and America in his early days, and who, in his unassuming lyrics and his humanitarianism, was a kind of later William Blake, lived at *No. 29* before the First World War.... Return to Albany Street.

13. Continue down Albany Street till you reach Chester Gate, intersecting from your right. Turn into it, reach Cambridge Terrace, on your left, and walk on through it, alongside the Outer Circle, till you

reach *Cambridge Gate*. The family of JOHN GALSWORTHY (1867-1933), Nobel Prize-winning novelist and dramatist, lived at *No. 8* when he was a young man, and he lived with them.

14. Return to *Albany Street*, and continue down it. *No. 55* was the home of HENRY MAYHEW (1812-87), humorous writer, one of the founders of *Punch*, author of *London Labour and the London Poor*— one of three brothers, all of whom were remarkably successful in humorous writing.

15. Near the bottom of Albany Street, turn left, into *Osnaburgh Terrace*. CHARLES DICKENS (see above) lived at *No. 9* in 1844.

16. Osnaburgh Terrace ends at *Osnaburgh Street*. On this street, at *No. 17*, was born the Fabian Society—a spiritual (or even spiritualistic) 'New Life' movement that immediately became social (or socialistic) in its aims, and subsequently attracted *George Bernard Shaw* (who attended early meetings here), *Sydney* and *Beatrice Webb, H. G. Wells*, and many other famous literatti.

Turn right, on Osnaburgh Street, and descend it a few steps to Euston Road. Here you will find the *Great Portland Street Underground Station*—and here this tour ends.

Tour 36
St John's Wood

Stacy Aumonier

Mathilde Blind

George Colman The Younger

Nora Hepworth Dixon

Herbert Farjeon

Ford Madox Ford

Laurence Gomme

Thomas Hood

William and Mary Howitt

Thomas Henry Huxley

W. W. Jacobs

John G. Lockhart

Louis MacNeice

Arthur Machen

Katherine Mansfield

John Middleton Murry

Barry Pain

Dorothy Richardson

William Michael Rossetti

Clement and Dora S. Shorter

Herbert Spencer

Francis Thompson

Arnold Toynbee

Leave the underground at the *St John's Wood Station.*

1. The station is at the corner of *Acacia Road.* At *No. 5* of this road
KATHERINE MANSFIELD (1888-1923), and JOHN MIDDLETON MURRY
(1889-1957), editor, critic, and biographer, were living in 1915—when
Katherine's beloved brother visited them on his way to the battle
front in France, where he was killed a short time later. Katherine
Mansfield, probably England's finest short-story writer, was the first
in English to free the short story, normally and consistently, of
emphasis on plot or idea, and concentrate on subtleties of pure
psychology.

The *bracketed* sections below outline an extensive walk. Before
you take this walk, glance over the sections to see whether you think
the persons involved are worth the exercise.

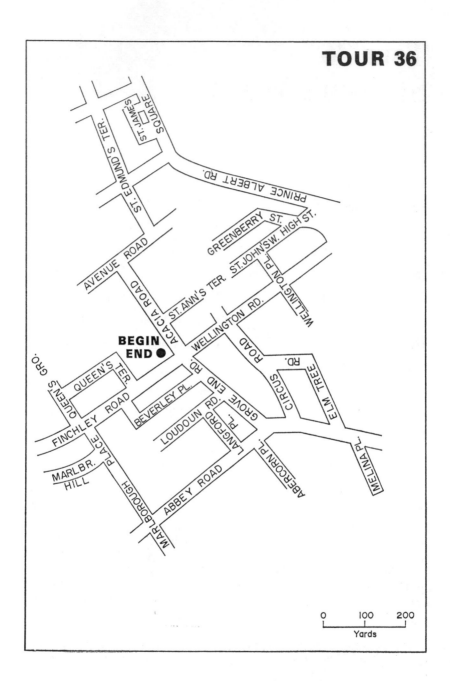

TOUR 36

[1A. Walk eastward on Acacia Road (away from the underground station). You will soon find *St Anne's Terrace* entering from your right. Here, at *No. 4*, lived briefly, in the autumn of 1854, the philosopher HERBERT SPENCER (1820-1903), who tried to apply Darwinian principles to philosophy and psychology. While here, he worked diligently on his *Principles of Psychology* (1855), which was based on Spencer's own ideas about evolution—four years before Darwin's great book appeared. Just opposite St Anne's Terrace there was once a short street called Upper York Place, where (at *No. 4*) THOMAS HENRY HUXLEY (1825-95) lived from 1851 to 1853. Biologist, essayist, defender of Darwinism, Huxley promoted the idea (revolutionary at the time) that science, as well as Greek and Latin literature, should be a major element in school and university curricula.

[1B. Continue along Acacia Road till you reach *Avenue Road*. To your left, the street was once called 'Upper Avenue Road'; and here, at *No. 28* (the modern number has not been certainly identified by the present writer) lived WILLIAM HOWITT (1792-1879), once a very popular descriptive and travel writer, and his even better-known wife MARY HOWITT (1799-1888), novelist, poet, and translator. Their house here was a kind of literary gathering-place for Victorian writers. Ironically, the only work of Mrs Howitt that remains in our cultural memory is the children's poem ' "Won't you walk into my parlour?" /Said the spider to the fly'.... Turn right on *Avenue Road*. HERBERT SPENCER (see above) lived at *No. 62* from 1889 till near the end of the 1890's.

[1C. After a very long block along Avenue Road, you will reach *St Edmund's Terrace*, entering from your left. At *No. 1* lived *Ford Madox Brown* (1821-93), the famous Pre-Raphaelite painter; and here with him lived his daughter and her son FORD MADOX HUEFFER (who later changed his name to FORD MADOX FORD) (1873-1939), the poet and novelist who collaborated with Joseph Conrad, and who (by the example of his own writing, and through his editorship of the *English Review*) strongly influenced literary developments in the twentieth century. In the late 1890's MATHILDE BLIND (1841-96), the German-born poet, and biographer of literary women, lived in this same *No. 1*. WILLIAM MICHAEL ROSSETTI (1829-1919), brother of Dante Gabriel and Christina Rossetti, lived, in the 1880's and 1890's, at *No. 3*. He was himself a son-in-law of the painter Ford Madox Brown, and was a poet, literary biographer and critic, novelist, translator, and editor.

[1D. Turn right, off St Edmund's Terrace, and reach Prince Albert Road, which runs alongside the Great Union Canal skirting Regent's Park. In passing, you may wish to pause by *St James's Terrace*, where, at *No. 6*, lived NORA HEPWORTH DIXON (d. 1932), novelist, dramatist, feminist, editor of the *Englishwoman* magazine.

[1E. Turn right, on Prince Albert Road, and trudge down it a long way—till you see a church on your right, and (just this side of the church) St John's Wood High Street. Turn into the latter, and then, almost immediately, turn right again, into *Greenberry Street*. The poet EDWARD FITZGERALD (1809-93) lived at *No. 24* while he was working on his translation of the *Rubaiyat* of Omar Khayyam.

[1F. Return to St John's Wood High Street, and turn right on it. At the next corner, turn left, into *Wellington Place*. In the mid-1940's, *No. 10* here was the home of the poet LOUIS MacNEICE (1907-63). A leftist in politics, and a rebel against traditional poetry, he was one of the most prominent and influential English poets of the 1930's and 1940's.
  [You will have noticed the traffic artery Wellington Road entering Wellington Place from your right. Turn into the former, ascend it to the Circus Road, and turn left.]

2. If you have decided against the long walk outlined in the sections above, walk straight down Wellington Road, as soon as you leave the underground station. Reach the *Circus Road*, and turn right. On your right you will soon see the buildings of the *Hospital of St John and St Elizabeth*. It was here that the religious poet FRANCIS THOMPSON (1859-1907) died (of tuberculosis). He is best remembered, no doubt, for his 'The Hound of Heaven', which many people regard as the finest short religious poem in the language.

3. Beyond the hospital, turn left, into *Elm Tree Road*, on which, at *No. 17*, the poet THOMAS HOOD (1799-45), author of 'The Bridge of Sighs' and 'The Song of the Shirt', spent his last years. It is ironic that he is best remembered for these melancholy poems—yet the mass of his work is humorous, and he made his living by humorous writing. From about 1937 until his death, W. W. JACOBS (1863-1943), lived at *Elm Tree Road Mansions* on this street.

4. Almost opposite the end of Elm Tree Road, on the far side of Grove End Road, is the entrance to *Melina Place*. ARNOLD TOYNBEE (b. 1889), the historian, lived at *No. 3* through most of the 1920's and 1930's, and

here his greatest work took shape, and was partly written. GEORGE COLMAN THE YOUNGER (1762-1836), dramatist and theatre manager, lived first (1811) at *No. 4*, and later (1824) at *No. 5*. ARTHUR MACHEN (1863-1947) who wrote novels of delicate fantasy, and also translated the *Memoirs* of the licentious *Casanova*, lived for a time at *No. 12*.

5. Return to Grove End Road, and turn left (northward) on it. Follow it till you find *Abbey Road* branching off to your left. At *No. 44* on this street lived JOHN LOCKHART (1794-1854) during his last years in London. He was a son-in-law of Sir Walter Scott, a literary critic, and editor-in-chief of the *Quarterly Review*. He is famous for his six-volume biography of his father-in-law, and infamous for having probably written (and certainly sanctioned) the *Quarterly*'s savage and tasteless attacks on John Keats and his poetry.

6. Walking up Abbey Road, you will find *Abercorn Place* entering from your left. This was formerly called Abbey Place. And here, at *No. 26*, lived (1861-72) THOMAS HENRY HUXLEY (see above).

7. Farther up Abbey Road, *Langford Place* enters from your right. *No. 8* here was the home (for about the first 15 years of the twentieth century) of BARRY PAIN (1865-1928), novelist and humorist, once famous for his humorously realistic 'Eliza' tales. (Ian Nairn describes the nearby *No. 12* as 'Sheer horror ... villa pickled in embalming fluid by some mad doctor ... radiates malevolence'!)

8. Return to Abbey Road, and continue up it till you reach the crossing with *Marlborough Place*. Turn left on the latter, and find *No. 4* (on your right, just beyond a church) where lived THOMAS HENRY HUXLEY (see above) from 1872 to 1890—in a house that he had had built for himself. *No. 16* was the long-time home (1900-11) of CLEMENT KING SHORTER (1857-1926), editor, literary biographer, with his wife DORA SIGERSON SHORTER (1866-1918), Irish poet. At *No. 20* lived SIR LAURENCE GOMME (1858-1921), anthropologist and historical novelist.

9. Turn around, and retrace your way along Marlborough Place—past Abbey Road, and beyond.
[9A. You will pass, on your left, the entrance of *Marlborough Hill*, up which, at *No. 35*, lived STACY AUMONIER (1887-1928), novelist, short-story writer, and painter.]
   Continue along Marlborough Place to *Finchley Road*, and turn left. The poet THOMAS HOOD (see above) was taken to *No. 28* to die.

10. By this time you will have noticed the entrance of Queen Anne's

Grove, leading away from Finchley Road almost opposite Marlborough Place. Enter Queen Anne's Grove, and then, almost at once, turn right, into *Queen's Terrace*. Here, at *No. 2*, DOROTHY RICHARDSON (1872-1957), the novelist who first brought the 'stream of consciousness' technique into English fiction, lived through most of the 1920's and all of the 1930's. Here she finished the last five of the twelve novels composing her major work, *Pilgrimage*.

11. Queen's Terrace winds about, and reaches Finchley Road. Cross over the latter, go a few steps to your right, and find the entrance of Finchley Place. Turn into it, and then left again, into *Waverley Place*, where at *No. 14*, THOMAS HENRY HUXLEY (see above) lived nearly seven years, 1855-61.

12. At the end of Waverley Place, turn right, go a block to *Loudoun Road*, and turn right. *No. 16* here was the home of HERBERT SPENCER (see above) from 1857 to 1859. He had moved here in order to be near Huxley, then living on Waverley Place. At *No. 34* lived HERBERT FARJEON (1887-1945) the dramatist. He was the son of the novelist and dramatist *Benjamin Farjeon* (1838-1903), and the brother of the dramatist *Joseph Jefferson Farjeon* and of the novelist, poet, and dramatist *Eleanor Farjeon*.

Now turn about, go back to Grove End Road, turn left, and reach *St John's Wood Underground Station*—where this tour began, and where it ends.

Tour 37
Paddington

George Arliss	Maurice Hewlett
James Blyth	John Masefield
Robert Browning	Sir Lewis Morris
John Davidson	James Payn
Ernest Christopher Dowson	Stephen Potter
Christopher Fry	Capt. Mayne Reid
Edmund Gosse	Herbert Spencer
Walter Jerrold	Stephen Spender

Leave the underground at the *Warwick Avenue Underground Station.* You will find yourself in a confusion of streets; but cross over Warwick Avenue, and make off down Clifton Villas.

1. *No. 1 Clifton Villas* was the home of GEORGE ARLISS (1868-1946) for many years, and at the time of his death. He was a famous actor on the stage until 1920, and even more famous on the screen in the 1920's and 1930's.

2. After a short block, turn right, into *Bristol Gardens. No. 15* was the home of the parents of ERNEST CHRISTOPHER DOWSON (1867-1900), the poet. He lived here (1889-94) before he became lost in the sad-gay bohemian life of France and London. Certainly the best of the younger poets of the 1890's, he was a contributor to the *Yellow Book*, member of the Rhymers' Club, writer of muted and delicate poetry of love and despair, friend of Yeats, Beardsley, Symons, Lionel Johnson, and other names of the aesthetic-decadent group of the century's end. He is remembered mostly for the acutely psychological and autobiographical poem whose refrain is, 'I have been faithful to thee, Cynara! in my fashion.'

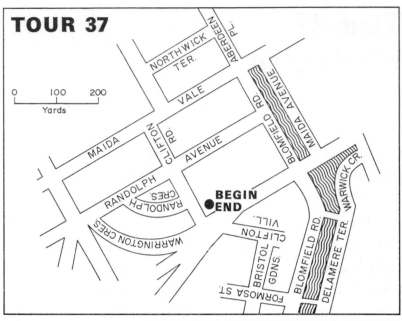

TOUR 37

NORTHWICK TER.

ABERDEEN PL.

VALE

BLOMFIELD RD.

MAIDA AVENUE

MAIDA

CLIFTON RD.

AVENUE

WARWICK CR.

0   100   200
Yards

RANDOLPH CRES.

RANDOLPH

WARRINGTON CRES.

BEGIN
END

CLIFTON VILL.

DELAMERE TER.

BLOMFIELD RD.

FORMOSA ST.

BRISTOL GDNS.

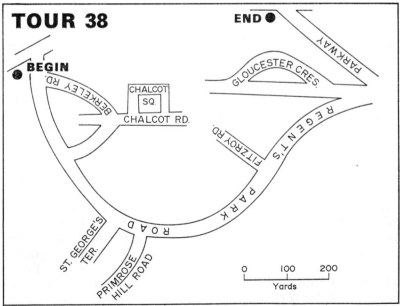

TOUR 38

END

BEGIN

PARKWAY

GLOUCESTER CRES.

BERKELEY RD.

CHALCOT SQ.

CHALCOT RD.

FITZROY RD.

REGENT'S

PARK

ROAD

ST. GEORGE'S TER.

PRIMROSE HILL ROAD

0   100   200
Yards

3. At the end of Bristol Gardens, turn left, on Formosa Street, and walk on along it to the bridge over the canal. Cross the bridge, and turn left on *Delamere Terrace*. EDMUND GOSSE (1849-1928), literary critic, historian, and biographer, and graceful verse writer, lived for more than twenty years at *No. 29*. His house is no longer here; but since it was a kind of mecca to which came most important writers of the 1880's and 1890's, the street here has left the footfalls of much English literature: *Henry James, Robert Browning, Max Beerbohm, George Moore, Arthur Symons, Algernon Swinburne, Henry Arthur Jones*, and many more.

4. Continue along Delamere Terrace till it becomes *Warwick Crescent*. At what was *No. 19* here (the house is gone) ROBERT BROWNING (1812-89), the poet, lived from shortly after his wife's death (1861) until 1887. Here he wrote *The Ring and the Book, Dramatis Personae*, and the two volumes of *Dramatic Idyls*. (These last works include the familiar 'Rabbi ben Ezra', 'Prospice', 'Caliban upon Setebos', and 'Abt Vogler'.)

5. Continue to the end of Warwick Crescent, and turn left, on *Warwick Avenue*. *No. 6* was the home of WALTER JERROLD (1865-1929), journalist, editor, literary biographer, grandson of Douglas Jerrold, the dramatist, humourist, and friend of Dickens.

6. You will very soon pass, on your right, the entrance to *Maida Avenue*, which runs alongside the canal. Just down this street, at *No. 30*, lived JOHN MASEFIELD (1878-1967), who became Poet Laureate, and who was living here at the time he was working on the poem that first made him famous: *The Everlasting Mercy*.

7. Return to Warwick Avenue, cross the bridge, and find yourself on *Blomfield Road*. At *No. 12* CAPTAIN MAYNE REID (1818-83), the adventure novelist, lived and died. At *No. 27* and then at *No. 37* lived CHRISTOPHER FRY (b. 1907), the dramatist who wrote *The Lady's Not for Burning*, during the 1950's and 1960's. When he first appeared in the 1930's, he was hailed as a bright new dramatic star —but, perhaps, he never quite lived up to his early reputation.

8. Continue along Blomfield Road till it crosses Maida Vale-Edgware Road.
[8A. To your left, at *No. 23 Maida Vale*, the novelist, literary historian, and biographer STEPHEN POTTER (b. 1900) was living in the 1960's.]

Continue, in a straight line with Blomfield Road, into Aberdeen Place. Walk a block, and then turn left into *Northwick Terrace*. Here, at *No. 7*, lived MAURICE HEWLETT (1861-1923), novelist, poet, essayist and art historian, who tried valiantly but vainly to restore dead romanticism to English literature.

9. At the end of Northwick Terrace (one block) turn left, on St John's Wood Road, reach Maida Vale again, and cross over it. Then turn right, walk a few steps, and reach *Clifton Road*, intersecting from your left. Turn into it. *No. 20* was the lodging place (off and on for several years in the early 1850's) of HERBERT SPENCER (1820-1903), the philosopher of Darwinism. *No. 31* was the home of JAMES BLYTH (1864-1933), a prolific and once very popular novelist.

10. Continuing along Clifton Road, you will soon find *Randolph Crescent* entering it from your right. Turn into it, *No. 25* was the residence of STEPHEN SPENDER (b. 1909), poet, critic, and novelist, in the mid-1930's, just when he was gaining his first fame as a new 'modern' and leftist poet.

11. Go on to the far end of Randolph Crescent, and enter *Randolph Avenue*. On this street, at *No. 42* lived SIR LEWIS MORRIS (1836-1907), well respected in his day as a dignified poet of the traditional Tennysonian school. He was the subject of one of Oscar Wilde's best witticisms. Told about Sir Lewis complaining of the critics' 'conspiracy of silence' against him, Wilde answered promptly, 'He should join it!'

12. Turn left on Randolph Avenue, go one short block, and then turn back sharp left, into *Warrington Crescent*. At *No. 43* lived, from 1883 to 1896, JAMES PAYN (1830-98), who succeeded Sir Leslie Stephen as editor of *Cornhill Magazine*—and who wrote *over one hundred novels!* At *No. 19* JOHN DAVIDSON (1857-1909), poet, novelist, and dramatist, lived with his wife for a few years in the late 1890's. He left here to move to Penzance, where he drowned himself some years later. Davidson was well known among the *Yellow Book* group of writers. But he was a tragic figure—too serious-minded to be at home among the Aesthetic butterflies of his time, and too intensely humanitarian and bitterly revolutionary to be popular with the Establishment.

Continue to the end of Warrington Crescent, bear left, and find yourself once more at the *Warwick Avenue Underground Station*—and the end of this tour.

Tour 38
Chalk Farm Area

Nigel Balchin	**Thomas Moore**
F. J. Furnivall	**Vernon S. Pritchett**
Francis Jeffrey	**Henry Handel Richardson**
Louis MacNeice	**H. G. Wells**
William Cosmo Monkhouse	**William Butler Yeats**
Arthur Moore	

Leave the underground at the *Chalk Farm Station*. Find Regent's Park Road, and start out on it.

1. Somewhere about here, as well as ahead of you and to your left, was the once well-known *Chalk Farm*—a favourite spot for duellers in the early eighteenth century. A famous literary duel occurred here in 1806 between the Irish poet THOMAS MOORE (1779-1852) and FRANCIS JEFFREY (1773-1850), Scottish lawyer, literary critic, and editor of the *Edinburgh Review*. The latter was a tough-minded, hard-headed anti-romantic who verbally bludgeoned Byron, Wordsworth, Leigh Hunt, Keats—and Thomas Moore. Moore challenged Jeffrey to a duel; but it was stopped here by the police before any damage was done to anybody. Byron (who had not met Moore and did not love Jeffrey) ridiculed the affair, saying the pistols were never loaded. Thereupon Moore wrote to Byron demanding an explanation and an apology for the insult. The letter led to a friendly meeting between Byron and Moore, and to the beginning of a warm friendship that had significant consequences for both men. Moore was a musician and a singer who put many of his own poems to music—among them 'Believe Me if All Those Endearing Young Charms', 'Oft in the Stilly Night', 'The Harp that Once through Tara's Halls', and many more.

2. Though you will not find all the following numbers immediately as

you walk down *Regent's Park Road*, they had best be given now. NIGEL BALCHIN (1908-70) was living at *No. 48* in the last five or six years of his life. Like C. P. Snow, he was both a scientist and a novelist. ARTHUR MOORE (1866-1952), novelist, collaborator with the poet Ernest Dowson in writing two novels, lived at *No. 72* during the 1920's. At *No. 90* the Australian-born novelist HENRY HANDEL RICHARDSON (whose real name was HENRIETTA RICHARDSON ROBINSON) (1870-1946), lived for 24 years, 1910-34. Her chief work (written at this place) was the trilogy *The Fortunes of Richard Mahony* (1917, 1925, 1929).

3. But before you find all the numbers just listed, turn aside (to your left) into *Berkeley Road*, where, at *No. 6*, WILLIAM BUTLER YEATS (1865-1939) lived in 1887.

4. Continue along Berkeley Road the short distance to its end, and bear left, into *Chalcot Square*. Here lived, at *No. 3*, the scholar F. J. FURNIVALL (1825-1910), whose work is familiar to everyone interested in medieval English literature. He helped his friend F. D. Maurice found the Christian Socialist Movement and the Working Men's College in London, helped promote the *Oxford English Dictionary*, edited many early English texts, and founded the following scholarly societies: Early English Text; Ballad; Chaucer; New Shakespeare; and Wyclif.

5. Now turn about, and seek Regent's Park Road once more, via Sharples Hall Street. Turn left on Regent's Park Road, and soon find (on your right) *St. George's Terrace*. Here, at *No. 11*, lived, during his later years, WILLIAM COSMO MONKHOUSE (1840-1901), a poet in the Tennysonian tradition, but a better historian and art critic than poet.

6. Not far down Regent's Park Road *Primrose Hill Road* enters from your right. Up this road, at *No. 16A*, the poet LOUIS MACNEICE (1907-63) settled for a few years in the late 1930's and early 1940's.

7. Still farther down Regent's Park Road, *Fitzroy Road* enters from your left. At *No. 23* the parents of WILLIAM BUTLER YEATS (see above) lived with the future poet from 1867 to 1875. The poet's father, *John Butler Yeats*, was a painter. In his later years he migrated to America because (he said) he wanted to be in a place where he would be known for himself, not as the father of William Butler Yeats. He and the poet had a long and stimulating correspondence (since published) on matters literary and aesthetic. H. G. WELLS lived at *No.*

46 from 1889 to 1891. Here he boarded with his aunt, and fell in love with his cousin—whom he married a few years later, and was divorced from a few years after that.

8. Walk on to the end of Regent's Park Road, and its continuation as Gloucester Avenue; then double back sharply, to your left, into the Oval Road. Alongside the latter, you will find *Regent's Park Terrace.* V. S. PRITCHETT (b. 1900), short-story writer and critic, was living at *No. 12* in the 1960's and 1970's.

Now return to Gloucester Avenue, turn sharp left into the Parkway —and follow the latter to its end. Here you will find the *Camden Town Underground Station,* and the end of this tour.

Appendix

Isolated Locations
Below are names of some authors in whom the literary explorer may have a special interest—even though places associated with these authors may lie off the routes outlined in the previous pages.

After each name the following items are given in this order: address, or addresses, associated with the writer named; a year of the writer's association with this address; the underground station nearest the address. If the place is not easily reached by the underground system, the nearest railway station ('Ry.') is indicated.

ABERCROMBIE, LASCELLES, poet, playwright, and critic: No. 7A Stanley Gardens, W.11; 1930; Holland Park Station.

AMIS, KINGSLEY, poet and fiction writer: No. 108 Maida Vale, W.9; 1965-8; Maida Vale Station. (Living with Amis here was his wife, ELIZABETH JANE HOWARD, a novelist).

BACON, SIR FRANCIS, essayist and philosopher: died in a house where now stands St Michael's Church, South Grove St., N.6; Highgate Station. (See also COLERIDGE, below.)

BENNETT, ARNOLD, novelist: No. 46 Alexander Road, N.W.8; 1890; West Hampstead Station.
No. 9 Fulham Park Gardens, S.W.6; 1897-1900; Putney Bridge Station, or Parson's Green Station.

BENSON, STELLA, poet and novelist: No. 13 Drayton Court, Drayton Gardens, S.W.10; 1927-32; Gloucester Road Station.

BLOUNT, MARTHA and TERESA, friends of Alexander Pope, who may have been in love with Martha: buried in Old St Pancras Church, N.W.1; King's Cross station.

CAVE, EDWARD, editor: St John's Gate, St John's Square, E.C.1; Aldersgate Station. The first number of the *Gentleman's Magazine* was issued from here, 1731. (See also GARRICK, below.)

CHURCH, RICHARD, poet, novelist, essayist: No. 19 Holland Park, W.11; mid 1930's; Holland Park Station.

COLERIDGE, SAMUEL TAYLOR, poet, critic, philosopher: No. 7 Addison Bridge Place, W.14; 1811-12; Olympia Station.

No. 3 The Grove, No. 6; 1816-34; Highgate Station. Coleridge died here.

St Michael's Church, South Grove Street, N.6; Highgate Station. Coleridge's grave is here.

CORVO, BARON (Frederick William Rolfe), baroque romancer: No. 69 Broadhurst Gardens, N.W.6; 1900-3; West Hampstead Station.

CRUIKSHANK, GEORGE, artist associated with Dickens: No. 23 Amwell Street, E.C.1; 1841; Angel Station.

DAVIES, W. H., poet: No. 11 Aldwych, W.C.2; 1915-16; Aldwych Station.

DEFOE, DANIEL, novelist and journalist: No. 95 Stoke Newington Church Street, N.16; Stoke Newington Ry. Station.

DE LA MARE, WALTER, poet: No. 14 Thornsett Road, S.W.18; early 1920's; Earlsfield Ry. Station.

DICKENS, CHARLES, novelist: No. 16 Somers Place, S.W.2; 1865; no nearby station.

DOBSON, AUSTIN, poet and critic: No. 76 Eaton Rise, W.5; 1900-21; Ealing Broadway Station.

DOYLE, CONAN, novelist and story writer: No. 17 Tennison Road, S.E.25; 1890-3; Norwood Junction Ry. Station.

DRINKWATER, JOHN, poet and dramatist: North Hall, Mortimer Crescent, N.W.6; 1930's; Kilburn Park Station.

No. 9 The Grove, N.6; 1935-7; Highgate Station.

DU MAURIER, GEORGE, novelist and artist: No. 44 Wharton Street, W.C.1; 1851-6; Angel Station, or King's Cross Station.

EDWARDS, J. PASSMORE, editor and philanthropist: No. 51 Netherhall Gardens, N.W.3; Finchley Road Station. He lived and died here.

ELIOT, GEORGE (Mary Ann Evans), novelist: No. 31 Wimbledon Park Road, S.W.18; Wimbledon Park Station.

ELLIS, HAVELOCK, psychological writer: No. 24 Holmende Avenue, S.E.24; 1930; Herne Hill Ry. Station.

FORD, FORD MADOX, novelist, poet, editor: No. 226 Finchley Road, N.W.3; West Hampstead Station. He lived here while recovering from a nervous breakdown.

No. 90 Brook Green, W.6; Hammersmith Station. He lived here as a child.

FREEMAN, JOHN, poet: No. 29 Weighton Road, S.E.20; 1920's; Anerly Ry. Station.

FREUD, SIGMUND, psychologist; No. 39 Elsworthy Road, N.W.3; Chalk Farm Station. This was his first home (to Nov. 1938) in London.

No. 20 Maresfield Gardens, N.W.3; Finchley Road Station. This was his last home (to Oct. 1939) in London.

GARRICK, DAVID, actor, dramatist, producer: St John's Gate, St John's Square, E.C.1; Farringdon Station. Here he first tried out as an actor in Edward Cave's rooms above the gate.

GEORGE, W. L., novelist, journalist, critic: 2 Hyde Park Terrace, W.2 (facing Bayswater between Clarendon Place and Albion Street); Lancaster Gate Station.

GIBSON, W. W., poet: No. 4 Ridge Hill, N.W.11; 1940's; Golders Green Station.

GISSING, GEORGE, novelist: No. 76 Burton Road, S.W.9; 1890's; Brixton Ry. Station.

GODWIN, WILLIAM, social philosopher and novelist: Old St Pancras Church, Pancras Road, N.W.1; King's Cross Station. Here he married, and here he was buried with his two wives—though he and his second wife, Mary Wollstonecraft (mother of Mary Shelley), were removed later.

GOULD, GERALD, poet, essayist, social critic: No. 1 Hamilton Terrace, W.8; c. 1925-35; Warwick Avenue Station.

HARDY, THOMAS, novelist and poet: No. 16 Westbourne Park Villas, W.2; 1862-7; Royal Oak Station.
No. 172 Trinity Road, S.W.17; Tooting Bec Station.
No. 1 Arundel Terrace, S.W.13; 1878-80; Hammersmith Station. Here he suffered a lung haemorrhage, and had to lie in bed, with his feet elevated, for several months.

HAWTHORNE, NATHANIEL, American novelist: No. 4 Pond Road, S.E.3; Blackheath Ry. Station. On a visit to England, 1856.

HENLEY, WILLIAM ERNEST, poet and editor: No. 4 Earl's Terrace, Devonshire Road, W.4; 1878; Turnham Green Station.
No. 51 Richmond Gardens, W.12; 1881-2; Shepherd's Bush Station.
No. 36 Loftus Road, W.12; Shepherd's Bush Station.
No. 9 Barnes Terrace, S.W.13; 1896; Barnes Bridge Ry. Station.

HENTY, G. A., historical novelist: No. 33 Lavender Gardens, S.W.4; Clapham Common Station.

HERBERT, A. P., humorous writer: No. 12 Hammersmith Terrace, W.6; 1950's and 1960's; Stamford Brook Station.

HEYWOOD, THOMAS, actor and dramatist, poet: St James's Church, Clerkenwell, E.C.1; Farringdon Station. His second marriage was here (1633), and he was buried here (1641).

HOUSEHOLD, GEOFFREY, novelist: No. 33 Hartington Road, W.4; 1950's; Chiswick Ry. Station.

HOUSMAN, A. E., poet and scholar: No. 82 Talbot Road, W.11; c. 1882, when he first settled in London; Royal Oak Station.
No. 17 North Road, N.W.6; 1886-1905; Highgate Station. Here he wrote *A Shropshire Lad*.

HUDSON, W. H., novelist, essayist, naturalist: No. 40 St Luke's Road, W.11; 1886-1922; Westbourne Park Station. Here nearly all his works were written.

HUNT LEIGH, poet, essayist, critic: No. 2 Phillimore Terrace, W.8; 1853-7; Kensington High Street Station.

HUXLEY, SIR JULIAN, biologist and philosopher: No. 31 Hillway, N.6; 1920-5; Highgate Station.

HUXLEY, LEONARD, biographer and editor, son of T. H. Huxley, and father of Aldous and Julian Huxley: No. 16 Bracknell Gardens, N.W.3; West Hampstead Station.

JACKSON, HOLBROOK, poet, editor, literary critic and biographer: No. 1 Winterstoke Gardens, Mill Hill, N.W.7; Mill Hill Station.

JONES, HENRY ARTHUR, dramatist: No. 6 Arkwright Road, N.W.3; 1910-11; Hampstead Station.
No. 10 Kidderpore Avenue, N.W.3; 1921-9; Hampstead Station.

KINGSLEY, HENRY, novelist: No. 88 Fortress Road, N.W.5; 1870's; Kentish Town Station.

LAMB, CHARLES, essayist: No. 45 Chapel Market (corner of Liverpool Road, N.1); 1797-1801; Angel Station.
No. 64 Duncan Terrace (formerly No. 19 Colebrook Row), N.1; 1823-7; Angel Station.

LE GALLIENNE, RICHARD, poet and critic: No. 16 Clifton Hill, N.W.9; St John's Wood Station.

LESSING, MRS DORIS, novelist: No. 60 Carrington Street, N.W.1; 1960's; Mornington Crescent Station.

LEWES, GEORGE HENRY, editor and critic: No. 7 Harrington Street, N.W.1; 1837; Euston Station.

LEWIS, WYNDHAM, painter, novelist, essayist, critic: No. 121 Gloucester Terrace, W.2; 1930's; Royal Oak Station.

MACAULAY, THOMAS BABINGTON, historian, essayist, poet: No. 5 The Pavement, S.W.4; Clapham Common Station. He lived here as a boy.

MACNEICE, LOUIS, poet: No. 52 Canonbury Park South, N.1; 1950's; Essex Road Station.

MARX, KARL, socialist philosopher: No. 9 Grafton Terrace, N.W.5; 1850's and 1870's; Chalk Farm Station.
No. 1 Maitland Park Road, N.W.3; Chalk Farm Station. He died here.

MAUGHAM, SOMERSET, novelist: No. 11 Vincent Square, S.W.1; 1892 and after; Victoria Station. He lived here as a medical student.

MILNE, A. A., dramatist and children's writer: No. 12 Dagnall Park, S.E.25; Selhurst Ry. Station.

Henley House, Mortimer Crescent, N.W.6; Kilburn Park Station. He lived here as a child.

MOORE, THOMAS, poet: No. 46 Wigmore Street, W.1; Marble Arch Station.

MOORE, T. STURGE, poet and artist: No. 20 St James's Gardens, W.11; Shepherd's Bush Station or Holland Park Station.

MORRIS, WILLIAM, poet, printer artist, socialist leader: No. 26 Lower Hammersmith Mall, W.6; the famous Kelmscott House from which Morris operated for many years; Hammersmith Station.

MURRY, JOHN MIDDLETON, editor, essayist, critic: No. 14A Whitehead's Grove, S.W.3; Sloane Square Station. He lived here with his second wife. (His first wife was Katherine Mansfield.)

NEWBOLT, SIR HENRY, poet, historian, critic: No. 26 Kensington Park Gardens, W.11; bef. 1911; Notting Hill Station.

'OUIDA' (MARY LOUISA DE LA RAMÉE), novelist: 11 Ravenscourt Square, W.6; Stamford Brook Station. She lived here before she acquired her tremendous popularity.
No. 41 Lansdowne Road, W.11; 1850's; Holland Park Station.

PAYNE, JOHN, poet: No. 10 Oxford Road, N.W.6; 1887-1910; Kilburn Park Station.

PEARSON, HESKETH, critic: No. 14 Priory Road, N.W.6; 1950-60; West Hampstead Station.

PHILLIPS, STEPHEN, poet and dramatist: No. 16 Featherstone Buildings, W.C.1; Holborn Station.

PINERO, ARTHUR WING, dramatist: No. 63 Hamilton Terrace, N.W.8; Warwick Avenue Station or Maida Vale Station.

PRIESTLEY, J. B., novelist, dramatist, essayist: No. 3 The Grove, N.6; 1935-9; Highgate Station.

READE, CHARLES, novelist: Nos. 12 and 19 Albert Gate, S.W.1; 1866-79; Knightsbridge Station.

RHYS, ERNEST, poet and editor: No. 48 West Heath Drive, N.W.11; Golders Green Station.

RITCHIE, ANNE THACKERAY, novelist: No. 109 St George's Square, S.W.1; 1902-12; no nearby station.

ROBERTSON, T. W., dramatist: No. 6 Eton Road, N.W.3; 1867-71; Chalk Farm Station.

RUSKIN, JOHN, art critic and social philosopher: No. 36 Herne Hill, S.E.24; Herne Hill Ry. Station. He lived here during much of his mature life.

SABATINI, RAFAEL, novelist: No. 25 Fitzjohns Avenue, N.W.6; 1925; Swiss Cottage Station.

SCHREINER, OLIVE, novelist: Women's Hospital, Endell Street, W.C.2; Covent Garden Station. Here she trained for midwifery.

SHARP, WILLIAM, poet: No. 46 Talgarth Road, W.14; 1886; West Kensington Station.
No. 13 Thorngate Road, W.9; 1883; Maida Vale Station.
SHELLEY, MARY GODWIN, novelist: No. 5 Bartholomew Road, N.W.5; 1824-7; Kentish Town Station.
SPENCER, HERBERT, philosopher: 24 Oakley Square, N.W.1; 1859; Mornington Crescent Station.
SMITH, JAMES and HORACE, satirists: No. 36 Basinghall Street, E.C.2; Bank Station or Moorgate Station. The brothers were born here, 1775 and 1779.
STEPHEN, LESLIE, scholar, editor: No. 18 Porchester Square, W.2; 1865; Royal Oak Station.
STRACHEY, LYTTON, historian and biographer: No. 67 Belsize Park Gardens, N.W.3; Belsize Park Station. Much of his time spent here till 1915.
No. 6 Belsize Park Gardens, N.W.3; after 1915; Belsize Park Station.
SWINBURNE, ALGERNON CHARLES, poet: No. 11 Putney Hill, S.W.15; 1879-1909 (died); Putney Ry. Station.
SWINNERTON, FRANK, novelist and literary historian: No. 150 Farringdon Road, E.C.1; 1890-9; Farringdon Station.
SYMONS, ARTHUR, poet and critic: No. 134 Maida Vale, W.9; 1901-6; Maida Vale Station.
No. 10 Clifton Hill, N.W.8; 1906; St John's Wood Station.
THOMAS, EDWARD, poet and essayist, killed in First World War: No. 61 Shelgate Road, S.W.11; Clapham Junction Ry. Station. He lived here for some years before the war.
TOMLINSON, H. M., novelist and essayist: No. 1 St Peter's Square, W.6; 1947-55; Stamford Brook Station.
TOYNBEE, ARNOLD, historian: 95 Oakwood Court, W.14; 1960's; Kensington Olympia Station.
USTINOV, PETER, actor, novelist, dramatist: No. 32 William Mews, S.W.1; 1947; Knightsbridge Station.
WATTS-DUNTON, THEODORE, novelist and critic: No. 11 Putney Hill Road, S.W.15; Putney Ry. Station.
WAUGH, ALEC and EVELYN, novelists, satirists, brothers: No. 11 Hillfield Road, N.W.6; West Hampstead Station. They were born here.
No. 145 North End Road, N.W.11; Golders Green Station. They lived here as children.
WEBB, SIDNEY and (his wife) BEATRICE, sociological writers: No. 41 Grosvenor Road, S.W.1; 1900-25; no nearby station.
WELLS, H. G., novelist, social philosopher: No. 28 Haldon Road, S.W.18; early 1890's; Putney Station.

WHISTLER, J. M., painter: No. 62, Sloane Street, S.W.1; Knightsbridge Station.

No. 454 Fulham Road, S.W.6; 1885; Parsons Green Station.

WILLIAMS, CHARLES, poet and religious writer: No. 28c Parkhill Road, N.W.3; 1930's; Belsize Park Station.

WILSON, ANGUS, novelist and dramatist: Grenville House, Dolphin Square, S.W.1; 1953-4; no nearby station.

YEATS, WILLIAM BUTLER, poet and dramatist: No. 3 Blenheim Road, Bedford Park, W.4; Turnham Green Station. Yeats was living here as a young man with his parents when Maud Gonne, who had read and admired one of his poems, visited him, and the two met for the first time; and here began that romantic association that inspired many of Yeats's poems during the rest of his life.

Some Burial Places

At least two cemeteries in London are worth visiting: *Kensal Green* and *Highgate*. Some of the literary personages buried in these two, as well as a few other writers, artists, and actors who are buried elsewhere, and are not mentioned in the text, are listed below:

HARRISON AINSWORTH, Kensal Green
ANNE BRACEGIRDLE, Westminster Abbey
WILKIE COLLINS, Kensal Green
CHARLES DICKENS's parents, wife, child, daughter, and sister-in-law (Mary Hogarth), Highgate
GEORGE ELIOT, Highgate
JOHN FORSTER, Kensal Green
BENJAMIN HAYDON, St Mary's Church, Paddington
THOMAS HOOD, Kensal Green
LEIGH HUNT, Kensal Green
CHARLES KEMBLE, Kensal Green
KARL MARX, Highgate
ALICE MEYNELL, St Mary's Roman Catholic Cemetery (Kensal Green)
JOHN MURRAY, Kensal Green
JOSEPH NOLLEKENS, St Mary's Church, Paddington
MACKWORTH PRAED, Kensal Green
HENRY CRABB ROBINSON, Highgate
CHRISTINA ROSSETTI, Highgate
MRS SARAH SIDDONS, St Mary's Church, Paddington
SYDNEY SMITH, Kensal Green
HERBERT SPENCER, Highgate

Appendix

WILLIAM MAKEPEACE THACKERAY, Kensal Green
FRANCIS THOMPSON, St Mary's Roman Catholic Cemetery (Kensal Green)
ANTHONY TROLLOPE, Kensal Green

Index of Persons

Abercrombie, Lascelles 104, 379
Ackland, Alice 173
Ackland, Rodney 181
Adams, John Quincy 56
Addison, Joseph 31, 61, 81, 86, 88, 89, 91, 105, 114, 152, 171, 172, 185, 199, 211, 287, 290, 303
Aders, Charles 131
Ainsworth, Harrison 186, 298, 385
Akenside, Mark 76, 88, 114, 126, 165
Albanesi, Effie 265
Aldington, Richard 204
Alleyn, Edward 45, 58, 65, 66
Ambler, Eric 234
Amis, Kingsley 379
Angell, Norman 119
Anne of Cleves 232
'Anstey, F.' see Guthrie, T. A.
Arbuthnot, John 152, 166, 175, 184, 211, 224, 230, 290
Archer, William 121, 210, 250, 317
Arliss, George 371
Armstrong, John 153, 214
Armstrong, Martin 250
Arne, Thomas 14, 81, 148, 156, 157, 211, 220
Arnold, Edwin 84, 309
Arnold, Matthew 137, 176, 333
Ascham, Roger 29, 33
Asquith, Cynthia 267
Asquith, Herbert 298
Asquith, Herbert H. 134, 163, 278
Asquith, Margot 135, 163, 278
Atterbury, Bishop Francis 223, 224
Atherton, Gertrude 164
Aumonier, Stacy 164, 369
Austen, Jane 137, 150, 265
Austin, Alfred 121

Bach, Johann Christian 211
Bacon, Francis 77-8, 105, 115, 137, 177, 280, 379
Baden-Powell, Baron R. 250
Bagnold, Enid 291
Baillie, Joanna 304
Baird, John L. 215
Bairnsfeather, Bruce 79
Balchin, Nigel 353, 376
Baldwin, Stanley 280
Barbauld, Laetitia 135, 303, 304
Barclay, Alexander 61
Barebone, Praise-God 94
Barham, Richard Harris 38, 41, 42
Baring, Maurice 104, 225
Barrie, James M. 79, 80, 108, 145, 146, 176, 184, 199, 202, 250, 252, 277, 345, 349, 357, 359
Barry, Elizabeth 114
Baugh, A. C. 241
Bax, Clifford 187, 327
Beadnell, Maria 61
Beardsley, Aubrey 61, 173, 185, 334
Beardsley, Mabel 231
Beaton, Cecil 234
Beattie, James 177, 318
Beauclerk, Topham 80, 136, 163, 210, 237-8, 239-40
Beaumont, Francis 16, 19, 49, 65, 84, 118, 122, 153, 154
Beckett, Arthur à 334
Beckford, William, Lord Mayor, 48, 214
Beckford, William, novelist 48, 184, 195, 214, 286
Beddoes, Thomas Lovell 31, 88
Bede, The Venerable 138
Beerbohm, Max 41, 202, 353, 358, 373
Behn, Aphra 19
Beith, John Hay ('Ian Hay') 260, 268

Bell, Clive 128-9, 316
Bell, Mackenzie 241, 343
Bell, Vanessa 129, 316
Belloc, Hilaire 210, 223, 344
Benedict, Julius, 284
Bennett, Arnold 87, 93, 114, 157, 163, 181, 187, 213, 222, 242, 267-8, 281, 333, 379
Benson, A. C. 233
Benson, E. F. 233, 266
Benson, R. H. 233
Benson, Stella 326, 379
Bentham, Jeremy 24, 58, 111, 240
Bentley, E. C. 106
Bentley, Phyllis 220
Bentley, Richard 21, 23, 174, 211, 239
Berkeley, George 137, 151, 166, 185, 196
Bernhardt, Sarah 81
Besant, Annie 13
Besant, Walter 41, 304
Betterton, Thomas 19, 98, 114, 153, 239
Binyon, Laurence 231, 334
Birrell, Augustine 45, 221
Birrell, Francis 130
Black, William 78
Blackmore, Richard 289
Blackmore, Richard D. 121
Blackstone, William 115
Blake, William 39, 41, 45, 82, 132, 157, 166, 208, 262
Blessington, Lady 292
Blind, Mathilde 135
Bloomfield, Robert 48
Blount, Martha and Teresa 168-9, 183, 184, 278, 379
Blunden, Edmund 104
Blunt, Reginald 220
Blunt, Wilfred S. 195, 344
Blyth, James 374
Bolingbroke, Viscount 209, 290

Index of Places

Places without literary associations are not indexed here.